ANGLO-SAXON STUDIES 15

THE ARCHAEOLOGY OF THE EAST ANGLIAN CONVERSION

The conversion to Christianity of the Anglo-Saxon kingdom of East Anglia left huge marks on the area, both metaphorical and real. Drawing both on the surviving documentary sources, and on the eastern region's rich archaeological record, this book presents the first multi-disciplinary synthesis of the process. It begins with an analysis of the historical framework, followed by an examination of the archaeological evidence for the establishment of missionary stations within the region's ruined Roman forts and earthwork enclosures. It argues that the effectiveness of the Christian mission is clearly visible in the region's burial record, which exhibits a number of significant changes, including the cessation of cremation. The conversion can also be seen in the dramatic transformations which occurred in the East Anglian landscape, including changes in the relationship between settlements and cemeteries and the foundation of a number of different types of Christian cemetery. Ultimately, it shows that, far from being the preserve of kings, the East Anglian conversion was widespread at a grassroots level, changing the nature of the Anglo-Saxon landscape forever.

Dr Richard Hoggett is currently Coastal Heritage Officer with Norfolk County Council.

Anglo-Saxon Studies
ISSN 1475-2468

General Editors
John Hines
Catherine Cubitt

'Anglo-Saxon Studies' aims to provide a forum for the best scholarship on the Anglo-Saxon peoples in the period from the end of Roman Britain to the Norman Conquest, including comparative studies involving adjacent populations and periods; both new research and major re-assessments of central topics are welcomed.

Books in the series may be based in any one of the principal disciplines of archaeology, art history, history, language and literature, and inter- or multi-disciplinary studies are encouraged.

Proposals or enquiries may be sent directly to the editors or the publisher at the addresses given below; all submissions will receive prompt and informed consideration.

Professor John Hines, School of History and Archaeology, Cardiff University, Colum Drive, Cardiff, Wales, UK CF10 3EU

Dr Catherine Cubitt, Centre for Medieval Studies, University of York, The King's Manor, York, England, UK YO1 7EP

Boydell & Brewer, PO Box 9, Woodbridge, Suffolk, England, UK IP12 3DF

Previously published volumes in the series
are listed at the back of this book

The Archaeology
of the
East Anglian Conversion

Richard Hoggett

THE BOYDELL PRESS

First published 2010
The Boydell Press, Woodbridge

ISBN 978-1-84383-595-0

The Boydell Press is an imprint of Boydell & Brewer Ltd
PO Box 9, Woodbridge, Suffolk IP12 3DF, UK
and of Boydell & Brewer Inc.
668 Mt Hope Avenue, Rochester, NY 14620, USA
website: www.boydellandbrewer.com

The publisher has no responsibility for the continued existence or accuracy of URLs for
external or third-party internet websites referred to in this book, and does not
guarantee that any content on such websites is, or will remain, accurate or appropriate.

A catalogue record of this publication is available
from the British Library
This publication is printed on acid-free paper

MIX
Paper from
responsible sources
FSC® C013604

Typeset by Tina Ranft, Woodbridge, Suffolk
Printed in Great Britain by
CPI Antony Rowe, Chippenham and Eastbourne

For my family

and

for Alice

Contents

Illustrations

Plates

Acknowledgements

This book owes a great debt to Professors Tom Williamson and Stephen Church of the School of History, University of East Anglia, and I am also grateful to Professors Carole Rawcliffe and Mick Aston for their insightful and positive responses to this material. The comments of the two anonymous readers provided by Boydell have greatly improved the text, as have the encouragement and support of John Hines and Caroline Palmer.

A number of individuals have assisted me in the completion of this work, freely offering advice, comments, references or sight of their own unpublished work. They are: Emily Archer, David Abraham, John Blair, Paul Blinkhorn, Sophie Cabot, Quinton Carroll, Jo Caruth, Alice Cattermole, Mary Chester-Kadwell, Pete Crawley, Gareth Davies, Chris Gerrard, Jenny Glazebrook, David Gurney, Sarah Harrison, Sarah Horlock, Sarah Hornbrook, Nick Higham, Trefor Jones, Sam Lucy, Sam Newton, Kenneth Penn, John Percival, Tim Pestell, Andrew Rogerson, Chris Scull, Andrew Tester, Jess Tipper, Keith Wade, Peter Watkins, Nicola Whyte and Howard Williams. John Newman deserves special thanks for providing me with the unpublished data from his Deben Valley fieldwalking survey, as does Will Bowden for providing early access to the results of the archaeological evaluation in Caistor St Edmund churchyard. A particular debt of gratitude is owed to Alice Cattermole at the Norfolk Historic Environment Record and Colin Pendleton at the Suffolk Historic Environment Record for their continual assistance.

Part of the research upon which this book is based was funded by a postgraduate scholarship from the School of History at the University of East Anglia. I am also grateful for the support of Jayne Bown and my other former colleagues at NAU Archaeology, who graciously accommodated my writing of this book.

Permission to reproduce figures and plates has kindly been granted by East Anglian Archaeology, NAU Archaeology, the Norfolk Museums and Archaeology Service, the Norfolk and Norwich Archaeological Society, the Ordnance Survey, the Sedgeford Historical and Archaeological Research Project, the Society of Antiquaries of London, the Society for Medieval Archaeology and the Trustees of the British Museum.

Finally, personal thanks are due to my family, who have always supported me, and to Alice Cattermole, with whom I can finally look to the future after too much time spent dwelling on the past. This book is dedicated to them.

The Ann Ashard Webb bequest

This volume has been published with the support of the Centre of East Anglian Studies and the School of History of the University of East Anglia, and with the aid of a grant from the Ann Ashard Webb bequest. Ann Ashard Webb (1902–1996) made her bequest to the School with the express purpose of funding an accessible series of works on the history of Suffolk which would appeal to a wide readership. In addition to the main volumes in the series, it is intended to produce a number of more specialised titles, of which *The Archaeology of the East Anglian Conversion* is one. Others which have already appeared with support from the bequest are:

JUDITH MIDDLETON-STEWART *Inward Purity and Outward Splendour: Death and Remembrance in the Deanery of Dunwich, Suffolk, 1370–1547*

CHRISTOPHER HARPER-BILL, CAROLE RAWCLIFFE, R. G. WILSON (eds) *East Anglia's History: Studies in Honour of Norman Scarfe*

CHRISTOPHER HARPER-BILL (ed.) *Medieval East Anglia*

DAVID BUTCHER *Lowestoft, 1550–1750: Development and Change in a Suffolk Coastal Town*

MARK BAILEY *Medieval Suffolk: An Economic and Social History, 1200–1500*

LUCY MARTEN *Late Anglo-Saxon Suffolk* (forthcoming)

Abbreviations

BAR   British Archaeological Reports

CAU   Cambridge Archaeological Unit

CBA   Council for British Archaeology

EAA   East Anglian Archaeology

HE   *Historia Ecclesiastica Gentis Anglorum* (B. Colgrave and R. Mynors (eds), *Bede's Ecclesiastical History of the English People* (Oxford, 1969)

LDB   Little Domesday Book. Alecto, *The Digital Domesday Book* (Hampshire, 2002)

NHER   Norfolk Historic Environment Record

NMAS   Norfolk Museums and Archaeology Service

PPG16   *Planning Policy Guidance Note 16: Archaeology and Planning* (Department of the Environment, 1990)

SCCAS   Suffolk County Council Archaeological Service

SHARP   Sedgeford Historical and Archaeological Research Project

SHER   Suffolk Historic Environment Record

SMA   Society for Medieval Archaeology

A Note on Burial Alignments

When describing the orientation of burials the convention of giving the head-end first has been followed. Thus a west–east burial lies with its head to the west and feet to the east.

A Note on Footnotes

Where no specific page references are given in footnotes this is because the entire cited work is relevant to the arguments developed there.

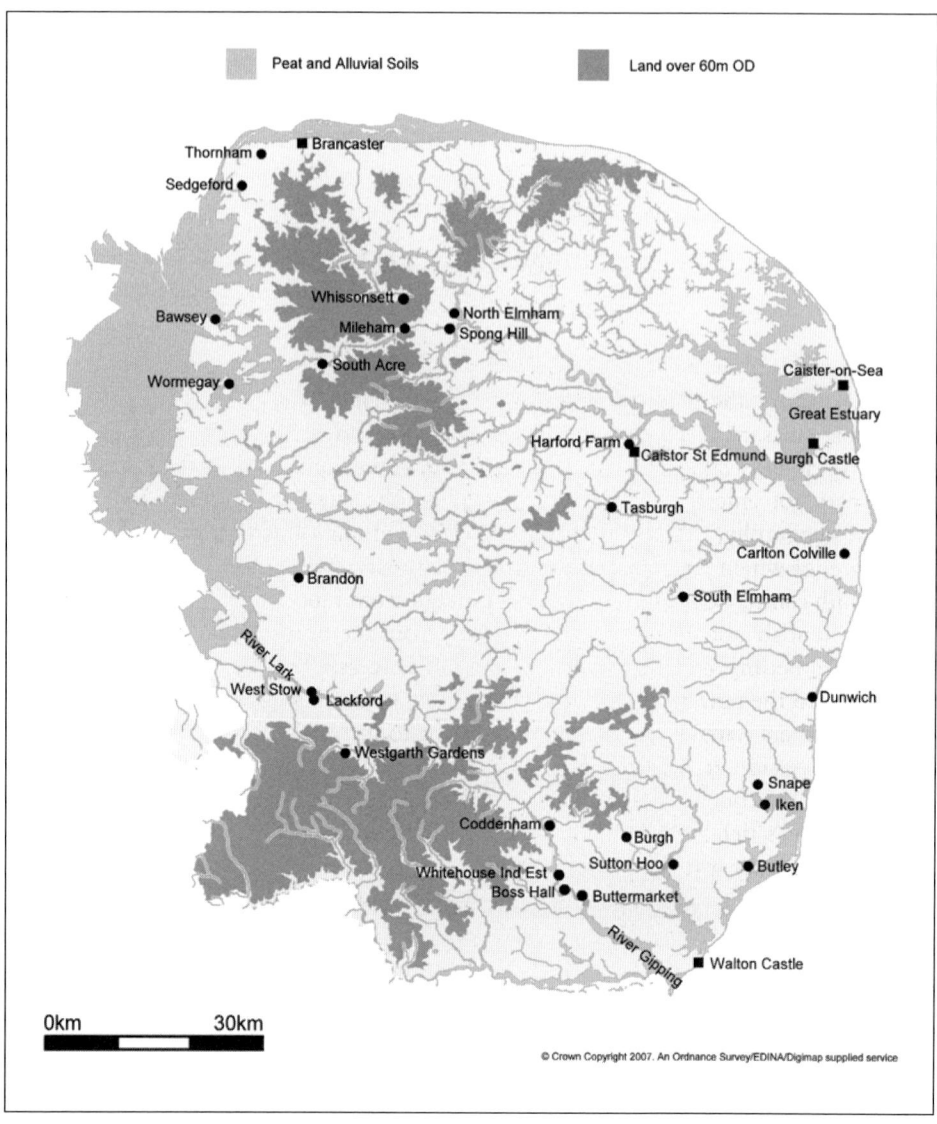

Fig. 1: Map of East Anglia, showing the principal places mentioned in the text set against the topography of East Anglia and areas of peat and alluvium.

Introduction

The Christianisation of the Anglo-Saxons was one of the most significant events in this country's history, the effects of which continue to shape society to this day. When Pope Gregory's emissary Augustine and his entourage landed in Kent in AD 597 — the event traditionally taken to mark the beginning of the conversion of the Anglo-Saxons — he was not entering a unified country.[1] In the late sixth century the country's political geography comprised a number of kingdoms of varying size and political allegiance, of which Kent was then among the most powerful. During the first half of the seventh century Christianity began to spread from kingdom to kingdom, radiating from its Kentish bridgehead and percolating from the north as members of the Irish church also became engaged in the conversion process.[2] The people of each kingdom responded to the new religion in different ways, with some readily accepting the new faith and others remaining steadfastly opposed to it, but by c. AD 700 the first stage of the conversion had effectively been completed across all of the Anglo-Saxon kingdoms.[3] This book is the first to use both the surviving historical sources and the eastern region's rich and varied archaeological record to examine the mechanisms by which Christianity was introduced into the Anglo-Saxon kingdom of East Anglia and to assess the rate at which and extent to which it spread throughout society.

Anglo-Saxon East Anglia

The Anglo-Saxon kingdom of East Anglia, which comprised most of modern-day Norfolk and Suffolk and perhaps the eastern part of the fen basin (Fig. 1), appears to have emerged as a political entity in the second half of the sixth century and by the early seventh century the Wuffing kings of south-eastern Suffolk had risen to prominence.[4] Some of the boundaries of the kingdom are relatively easy to identify, others less so. To the north-west, north and east the kingdom was bordered by the North Sea, at once both a natural boundary and a thriving maritime link to

[1] Mayr-Harting, *The Coming of Christianity*, pp. 51–68; Gameson, 'Augustine of Canterbury'; Yorke, *Kings and Kingdoms*, pp. 9–15; Bassett, 'In Search of the Origins', pp. 3–27.
[2] Mayr-Harting, *The Coming of Christianity*, pp. 69–77 and 94–102; Brown, *How Christianity Came to Britain*, pp. 118–37; Yorke, *Conversion of Britain*, pp. 122–8; Dunn, *Christianization of the Anglo-Saxons*, pp. 43–56.
[3] Mayr-Harting, *The Coming of Christianity*, pp. 13–113; Yorke, *Conversion of Britain*, pp. 98–148; Dunn, *Christianization of the Anglo-Saxons*, pp. 187–94.
[4] Bassett, 'In Search of the Origins', pp. 26–7; Carver, 'Kingship and material culture'; Yorke, *Kings and Kingdoms*, pp. 1–24 and 58–71; Scull, 'Before Sutton Hoo', pp. 1–7; Williamson, *Origins of Norfolk*, pp. 73–83; Plunkett, *Suffolk in Anglo-Saxon Times*, pp. 55–96.

Scandinavia and the northern reaches of Germany.[5] The processes of coastal erosion and deposition have greatly altered the shape of the coastline since the Anglo-Saxon period, with deposits having accrued along the central northern coast while at the same time the east coast has suffered erosion, most famously around Dunwich.[6] Sea levels apparently rose slightly during the Roman period, inundating much of the fens throughout the Early and Middle Saxon periods, before receding again in the Late Saxon period, leaving large areas of alluvial deposits bordering the Wash and the Norfolk and Suffolk coasts.[7] Throughout the Iron Age and Roman periods a large estuary existed in the vicinity of present-day Great Yarmouth (Fig. 2), but during the Late Saxon period the sea retreated and a shingle spit built up across the estuary's entrance.[8] This 'Great Estuary' was flanked to the north and south by a pair of Roman forts — at Caister-on-Sea and Burgh Castle — which, as explored in Chapter 3, were to play a significant role in the Christianisation of the kingdom.

To the west lay the natural barrier of the fens, although it is not clear exactly where the Anglo-Saxon political boundary lay. The Tribal Hidage, a record of the relative sizes of the tribal territories of seventh-century England, listed several small territories lying within the area of the fens, including the North and South Gyrwe, the Winxa and the Willa.[9] Their existence would seem to suggest that during the seventh century the boundary of East Anglia lay somewhere to the east of the fens, yet in the early eighth century Bede described Ely as lying within the East Anglian kingdom, suggesting that the smaller territories recorded in the Tribal Hidage had been subsumed by this date.[10] A fluctuating western boundary to the kingdom is also suggested by the series of Anglo-Saxon linear earthworks, thought to have marked territorial boundaries, which crowd the landscape to the south of the fens in Cambridgeshire, the most famous of which is the Devil's Dyke.[11]

To the south, the border with the neighbouring kingdom of the East Saxons has traditionally been assumed to have followed the line of the River Stour, which forms the modern boundary between Suffolk and Essex. However, recent scholarship has challenged this assumption and demonstrated convincingly that the rivers Gipping and Lark, which form a navigable corridor running north-west–south-east approximately between Bury St Edmunds and Ipswich, marked a much more substantial cultural boundary throughout later prehistory, the Anglo-Saxon period and well into the medieval period (Fig. 1).[12] Consequently, much of what is now

---

[5] cf. Hines, *Scandinavian Character*, pp. 286–91; Carver, 'Pre-Viking traffic'.

[6] Murphy, 'Coastal Change', p. 7; Williamson, *Sandlands*, pp. 128–32; Chester-Kadwell, *Early Anglo-Saxon Communities*, p. 51.

[7] Chatwin, *British Regional Geology*, pp. 95–8; Martin, 'Soil Regions'; Williamson, 'Soil Landscapes'.

[8] Green, 'East Anglian Coast-line Levels'; Murphy, 'Coastal Change'; Albone *et al.*, 'Archaeology of Norfolk's Coastal Zone', p. 14.

[9] Hill, *Atlas of Anglo-Saxon England*, pp. 76–7; Yorke, *Kings and Kingdoms*, pp. 9–15; Higham, *English Empire*, pp. 74–111.

[10] *HE*, iv, 19; Williamson, *Origins of Norfolk*, pp. 63–4; Bassett, 'In Search of the Origins', pp. 17–20; Yorke, *Kings and Kingdoms*, pp. 9–15.

[11] Malim *et al.* 'New Evidence on the Cambridgeshire Dykes'; Pestell, *Landscapes of Monastic Foundation*, pp. 11–12.

[12] Parker Pearson *et al.*, 'Three Men and a Boat', pp. 28–41; Newman, 'Exceptional Finds', pp. 99–100; Williamson, *England's Landscape: East Anglia*, pp. 29–30; Martin and Satchell, *Where Most Inclosures Be*, pp. 198–206; Rippon, *Beyond the Medieval Village*, pp. 140–43.

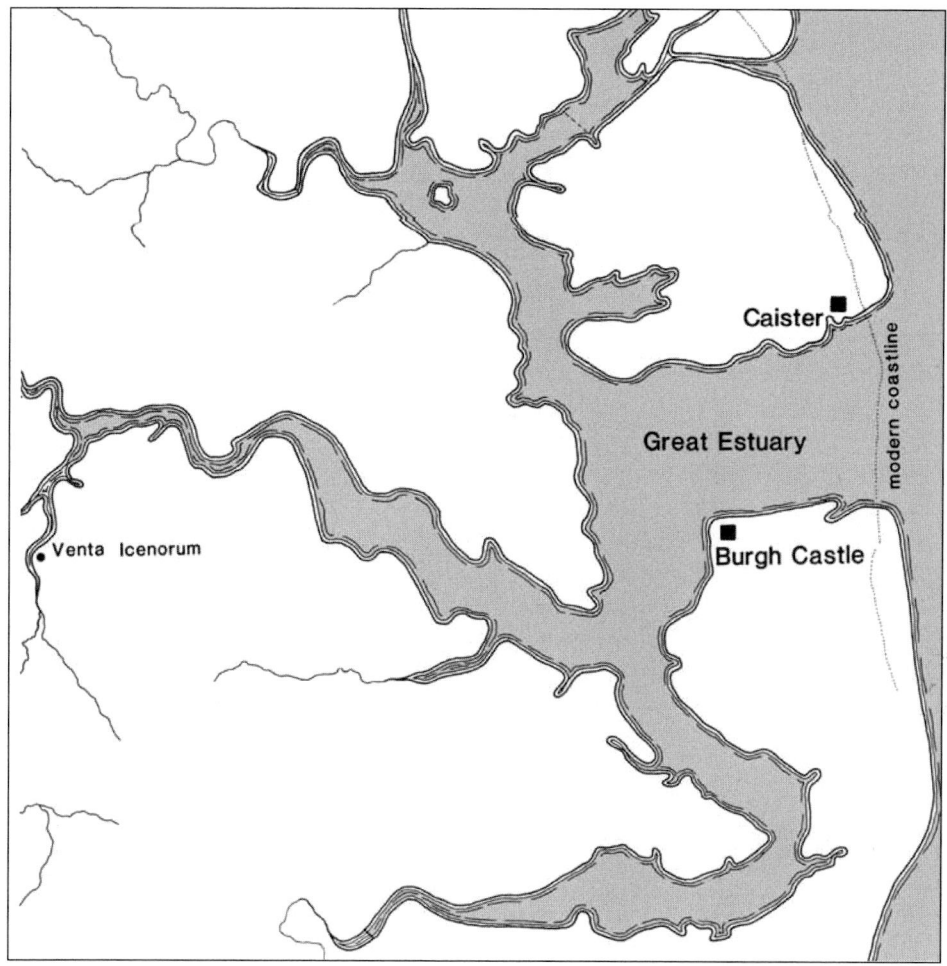

Fig. 2: The Great Estuary, showing the probable extent of the Roman coastline and the locations of Burgh Castle, Caister-on-Sea and *Venta Icenorum* (after Darling with Gurney, *Caister-on-Sea*, fig. 168). © *NMAS*

south-west Suffolk may once have lain outside the kingdom and therefore been subject to different cultural influences. Indeed, such differences are visible in the material discussed in later chapters, not least in the burial practices which were employed across the region during the Anglo-Saxon period.

The archaeological record

As is explored thoroughly in Chapter 2, Anglo-Saxon East Anglia is particularly poorly represented in the surviving historical sources, yet the kingdom's archaeological record is exceptional in both its quality and its quantity. This means that the archaeological record of Anglo-Saxon East Anglia is exceptionally well suited to answering questions such as those posed here. We are additionally fortunate that discoveries began to be recorded at a relatively early date, as

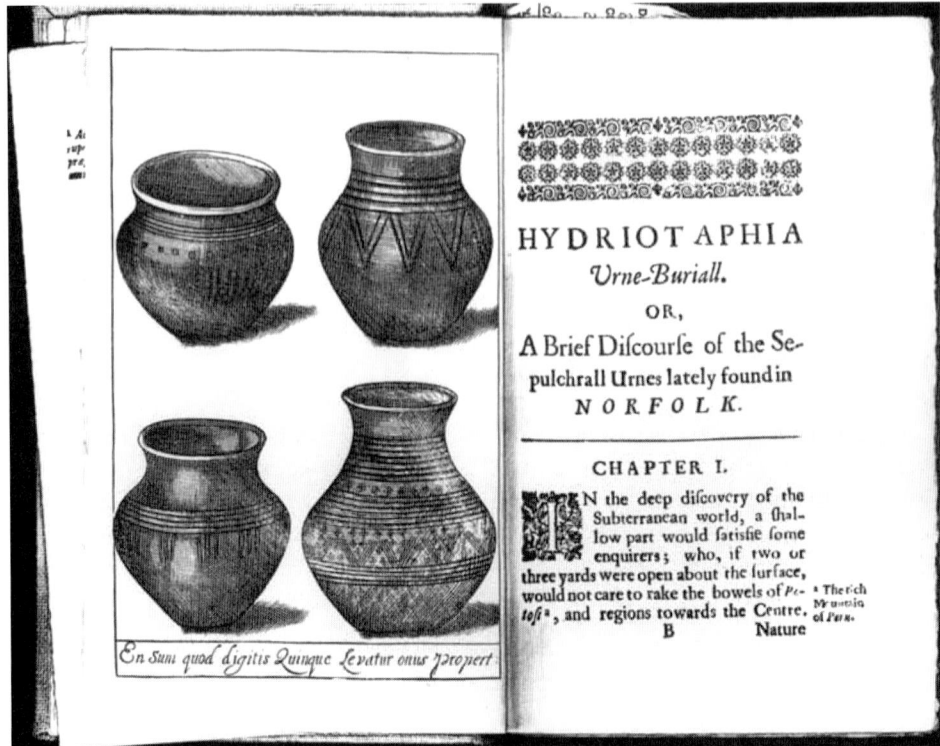

Fig. 3: The opening pages of Sir Thomas Browne's *Hydriotaphia*, published in 1658, which contained the earliest illustrations of East Anglian cremation urns.

demonstrated by the publication by Sir Thomas Browne in 1658 of *Hydriotaphia*, which recorded how at a site near Little Walsingham (Norfolk) 'were digged up between fourty and fifty Urnes, deposited in a dry and sandy soile, not a yard deep, nor farre from one another' (Fig. 3).[13] Many other important archaeological discoveries were made in East Anglia throughout the nineteenth and twentieth centuries, with the post-war period seeing a particularly dramatic rise in the number of archaeological discoveries owing to strategies instigated by the authorities in Norwich, Ipswich and Bury St Edmunds during the redevelopment of these towns and cities.[14] These strategies presaged the introduction in 1990 of *Planning Policy Guidance Note 16: Archaeology and Planning* (PPG16), which resulted in a vast increase in the quantity (if not the quality) of archaeological fieldwork in the region.[15] We are fortunate that many of these sites have been comprehensively published in the regional archaeological journals and the monograph series *East Anglian Archaeology*.

We are additionally fortunate that East Anglia's largely arable agricultural

[13] Browne, *Hydriotaphia*, p. 14.
[14] e.g. Scole Committee, *Ipswich*; Carr, 'Archaeological potential'; Norwich Survey, *Norwich Survey*.
[15] Darvill and Russell, *Archaeology After PPG16*, pp. 12–50.

economy makes fieldwalking surveys — the systematic collection of artefacts from the ploughsoil — particularly effective; several large-scale campaigns, such as the Deben Valley Survey in south-east Suffolk and the Fenland Survey in west Norfolk, Cambridgeshire and Lincolnshire, have produced results significant to this discussion (see Chapter 5).[16] Allied to fieldwalking is metal-detecting: vast areas of Norfolk and Suffolk have been examined by amateur metal-detectorists since the emergence of the hobby in the 1970s. Thanks primarily to the positive relationship developed between detectorists and the region's archaeological authorities, this information has greatly enhanced our understanding of many archaeological periods, the Anglo-Saxon period being foremost amongst them (see Chapter 4).[17] The archaeological record of the Early Saxon period (*c.* AD 411–650) is broadly characterised by artefacts from funerary contexts — cremations urns, grave-goods and human remains — and many Early Saxon cemeteries have been excavated across the region, as at Spong Hill (Norfolk) and Snape (Suffolk).[18] Two extensively excavated Early Saxon settlements also lie in Suffolk, at West Stow and Carlton Colville, although very few other Early Saxon settlements have been excavated across the region.[19] The archaeological record of the Middle Saxon period (*c.* AD 651–850) presents a complete reversal of the Early Saxon picture. Middle Saxon cemeteries are rare discoveries in East Anglia, the handful of excavated examples including the cemeteries at Harford Farm and Burgh Castle (both Norfolk).[20] The Middle Saxon settlements of East Anglia, by contrast, are easily recognised archaeologically because of the prevalence of Ipswich ware, a well-fired and robust domestic pottery produced at the eponymous *wic* during the Middle Saxon period.[21]

The extent of the period during which Ipswich ware was produced has been the subject of much debate. Initially its production was thought to span *c.* AD 650–850 on the basis of its associations with other seventh- to ninth-century artefacts.[22] More recently, Blinkhorn has argued that production did not begin until *c.* AD 700–720,[23] although the discovery of several hundred Ipswich ware sherds in seventh-century contexts at West Stow provides a compelling argument for the earlier dates.[24] It would seem that the production of Ipswich ware began perhaps as little as a generation after

---

[16] Newman, 'Sutton Hoo before Rædwald' and 'Survey in the Deben Valley'.

[17] Gurney, 'The Distribution of Metal-Detecting'; Chester-Kadwell, 'Metallic Taste', 'Metal-Detector Finds in Context' and *Early Anglo-Saxon Communities*, pp. 62–90; Newman, 'Metal Detector Finds' and 'Exceptional Finds'; Rogerson, 'Six Middle Anglo-Saxon Sites'.

[18] Smith, 'Anglo-Saxon Remains' (1901) and 'Anglo-Saxon Remains' (1911); Clarke, 'Norfolk in the Dark Ages II'; Meaney, *Gazetteer*, pp. 169–85 and 224–36; Myres, *Corpus*; Myres and Green, *Anglo-Saxon Cemeteries*, pp. 258–62; O'Brien, *Post-Roman Britain*, pp. 105–17; West, *Corpus*; Penn and Brugmann, *Aspects of Anglo-Saxon Inhumation Burial*, pp. 101–11; Chester-Kadwell, *Early Anglo-Saxon Communities*, pp. 173–212; Hills, *Anglo-Saxon Cemetery at Spong Hill I*; Hills and Penn, *Anglo-Saxon Cemetery at Spong Hill II*; Hills *et al.*, *Anglo-Saxon Cemetery at Spong Hill III*; *Anglo-Saxon Cemetery at Spong Hill IV* and *Anglo-Saxon Cemetery at Spong Hill V*; Filmer-Sankey and Pestell, *Snape*.

[19] West, *West Stow* and *West Stow Revisited*; Lucy *et al.*, *Anglo-Saxon Settlement and Cemetery*.

[20] Penn, *Excavations on the Norwich Southern Bypass*; Johnson, *Burgh Castle*.

[21] Hurst and West, 'Middle Saxon Ipswich Ware'; Smedley and Owles, 'Some Suffolk Kilns'; West, 'Excavations at Cox Lane'.

[22] Hurst and West, 'Middle Saxon Ipswich Ware'; Hurst, 'The Pottery'.

[23] Blinkhorn, 'Of Cabbages and Kings', pp. 8–10.

[24] West, *West Stow*, pp. 137–8, *Corpus*, p. 317, and *West Stow Revisited*, pp. 28–32.

the East Anglian conversion began in earnest in the mid-seventh century and its presence at a number of the region's key early ecclesiastical sites is of fundamental importance to the arguments developed later in this book (Chapters 4 and 5).

The current approach

Anglo-Saxon religious practices have attracted a considerable degree of academic interest: the evidence for the nature of Anglo-Saxon paganism has been presented numerous times,[25] while the history and archaeology of the Anglo-Saxon Church have received even greater attention because of the better survival of the evidence.[26] Yet, despite this high level of interest, relatively few studies have addressed the Anglo-Saxons' conversion from one set of religious beliefs to another, although it is extremely encouraging that the last few years have seen a number of new publications on the subject.[27] Within this limited set of studies the conversion of individual Anglo-Saxon kingdoms has been subject to disproportionate degrees of study: Kent's connections with Augustine's mission and the archiepiscopal see at Canterbury have attracted a great deal of attention, not least around the time of the 1500th anniversary of Augustine's landing in 1997,[28] while the Northumbrian conversion has been well studied because of its central place in Bede's writing and the region's high number of architectural and archaeological survivals.[29]

The conversion of the East Anglian kingdom, by contrast, has not yet been studied in any great depth, although several authors have considered individual aspects of the subject or taken broad-brush approaches to the Anglo-Saxon period. For example, an assessment of the surviving historical evidence for the pre-Viking East Anglian church was published by Dorothy Whitelock in 1973 and was subsequently built upon by James Campbell within the context of a wider study of the pre-Conquest history of the East Anglian diocese published in 1996.[30] Other authors, such as Margaret Gallyon and Trefor Jones, have focused on the lives and deeds of the East Anglian saints, placing them into their appropriate historical and social contexts.[31] On a broader scale, the mid-1990s saw the publication of a pair of books in which Tom Williamson and Peter Warner considered the historical and archaeological evidence for Anglo-Saxon Norfolk and Suffolk respectively. However, although the conversion was discussed in both cases, the division of the discussion between the two counties rather limited its effectiveness.[32] A similar

---

[25] e.g. Branston, *Lost Gods of England*; Owen, *Rites and Religions*; Wilson, *Anglo-Saxon Paganism*; Hutton, *Pagan Religions*; Ewing, *Gods and Worshippers*.

[26] e.g. Thomas, *Early Christian Archaeology*; Butler and Morris, *The Anglo-Saxon Church*; Morris, *Churches in the Landscape*, pp. 93–167; Blair, *The Church in Anglo-Saxon Society*; Foot, *Monastic Life*.

[27] e.g. Mayr-Harting, *The Coming of Christianity*; Fletcher, *Conversion of Europe*, pp. 108–29; Cusack, *Conversion*, pp. 88–118; Carver, *The Cross Goes North*, pp. 227–411; Yorke, *Conversion of Britain*; Dunn, *Christianization of the Anglo-Saxons*.

[28] e.g. Mayr-Harting, *The Coming of Christianity*, pp. 51–68; Wood, 'The Mission of Augustine' and 'Some Historical Re-identifications'; Gameson, 'Augustine of Canterbury'.

[29] e.g. Mayr-Harting, *The Coming of Christianity*, pp. 148–67; Blair, *The World of Bede*; Hawkes and Mills, *Northumbria's Golden Age*; Cramp, *Wearmouth and Jarrow*.

[30] Whitelock, 'The Pre-Viking Age Church'; Campbell, 'The East Anglian See'.

[31] Gallyon, *The Early Church*; Jones, *The English Saints*.

[32] Williamson, *Origins of Norfolk*, pp. 137–61; Warner, *Origins of Suffolk*, pp. 108–43.

geographical restriction besets Steven Plunkett's otherwise masterly synthetic summary of Anglo-Saxon Suffolk published in 2005, a volume of great interest and with much to offer, but which is crying out for a sister volume covering Norfolk.[33]

This book aims to provide an overarching synthesis of the relevant historical and archaeological evidence pertaining to the conversion of the kingdom of East Anglia, in particular dealing with the mechanisms by which the new religion may have spread and the speed and scale of its adoption throughout the kingdom. In doing so, it complements the significant contribution to the subject made by Tim Pestell in another volume in this series published in 2004, in which he examined the development of the monastic landscape of Anglo-Saxon East Anglia.[34] Pestell's book was primarily concerned with the period after Christianity had been established, rather than the conversion period *per se*, and the beginning of his period of interest effectively marks the end of that considered here.

Chapter 1 presents the theoretical frameworks which underpin this work, considers various archaeological approaches to the study of religion and religious conversion, and develops a series of archaeological indicators though which religious practices might be recognised in the archaeological record. Chapter 2 focuses on Anglo-Saxon East Anglia, beginning with an analysis of the surviving documentary evidence and establishing a historical framework within which the archaeological record can be studied. Bede's accounts of the conversion of the East Anglian royal dynasty and other missionary activities are examined and placed within their wider contexts. Chapter 3 turns to the archaeological record and considers the means by which the region's early ecclesiastical sites were established, starting with the reuse of Roman enclosures as missionary stations and encompassing other missionary foundations established within earthwork enclosures and at topographically isolated locations. Chapter 4 continues the archaeological theme by focusing on the archaeological evidence for the burial rites which were performed during the conversion period — specifically inhumation and cremation — in an attempt to recognise material traces of the new religion. Particular attention is paid to the cessation of cremation, the changing use of pyre- and grave-goods and the alignment of inhumations. A broader approach is taken in Chapter 5, which examines the restructuring of the Middle Saxon landscape brought about by the coming of Christianity. The landscape settings of Early and Middle Saxon settlements and cemeteries are contrasted to demonstrate the degree to which the conversion affected the population of Anglo-Saxon East Anglia. Attempts are also made to overcome the difficulty of exploring the archaeological evidence which lies sealed beneath parish churches via the use of surface finds made in churchyards and data from the many fieldwalking surveys which have taken place in the vicinity of churches. Finally, the Conclusion to this work describes the development of Christianity in East Anglia as it can be reconstructed from the archaeological and historical sources, and presents an agenda for further research.

---

[33] Plunkett, *Suffolk in Anglo-Saxon Times*, pp. 97–126.
[34] Pestell, *Landscapes of Monastic Foundation*, especially pp. 18–64.

1

The Archaeology
of Religious Conversion

Timothy Insoll has recently described the relationship between archaeology and religion as having been 'predominantly one of neglect'.[1] As is explored in this chapter, archaeologists have generally considered religion and religious conversion to lie at the limits of archaeological knowledge. Although the processualist movement went some way towards challenging this assumption, in the end its efforts had very little effect, while the post-processualist movement has also done little to address the archaeological study of religion. Greater hope is offered by 'cognitive archaeology', an amalgamation of the more successful aspects of both schools of thought, although this approach too has yet to achieve its full potential and is not without its own flaws.

This chapter also examines religious conversion as a process and considers the different approaches which might be taken to its study. As is discussed below, the archaeological record is particularly well suited to the study of conversion as the material traces of changing religious practices are made manifest in a number of different ways and on a number of different scales, ranging from individual artefacts to entire landscapes. Comparative studies demonstrate that the highly adaptive nature of Christianity means that any given conversion episode can only really be understood and appreciated within its own, highly regionalised, terms. To this end, the chapter concludes with a consideration of how we might attempt to recognise conversion in the archaeological record of Anglo-Saxon East Anglia.

Archaeological approaches to religion

Religion is an abstract concept, concerning individual experience, faith and spirituality, and existing only in the minds of its subscribers; it cannot in itself be preserved in the archaeological record or accessed materially.[2] Sometimes dubbed 'the numinous', this abstract element is only one aspect of religion, and, fortunately, there are many other aspects, such as the rituals enacted as a part of religious observance, which can and do leave strong material traces.[3] Archaeologists study the material traces of religious acts: the artefacts created for and used in them, the

---

[1] Insoll, 'Are Archaeologists Afraid of Gods?', p. 1.
[2] Renfrew, *Archaeology of Cult*, p. 12, and 'Archaeology of Religion', p. 48; Insoll, *Archaeology, Ritual, Religion*, pp. 19–20.
[3] Clark, *Archaeology and Society*, p. 232; Otto, *Idea of the Holy*, pp. 5–11; Insoll, *Archaeology, Ritual, Religion*, p. 19.

places in which they were enacted and the deposits which resulted from them. From such evidence we may attempt to reconstruct something of the religiously motivated practices which produced it, although this is by no means an easy task to accomplish. The difficulties inherent in attempting to infer religious beliefs from the material record alone were exemplified by Philip Barker, whose pithy observation that 'the site of the Crucifixion would be merely three large post-holes' starkly highlights the difficulty which we would have in interpreting the material remains of Christianity without the benefit of explanatory historical sources.[4] In this sense archaeological attempts to study religion cut right to the heart of what the discipline is arguably all about, in that they are an attempt to use material culture to get as close as possible to the inner workings of the 'ancient mind'.[5]

In 1954, Christopher Hawkes presented the 'Ladder of Inference', in which he ranked human activities according to the ease with which they could be inferred from the archaeological record. He summarised his hierarchy thus: 'material techniques are easy to infer to, subsistence-economies fairly easy, communal organization harder, and spiritual life hardest of all'.[6] In placing religion on the top rung Hawkes was not saying that attempts to study past religion archaeologically were futile, simply that they were more difficult than attempts to understand other aspects of society, although many archaeologists appear to have misunderstood his message. The problem, then, did not stem from any lack of material evidence; rather, it stemmed from the lack of a body of theory with which such remains could be interpreted.

The processualist 'New Archaeology' of the 1960s and 70s went some way to addressing this theoretical vacuum. The emphasis its practitioners placed on unpicking the formation processes behind the archaeological record showed great potential for increasing the understanding of the religious acts responsible for some material remains.[7] Foremost among the New Archaeologists was Lewis Binford, who was among the first to acknowledge that religion was a significant factor in the creation and structuring of archaeological deposits.[8] Within the model of cultural and social systems that he propounded, Binford identified three functional sub-classes of material culture, one of which comprised those artefacts that were primarily used in ideological practices, and he argued that once such artefacts were fully contextualised it would be possible to use them to reconstruct something of the religious practices and ideology behind them.[9]

Binford's work is typical of the attempts made by the processualist movement to interpret past societies in terms of a series of interrelated cultural subsystems, of which religion was often thought to be one. Regardless of the shortcomings of their ideological stance regarding the structure of society, it has often been said of the New Archaeologists that they ultimately remained more interested in what people *did*, rather than what they *thought*.[10] Therefore, although they considered the

---

[4] Barker, *Techniques*, p. 237.
[5] Renfrew and Zubrow, *The Ancient Mind*; Edwards, 'Archaeology of Religion'.
[6] Hawkes, 'Archaeological Theory', p. 162.
[7] Trigger, *History of Archaeological Thought*, pp. 294–300.
[8] Insoll, *Archaeology, Ritual, Religion*, p. 47.
[9] Binford, 'Archaeology as Anthropology', pp. 219–20.
[10] e.g. Trigger, *History of Archaeological Thought*, pp. 312–19; Renfrew, 'Towards a Cognitive Archaeology', p. 3; Parker Pearson, *Archaeology of Death*, p. 32.

archaeological study of religion to be theoretically possible, in effect they gave it little consideration and remained firmly on the lower, more functional rungs of Hawkes' Ladder of Inference.

During the 1980s growing criticism of the processualist approach to archaeology gave rise to a diverse but broadly unified range of post-processualist archaeological theories.[11] Rejecting most of the main tenets of processualism, post-processual archaeologists adopt a more relativistic stance and are particularly interested in studying the deliberate human actions — agency — behind the creation and use of material culture.[12] With such an outlook, one would expect post-processual archaeology to be particularly well suited to the archaeological study of religion, yet opinion is divided over whether or not this has proved to be the case. Some scholars have credited post-processualists with advancing archaeological approaches to religion by emphasising the meaningfully constructed nature of the archaeological record and developing methods for its interpretation.[13] However, despite the many benefits that their work has brought to archaeological interpretation, post-processualists have largely neglected religion, Insoll describing the near-total absence of religion from post-processualist analyses as 'a glaring omission within a theoretical approach otherwise concerned with recovering the maximum amount of information on all aspects of the past'.[14]

While both the processualist and post-processualist schools were and are theoretically equipped to make inroads into the archaeological study of religion, neither can be said to have achieved this successfully. However, there is a school of archaeological thought which grew out of the processualist tradition, but which incorporates some of the theoretical doctrine of the post-processualists, that has been actively addressing the archaeology of religion for the past twenty-five years: cognitive archaeology.

Cognitive Archaeology: 'the archaeology of the mind'

During the 1980s a number of archaeologists began to investigate ways in which the cognitive and ideological aspects of society could be addressed properly within the processualist mould.[15] In 1982 Colin Renfrew outlined the tenets of cognitive archaeology, which he defined as 'the study of past ways of thought as inferred from material remains'.[16] Cognitive archaeology focuses on the study of perception, attention, learning, memory and reasoning in the past and lists among its objectives the identification and interpretation of religious behaviour in the archaeological record, a task which Renfrew acknowledged was difficult, but not impossible.[17] In a series of publications Renfrew has developed a methodology for recognising religion archaeologically and argued that two main approaches to the material record may be taken in order to recognise the archaeological remains of

---

[11] Hodder, 'Post-Processual and Interpretative Archaeology', pp. 207–9.
[12] Whitley, 'New Approaches', pp. 5–7; Barrett, 'Agency', pp. 141–62.
[13] Wilkins, *Approaches to the Study of Ritual*, pp. 2–3; Bertemes and Biehl, 'Archaeology of Cult', p. 13.
[14] Insoll, *Archaeology, Ritual, Religion*, pp. 77–8.
[15] Johnson, *Archaeological Theory*, pp. 89–90.
[16] Renfrew, *Towards an Archaeology of the Mind*, p. 2, and 'Towards a Cognitive Archaeology', p. 3.
[17] Zubrow, 'Cognitive Archaeology', p. 187; Renfrew, *Towards an Archaeology of the Mind*, pp. 19–21.

religion: the search for the material residue of ritual practices and the use of iconography to understand past societies' religious beliefs. To this end he has identified five key aspects of religiously motivated ritual behaviour for which material evidence might be found.[18]

Renfrew's first aspect pertains to the focusing of attention. In communal worship, in particular, a range of devices might be employed to focus the attention of the worshippers: for example, the ritual may be conducted with a natural feature, such as a cave or a spring, acting as a focal point, or in a specific building, such as a temple or a church. Within such places one might expect to find additional attention-focusing features, such as an altar or directional seating, and see the repeated use of religious symbols. Movable objects, such as ritual vessels or special clothing, may also have been used, although these might not remain in the sacred area.[19]

The second aspect acknowledges that religious rituals often involve a degree of communication between this world and the supernatural 'Other World', meaning that the area in which such rituals were enacted is regarded as a liminal zone and is often treated differently from other social spaces. Consequently, such areas might feature overt displays of conspicuous consumption or they may be hidden and subject to exclusive access. They might also have required special preparation before entry was allowed — washing, for example — and surviving features such as basins or pools might indicate this.[20]

Renfrew's third aspect concerns the symbolic presence of the deity or deities which form the focus of the religious practices in question. Archaeologically this might result in two- or three-dimensional representations of the deity in either a symbolic or realistic form. One might also expect the repeated religious symbols referred to above to reflect the iconography of the deity, although some of these connections might not be easily understood without the benefit of explanatory texts.[21]

The fourth aspect, participation and offering, pertains mainly to the activities performed by the worshippers, which may or may not leave material traces. Worship may involve specific gestures or activities, such as prayer or dance, which might be reflected in the iconography employed in the sacred area. The sacrifice of animals or humans might be practised. Food and drink might be offered to the deity, as might other classes of material or artefact, either whole or broken.[22] Many of the activities designated as 'participation and offering' overlap heavily with the fifth aspect, funerary practices. Renfrew highlights the potential for funerary activities to be particularly indicative of religious beliefs, as the very act of burial is in itself highly symbolic, regardless of the additional symbolism and iconography employed in its execution, and the connection between religion and the explanation of death is often very strong.[23]

---

[18] Renfrew, *Towards an Archaeology of the Mind*, p. 21, *Archaeology of Cult*, pp. 14–21, 'Towards a Cognitive Archaeology', 'Archaeology of Religion', 'Cognitive Archaeology' and 'Ritual and Cult'; Renfrew and Bahn, *Archaeology: Theories, Methods and Practice*, pp. 414–20.
[19] Renfrew, *Archaeology of Cult*, pp. 18–19; Renfrew and Bahn, *Archaeology: Theories, Methods and Practice*, pp. 416–17.
[20] *Ibid.*
[21] *Ibid.*
[22] *Ibid.*
[23] Renfrew, 'Archaeology of Religion', p. 52.

Such are the aspects of the archaeological record that the cognitive archaeology school of thought promotes as being key to identifying the material traces of religiously motivated behaviour.[24] As is explored more thoroughly in the remainder of this book, each of these aspects is well represented in the archaeological record of Anglo-Saxon East Anglia, where they are strongly indicative of both pre-conversion 'pagan' practices and the Christian practices which ultimately superseded them. However, before we begin to examine the East Anglian material record, we must first consider the mechanics of religious conversion and examine some of the ways in which we might be able to see the transition from one religion to another in the archaeological record.

The conversion process

Mission — the act of bringing Christianity to non-Christians — has always played a significant part in the history of Christianity.[25] Having survived the persecutions of the third and early fourth centuries, Christianity became the official religion of the Roman Empire under Constantine's rule in AD 325.[26] From the late fourth century AD missionary activity began in earnest within the confines of the Western Roman Empire as an increasing number of barbarian peoples entered the Empire from beyond its eastern borders.[27] Many of these new peoples subsequently became Christians, as was the case in AD 376 with the Visigoths and, later, the Franks, whose King Clovis was baptised *c.* AD 500 as part of the wider conversion of his people.[28] Throughout the fifth and sixth centuries the influence of Christianity began to spread to areas that lay beyond the edges of the Roman Empire.[29] In AD 431 Pope Celestine sent Palladius to Ireland to consolidate evangelisation which had already occurred via Irish contact with Britain and Gaul, and his work was subsequently augmented when Patrick arrived from Britain.[30] Most famously, Pope Gregory sent Augustine to convert the Anglo-Saxons in AD 596, the vestiges of Romano-British Christianity having been largely driven out by the arrival of Anglo-Saxons in the early fifth century.[31] The remarkable and dramatic impact which Augustine's mission had on Anglo-Saxon society, and the East Anglian kingdom in particular, forms the focus of the rest of this book, but the spread of Christianity throughout western Europe did not end with the Anglo-Saxons.

The new converts in Ireland and England began, in turn, to send out missions of their own. Columba left Ireland and founded the monastery of Iona in AD 563,

---

[24] Renfrew, *Archaeology of Cult*, pp. 18–20, and 'Archaeology of Religion', pp. 51–2; Renfrew and Bahn, *Archaeology: Theories, Methods and Practice*, pp. 414–20.

[25] Lane, 'Archaeology of Christianity', p. 153.

[26] Frend, *Rise of Christianity*, pp. 439–517; Wood, *Missionary Life*, pp. 6–7; Rousseau, *Early Christian Centuries*, pp. 153–86.

[27] Wood, 'Conversion', pp. 85–6, and *Missionary Life*, pp. 7–8.

[28] Wallace-Hadrill, *The Frankish Church*, pp. 17–36; James, *The Franks*, pp. 121–61; Cusack, *Conversion*, pp. 63–87.

[29] Wood, *Missionary Life*, pp. 8–10.

[30] Mayr-Harting, *The Coming of Christianity*, pp. 78–93; Paor, *Saint Patrick's World*, pp. 8–45; Dales, *Light to the Isles*, pp. 27–37.

[31] Mayr-Harting, *The Coming of Christianity*, pp. 51–77.

from where he set about converting the Picts.[32] The monks of Iona — Aidan in particular — subsequently played a major role in the conversion of the Northumbrian kingdom in the seventh century.[33] In conjunction with the Franks, another Irishman, Columbanus, helped to Christianise eastern Gaul during the late sixth century, before turning his attention to Lombard Italy.[34] The newly converted Anglo-Saxons sent missionaries to their Continental homelands in the late seventh and eighth centuries.[35] In the late AD 670s the Northumbrian Wilfrid spent time preaching among the Frisians on his way to Rome, and on his return to England was instrumental in the conversion of Sussex.[36] He was followed by fellow Northumbrian Willibrord, who, after a period in Ireland, arrived in Francia in AD 690 and worked among the Frisians, remaining their archbishop until he died in AD 739.[37] The missionary work of Boniface began in central Germany in AD 718 and is well evidenced in letters to, from and about him that were collected together after his death.[38] With papal support Boniface spent his life evangelising Thuringia, Frisia, Hessen, Franconia and Bavaria, became archbishop of Germany and established a network of episcopal sees before his martyrdom in AD 754.[39]

Willibrord attempted to evangelise the Danish in the early eighth century, with little success. Christianity finally took hold in both Denmark and Sweden under the auspices of Bishop Anskar of Hamburg during the early ninth century, although his work was undone shortly afterwards by the rise to prominence of the pagan Vikings.[40] They, too, were eventually converted, however; Danish king Harald Gormsson became Christian in AD 965, although it is clear that many in his country were already familiar with Christian beliefs and practices before that date.[41] The conversion of Norway began in the last years of the tenth century and Christianity was established after much conflict between the Norwegian kingdoms about whether or not to accept the new faith. The English court of Athelstan appears to have played an important role in this process, as the Norwegian prince Håkon, an influential figure in the Norwegian conversion, had been educated there before returning to his homeland.[42] Elsewhere in Scandinavia Bishop Anskar's ninth-century attempts to evangelise Sweden enjoyed only limited success, but the thousands of Swedish runestones dating from the end of the tenth to the twelfth century suggest that Christianity ultimately became widespread and popular.[43] In Iceland Christianity had been familiar since the country was settled in the ninth century, although the Icelandic

[32] Dales, *Light to the Isles*, pp. 55–67.
[33] *Ibid.*, pp. 93–112.
[34] *Ibid.*, pp. 67–74; Wood, *Missionary Life*, pp. 31–5.
[35] Cusack, *Conversion*, pp. 119–34.
[36] Mayr-Harting, *The Coming of Christianity*, pp. 129–47; Thacker, 'Wilfrid'.
[37] Dales, *Light to the Isles*, pp. 145–60; Costambeys, 'Willibrord'.
[38] Tangl, *Die Briefe*; Emerton, *Letters*.
[39] Parsons, 'Sites and Monuments', pp. 280–84; Wood, 'Boniface'.
[40] Wood, 'Conversion', p. 88; Cusack, *Conversion*, pp. 135–41; Gelting, 'Kingdom of Denmark'; Blomkvist *et al.*, 'Kingdom of Sweden'.
[41] Sawyer, 'The Process of Scandinavian Christianization', pp. 69–70.
[42] *Ibid.*, pp. 70–74; Abrams, 'The Anglo-Saxons', pp. 216–23; Cusack, *Conversion*, pp. 146–8; Bagge and Nordeide, 'Kingdom of Norway'.
[43] Gräslund, 'Conversion of Scandinavia'; Lager, 'Runestones'.

people were subject to a number of tenth-century missions before officially adopting Christianity at the Althing of AD 999/1000.[44]

As is clear even from this simplified narrative framework of the conversion of western Europe and Scandinavia, the surviving historical sources present a decidedly 'top-down' view of conversion; that is, missionaries would target the ruler of any given society and, once the individual ruler had converted, their subjects followed suit.[45] Undoubtedly there were a number of political and social benefits which Christianity would have afforded a convert king, foremost among them greater integration with the powerful political entities of mainland Europe; and, similarly, from the missionaries' perspective, kings would have been powerful allies. But in reality this 'top-down' element was only ever one part of the wider conversion process, which began before any direct missionary approaches were made, continued long after they had occurred and affected all tiers of society.

When considering the mechanics of the conversion process it is important to think about how one recognises the point at which conversion might be said to have been achieved. There are no easy answers to this question and a great deal of uncertainty remains about conversion in the past in terms of what it entailed and how it was made manifest. In his work on the conversion of Norway, published in 1973, Birkeli divided the conversion process into three distinct phases (Fig. 4). The first of these was the 'infiltration' phase, a period of time during which a given people might become passively acquainted with Christianity through cultural or economic contacts. Second was the 'mission' phase, during which Christianity was actively introduced to the population by missionaries and the adoption of Christianity effected. This was followed by a third, 'institution', phase, which saw the establishment of an ecclesiastical infrastructure and the foundation of churches.[46] Birkeli's three-phase model was echoed by Foote, who was also working on Scandinavian material and who argued for three similar phases of conversion (Fig. 4). Foote's equivalent of the 'infiltration' phase was the 'familiarisation' phase, which included the same passive contacts with Christianity, but which also encompassed Birkeli's more active 'mission' phase. Foote then highlighted the 'conversion moment' itself, perhaps marked by the ruler of a society changing beliefs and declaring their people Christian. This is the point of the process most closely identified with the 'top-down' model of conversion. Lastly, Foote identified a subsequent period of consolidation, akin to Birkeli's 'institution' phase, which, Foote argued, might be said to have ended when metropolitan bishoprics were established.[47]

A phased interpretation of the conversion process is also supported by Insoll, who argues that the initial stages of the 'institution/consolidation' period advocated by Birkeli and Foote should be divided into three sub-phases (Fig. 4). The first of these was the 'inclusion' period, during which the new religion became integrated into the existing social and religious infrastructures. Second came an 'identification' period, during which the population began to identify and realign themselves with

---

[44] Cusack, *Conversion*, pp. 158–72; Vésteinsson, *Christianization of Iceland*.
[45] cf. Chaney, *Cult of Kingship*; Higham, *The Convert Kings*; Urbańczyk, 'Christianisation'; Yorke, 'Reception of Christianity' and 'Adaptation of the Anglo-Saxon Royal Courts'; Berend, *Christianization*.
[46] The structure of Birkeli's framework is explained in Lager, 'Runestones', p. 497.
[47] Foote, 'Historical Studies', p. 137.

	Birkeli (1973)	Foote (1993)	Insoll (2001)
1st Phase	Infiltration	Familiarisation	
2nd Phase	Mission		
		Conversion Moment	
3rd Phase	Institution	Consolidation	Inclusion
			Identification
			Displacement

Fig. 4: The phased models of conversion propounded by Birkeli, Foote and Insoll.

the teachings of the new religion. Finally, there was a 'displacement' period, during which the new religion successfully ousted the old and proceeded to build infrastructures of its own.[48]

Conversion should therefore be viewed as a multi-phased process which took time to accomplish, sometimes a considerable length of time, a conclusion that is rather at odds with the focus on the 'conversion moment' which is prevalent in the historical accounts of European conversions summarised above.[49]

Multiple Christianities

Since the nineteenth century studies of Christian missionary activity, both historical and contemporary, have become increasingly secular and academic. The last few decades, in particular, have seen a number of publications presenting a broad range of studies of Christianisation drawn from around the world and from throughout history. Examples include the Christianisation of the classical world,[50] early medieval Europe,[51] Scandinavia,[52] the New World,[53] Russia,[54] Africa and the Colonies.[55] Further publications have examined the methodological aspects of studying conversion or presented an eclectic mixture of conference papers.[56] With so many historical and contemporary instances of conversion so widely separated

[48] Insoll, 'Introduction'.
[49] Foote, 'Historical Studies', p. 137; Urbańczyk, 'Christianisation', p. 129.
[50] e.g. Frend, *Rise of Christianity*; Lane-Fox, *Pagans and Christians*; Brown, *Rise of Western Christendom*; Mills and Grafton, *Conversion in Late Antiquity*.
[51] e.g. Parsons, 'Sites and Monuments'; Crawford, *Conversion and Christianity*; Mayr-Harting, *The Coming of Christianity*; Russell, *Germanization*; Cusack, *Conversion*; Wood, *Missionary Life*; Bartlett, 'From Paganism to Christianity'; Yorke, *Conversion of Britain*; Dunn, *Christianization of the Anglo-Saxons*.
[52] e.g. Sawyer *et al.*, *Christianization of Scandinavia*; Vésteinsson, *Christianization of Iceland*; Brink, 'New Perspectives'; Berend, *Christianization*.
[53] e.g. Traboulay, *Columbus*; Mills and Grafton, *Conversion: Old Worlds and New*.
[54] e.g. Hamant, *Christianization*.
[55] e.g. Finneran, *Archaeology of Christianity*; Neill, *History of Christian Missions*.
[56] e.g. Cuming, *Mission of the Church*; Hofstra *et al.*, *Pagans and Christians*; Armstrong and Wood, *Christianizing Peoples*; Holtrop and McLeod, *Missions and Missionaries*.

by space and time, and such a large number of ways of approaching the subject, it is clear that no single methodology is ever going to be able to address the subject of conversion in its entirety. As Cusack states, 'the missionary historian should ideally be to some extent a social, political and economic historian; a geographer, ethnologist and historian of religions; as well as a Christian historian in the more usual sense'.[57] Cusack's list could be expanded further: 'anthropologist' is noticeably absent, as, indeed, is 'archaeologist'. The existence of such a large number of historical examples of conversion also makes it tempting to draw comparisons between conversions, although this is not as straightforward a process as we might hope.

In discussing the spread of Islam, Insoll describes the religion as a set of fundamental beliefs which have been adapted and interpreted within different cultural contexts around the world. Ultimately this has resulted in a diverse range of practices, cultures and material manifestations, all of which, however different, are considered to be Muslim.[58] These observations are equally applicable to Christianity, for in its long history Christianity has demonstrated a remarkable ability to take on different cultural shadings as different peoples have adapted it to their different world-views.[59] As a consequence there is no universal set of Christian ideals or practices, for in every instance of conversion these ideals and practices varied in response to the existing ideals and practices of the converting population. During the course of many conversions compromises were made with existing beliefs and many existing practices integrated and adapted to suit the new religion.[60] Certainly this was the case in first-millennium western Europe, where, as James Russell has argued, as the Germanic peoples gradually became Christian their versions of Christianity became progressively more Germanic.[61] A good illustration of this integrative approach to conversion is the appropriation into the new religion of existing religious festivals or deities, such as the adoption of the name of the Anglo-Saxon goddess Eostre, whose name the Anglo-Saxons gave to the month of April, for the Christian festival of Easter.[62] Such amalgamations might also be recognised materially via syncretic artworks in which local artistic styles are used to depict Christian iconography, a phenomenon recognised throughout the Christian world.[63] Among the many examples of such syncretic artworks from Anglo-Saxon East Anglia are a pair of seventh-century pectoral crosses executed in a demonstrably pre-Christian style (Plate 10); these artefacts, and others like them, are discussed in Chapter 4 (pp. 108–14).

The tendency for conversions to be adaptive in this way, with the new religion mapping itself onto the existing social and economic structures of the converting society and absorbing aspects of existing cultures, means that, even from the same starting point, no two conversion processes will follow the same path or have the same result. Consequently there are many Christianities rather than one single

[57] Cusack, *Conversion*, p. 2.
[58] Insoll, *Archaeology of Islam*, p. 1.
[59] Sawyer *et al.*, *Christianization of Scandinavia*, p. 1; Hefner, 'Introduction', p. 5.
[60] Pluskowski and Patrick, 'How do you Pray to God?'.
[61] Russell, *Germanization*, pp. 134–214.
[62] Mayr-Harting, *The Coming of Christianity*, p. 22; Wallis, *Bede*, pp. 53–4.
[63] Lane, 'Archaeology of Christianity', p. 168.

Christianity and, although they are linked by overarching beliefs, the fundamental differences between them mean that the conversion of a people from one place and time cannot be used easily as an analogy to explain the circumstances of the conversion of a different people in another place and time.[64]

Scholars of conversion have long been aware of this variation between Christianities and the difficulties which it presents.[65] Within the context of the conversion of the Scandinavians, Roesdahl was at pains to remind us that Scandinavia comprised a number of different kingdoms, each with different religions, languages and cultures, and that its various regions were exposed to Christianity at different times.[66] The highly regionalised nature of this area, she argued, requires that the conversion of each kingdom be studied individually in order to be properly understood, meaning that one cannot readily talk of a 'Scandinavian conversion'. Similarly, Staecker compared the conversions of three adjacent peoples in the Schleswig-Holstein region of northern Germany — the Saxons, the West Slavs and the Danes — and concluded that, despite their geographical closeness, each region saw the employment of a different conversion strategy that was entirely dependant on local circumstances.[67] Taking a broader geographical approach, Cusack attempted to develop a theory of conversion which might apply to the Germanic peoples of early medieval Europe via a comparative study of the Goths, Franks, Anglo-Saxons, continental Saxons, Scandinavians and Icelanders, but was eventually forced to conclude that each conversion was very different and could only be understood in its own immediate context.[68]

Closer to home, a strong reminder that different versions of Christianity existed alongside one another during the Anglo-Saxon period is recorded in the pages of Bede's *Historia Ecclesiastica*. Well into the seventh century there were distinct differences between the British forms of Christianity and their Roman counterpart which indicate that, although all forms were nominally Christian, there was no uniform version of Christianity in the British Isles.[69] The Synod of Whitby of AD 664 — at which various ecclesiastical differences, including disagreements about the manner of calculating Easter and the correct form of tonsure, were argued out between adherents of the British and Roman churches — is a testament to the strength of feeling on both sides and demonstrates that, occasionally, steps were taken to unify some of the divergent branches of Christianity.[70]

Every conversion to Christianity is unique, being shaped by any number of factors including the missionaries' own brand of Christianity, the nature of the society being converted and the various local practices which were rejected by or adapted into the emerging Christian doctrine. Therefore, while all the conversions referred to here took place under the nominal banner of Christianity, realistically each conversion can ultimately only be understood and appreciated within its own,

---

[64] Urbańczyk, 'Christianisation', p. 129.
[65] e.g. Wood, 'Afterword', p. 305; Mayr-Harting, *Two Conversions*.
[66] Roesdahl, 'Archaeological Evidence for Conversion', p. 2–3.
[67] Staecker, 'Mission to the Triangle'.
[68] Cusack, *Conversion*, pp. 30–62 and 173–80.
[69] Hughes, 'The Celtic Church'; Davies, 'The Myth of the Celtic Church'; Yorke, *The Conversion of Britain*, pp. 115–22.
[70] *HE*, iii, 25; Mayr-Harting, *The Coming of Christianity*, pp. 103–13.

highly regionalised terms, as Rosedahl, Staecker and Cusack discovered.[71] In fact, once the extent of the potential for local variation is accepted, many of the difficulties encountered in the traditional attempts to understand conversion can be surmounted. For example, much previous discussion has centred upon explaining why the conversion to Christianity in the Frankish kingdoms coincided with the origin of the practice of richly furnishing burials, while in Anglo-Saxon England it was associated with the waning of the practice, as is fully explored in Chapter 4.[72] Viewed in the context of the discussions above, it is not so surprising that two different peoples should respond to conversion in two different ways; indeed, in such circumstances we might be more surprised if they responded similarly. In the light of such arguments the analysis of the conversion of East Anglia presented in this book focuses on the evidence which survives from East Anglia itself and interprets that material within its own, regional frame of reference. While not denying the usefulness of looking to other episodes of conversion in order to assist and inspire interpretation, ultimately we should not expect to find the answers to such regionally specific questions anywhere but in East Anglia.

Archaeological approaches to conversion

We have already seen that archaeologists wishing to study religion must accept that the 'numinous', that part of religious belief which is entirely in the mind, is beyond the limits of our knowledge. Similarly, at its most fundamental level religious conversion is also 'all in the mind', and we cannot hope to understand the motivations of those converted individuals. Yet it is possible, despite these difficulties, to recognise some material traces of conversion in the archaeological record. Indeed, Martin Carver has gone so far as to argue that the study of material remains is the only viable option when attempting to understand the process of conversion and gauge its progress.[73] Material culture, unlike documentary sources, was created and used by both pagans and Christians alike and so provides evidence for the periods both before and after conversion.[74] Therefore, we are able to examine these material remains for signs of change which might indicate religious conversion. Such arguments have gathered strong support in some quarters; for example, Else Roesdahl is in no doubt that the conversion of the Scandinavian countries had a great effect on the material expression of religious beliefs, making the process particularly visible in changing burial customs, burial memorials, changes in iconography and the introduction of churches, among other aspects.[75] As is explored in Chapters 3 and 4, all the material changes highlighted by Roesdahl have parallels in the archaeological record of Anglo-Saxon East Anglia, and are argued here to be strong material indicators of the conversion.

[71] Roesdahl, 'Archaeological Evidence for Conversion'; Staecker, 'Mission to the Triangle'; Cusack, *Conversion*, pp. 30–62 and 173–80.
[72] e.g. James, 'Cemeteries' and 'Burial and Status'; Young, 'Myth of the Pagan Cemetery'; cf. Geake, *The Use of Grave-Goods*.
[73] Carver, 'Conversion and Politics', p. 12.
[74] Insoll, 'Introduction', p. 19; Lane, 'Archaeology of Christianity', p. 150; Burnell and James, 'The Archaeology of Conversion'.
[75] Roesdahl, 'Archaeological Evidence for Conversion', p. 2.

The search for archaeological traces of conversion should not, however, be limited to individual artefacts and features; we must also look to the wider landscape, for, as Carver also notes, 'the documented conversion was coincident with a radical reorganisation of the way that agricultural resources were exploited and people lived'.[76] This notion has recently been developed by Sam Turner, who has examined the conversion-period landscapes of Cornwall and Wessex and identified a number of significant landscape changes which can be directly linked to the conversion process, including the foundation of churches, the restructuring of agricultural resources, and the distribution of settlements and ritual sites.[77] Picking up on some of these themes, Chapter 5 argues that the well-documented changes which occurred in the ordering of the Anglo-Saxon East Anglian landscape were closely linked to conversion and that it is possible to use them to chart its progress. In particular, the changing relationship between settlements and cemeteries and the different locations chosen for the disposal of the dead can both be demonstrated to provide strong archaeological indications of the adoption of the new religion in the region.

Conclusion

We cannot hope to be able to understand completely the nature of Anglo-Saxon religions, either pagan or Christian, from the archaeological record alone, as intimated above. Unfortunately, this has caused archaeologists to take a very pessimistic view of attempts to infer religious beliefs from the archaeological record. We may not be able to see the material remains of religion, but we can and do find traces of rituals which were performed as a part of religious observance. These traces can tell us a great deal, particularly when used in conjunction with surviving explanatory texts. Renfrew has identified a number of material signatures by which ritual practices might be recognised archaeologically and the following chapters explore how these criteria might be readily applied to the East Anglian archaeological record.

We are similarly unable to study archaeologically the numinous aspect of conversion, but again we are able to study the material traces of religious change and identify something of the process and progress of the conversion to Christianity. In studying conversion we must reconcile the available historical evidence, with its Christian bias and emphasis on the upper echelons of society, with the body of archaeological, anthropological and sociological evidence which indicates that conversion is a long-drawn-out, multi-phased process which affects many different tiers of society. As is clearly demonstrated in the following chapters, the archaeological record is particularly suited to the study of conversion, for the material traces of religion and religious conversion are made manifest in many different ways and on many different scales.

Christianity is a highly adaptive religion and one of the keys to its success is the ease with which it has moulded itself to existing social, political, economic and

---

[76] Carver, 'Conversion and Politics', p. 19.
[77] Turner, 'Making a Christian Landscape' and *Making a Christian Landscape*, pp. 71–170.

religious structures of converting societies, even going so far as to integrate existing religious practices into its doctrine. In each case the mechanism of conversion will vary and the end result will be a uniquely regionalised version of Christianity, tailor-made for the population in question. Consequently, the questions posed in this book can only be answered by taking a detailed look at the *East Anglian* historical and archaeological records. With these theoretical and methodological concerns in mind, the following chapter examines the surviving historical evidence for the conversion of East Anglia.

2

The Historical Framework

Any attempt to study the history of Anglo-Saxon East Anglia is hindered by the very poor survival of documentary material and the incomplete and unreliable coverage provided by the few extant sources. This lack of documentary material only serves to emphasise the importance of the region's rich archaeological record, which is explored in the following chapters. This chapter presents the surviving historical sources and examines their provenance before placing them within their wider context. The majority of what follows is drawn from Bede's *Historia Ecclesiastica Gentis Anglorum* (*HE*), so the first part of this chapter examines Bede's motivation for writing this work and the sources which he used. The *HE* emphasises the important role that the East Anglian kings played in the Christianisation of the region, so the pertinent events which occurred during their reigns are also examined here. The few other surviving sources are introduced here where they are relevant.

The most important step towards the Christianisation of the East Anglian kingdom was the establishment of the episcopal see, at *Dommoc* in the first instance, although the see was later divided and a second bishopric established at Elmham. Debates have raged for a number of years about the locations of both *Dommoc* and Elmham; these arguments are considered here, and assessments made of the historical and archaeological evidence. The place of historically attested missionaries in the conversion process — Fursa, founder of the unidentified monastery of *Cnobheresburg*, and Botolph, founder of the monastery of Icanho — is also addressed. The chapter concludes by summarising the chronological framework of the East Anglian conversion as it can be inferred from the surviving historical sources.

The fate of the East Anglian sources

The dearth of East Anglian Anglo-Saxon documentary sources is made abundantly clear when the relatively large quantities of extant documentary evidence — charters, genealogies, regnal lists, administrative records and chronicles — from the other major Anglo-Saxon kingdoms are considered.[1] There is no reason to assume that the East Anglian paucity is the result of the kingdom having been any less literate than other kingdoms; indeed, there is strong evidence to the contrary. Prestigious manuscripts were certainly produced in East Anglia: for example, the

---

[1] Yorke, *Kings and Kingdoms*, pp. 58–60.

Vita Sancti Guthlaci Auctore Felice was commissioned by the East Anglian king Ælfwald (AD 713–49) and written *c*. AD 730–40 by Felix, an East Anglian monk of an unspecified house, who was clearly familiar with a wide range of the scholarly texts of the day.[2] It would seem that the lack of East Anglian documentary sources is a result of such material not having survived rather than never having existed.

Traditionally this poor survival rate has been attributed to the predations of ninth-century Viking raiders on most of the region's principal episcopal and monastic institutions, as recorded in the Peterborough Manuscript of the *Anglo-Saxon Chronicle*.[3] After the reconquest of the Eastern Danelaw in the early tenth century further incursions occurred during the eleventh century, when both Norwich and Thetford were attacked.[4] But were the Vikings solely responsible for the destruction of East Anglia's documentary sources? Apparently not, for the shortage of surviving documents is not confined to the pre-Viking period, as one would expect if this were the case; the post-Viking period of East Anglian history is equally poorly represented for what must be entirely different reasons.[5] It would seem that the impact of the Vikings has been overstated, and it is much more likely that the lack of proper curation was the major contributing factor.[6] By the time of the first Viking raids the East Anglian diocese had already been divided into two parts, with each see presumably producing documents of its own. Of the two bishoprics, only Elmham was re-established after the reconquest of the Danelaw and the see was subsequently transferred to Thetford in AD 1071/2 and from there to Norwich *c*. AD 1095.[7] We do not know exactly what implications these divisions, dislocations and relocations had for the survival of documentary material, but we can be sure that by the time the bishopric became permanently established in Norwich very little pre-Norman Conquest material survived in the episcopal archives.[8] This conclusion is supported by the fact that the early post-Conquest historians who considered the history of East Anglia all clearly relied upon the same sources that are available to us now.[9]

To complicate matters further, the majority of the surviving documentary sources pertaining to the East Anglian conversion were written in other parts of the country, often many years after the events they describe. Bede's *HE*, for example, was completed in the Northumbrian monastery of Jarrow in *c*. AD 731. Despite this, our reliance upon Bede's work is so great that without him, as Yorke states, 'we would scarcely be able to attempt the history of the East Anglian kingdom'.[10]

---

[2] Colgrave, *Felix's Life of St Guthlac*, pp. 15–19; Roberts, *Guthlac*, pp. 4–7.

[3] Plummer and Earle, *Two of the Saxon Chronicles*, p. 71; Whitelock, 'The Pre-Viking Age Church', p. 1.

[4] Plummer and Earle, *Two of the Saxon Chronicles*, pp. 135–6 and 140–41.

[5] Campbell, 'The East Anglian Sees', p. 9.

[6] Pestell, *Landscapes of Monastic Foundation*, pp. 72–6; Foot, *Monastic Life*, pp. 339–49; Lapidge, *Anglo-Saxon Library*, pp. 44–6.

[7] Whitelock, 'The Pre-Viking Age Church', p. 1.

[8] Campbell, 'The East Anglian sees', p. 9.

[9] Yorke, *Kings and Kingdoms*, p. 58.

[10] *Ibid.*

Bede's East Anglian sources

Bede's *HE* is widely recognised as the most important source for early English history. Indeed, for much of the history of early England the *HE* is the *only* source, making it difficult to verify much of the material contained within it.[11] The two main themes which Bede explored in the *HE* were the gradual conversion of the Anglo-Saxon kingdoms — a feat most often achieved via royal patronage and the establishment of the episcopal sees — and the unification of different Christian entities into a single whole.[12] In the process, he also described how the disparate Christian kingdoms overcame the initial difficulties in sustaining their new faith, eventually became united under the Kentish church and ultimately settled their many differences with the British church.[13] However, we must tread carefully when using the *HE* as an historical source, for Bede was primarily a theologian and an educator, and the dominant purpose of all of his works was theological instruction.[14]

In recounting his history Bede placed a great emphasis on the collection of documents, the clear citation of sources and the inclusion of sometimes lengthy extracts from original texts,[15] allowing us to see that the source materials that were available to him varied widely in their nature and geographical coverage. As might be expected, Bede's native Northumbria was particularly well represented, while Mercia, for example, was hardly represented at all.[16] Bede frequently referred to the East Anglian kingdom, and the nature of Bede's East Anglian sources can be reconstructed with some certainty, for he outlined some of them in his preface and conclusion and occasionally acknowledged his informants in the text. Additional sources can also be inferred.

Bede stated in his preface that much of what he had learned of the Gregorian mission of AD 597 and the subsequent spread of Christianity was derived from the academic efforts of Albinus, abbot of the monastery of SS Peter and Paul in Canterbury. Nothhelm, a priest of the London church, had acted as their intermediary and travelled to Rome on Bede's behalf, where he searched the papal archives for copies of letters pertaining to the English conversions. Bede also indicated that Albinus and Nothhelm provided him with details of the East Anglian episcopal lists and the division of the East Anglian diocese in the late seventh century.[17] It seems likely that Canterbury was also the original source for the passages of the *HE* which recount the East Anglian king Rædwald's Kentish baptism and Sigeberht's relationship with the Burgundian Bishop Felix (see below, pp. 28–32).[18]

Bede was explicit about the provenance of the material which interests us here, explaining that he 'learned the history of the church of East Anglia, partly from the writings or the traditions of men of the past, and partly from the account of the

---

[11] Kirby, *Bede's Historia Ecclesiastica*, pp. 2–5; Gransden, *Historical Writing*, p. 17.

[12] Barnard, 'Bede and Eusebius', p. 107; Foot, *Monastic Life*, pp. 20–25.

[13] Markus, *Bede and the Tradition of Ecclesiastical History*, p. 9.

[14] Brown, *Bede the Educator*, pp. 1–4; Campbell, 'Bede I', p. 25, 'Bede II', p. 46.

[15] Markus, *Bede and the Tradition of Ecclesiastical History*, pp. 3–5; Campbell, 'Bede II', p. 34; Meyvaert, 'Bede the Scholar', pp. 42–3; Lapidge, *Anglo-Saxon Library*, pp. 191–228.

[16] Kirby, 'Bede's Native Sources', p. 342.

[17] *HE*, iii, 20 and iv, 5.

[18] *HE*, ii, 15 and iii, 18.

esteemed Abbot Esi'.[19] The singling out of Esi in this fashion suggests that he was a major source for Bede's East Anglian material, and can in turn be taken to indicate that Bede had no direct contact with the East Anglian bishops during the compilation of the *HE*, for he would surely have acknowledged that if he had. It is reasonable to assume that Esi was the abbot of an East Anglian monastery in the eighth century, but unfortunately nothing more is known about him.[20] One possible explanation for the connection between the two men might lie in another reference to East Anglia which Bede made in his *De octo quaestionibus*, in which he described an illustration in 'the book which the most reverend and most learned Cuthwine, Bishop of the East Angles, brought with him when he came from Rome to Britain'.[21] Cuthwine was bishop of *Dommoc* at some point between AD 716 and AD 731; as there is no evidence to suggest that Bede ever visited East Anglia, the means by which he obtained the book remain open to conjecture. Therefore, Dorothy Whitelock suggested that the book in question may have been brought to Northumbria by Abbot Esi, thus explaining Bede's contact with him.[22] Of course, we will never know, but the idea is an attractive one.

Bede referred to a handful of other sources within the *HE*. In the famous passage concerning King Rædwald's two-altared temple (see below, pp. 28–9) he stated that 'Ealdwulf, who was ruler of the kingdom [of East Anglia] up to our time, used to declare that the temple lasted until his time and that he saw it when he was a boy.'[23] Bede's tone suggests that, if he had not met Ealdwulf himself, then he had at least met someone who had. Ealdwulf died in AD 713, eighteen years before the completion of the *HE*, but his link with the Northumbrian royal house — Bede's probable source — can be clearly identified. Elsewhere in the *HE* Bede records that Ealdwulf's mother, Hereswith, was a member of the Northumbrian royal house who had married into the East Anglian royal dynasty, the Wuffingas.[24] Bede did not give her husband's name, but he is thought to have been Æthelric, who reigned in East Anglia around AD 630–40, but about whom little else is known (Fig. 5).[25] Sam Newton suggests that Æthelric should actually be equated with Ecgric, who, according to Bede, succeeded Sigeberht and was killed alongside him in battle.[26] Although Bede had nothing more to say about Ealdwulf, it is possible that he also supplied Bede with details of his royal ancestors stretching back as far as Rædwald.

Another East Anglian source was acknowledged in Bede's account of Fursa, the Irish missionary who founded a monastery in the kingdom in the early AD 630s (his role in the East Anglian conversion is discussed further below (pp. 44–6)). By way of provenance, Bede wrote that 'an aged brother is still living in our monastery who is wont to relate that a most truthful and pious man told him that he had seen Fursa himself in the kingdom of East Angles'.[27] This 'aged brother' may have been a

[19] *HE*, Preface.
[20] Colgrave and Mynors, *Bede's Ecclesiastical History*, p. 6.
[21] Foley and Holder, *Bede*, pp. 145–7 and 151; Lapidge, *Anglo-Saxon Library*, pp. 26–7.
[22] Whitelock, 'Bede and his Teachers', p. 30.
[23] *HE*, ii, 15.
[24] *HE*, iv, 23.
[25] Stenton, 'East Anglian Kings', pp. 48–9.
[26] Newton, *The Reckoning of King Rædwald*, p. 44; *HE*, iii, 18.
[27] *HE*, iii, 19.

source of some of Bede's East Anglian knowledge, but Bede clearly also had access to a copy of the anonymous *Vita Sancti Fursei*, which he incorporated into the *HE*, embellishing it in places with information derived from his other sources.[28] Comparison with the earliest surviving manuscript of the *Vita Sancti Fursei*, thought to date from the early seventh century, demonstrates it to be a close, or more probably identical, copy of the version in Bede's possession.[29]

In addition to the overtly acknowledged sources, it is also possible to offer some conjecture with regard to other possible sources for Bede's East Anglian material. There were a number of connections between the East Anglian and Northumbrian royal dynasties and Bede would have been able to use Northumbrian material to reconstruct some of the history of East Anglia. Most notably, Rædwald had protected the Northumbrian prince Edwin during the period of his exile and East Anglian military forces helped to deliver Edwin's kingdom at the Battle of the River Idle in AD 617.[30] On a less positive note, Bede was also aware that Æthelhere of East Anglia had fought alongside Penda of Mercia *against* the Northumbrian king Oswiu at the battle of Winwæd in AD 655. Bede even cited Æthelhere as the cause of the war, although he did not elaborate, and the *HE* records that Æthelhere was killed in the conflict.[31] Doubtless details of these events, and many others, were preserved in the Northumbrian traditions with which Bede would have been familiar.

Bede also recorded two kingly baptisms which took place in East Anglia. The first was that of Cenwealh of Wessex, who spent three years exiled in King Anna's East Anglian court *c.* AD 645–8, where in Bede's words he 'accepted the true faith'.[32] The second was the baptism of Swithhelm, king of the East Saxons, which was sponsored by Anna's brother and successor Æthelwold (Fig. 5). The ceremony was conducted *c.* AD 661 by the East Saxons' own Bishop Cedd, but apparently took place in the royal vill of Rendlesham in south-east Suffolk.[33] Both accounts are likely to have been derived from information supplied to Bede by institutions in Wessex and Essex respectively, rather than directly from East Anglian sources. In the case of Swithhelm's baptism a further Northumbrian connection is possible, for Bishop Cedd was a Northumbrian and was instrumental in founding the abbey at Lastingham, a monastic house with which Bede was in contact.[34]

Ultimately, it is clear that very little of Bede's East Anglian material was actually derived directly from East Anglian sources. Many of the details he included in the *HE* can be shown to be drawn from Northumbrian traditions, while the traditions of Wessex and Essex also informed his narrative. The episcopal lists and an outline diocesan history doubtless came from Canterbury. First-hand accounts of East Anglia were apparently provided by Abbot Esi, King Ealdwulf and the 'aged brother' who claimed to have met Fursa, although Bede's account of Fursa was clearly derived from a copy of the *Vita Sancti Fursei* which was in his possession.

---

[28] Kirby, 'Bede's Native Sources', pp. 361–2; Plummer, *Venerabilis Baedae*, pp. 163–8; Brown, *Life of Fursey*.
[29] Krusch, *Monumenta Germaniæ*, pp. 434–49; Bieler, 'Ireland's Contribution', pp. 222–3; Rackham, *Transitus*, vi–vii.
[30] *HE*, ii, 12.
[31] *HE*, iii, 24 and v, 24.
[32] *HE*, iii, 7; Keynes, 'Rulers', p. 512.
[33] *HE*, iii, 22; Newton, *The Reckoning of King Rædwald*, p. 44.
[34] *HE*, iii, 23; Kirby, 'Bede's Native Sources', p. 347.

Tellingly, Bede does not appear to have been in contact with either of the East Anglian bishoprics, presumably the result of their not having responded to his enquiries, as he surely would have made an effort to contact them. Indeed, with the exception of the unidentified house of Abbot Esi, none of the region's monastic houses appear to have provided Bede with information, although he was clearly aware of the existence of some of them. Therefore, far from providing a comprehensive history of the East Anglian conversion, 'Bede's account of the kingdom is fragmentary, the traditions scattered in time and space'.[35] Having examined the sources upon which Bede drew, we now turn to consider the East Anglian historical framework which he presented.

The kings of East Anglia

The earliest surviving East Anglian regnal list is contained within a late-eighth-century Mercian collection of royal genealogies (Fig. 5).[36] Consequently, Bede is our main source for the history of the East Anglian kings, and the narrative of the *HE*

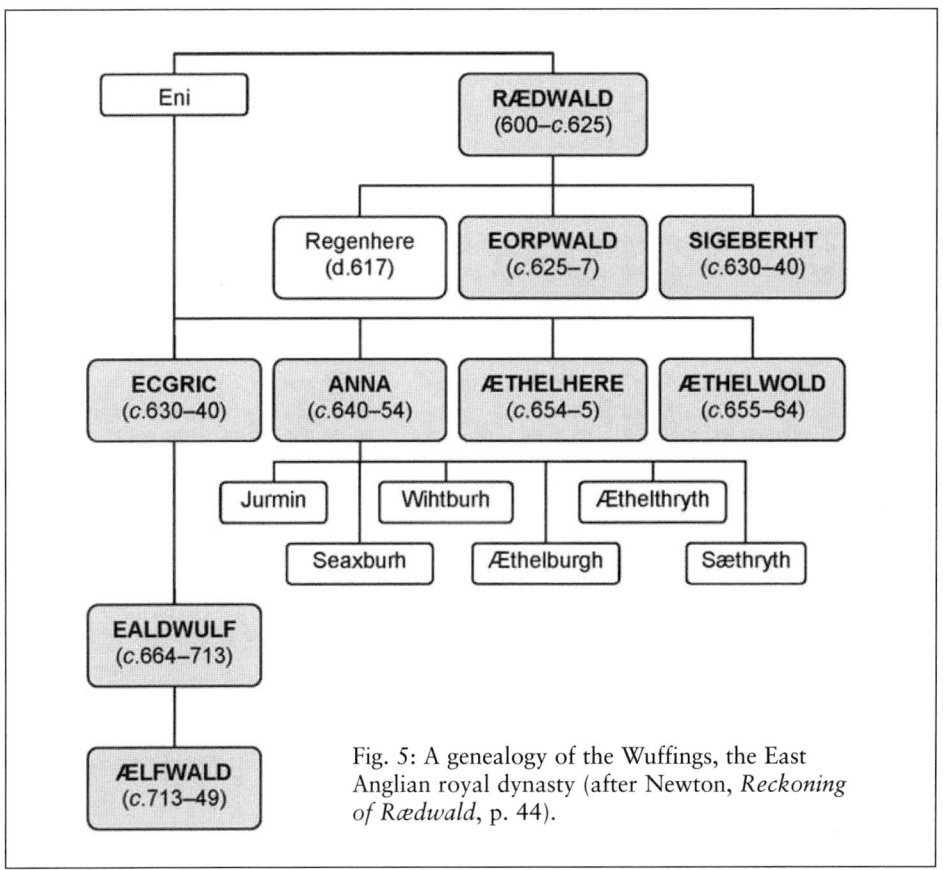

Fig. 5: A genealogy of the Wuffings, the East Anglian royal dynasty (after Newton, *Reckoning of Rædwald*, p. 44).

[35] Kirby, 'Bede's Native Sources', p. 363.
[36] Dumville, 'Anglian Collection', pp. 33–4.

is intimately bound up with their affairs. The achievements of each king, as presented in the *HE* and other sources, are examined here chronologically.

Rædwald (ante AD 600–c. 625)

The first East Anglian king to feature in the historical record as anything more than a name in a regnal list is Rædwald, who ruled the region during the first quarter of the seventh century.[37] Rædwald was also the first East Anglian king to come into contact with Christianity. This initial contact, and Rædwald's reaction to it, have since made him one of the most widely discussed kings of East Anglia, not least because of his possible connection with the Sutton Hoo ship burial. Despite these credentials, history actually tells us relatively little about Rædwald. Bede referred to him in four passages of the *HE* and he was briefly mentioned in the *Vita Gregorii*, written by an anonymous monk of Whitby in the first or second decade of the eighth century.[38]

According to Bede, Rædwald was the son of Tytil and the grandson of Wuffa, 'from whom the East Anglian kings are called the Wuffingas'.[39] During his account of the conversion of Rædwald's son Eorpwald by Edwin of Northumbria, Bede stated that Rædwald had 'long before been initiated into the mysteries of the Christian faith in Kent'.[40] Bede did not give a date for this Kentish baptism, but it must have taken place after both the arrival of the Gregorian mission in AD 597 and the establishment of the episcopal see of Canterbury.[41] In AD 601 Pope Gregory wrote a letter to Æthelberht of Kent in which he encouraged him to 'hasten to extend the Christian faith among races subject to you',[42] papal advice upon which Æthelberht clearly acted, for in AD 604 his nephew Sæberht, then king of the East Saxons, was baptised.[43] On this basis, it has been suggested that Rædwald's baptism may also date to around AD 604. Although the details of the baptism remain a mystery, it has been suggested that Æthelberht may have acted as Rædwald's godfather and that Augustine himself may even have conducted the ceremony.[44]

As might be expected given his motivation for writing the *HE*, Bede presented Rædwald's baptism as a profoundly spiritual undertaking, but it can also be interpreted as an overtly political gesture. Although a king in his own right, at this time Rædwald as king of East Angles was a subordinate king to Æthelberht of Kent; his acceptance of the new faith should be seen, therefore, as a statement of allegiance to Kent as much as a genuine spiritual conversion. This interpretation is lent credence by the subsequent unfolding of events, for Rædwald's conversion did not last long. The *HE* states that 'on his return home, he was seduced by his wife and by certain evil teachers and perverted from the sincerity of his faith, so that his last state was worse than his first'.[45] Rædwald's situation was resolved with what Nicholas Higham describes as 'a balancing act of some subtlety', which allowed

---

[37] Stenton, 'East Anglian Kings'; Dumville, 'Anglian Collection'; Campbell, 'Rædwald'.
[38] *HE*, ii, 5, 12 and 15 and iii, 18; Colgrave, *Earliest Life of Gregory*, p. 99.
[39] *HE*, ii, 15.
[40] *HE*, ii, 15.
[41] *HE*, i, 25 and 26.
[42] Martyn, *Letters of Gregory*, 11.37; see also *HE*, i, 32.
[43] *HE*, ii, 3.
[44] Newton, *The Reckoning of King Rædwald*, pp. 9–10.
[45] *HE*, ii, 15.

both the old and the new gods to be served.[46] As Bede put it, Rædwald 'seemed to be serving both Christ and the gods whom he had previously served; in the same temple he had an altar for the Christian sacrifice and another small altar on which to offer victims to devils'.[47] The two-altared temple apparently survived until at least the late seventh century, for Bede records that Ealdwulf remembered seeing it when he was a boy (see above, p. 25).[48]

Was Rædwald really an apostate? Bede clearly thought so, branding Rædwald 'noble by birth though ignoble in his deeds'.[49] Certainly, he did not adhere exclusively to his new faith, but it would appear that he did not reject it outright either. By balancing the two religions, it could be argued that Rædwald considered himself a Christian of sorts.[50] Despite this, there is little evidence to suggest that Rædwald became a Christian in anything more than name. During his reign Christianity did not become the sole, or even the dominant, religion of East Anglia and no steps were taken towards developing any kind of diocesan infrastructure. In addition, the artefacts and rites employed in Rædwald's probable burial at Sutton Hoo displayed strong pre-Christian imagery, suggesting that those who buried him did not consider him to be truly Christian.[51] Indeed, given Bede's motives for writing the *HE*, it seems incongruous that he should have included Rædwald's story at all, but his inclusion may be explained by the role which he played in protecting and enthroning Edwin, the king who brought Christianity to Bede's native Northumbria.

Bede recorded that Æthelberht of Kent died in AD 616 and described how he had been the third English king to hold *imperium* or overlordship over all of the southern kingdoms.[52] Bede continued: 'the fourth was Rædwald, king of the East Angles, who even during the lifetime of Æthelberht was gaining the leadership for his own people'. This sentence has proved difficult to translate, but is now widely taken to mean that while Rædwald remained subordinate to his overlord, he was growing in might even before Æthelberht's death.[53] Certainly, once Æthelberht was dead, Rædwald emerged from his shadow as one of the most powerful rulers of his day and the rejection of his former overlord's religion can be seen as a statement of new-found independence. During Rædwald's *imperium* a subject-king would have gained little by pursuing Christianity.

At this point in the early seventh century the Gregorian mission headed by Augustine appears to have lost its impetus. While Rædwald's power grew, Æthelberht was succeeded by his unbaptised son Eadbald, under whose rule the kingdom of Kent also lapsed from Christianity.[54] Eadbald followed the Anglo-Saxon tradition and took his dead father's wife, making him doubly unholy in the eyes of the church, the practice having been the subject of disapproving correspondence between Augustine and

---

[46] Higham, *English Empire*, pp. 183–217, quote at p. 190.
[47] *HE*, ii, 15.
[48] *HE*, ii, 15.
[49] *HE*, ii, 15.
[50] Newton, *The Reckoning of King Rædwald*; Kilbride, 'Why I Feel Cheated', pp. 5–7.
[51] Carver, *Sutton Hoo: Burial Ground of Kings?* and *Sutton Hoo: A Seventh-Century Princely Burial Ground*, pp. 177–99.
[52] *HE*, ii, 5; Higham, *English Empire*, pp. 47–73.
[53] Wallace-Hadrill, *Bede's Ecclesiastical History*, pp. 59 and 220–22.
[54] *HE*, ii, 5.

Gregory the Great.[55] And Sæberht of Essex, whom Æthelberht had baptised in AD 604, died *c.* AD 616, after which his three sons are reported to have quickly steered the kingdom back into idolatry, even going so far as to exile the bishop and his retinue.[56]

Meanwhile, in the north, Æthelfrith of Bernicia was growing in might, prompting the appearance of Edwin of Deria at the East Anglian court in the AD 610s. The events of Edwin's stay are recounted in both the *HE* and the anonymous *Vita Gregorii*. Rædwald was offered money to kill Edwin, but his wife persuaded him not to and in AD 617 the new overlord and his army marched north to meet Æthelfrith. Battle was joined on the banks of the River Idle (in modern Nottinghamshire), where Rædwald's son Regenhere was killed, along with Æthelfrith.[57] As a result of the victory Edwin was installed as king of Northumbria; he would have remained indebted to Rædwald, his protector and deliverer, for the rest of his life. After recounting this episode Bede made no further mention of Rædwald, although once he had become overlord of the English kingdoms he appears to have enjoyed a period of political stability, peace and prosperity. In breaking off his narrative at this point Bede also confirmed the supposition presented earlier that Rædwald's story was included because of its importance to the success of Edwin. We are not told when or how Rædwald died, but it would appear that he died *c.* AD 625, if not slightly before,[58] later becoming associated, as mentioned above, with the high-status ship burial under Mound 1 at Sutton Hoo.[59]

Eorpwald (c. AD 625–7)

After Rædwald's death his surviving son, Eorpwald, became king of the East Angles. We know very little about him beyond the sparse details which Bede provided. In AD 627, some time after his investiture and, significantly, after the death of his overlord and sponsor Rædwald, Edwin of Northumbria converted to Christianity and, we are told, 'so great was Edwin's devotion to the true worship, that he also persuaded Eorpwald, son of Rædwald and king of the East Angles, to abandon his idolatrous superstitions and, together with his kingdom, to accept the Christian faith and sacraments'.[60] By then Edwin had become an overlord in his own right and Eorpwald's acceptance of Christianity needs to be viewed in the same context as both Sæberht and Rædwald's baptisms under Æthelberht — that is, that of a subordinate king accepting his overlord's faith. Again, there is no evidence to suggest that the East Anglian kingdom under Eorpwald was converted in anything more than a nominal sense, for there was no development of an episcopal infrastructure and Eorpwald's conversion was, literally, short-lived. Bede reported that 'Eorpwald was killed not long after he had accepted the faith, by a heathen called Ricberht. Thereupon the kingdom remained in error for three years, until Eorpwald's brother Sigeberht came to the throne.'[61] It is not clear whether this coup

[55] Chaney, *Cult of Kingship*, pp. 25–8; Martyn, *Letters of Gregory*, 8.37; *HE*, i, 27.
[56] *HE*, ii, 5.
[57] *HE*, ii, 12; Colgrave, *Earliest Life of Gregory*, p. 99.
[58] Chadwick, 'Sutton Hoo Ship Burial', p. 85; Kirby, *Earliest English Kings*, pp. 66 and 77.
[59] Chadwick, 'Sutton Hoo Ship Burial', p. 87; Bruce-Mitford, *The Sutton Hoo Ship-Burial*, vol. I, pp. 683–717.
[60] *HE*, ii, 15.
[61] *HE*, ii, 15.

should be viewed as a backlash against the new Christian religion or merely as an unfortunate moment in secular politics. Whether Ricberht subsequently ruled the kingdom for the three 'erroneous' years is also unknown, but what we do know is that the accession of Sigeberht in AD 630/31 marked the beginning of the East Anglian conversion proper.

Sigeberht and Ecgric (AD 630/1–c. 640)

Bede discussed Sigeberht's story twice in the *HE*.[62] Bede described Sigeberht as 'a good and religious man' and 'a devout Christian and a very learned man in all respects', and recorded that during his brother's reign Sigeberht had been in exile in Gaul, having fled from Rædwald's enmity.[63] The precise reason for his exile was not disclosed, but his being described as Eorpwald's brother and not Rædwald's son has led some to suggest that he was actually Rædwald's stepson and consequently out of favour.[64] Sigeberht had become a Christian while in Gaul and 'as soon as he began to reign he made it his business to see that the whole kingdom shared his faith'.[65]

Returning to the phased model of the conversion process discussed in the previous chapter and illustrated in Figure 4, Foote's 'familiarisation' or Birkeil's 'infiltration' phase might be thought of as spanning the period between Rædwald's short-lived baptism and Sigeberht's accession, during which the East Anglian kingdom was passively exposed to Christianity through economic and political ties, but not through direct missionary contact. However, once Sigeberht was enthroned the East Anglian conversion process quickly progressed into the second, 'mission', phase.[66]

Sigeberht was aided in his efforts by Felix, who became the first bishop of the East Angles. Born and consecrated in Burgundy, he was sent to East Anglia by Archbishop Honorius.[67] Little is known of Felix's Continental background, although a Bishop Felix was recorded as holding the Burgundian see of Châlons in AD 626/7 and it has been suggested that he may have become a political exile after the death of the Frankish king Chlotar II in AD 629.[68] Sigeberht and Felix may have previously encountered one another in Gaul, and it is probable that Honorius sent Felix to East Anglia in response to a request for assistance from Sigeberht.[69] As both men were familiar with the Frankish church and doubtless had languages in common, Felix would have been the obvious candidate. Sigeberht was apparently keen to 'imitate some of the excellent institutions which he had seen in Gaul, and established a school where boys could be taught letters' and Bishop Felix was able to provide him with 'masters and teachers as in the Kentish school'.[70] The subsequent foundation of the diocese (considered further below, on pp. 35–44) marked the beginning of the third 'institution/consolidation' phase of the conversion process (Fig. 4).

---

[62] *HE*, ii, 15 and iii, 18.
[63] *HE*, iii, 18; *HE*, ii, 15.
[64] Colgrave and Mynors, *Bede's Ecclesiastical History*, p. 266 n. 3; Campbell, 'Sigeberht'.
[65] *HE*, ii, 15.
[66] Lager, 'Runestones', p. 497; Foote, 'Historical Studies', p. 137.
[67] *HE*, ii, 15.
[68] McClure and Collins, *Bede*, pp. 381–2.
[69] Yorke, 'Adaptation', pp. 246–7.
[70] *HE*, iii, 18.

Bede also recorded that Sigeberht welcomed at least one missionary, Fursa, to the kingdom and encouraged him to found a monastery at *Cnobheresburg* (pp. 44–6).[71] Fursa's missionary activities were by no means unique, however, and it is likely that he was included in the *HE* only because Bede had a convenient source. We can be certain that there were other missionaries at work in East Anglia who were not mentioned in the *HE*, the most notable being Botolph, whose founding of a monastery at Iken is recorded in the *Anglo-Saxon Chronicle* for the year AD 653 (see pp. 47–50).[72]

After setting a number of religious developments in motion, Sigeberht wished to pursue holy matters on a more personal level and so 'resigned his kingly office and entrusted it to his kinsman Ecgric, who had previously ruled over a part of the kingdom'.[73] Once again, historical details are lacking, but this presumably occurred in the mid- to late AD 630s and Ecgric is thought to have been Sigeberht's cousin. There are two possible readings of this situation: either Ecgric had ruled during the three 'erroneous' years after Eorpwald's death, before Sigeberht's return from exile; or perhaps he had shared in Sigeberht's rule, probably by ruling over a subdivision of the East Anglian kingdom. Such arrangements were certainly common in Kent and Northumbria, and it may well be that the arrangement was more common in East Anglia than the historical sources suggest.[74] It is even possible that we are being afforded an early glimpse of the existence of the North-folk and the South-folk, from whom the later county names of Norfolk and Suffolk were derived.

After his abdication Sigeberht 'entered a monastery which he himself had founded. He received the tonsure and made it his business to fight instead for the heavenly kingdom.'[75] We are not given the name of this monastery, although a later tradition, interlineated into the twelfth-century *Liber Eliensis*, records that it was *Betrichesworde* (Bury St Edmunds); this evidence is unreliable, however.[76] Entering the cloister did not remove Sigeberht from the public consciousness, for *c.* AD 640, when Sigeberht had been in his monastery for 'some considerable time', the East Anglian kingdom was attacked by Penda of Mercia and the East Anglians asked Sigeberht, as their 'most vigorous and distinguished leader', to join the fight. He refused, however, and was forcibly dragged from his monastery to the battlefield. True to his new vocation, Sigeberht refused to carry anything but a staff into battle and, unsurprisingly, was killed, along with Ecgric and much of the East Anglian army.[77] The location of the battlefield is unknown, although it presumably lay towards the western border of the kingdom. Despite losing the battle, the East Anglian kingdom survived this attack and the two cousins were succeeded by Anna, another of Eni's sons and nephew of Rædwald (Fig. 5).

---

[71] *HE*, iii, 19.
[72] Plummer and Earle, *Two of the Saxon Chronicles*, pp. 28–9.
[73] *HE*, iii, 18.
[74] Yorke, *Kings and Kingdoms*, pp. 32–9 and 74–81.
[75] *HE*, iii, 18.
[76] Blake, *Liber Eliensis*, p. 11; Whitelock, 'The Pre-Viking Age Church', p. 4; Pestell, 'An Analysis of Monastic Foundation', p. 321.
[77] *HE*, iii, 18.

Anna (c. AD 640–54)

Bede wrote of Anna in approving tones, calling him 'a good man and blessed with a good and saintly family'.[78] We are told that Anna continued the developments begun during Sigeberht's reign, adding greatly to the endowments of *Cnobheresburg* and presumably also to those of many of the other religious houses that existed at that time.[79] After Fursa's death *c.* AD 650 Anna was expelled by the Mercians and *Cnobheresburg* was despoiled, but it is appropriate to consider here the other ways in which Christianity flourished during his reign. Bede recorded, for instance, that Anna was responsible for the baptism of King Cenwealh of Wessex.[80] Cenwealh had been attacked by Penda of Mercia for slighting his sister and had been driven into exile in East Anglia. He stayed at Anna's court for three years, during which time he was converted to Christianity, yet another example of a royal exile adopting his protector's faith.

Bede did not record any other examples of Anna's Christian deeds, although there were surely many, but he did write about Anna's daughters, who were all important religious figures in their own right. After marriages to Tondberht, an ealdorman of the South Gyrwe, and King Ecgfrith of Northumbria, Anna's daughter Æthelthryth entered the monastery at Coldingham *c.* AD 672, but a year later was appointed the founding abbess of Ely.[81] On her death she was succeeded at Ely by her sister Seaxburh, who had previously been married to King Eorcenberht of Kent.[82] Another of Anna's daughters, Æthelburh, became the abbess of the Continental monastery of Faremoutiers-en-Brie, as did her step-sister Sæthryth.[83]

In AD 653 Anna was killed in battle by Penda of Mercia. The later *Liber Eliensis* records the tradition that he was buried at Blythburgh, where his remains continued to be venerated into the twelfth century.[84]

Anna's successors (AD 653–713)

Anna was succeeded by his short-lived brother Æthelhere (Fig. 5), who reigned as Penda's client-king from AD 653 and fought alongside Penda at the Battle of the Winwæd in AD 655, where he was killed along with Penda by Oswiu of Northumbria. Bede stated that Æthelhere was the cause of the battle, although he did not specify in what way.[85] Æthelhere was succeeded by a second brother, Æthelwold (Fig. 5), who, free from Penda's power, continued the Christian traditions of his kinsmen in a reign which lasted until around AD 664.[86] Æthelwold sponsored the baptism of Swithhelm of Essex, which took place at the royal vill of Rendlesham *c.* AD 661 and was conducted by Bishop Cedd of the East

---

[78] *HE*, iii, 7.
[79] *HE*, iii, 19.
[80] *HE*, iii, 7.
[81] Campbell, 'Bede's Words for Places', p. 5.
[82] *HE*, iv, 19.
[83] *HE*, iii, 8.
[84] *HE*, iii, 18; Plummer and Earle, *Two of the Saxon Chronicles*, pp. 28–9; Blake, *Liber Eliensis*, p. 18; Pestell, *Landscapes of Monastic Foundation*, pp. 91–2; Fairweather, *Liber Eliensis*, pp. 21–3.
[85] *HE*, iii, 24.
[86] Newton, *The Reckoning of King Rædwald*, p. 44.

Saxons.[87] Æthelwold was succeeded by his son Ealdwulf (Fig. 5), whose very long reign between AD 664 and 713 saw the creation of the new diocese of Elmham (see below, pp. 40–4).

This, then, except for a few incidental details about the episcopal succession and Fursa's monastery at *Cnobheresburg* (see below, pp. 44–61) is the sum total of Bede's contribution to our understanding of East Anglian history. Clearly, these brief descriptions do not constitute a comprehensive history of the kingdom, or even its episcopal development, yet many have seen Bede's work as being sufficiently detailed to negate the need for further research. However, the desirability of more research is highlighted by a reassessment of one of the few original sources for East Anglian ecclesiastical history, Ælfwald's letter to Boniface.

Ælfwald (AD 713–49)

Ælfwald was the son of Ealdwulf and is famed for commissioning one of the earliest English saint's lives, Felix's *Vita Sancti Guthlaci*.[88] However, he is also remembered for the letter which he wrote to Boniface at some point between AD 742 and 749. Boniface was an Anglo-Saxon missionary active on the Continent in the first half of the eighth century and widely known as the Apostle to the Germans.[89] In response to a request for support from Boniface, Ælfwald wrote to assure him that his name was being remembered 'in septenis monasteriorum nostrorum sinaxis' and suggested that they exchange the names of their dead so that mutual prayers could be said.[90] It is clear from this letter that Ælfwald had a sound understanding of Latin grammar, but the quoted phrase has caused difficulties for those trying to understand the early East Anglian church. Dorothy Whitelock's view was that the phrase meant that prayers were being said for Boniface in seven East Anglian monasteries; this reading has percolated through a number of other works,[91] the authors of which all acknowledge that by this time there must have been more than seven monasteries in East Anglia and are at pains to explain this reference. However, their efforts were unnecessary, since the various pieces of this puzzle have been in print for a long time, although they have only recently been brought together and published.[92]

A footnote to the Latin transcription of Ælfwald's letter published by Haddan and Stubbs in 1871 clearly states that the letter refers to the seven canonical hours and not seven monasteries, and Emerton's 1940 translation renders the problematic sentence thus: 'Your name is to be remembered forever in the seven-fold recitation of the office of our monasteries'.[93] Rather than referring to seven monasteries, as many have supposed, Ælfwald was in fact referring to the manner in which

---

[87] *HE*, iii, 22.

[88] Colgrave, *Felix's Life of St Guthlac*, pp. 15–19; Roberts, *Guthlac*, pp. 4–11.

[89] Wood, 'Boniface'.

[90] Haddan and Stubbs, *Councils and Ecclesiastical Documents*, pp. 387–8; Tangl, *Die Briefe*, pp. 181–2; Emerton, *Letters*, pp. 149–50.

[91] Whitelock, 'The Pre-Viking Age Church', pp. 16–17; Williamson, *Origins of Norfolk*, pp. 143–9; Newton, *Origins of Beowulf*, pp. 134–5, and *The Reckoning of King Rædwald*, p. 44; Pestell, *Landscapes of Monastic Foundation*, p. 21.

[92] Plunkett, *Suffolk in Anglo-Saxon Times*, p. 153; Foot, *Monastic Life*, p. 197.

[93] Haddan and Stubbs, *Councils and Ecclesiastical Documents*, p. 388; Foot, 'What was an Early Anglo-Saxon Monastery?', p. 52; Emerton, *Letters*, p. 149.

Boniface's name and those of others were to be praised during the monastic day.[94] Unfortunately, this is not the only instance of a mistaken interpretation of the surviving sources becoming an accepted fact, as is made clear in the following examination of the foundation of the East Anglian dioceses.

The East Anglian dioceses

In AD 630/1 Sigeberht granted Felix a site for his bishopric at *Dommoc*, where he abided until his death seventeen years later.[95] On Felix's death Archbishop Honorius of Canterbury consecrated a deacon named Thomas who belonged to the nation of the Gyrwe. When he died five years afterwards, Honorius appointed Berhtgisl, also named Boniface, from the kingdom of Kent.[96] *Dommoc* remained the sole East Anglian see under these bishops until *c.* AD 673, when Boniface's successor Bisi became too infirm to minister to the diocese; Archbishop Theodore then divided the diocese and consecrated two bishops in Bisi's place. One bishopric continued at *Dommoc* under Æcci, while the other was established under Baduwine.[97] Bede did not name the new see, but evidence from the Council of Cloveshо identifies it as Elmham.[98] This division prevailed until the ninth century, when both dioceses were apparently disrupted by Viking incursions. After the English reconquest of the region in the early tenth century only the see of Elmham was restored, and the new incumbents began to style themselves bishop of the East Angles.[99]

The lack of East Anglian documents means that the earliest episcopal lists are preserved in a ninth-century Mercian compilation based on lists compiled in the last decade of the eighth century.[100] The details contained within these lists are complemented by a handful of other sources: the Canterbury bilingual manuscript of the *Anglo-Saxon Chronicle* for AD 798, which records the death of Bishop Ælfhun at Sudbury, his subsequent burial at *Dommoc* and his succession by Tidfrith;[101] a letter written by Alcuin to the East Anglian bishops Alhheard and Tidfrith at the turn of the ninth century;[102] three other bishops' professions of faith to the archbishops of Canterbury, which shed a little more light on the episcopal succession;[103] the records of numerous eighth- and ninth-century synods and councils attended by the bishops of *Dommoc* and Elmham; and charters witnessed by the East Anglian bishops.[104] Although we can be reasonably confident of the names of the bishops and the order of their succession, a great deal of uncertainty remains about the precise dates of their episcopates.

---

[94] Foot, *Monastic Life*, pp. 197–8; Cubitt, *Anglo-Saxon Church Councils*, pp. 99–110.
[95] *HE*, ii, 15.
[96] *HE*, iii, 20.
[97] *HE*, iv, 5.
[98] Haddan and Stubbs, *Councils and Ecclesiastical Documents*, p. 547.
[99] Pestell, *Landscapes of Monastic Foundation*, p. 72; Foot, *Monastic Life*, pp. 343–4; Wade-Martins, *Excavations in North Elmham Park*, pp. 3–11.
[100] Whitelock, 'The Pre-Viking Age Church', pp. 15 and 19–20.
[101] Whitelock *et al.*, *Anglo-Saxon Chronicle*, p. 38.
[102] Haddan and Stubbs, *Councils and Ecclesiastical Documents*, pp. 551–2.
[103] *Ibid.*, pp. 511, 591 and 659.
[104] Whitelock, 'The Pre-Viking Age Church', pp. 17–18; Haddan and Stubbs, *Councils and Ecclesiastical Documents*, pp. 360–76, 447–62, 541–8, 579–86, 592–607 and 624–5.

The last known bishop of Elmham was Hunberht, who attended a meeting in London in November 845.[105] After this date nothing more was heard of the bishops of Elmham for over a century. Similarly, the final historically attested bishop of *Dommoc* was Æthilwald, whose profession of obedience to Archbishop Ceolnoth of Canterbury dates from between AD 845 and AD 870.[106] This suggests that either or both of the East Anglian bishoprics could have been disrupted as early as AD 845. However, the Peterborough Manuscript of the *Anglo-Saxon Chronicle* records that the Danes conquered the region in AD 870, a much more likely date for, and cause of, the diocesan disruptions.[107]

So much for the bishops themselves, but what of their sees? The location of *Dommoc* has never been satisfactorily established. The two main contenders are Dunwich and Walton Castle, both on the Suffolk coast, but as both sites have since been eroded by the sea further archaeological investigations are impossible. Of the two sites, Dunwich is the more popular identification, although a much stronger case can be made for Walton Castle (Fig. 1). The location of Elmham is only marginally less problematic: there is a North Elmham in Norfolk and a South Elmham in Suffolk, both of which feature significant ecclesiastical remains (Fig. 1).[108] Once again, opinion is divided, hence Campbell's witty summation of the matter as being an 'East Anglian game of musical *sedes episcopales*'.[109]

Dommoc

The location of the see of *Dommoc* has traditionally been identified with Dunwich, despite the fact that Stuart Rigold pronounced this identification to be 'unwarranted' over forty years ago.[110] However, further research has led more recently to a growing consensus that the Roman fort at Walton Castle was actually the site of *Dommoc*.[111] But how did this erroneous identification arise?

The name '*Dommoc*' appears in only four primary sources. Of these, the earliest is the *HE*, the others being a reference in the Peterborough Manuscript of the *Anglo-Saxon Chronicle* for the year AD 798 concerning Ælfhun's burial at the site, the signatories to the Council of Clovesho from AD 803, and Bishop Æthilwald's profession of obedience to Archbishop Ceolnoth of Canterbury in the ninth century.[112] The name itself, which Ekwall suggests is derived from the Celtic *dubno-* 'deep', may be of Romano-British origin, or it could be derived from the Celtic *domnach*, a word for church widely used in Ireland.[113]

---

[105] Whitelock, 'The Pre-Viking Age Church', p. 22.
[106] Haddan and Stubbs, *Councils and Ecclesiastical Documents*, pp. 659–60.
[107] Plummer and Earle, *Two of the Saxon Chronicles*, p. 71; Pestell, *Landscapes of Monastic Foundation*.
[108] Wade-Martins, *Excavations in North Elmham Park*; Smedley and Owles, 'Excavations at the Old Minster'.
[109] Campbell, 'Bede's Words for Places', p. 36 n. 6.
[110] Rigold, 'The Supposed See of Dunwich', p. 55; Examples include Colgrave and Mynors, *Bede's Ecclesiastical History*, p. 191; Whitelock, 'The Pre-Viking Age Church', p. 4; Mynors *et al.*, *Gesta regum Anglorum*; Preest, *Deeds of the Bishops*; Dunn, *Christianization*, p. 129.
[111] Haslam, '*Dommoc* and Dunwich'; Newton, *Origins of Beowulf*, p. 134; Pestell, 'An Analysis of Monastic Foundation', pp. 299–305; Foot, *Monastic Life*, p. 78, n. 14.
[112] *HE*, ii, 15; Rigold, 'The Supposed See of Dunwich', p. 56; Haddan and Stubbs, *Councils and Ecclesiastical Documents*, pp. 547 and 659–60.
[113] Ekwall, *Concise Oxford Dictionary of English Place-Names*, p. 154; Rees, *Celtic Saints*, p. 7.

The use of *Dommoc* and variations upon it was commonplace well into the twelfth century and continued into the fourteenth century, with a couple of miscopied exceptions. In the first quarter of the twelfth century William of Malmesbury made three references to the see in his *Gesta regum Anglorum* and *De gestis pontificum Anglorum*.[114] Significantly, a late-twelfth-century manuscript copy of *De gestis pontificum Anglorum* includes an instance where the intended *Domoc* was given as *Donewyc*, with an additional instance of *Dammucensem* altered to *Donuycensem* in a later ink.[115] The fourteenth-century manuscript of Ranulf Higden's *Polychronicon* used *Donmic*, which later copies rendered as *Donwik* and *Dunwik* and which Trevisa's English translation eventually gave as *Domnyk*. It was not until the publication of Caxton's edition of the *Polychronicon* in 1482 that *Donwyck* was first used, although by then an unequivocal identification of *Dommoc* with *Dunwich* had been made elsewhere.[116]

The first explicit identification of *Dommoc* with *Dunwich* was made in the early fifteenth century by Thomas of Elmham, a monk of Canterbury. In his *Historia Monasterii S. Augustini Cantuariensis* he wrote that Felix 'acceptique sedem episcopatus in civitate Donwichnica, id est, Donwiche'.[117] It is possible that Thomas hailed from North or South Elmham, and may have substituted Dunwich, with which he would have familiar, for *Dommoc* as an independent act of scholarship. This identification was apparently picked up by Caxton and used in the *Polychronicon*, subsequently being adopted by Leland and Camden, whence it has become an accepted fact.[118]

So, if the traditional association between *Dommoc* and Dunwich is ignored and we return to the primary sources, what evidence do we have as to the actual location of *Dommoc*? In fact, one of our only real clues comes from the fact that Bede referred to *Dommoc* as being a *civitas*.[119] Bede did not refer to every episcopal see as such, so he was not using the term as a reflection of the current status of the see, but it is telling that all of the identifiable places that Bede referred to as *civitates* all had a significant Roman past.[120] In addition, a high proportion of these *civitates* also had vernacular names ending in -caestir, which in the Old English vernacular generally refers to a Roman town or city. The distinction between sees with and without a Roman connection was also made in the signatories of the Council of Clovesho of AD 803: of the thirteen signatory bishops, eight described their sees as *civitates*, *Tidfrith Dummucae civitas* among them, while the remaining five, including Alhheard, bishop of Elmham, described their sees as *ecclesiae*.[121] In every identifiable instance the sees described as *civitates* had Roman connections, while those described as *ecclesiae* did not.[122]

---

[114] Mynors *et al.*, *Gesta regum Anglorum*, pp. 122 and 534; Hamilton, *Willelmi Malmesbiriensis*, pp. 16 and 147–8.
[115] Hamilton, *Willelmi Malmesbiriensis*, pp. 16 and 148.
[116] Lumby, *Polychronicon*, pp. 6–7; Rigold, 'The Supposed See of Dunwich', p. 57.
[117] Hardwick, *Thomas of Elmham*, p. 166.
[118] Rigold, 'The Supposed See of Dunwich', p. 57.
[119] *HE*, ii, 15.
[120] Campbell, 'Bede's Words for Places', p. 35.
[121] Haddan and Stubbs, *Councils and Ecclesiastical Documents*, pp. 546–7.
[122] Campbell, 'Bede's Words for Places', p. 40.

Perhaps the most significant statement regarding the location of *Dommoc* was made by Bartholomew Cotton in the late thirteenth century in his *Historia anglicana*. His passage on Felix began by following Bede, but, crucially, he added 'et in civitate Donmoc sedem habuit, quæ nunc Filchstowe vocatur, super mare in orientali parte Suthfolchiæ'.[123] Here, then, was a clear identification of *Dommoc* with Felixstowe, lent weight by the fact that Cotton was a Suffolk-born monk of Norwich Cathedral Priory and therefore likely to be well informed on the matter.[124] A further identification of Felixstowe as *Dommoc* is contained within documents copied from Rochester Priory dating from before the mid-thirteenth century and possibly as early as the mid-twelfth century.[125] A third reference, contained within notes made by John Leland from a lost chronicle of Jervaulx Abbey dating from *c*.1200, again equated *Dommoc* with Felixstowe.[126] That three independent sources should have explicitly identified *Dommoc* with Felixstowe is clearly of immense significance, for there is a site in the vicinity of that town which fits the available evidence and could well have been *Dommoc*.

Walton Castle was a Roman fort which stood on the coast at Felixstowe and was destroyed by the sea in the eighteenth century (traces of the rubble of the fort can still be seen at very low tide), but not before the site was recorded by a number of antiquarians. Their accounts describe a fort over 100 yards long, with round corner-bastions and bands of decorative red brick in its walls, making it broadly comparable with the extant fort at Burgh Castle (Fig. 6).[127] As a standing Roman masonry structure Walton Castle would certainly have warranted Bede's description as a *civitas*, a distinction reinforced by the signatory at Clovesho, and the reuse of Roman buildings as early ecclesiastical sites is a well-attested phenomenon which is explored more fully in Chapter 3.[128] Walton Castle's location also supports its identification as *Dommoc*: after the Roman withdrawal it would have remained a significant coastal landmark which Felix would have passed if he made his way from Kent to East Anglia by sea. The site stood at the gateway to the Wuffingas' heartland in south-east Suffolk, for the Deben valley was the site of both the royal vill at Rendlesham and the royal burial-ground at Sutton Hoo, making Walton Castle a fitting site for the king's new bishopric and one which he was well within his rights to gift to Felix.

In addition to the presence of the Roman fort, there are other archaeological indicators that the Walton Castle area was host to a significant degree of Middle Saxon activity: a number of items of metalwork have been recovered from the area of the fort and it is possible that a hoard of Middle Saxon coins identified as the 'Woodbridge Sceatta Hoard' might have been discovered in the vicinity.[129] There is also documentary evidence which suggests that a pre-Conquest church stood within the walls of Walton Castle and, although it is difficult to ascertain when this church was founded, it may

[123] Luard, *Bartholomew Cotton*, p. 387.
[124] Rigold, 'The Supposed See of Dunwich', pp. 57–8; Rigold, 'Further Evidence', p. 9.
[125] Rigold, 'Further Evidence', pp. 98–100.
[126] *Ibid.*
[127] Fox, 'Romano-British Suffolk', pp. 287–91; Fairclough and Plunkett, 'Drawings of Walton Castle', pp. 419–26.
[128] *HE*, iii, 21; Rigold, '*Litus Romanum*'; Bell, 'Churches on Roman Buildings'.
[129] Newman, 'Exceptional Finds', p. 109.

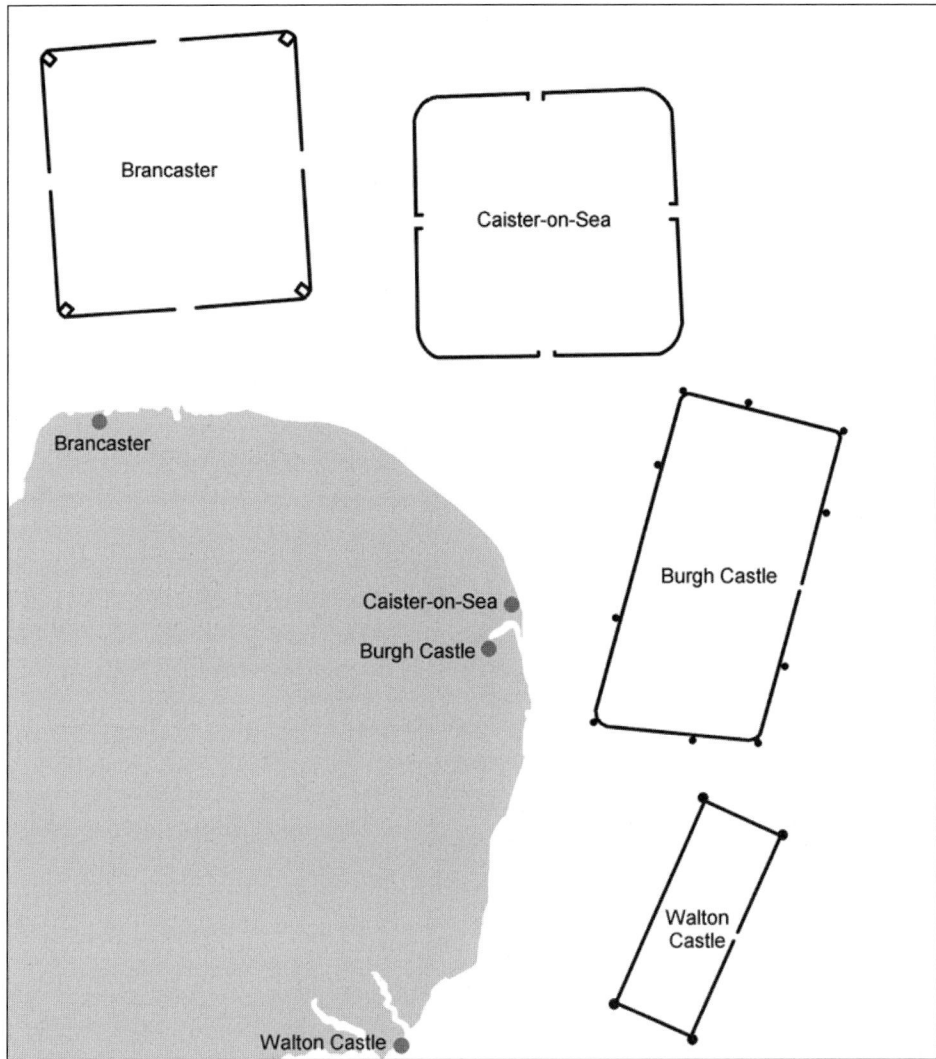

Fig. 6: Comparative plans of the East Anglian Saxon Shore forts at Brancaster, Caister-on-Sea, Burgh Castle and Walton Castle at 1:5,000.

well have been a remnant of the original episcopal buildings. Shortly after the Norman Conquest Roger Bigod built a castle inside the Roman fort and, during the reign of William II (1087–1100), granted Rochester Priory the church of Walton St Felix;[130] in 1154 Roger's son, Hugh, was recorded granting the priory land elsewhere in Walton in exchange for 'the land of their church where he built his castle', which strongly suggests that the original church of St Felix stood inside the fort.[131] While the dedication to St

[130] Rigold, 'Further Evidence', pp. 98–100; Davison, 'History of Walton Priory', pp. 142–3; Pestell, 'An Analysis of Monastic Foundation', pp. 303–4; Fairclough and Plunkett, 'Drawings of Walton Castle', pp. 451–2.
[131] Davison, 'History of Walton Priory', p. 143.

Plate 1: An aerial view of North Elmham from the north-east, 26 April 1984. Note the ruined church (centre) and the later parish church (top left). TF9821/ABS/AWE2 (Derek Edwards). © *NMAS*

Felix must post-date his episcopate, perhaps by some time, it certainly suggests that a church dedicated to the founding bishop of East Anglia stood within the walls of one of the probable candidates for his see.

Dommoc remained the sole East Anglian bishopric until *c*. AD 673, when Archbishop Theodore divided the see into two parts. *Dommoc* continued under Bishop Æcci and a new see was established under Bishop Baduwine.[132] Fortunately, identifying the location of this second see has not proved to be quite as difficult as identifying *Dommoc*, although it, too, is not without its problems.

Elmham

The earliest documentary reference to the see of Elmham is found in the signatories of the Council of Clovesho from AD 803.[133] Unfortunately, there are no contemporary documentary sources which conclusively prove whether this was North Elmham in Norfolk (Plate 1) or South Elmham in Suffolk (Fig. 13), and both Elmhams house the architectural ruins of apsidal churches, each of which has been argued to have Anglo-Saxon origins.[134] Neither are we comparing like with like, for,

---

[132] *HE*, iv, 5.
[133] Haddan and Stubbs, *Councils and Ecclesiastical Documents*, p. 547.
[134] Wade-Martins, *Excavations in North Elmham Park*, p. 3; Harrod, 'On the Site of the Bishopric'; Howlett, 'Ancient See'.

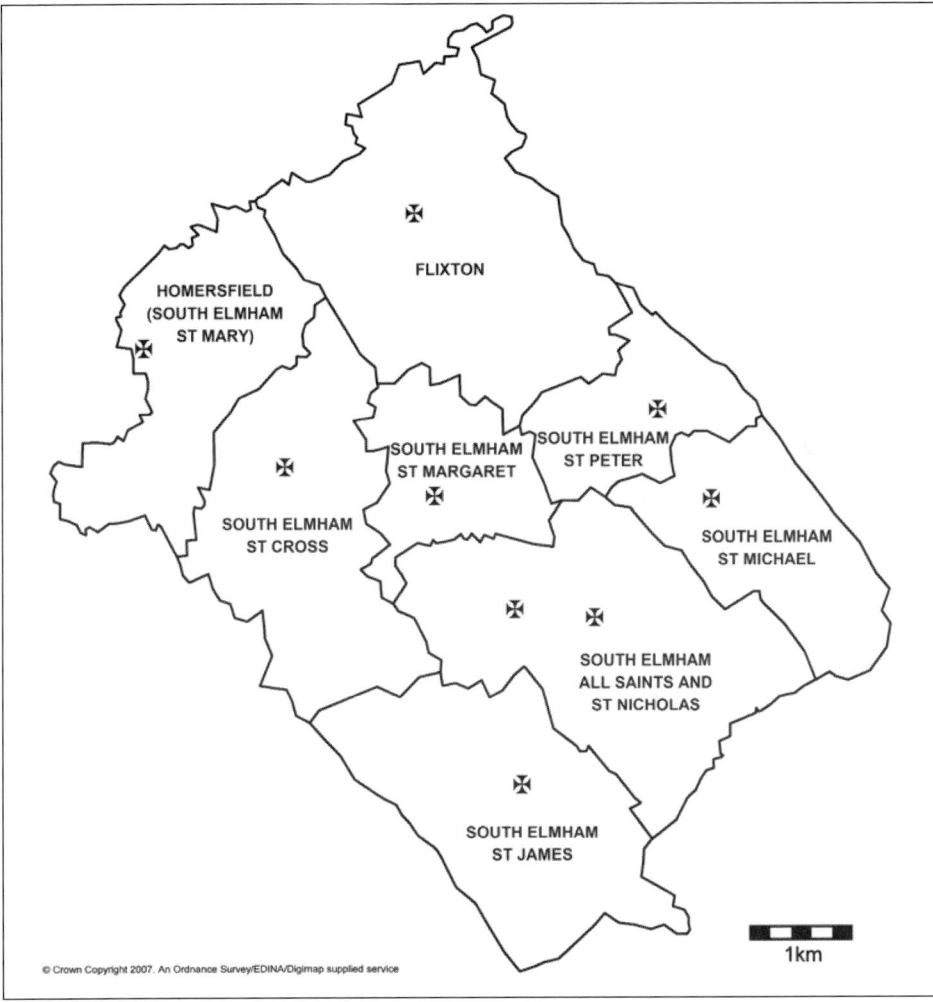

Fig. 7: The South Elmham parishes and Flixton, showing the relative locations of their parish churches.

unlike Norfolk's Elmham, which is a distinct single settlement, Suffolk's Elmham is actually a group of seven parishes which share the name, each now differentiated by the dedication of its church. Together with the parish of Flixton, the South Elmhams form a rectangular block of land measuring some 5km SW–NE by 6.5km NW–SE, and there can be little doubt about their having once been a single large estate which subsequently fragmented (Fig. 7).[135]

Elmham is described in the signatories of the Council of Clovesho as an *Ecclesiæ*, suggesting that the site did not have a Roman past.[136] This would certainly apply to North Elmham, which has been extensively investigated and found to have had no

---

[135] Harrold, *Enigma of Ancient Suffolk*, pp. 38–9 and 48.
[136] Haddan and Stubbs, *Councils and Ecclesiastical Documents*, p. 547.

Roman antecedent.[137] By contrast, the church known as the 'Old Minster' in South Elmham (the focus of the argument for its having been the bishopric) stands within the earthworks of a square enclosure to which its excavators have ascribed a Roman date (Fig. 13).[138] This conclusion is supported by Wade-Martins as a result of his own fieldwork at the site, although Fairclough and Hardy suggest that the enclosure may actually be a later feature dug through an area of Roman settlement.[139] North Elmham would thus appear to be the better candidate for the episcopal see on this evidence.

We can at least be certain that the bishopric was based at North Elmham after the refoundation of the diocese in the tenth century. Domesday Book records that North Elmham (*Elmenham*) was owned by the bishop of Thetford and had been held by the bishopric in 1066.[140] The entry also records that Stigand, archbishop of Canterbury until 1072, had twenty-four sokemen in North Elmham in 1066. These presumably remained from his period as bishop of Elmham, which was begun in 1043 and briefly interrupted in 1044 before ending in 1047, when he moved on to the see of Winchester.[141] The estate stayed in the hands of the bishopric until 1536, remaining an episcopal residence after the transference of the see itself to Thetford and then Norwich.[142]

Domesday Book also records the bishop holding one manor in South Elmham, at Homersfield, now known as South Elmham St Mary.[143] Scarfe suggests that the name is derived from that of Hunberht, the last recorded bishop of Elmham before the disruption of the dioceses.[144] The same Domesday entry records that the bishop had jurisdiction over the whole ferding (a quarter of a hundred) of South Elmham. Clearly the bishops held some sway in South Elmham at Domesday, almost certainly a result of its having been held as a large estate prior to its fragmentation. However, this does not mean that South Elmham was the bishopric.

Confirmation that South Elmham was not the bishopric from the tenth century onwards is provided by two sources, both of which identify nearby Hoxne as the episcopal see of Suffolk, *Dommoc* having fallen out of use. After the reconquest of the Danelaw the first claim to East Anglian episcopal authority is found in the will of Theodred dated AD 942 × 951.[145] Theodred was bishop of London, but in his will he also made reference to his bishopric at Hoxne, meaning that in the first instance the diocese was united with that of London. No indication is given as to whether his authority extended to Elmham or for how long he had held the position, but he was bishop of London by AD 926 and the East Anglian diocese was presumably refounded shortly after this.[146] Hoxne is also the first Suffolk holding listed in Domesday Book for the bishop of Thetford and the entry explicitly refers to Hoxne having been the episcopal see of Suffolk at the time of the Norman

---

[137] Rigold, 'Anglian Cathedral'; Wade-Martins, *Excavations in North Elmham Park*.
[138] Woodward, 'The Old Minster'; Smedley and Owles, 'Excavations at the Old Minster', pp. 5–6.
[139] Wade-Martins, *Excavations in North Elmham Park*, p. 5; Fairclough and Hardy, *Thornham*, p. 85.
[140] LDB f.191v.
[141] Cowdrey, 'Stigand'.
[142] Rigold, 'Anglian Cathedral', p. 71.
[143] LDB f.379.
[144] Scarfe, *Suffolk Landscape*, p. 123.
[145] Whitelock, *Anglo-Saxon Wills*, pp. 2–5.
[146] Wade-Martins, *Excavations in North Elmham Park*, p. 7.

Conquest.[147] Despite being nominally a separate see from that of Elmham, it would appear that the two sees were held in plurality, with the incumbents styling themselves the bishop of the East Angles.[148]

The remains of the church at North Elmham had traditionally been thought to be the remains of the Anglo-Saxon cathedral, much altered when Bishop Henry le Despenser (1370–1406) converted the building into a fortified residence and caused the elaborate earthwork defences surrounding the site to be made (Plate 1).[149] However, excavations in the 1950s revealed a number of earlier phases of Late Saxon timber building beneath the stone structure.[150] Similarly, Stephen Heywood argues that the ruins contain no traces of Anglo-Saxon workmanship, suggesting that it was an unequivocally Norman structure and therefore post-dated the transference of the see to Thetford.[151] The visible remains are, therefore, not those of the Anglo-Saxon cathedral, although they probably stand on the site of its later timber incarnations. A lack of Middle Saxon evidence from the trenches might suggest that earlier phases of the cathedral may have been constructed on a different site in the vicinity. Between 1967 and 1972 an area of North Elmham Park adjacent to the standing ruins was excavated, revealing three increasingly intensive phases of Middle Saxon settlement. Although these did not produce much Middle Saxon Ipswich ware or metalwork, the evidence was sufficient to convince the excavator that North Elmham had truly been the site of the bishopric since the foundation of the diocese.[152] By the eleventh century the population of this rural centre had grown, requiring the expansion of the cathedral cemetery over some of the settlement area, an event which seems to have coincided with alterations made to the cathedral itself.[153]

An explanation for this intriguing archaeological sequence is found in the first register of Norwich Cathedral, which records that Bishop Herbert de Losinga (AD 1091–1119) founded a church at North Elmham.[154] This was the present parish church, situated immediately to the south of the main earthwork enclosure (Plate 1). Having provided for the spiritual needs of the population with this new church, Bishop de Losinga then seems to have built his own private chapel in stone on the site of the original cathedral.[155] In his assessment of the architectural remains at North Elmham, Heywood drew attention to some unusual characteristics: in particular, the nave and tower were of the same width and there was an external stair turret at the south-east corner of the tower. He argued that these characteristics are only paralleled at one other site in East Anglia, the 'Old Minster' at St Cross South Elmham. To Heywood this was proof enough that the remains at South Elmham must also be Norman, a conclusion supported by his architectural analysis of the site.[156] Again the first register provides us with an explanation, for it also

---

[147] LDB f.379.
[148] Wade-Martins, *Excavations in North Elmham Park*, pp. 3–11.
[149] Rigold, 'Anglian Cathedral', pp. 70–71; Emery, *Greater Medieval Houses*, pp. 129–31.
[150] Rigold, 'Anglian Cathedral', pp. 78–95.
[151] Heywood, 'Ruined Church at North Elmham', pp. 1–5.
[152] Wade-Martins 1980, *Excavations in North Elmham Park*, pp. 628–32.
[153] *Ibid.*, pp. 632–4.
[154] Saunders, *First Register*, pp. 32–3.
[155] Heywood, 'Ruined Church at North Elmham', pp. 5–10.
[156] *Ibid.*, pp. 5–9.

records that Bishop de Losinga bought the manor of St Cross South Elmham and gave it to the monks of Norwich Cathedral Priory.[157] As the bishop was also the prior, South Elmham therefore continued to be used as an episcopal residence, the closely paralleled designs of the two ruined buildings suggesting that the 'Old Minister' was another of de Losinga's private chapels.[158] Heywood's conclusions echo those of Smedley and Owles, who partially excavated the site of the 'Old Minister' in the 1960s and discovered the buried foundations of the external stair-turret and a carved stone built into the south-east corner of the nave, which they considered to be eleventh-century in date.[159] Significantly, neither the excavations or any subsequent fieldwork at the 'Old Minister' have produced any evidence for Anglo-Saxon occupation in the area of the enclosure.[160]

Although neither case is conclusive, the available historical and archaeological evidence seems to suggest that North Elmham was the site of the bishopric from the late seventh century until the disruption of the diocese and again from its refoundation until the eleventh-century translation to Thetford. Throughout this same period South Elmham was clearly an important episcopal estate (which had fragmented by Domesday), but it apparently did not function as the bishopric. After the reconquest there was a nominal Suffolk-based bishopric at Hoxne, complementing Norfolk's Elmham, but both were held by the same bishop under their title of bishop of the East Angles.

Missionaries

The creation of the dioceses of *Dommoc* and Elmham was not the only means by which Christianity was advanced within East Anglia. The kingdom also played host to a number of missionaries who founded their own monasteries under royal patronage. The two historically attested East Anglian missionaries were Fursa, the founder of *Cnobheresburg*, and Botolph, founder of Iken, both discussed below. However, it must be borne in mind that the archaeological record suggests that many other missionaries, whose exploits were not recorded in the documents, were also at work in the East Anglian region during this period.[161]

Fursa and Cnobheresburg

The establishment of *Dommoc* was not the only step towards the Christianisation of the region which occurred during Sigeberht's reign. In a chapter of the *HE* largely derived from a copy of the *Vita Sancti Fursei* Bede reported how the Irish missionary Fursa was honourably received by Sigeberht, who subsequently granted him the site of *Cnobheresburg* on which to build a monastery.[162] *Cnobheresburg* is described by Bede as having been 'pleasantly situated close to the woods and the sea, in a Roman camp which is called in English *Cnobheresburg*, that is the city of Cnobhere'.[163]

---

[157] Saunders, *First Register*, pp. 36–9.
[158] Heywood, 'Ruined Church at North Elmham', pp. 8–10; Fairclough and Hardy, *Thornham*, pp. 104–7.
[159] Smedley and Owles, 'Excavations at the Old Minster', pp. 9–14.
[160] *Ibid.*
[161] cf. Foot, *Monastic Life*, p. 90.
[162] *HE*, iii, 19; Rackham, *Transitus*.
[163] *HE*, iii, 18.

Fursa apparently then spent his life preaching the gospel to the population in the Irish tradition and, we are told, was responsible for the conversion of many individuals to the Christian faith.[164] He may even have founded other monasteries that have gone unrecorded. Of the later history of *Cnobheresburg*, Bede tells us that Anna (*c.* AD 640–54) and his nobles 'endowed it with still finer buildings and gifts', doubtless making it an institution of some standing.[165] After many years, wishing to free himself from worldly affairs, Fursa left *Cnobheresburg* in the care of his brother Foillán and two priests, Gobán and Dícuill, and went to live as a hermit with another of his brothers, Ultán. In response to the Mercian onslaught of AD 640 that saw the deaths of both Sigeberht and Ecgric on the battlefield, Fursa apparently left East Anglia and travelled to the court of Clovis, king of the Franks.[166] Once there Fursa founded another monastery at Lagny, where he resided until his death.[167] Unusually, at this point Bede's account can be supplemented by an account of Foillán's life written at Nivelles not later than AD 655.[168] This tells that after Fursa's death *c.* AD 650 Anna had been expelled by the Mercian advance and *Cnobheresburg* despoiled. Foillán himself would have been killed but for the timely return of Anna and his army, and afterwards the monks and their relics, altar equipment and books were loaded onto a boat and shipped to Francia.[169]

Cnobheresburg is another site identified by Bede the location of which is unknown, but about which there is much debate. In a manner reminiscent of the association of *Dommoc* with Dunwich, *Cnobheresburg* is now almost universally thought to have lain within the Roman fort at Burgh Castle (Fig. 6), although, if anything, the surviving documentary evidence contradicts this identification. In order to get to the heart of the matter it is first necessary to dissect the relevant passage of the *HE* in some detail.

Bede openly acknowledged that he relied heavily on a copy of the *Vita Sancti Fursei* when writing the *HE*, going so far as to copy it verbatim, adding details of his own derived from other sources.[170] Of Fursa's monastery the *Vita* states: 'Quod monasterium in quodam castro constructum, silvarum et maris vicinitate amoenum rex gentis illius Anna ac nubiles quique tectis et muneribus adornarunt.'[171] Here, then, are three of the elements of the story which Bede presented: the monastery was built in a *castrum*; it lay in the vicinity of woods and the sea; and Anna provided the site with further buildings and gifts. Significantly, the *Vita* did not give the name of the site. The phrase 'quod lingua Anglorum Cnobheresburg, id Vrbs Cnobheri' which Bede used is, therefore, his own addition and must be derived from one of his other East Anglian sources, perhaps Abbot Esi or the 'aged brother' who Bede reported as having met Fursa.[172]

Hagiography is notoriously difficult to use for historical purposes and, as the

[164] *HE*, iii, 19.
[165] *Ibid.*
[166] *HE*, iii, 18 and 19; Rackham, *Transitus*; Brown, *Life of St. Fursey*.
[167] *HE*, iii, 19.
[168] Whitelock, 'The Pre-Viking Age Church', p. 6.
[169] *Ibid.*
[170] Krusch, *Monumenta Germaniæ*, pp. 434–49; Bieler, 'Ireland's Contribution', pp. 222–3.
[171] Krusch, *Monumenta Germaniæ*, pp. 437; cf. Rackham, *Transitus*.
[172] *HE*, iii, 18.

author of the *Vita* remains anonymous, little can be said of its provenance and reliability. Anna surely did patronise the site during his reign and is also likely to have patronised other East Anglian monasteries which remain unrecorded. The topographical description — in the vicinity of woods and the sea — is quite general and could easily be applied to large tracts of East Anglia. Tellingly, Bede also described the monastery at Bosham on the Sussex coast as being similarly 'surrounded by woods and sea'.[173] In both instances the phrase has a poetic quality which suggests that it was being used to conjure a suitable image rather than provide a topographical guide. The word *castrum*, when used to describe the enclosure within which the monastery was founded, should, Campbell suggested, be translated as 'fortified place' rather than 'Roman camp', and Bede only used *castrum* in passages copied from other written sources.[174] Bede's description of *Cnobheresburg* as having been built within a *castrum*, therefore, is not one of his own devising and cannot be treated in the same manner as the additional information he provided. Bede's own description of *Cnobheresburg* as an *urbs* is much more telling: his use of the words *civitas* and *urbs* were very specific, the former signifying a site with a Roman past and the latter one without.[175] Unlike *Dommoc*, which Bede rightly called a *civitas*, his use of *urbs* for *Cnobheresburg* suggests that he was aware it was a non-Roman site.

Reference has already been made to the traditional association between the Roman fort at Burgh Castle and *Cnobheresburg*; the earliest equation of the two is in Camden's *Britannia*, published in 1586. In discussing Suffolk he wrote 'where Yare and Waveney meet in one streame, there flourished *Cnobersburg*, that is, as Bede interpreteth it, Cnobers City, we call it at this day Burgh-Castle'.[176] Whether Camden was reporting a local tradition or simply making an educated guess, his identification stuck and has since become accepted.[177] The tradition prevails, despite the fact that the evidence presented by Bede tends to contradict it by suggesting that *Cnobheresburg* lay within a non-Roman fortification.

Ultimately, the question of whether *Cnobheresburg* was or was not situated within the walls of Burgh Castle is one to which neither the historical nor the archaeological record can provide a comprehensive and conclusive answer. However, as is discussed in the next chapter, the archaeological record can and does demonstrate that Burgh Castle was indeed host to significant ecclesiastical occupation during the Middle Saxon period (AD 650–850) and undoubtedly played an important role in the East Anglian conversion, whether or not it was it was actually associated with Fursey.

---

[173] *HE*, iv, 13; Parsons, *Books and Buildings*, p. 12.
[174] Campbell, 'Bede's Words for Places', p. 36; Jones, *A Concordance to the Historia Ecclesiastica*, p. 73; *HE*, i, 5, 20, iii, 19 and v, 7.
[175] Campbell, 'Bede's Words for Places', pp. 35–7.
[176] Camden, *Britannia*, col. 376.
[177] Campbell, 'Bede's Words for Places', p. 36; Dahl, *The Roman Camp*; Rackham, *Transitus*, p. 54; Brown, *Life of St. Fursey*, pp. 17–18.

Botolph and Iken

We have seen in this chapter that the *HE* is not a complete and comprehensive history, although the lack of contemporary sources makes it difficult for us to gauge the extent of the omissions. However, there is one East Anglian example which sheds some light on the limitations and motivations of Bede's work: the total exclusion of Botolph and his monastery at Iken from the text. Turning from the *HE* to the *Anglo-Saxon Chronicle*, we find that the entry for the year AD 653 records that 'Her Anna cining werð of slagen and Botuulf ongan timbrian mynster æt Icanhoe'.[178] While this statement does not explicitly tell us that *Icanho* was East Anglian, its mention in the same sentence as the death of Anna strongly suggests that this was the case.

Further proof that *Icanho* is East Anglian is provided by the *Vita Ceolfridi*, written by an anonymous monk of Jarrow after AD 716 and before Bede used it to complete his *Historia abbatum* of c. AD 725.[179] The biographer recorded that, before he became the founding abbot of Jarrow, Ceolfrith began his monastic career at Ripon c. AD 670 and shortly afterwards visited Kent to learn more about the monastic way of life.[180] After leaving Kent Ceolfrith 'came also to East Anglia to see the monastic practices of Abbot Botwulf, whom report had proclaimed on all sides to be a man of unparalleled life and learning, and full of the grace of the Holy Spirit'.[181] As a result of his visit Ceolfrith 'returned home abundantly instructed, as far as he could be in a short time, so much so that no one could be found at that time more learned than he in either the ecclesiastical or the monastic rule'.[182] High praise indeed.

Historically there has been some debate about the location of *Icanho*, although considerably less than about the other sites discussed here. In the nineteenth and early twentieth centuries *Icanho* was thought to have been Boston (Lincolnshire), where there is a church dedicated to St Botolph,[183] but this is clearly contradicted by the *Vita Ceolfridi*. By the 1920s there was a growing consensus that Iken, in south-east Suffolk, was the real site of Botolph's minster.[184] Iken's church is dedicated to St Botolph and the name *Ycanho* was used for Iken in a fourteenth-century charter of nearby Butley Priory.[185] The *-ho* element of *Icanho* refers to a low spur of land projecting into a river or an area of more level ground — and the church at Iken is sited on just such a promontory.[186]

Since the 1930s the identification of Iken has been challenged only by Rodwell, who stated that 'a stronger case can be argued for the identification of Icanho with Hadstock [Essex] than any other place'.[187] His main evidence was Hadstock

---

[178] Plummer and Earle, *Two of the Saxon Chronicles*, pp. 28–9.
[179] Plummer, *Venerabilis Baedae*, pp. 388–404; Whitelock, *English Historical Documents*, pp. 758–70.
[180] Whitelock, *English Historical Documents*, pp. 758–70; Stevenson, 'St Botolph', p. 35.
[181] Whitelock, *English Historical Documents*, p. 759.
[182] *Ibid.*
[183] Stevenson, 'St Botolph'; Whitley, 'Botolph's Ycean-Ho'.
[184] e.g. Cox, 'Ecclesiastical History', p. 7.
[185] Stevenson, 'St Botolph', pp. 31–2; Whitley, 'Botolph's Ycean-Ho', pp. 233–7.
[186] Smith, *English Place-name Elements*, p. 256.
[187] Rodwell, 'Archaeological Investigation of Hadstock', p. 69.

church's dedication to Botolph and a twelfth-century charter of Bishop Nigel of Ely which stated that Hadstock (then called *Cadenho*) was the site of a foundation of Botolph and the location of his burial.[188] It is easy to see how a case might be made from this evidence, but it would appear that Bishop Nigel was simply equating his own *Cadenho* with the historical *Icanho*. Rodwell's suggestion provoked a detailed rebuttal from Martin in which he firmly restated the case for Iken and there the matter has rested ever since.[189]

The fabric of Iken church comprises a Norman nave, a fifteenth- or sixteenth-century tower and south porch, and a Victorian chancel. The recognition of a broken piece of carved Anglo-Saxon cross shaft built into the base of the tower prompted an archaeological excavation in 1977. Trenches inside the church revealed the Norman foundations of the nave, which cut a series of earlier graves, while excavation in the churchyard revealed a series of clay-filled trenches thought to have been the foundations of an earlier timber church. The excavations also produced three sherds of Middle Saxon Ipswich ware and two Late Saxon Thetford ware sherds.[190] During the work the carved stone was removed from the wall and revealed to be a 1.5m section of broken cross-shaft decorated with interlace, crosses and animals. The cross, which would have stood 3m high, is an unusual artefact in this region. It is stylistically dated to the late ninth or early tenth centuries and is thus later than the documented period of the monastery's occupation, but it may have been erected as a later monument to Botolph, whose remains were reportedly buried at Iken until the tenth century.[191]

In the later years of the tenth century royal consent was given for Botolph's body to be exhumed and divided into thirds, to be shared between the abbeys of Ely and Thorney and King Edgar, through Westminster Abbey.[192] This appears to have been related to Edgar's gifting the manor of Sudbourne, of which Iken was a part, to Bishop Æthelwold of Winchester in return for his translating the *Rule of St Benedict* into English.[193] Thorney clearly received its portion of the body, prompting Botolph's eleventh-century *Vita* to be written, but it is not clear whether Ely and Westminster received theirs. Tradition records that Botolph's body (or at least parts of it) rested for some time at nearby Grundisburgh, from where Cnut ordered it be transferred to Bury St Edmunds in 1020.[194] It has been argued that this stopping off en route resulted in the foundation of St Botolph's church within the earthwork enclosure at Burgh.[195] This later interest in Botolph's relics led to a revival of his cult, attested by the many churches which are dedicated to him nationwide; his cult even spread to Scandinavia, where it enjoyed wide support.[196]

---

[188] Rodwell, 'Archaeological Investigation of Hadstock', p. 68; Blake, *Liber Eliensis*, p. 336.
[189] Martin, 'St Botolph'; although Foot, *Monastic Life*, p. 257, fig. 11, depicts the location of Icanho as lying in Essex.
[190] West *et al.*, 'Iken', pp. 283–8.
[191] *Ibid.*, pp. 289–92.
[192] Stevenson, 'St Botolph', pp. 42–3; Blair, 'A Handlist', pp. 518–19.
[193] West *et al.*, 'Iken', p. 298.
[194] *Ibid.*, pp. 299–300.
[195] Stevenson, 'St Botolph', pp. 43–5; Martin, *Burgh*, p. 74.
[196] Blair, 'A Handlist', pp. 518–19; Toy, 'St Botolph'.

Botolph was clearly a significant religious figure and the practices observed at Iken must have been truly exemplary, judging by the praise in the *Vita Ceolfridi*. Why, then, is Botolph absent from the *HE*? Did Bede not know about him or was he deliberately excluded? We can be reasonably certain that Bede did know about both Botolph and Iken, for Ceolfrith's visit had clearly made a strong impression on him and Bede had a great affection for Ceolfrith, who was abbot when Bede was a young boy and was probably responsible for Bede's education.[197] By the time that Ceolfrith departed for Rome in AD 716, a journey from which he did not return, the two men had lived side-by-side at Jarrow for some forty years and Ceolfrith's departure caused Bede such grief that he was unable to work for some time.[198] It seems highly unlikely that Ceolfrith would not have told Bede of his travels in East Anglia and Bede certainly knew of the *Vita Ceolfridi*, for he used parts of it himself in both his *Historia abbatum* and the *HE*.[199] Indeed, some have even gone so far as to suggest that Bede himself might have written the *Vita Ceolfridi*.[200]

We are forced to conclude, therefore, that Bede deliberately chose not to mention Botolph. This omission has led some to suggest that Bede did not approve of Botolph and deliberately left him out, but this argument cannot be sustained. Whitley suggested that Botolph's exclusion may have been the result of his being a Scot (at least according to the unreliable eleventh-century *Vita*), as Bede held a vehement dislike of the British church.[201] This seems unlikely, as Ceolfrith was also a strong opponent of the British church and would not have visited a house which observed British practices.[202] Therefore, instead of questioning Bede's opinion of Botolph's practices, we must return to the motives behind his writing. In the first of his works which dealt with Ceolfrith, the *Historia abbatum*, Bede was more concerned with the history of his monastery than with detailing the lives of the abbots themselves. Bede made no mention of Ceolfrith's early life or career until after the death of his predecessor Benedict Biscop.[203] This approach would have automatically resulted in the exclusion of Ceolfrith's East Anglian visitation, undertaken early in his monastic life, and would explain the lack of references to either Botolph or Iken. By contrast, the *HE* would appear to be the obvious context for Bede to have imparted his knowledge of Botolph and Iken, yet he chose not to do so. The answer lies in the focus of his work: Bede was writing a history of the English Church and thus did not concern himself with people and places which were not directly related to the principal characters in his narrative, most often royalty, but occasionally also important bishops.[204] Consequently Fursa, who was sponsored by Sigeberht, the king responsible for introducing both Bishop Felix and Christianity to the East Anglian kingdom, was therefore

---

[197] Whitelock, *English Historical Documents*, p. 762; McClure, 'Bede', pp. 81–2.
[198] Whitelock, 'Bede and his Teachers', pp. 22–3.
[199] Campbell, 'Bede II', p. 44; Plummer, *Venerabilis Baedae*, pp. 364–87; Webb and Farmer, *Age of Bede*, pp. 185–210.
[200] e.g. McClure, 'Bede'; Wood, *The Most Holy Abbot Ceolfrid*, pp. 18–19.
[201] Whitley, 'Botolph's Ycean-Ho', pp. 236–7.
[202] Whitelock, 'The Pre-Viking Age Church', pp. 10–11, and *English Historical Documents*, pp. 759–61.
[203] Wood, *The Most Holy Abbot Ceolfrid*, p. 9.
[204] Campbell, 'Bede II', p. 40.

included, while Botolph, whose monastery was begun well after the major apparatus of the diocese was in place and who is linked to Anna only by a shared entry in the *Anglo-Saxon Chronicle*, was not included. Botolph's story was simply not relevant to Bede's narrative.

Conclusions

East Anglia is among the most poorly represented Anglo-Saxon kingdoms in terms of its historical sources and it is fortunate that the vast majority of the material which has been preserved is of an ecclesiastical nature. This material is not without its difficulties, for very few of the surviving sources are contemporary, having been preserved in the records of other Anglo-Saxon kingdoms or collected, compiled and edited by Bede at least a century later. One should not fall into the trap of believing that Bede was an historian; he was first and foremost a theologian, who used his historical writing to present object lessons on good Christian living. He was not writing history for its own sake. Neither was he writing a history of Anglo-Saxon England; he was specifically interested in recording the development of his own, English, Church. As such, the *HE* focuses on the conversion of individual kings and kingdoms, the creation of the dioceses and the unification of disparate strands of Christianity into a single entity. In pursuing these aims Bede made judicious use of his sources, including only those details which helped fulfil his purpose.

There has been a tendency among those studying Anglo-Saxon East Anglia to rely heavily and unquestioningly on the material presented by Bede. Such reliance on and acceptance of the veracity of Bede's writing have resulted in a decided lack of scholarly interest in the subject of the conversion of East Anglia. This manifests itself in two main ways: first, the lack of detail in the *HE* has made scholars reluctant to look beyond the written word and consider those aspects of the conversion about which history is silent; secondly, the few 'facts' which Bede does present have become the focus of such intensive debate that any attempt to place them within a wider framework is obfuscated by the need to identify a certain grave or pinpoint a particular name on a map.

It has been necessary to engage with such debates, particularly those surrounding the identification of *Dommoc*, Elmham and *Cnobheresburg*. Despite the lack of evidence, the site of the bishopric founded at *Dommoc* in the AD 630/1 has erroneously become associated with Dunwich; however, there *is* overwhelming evidence in favour of its having been at Walton Castle. Similarly, the more easily resolved debate surrounding the second diocese of Elmham, established in AD 673, has focused upon the remains of two buildings, both widely considered to be Anglo-Saxon and yet both demonstrably Norman on closer examination. In this case the evidence supports the identification of North Elmham, although clearly South Elmham was at least partially in the hands of the bishopric, along with nearby Hoxne. A similar debate concerns the location of the monastery which Fursa established at *Cnobheresburg* in the AD 630s, which is widely believed to have been sited at Burgh Castle despite evidence to the contrary. Less problematic is Botolph's monastery at *Icanho*, begun in AD 654, now firmly accepted to have been situated at Iken. In this instance, we have had to engage with a different historical problem, that of Bede's silence on the matter of the man and his monastery when we can be certain that he must have known of both.

Ultimately one has to question the use of trying to identify sites named in incomplete sources when time can be spent much more productively trying to develop an understanding of a wider range of issues. Burgh Castle is a good case in point: despite being erroneously identified as Fursa's monastery, it is clear from the archaeological evidence that Burgh Castle *was* a site of great religious significance during the Middle Saxon period.[205] Irrespective of which name the site may have had, its being reused in this way is more relevant and makes much greater sense when viewed within the wider context of the reuse of Roman structures by early ecclesiastics.[206] It is clear that the account of the East Anglian conversion derived from the documentary sources does not provide a comprehensive explanation of events; rather, it provides a framework against which the contemporary archaeological evidence can be measured, compared and contrasted.

Having himself attempted to summarise the evidence for early Christian Norfolk, Williamson stated that 'the development of ecclesiastical organisation in the county remains truly mysterious. The evidence of documents will probably contribute little to our understanding in the future: the challenge is one for archaeology to answer.'[207] This rest of this book answers that challenge.

---

[205] Johnson, *Burgh Castle*, pp. 60–65.
[206] Bell, 'Churches on Roman Buildings' and *Religious Reuse.*
[207] Williamson, *Origins of Norfolk*, p. 161.

3

The Establishment
of Missionary Stations

One of the conclusions which can be drawn from the detailed analysis of the historical evidence for the conversion of East Anglia is the important role played by the bishops and missionaries in the establishment and maintenance of the region's episcopal structure, a pattern repeated in the conversions of other Anglo-Saxon kingdoms.[1] Building on the framework presented by the historical evidence, this chapter examines the archaeological evidence from a series of East Anglian sites, all of which can be demonstrated to have been instrumental in the conversion effort.

Any analysis of the Middle Saxon ecclesiastical landscape is inevitably dominated by discussion of minster churches. The term 'minster' is derived from the Old English translation of the Latin *monasterium*[2] and appears to have been used by the Anglo-Saxons to describe a wide range of early ecclesiastical foundations ranging from a small isolated community, perhaps with a timber church, to a large enclosed establishment focused around a stone church.[3] Following their Anglo-Saxon subjects, modern scholars use minster in a similarly broad sense and it is the generally preferred term because it carries none of the later medieval connotations of the Anglicised 'monastery'.

The development of the ecclesiastical system throughout the Anglo-Saxon period and the eventual emergence of the parochial system have frequently been the subject of often quite heated debate.[4] Differences of interpretation aside, one thing on which all parties agree is that the first religious sites to be founded during the conversion period were different from those founded later and by definition must have housed ecclesiastics who combined a traditional life of monastic devotion with proactive missionary and pastoral work within the local lay community.[5] John Blair

---

[1] Mayr-Harting, *The Coming of Christianity*, pp. 13–113; Foot, *Monastic Life*, pp. 75–137.
[2] e.g. Radford, 'Pre-Conquest Minster Churches'; Morris, *Churches in the Landscape*, pp. 93–139; Blair, 'Minster Churches in the Landscape', 'Anglo-Saxon Minsters', 'Ecclesiastical Organization' and *The Church in Anglo-Saxon Society*, pp. 79–134; Hall, *Minster Churches*; Foot, 'What was an Early Anglo-Saxon Monastery?', 'Anglo-Saxon Minsters' and *Monastic Life*.
[3] Foot, 'Anglo-Saxon Minsters' and *Monastic Life*, pp. 5–10.
[4] e.g. Everitt, *Continuity and Colonization*, pp. 181–224; Morris, *Churches in the Landscape*, pp. 93–226; Cambridge and Rollason, 'Pastoral Organisation'; Holdsworth, 'Bishoprics'; Pestell, *Landscapes of Monastic Foundation*, pp. 18–151; Blair, *The Church in Anglo-Saxon Society*, pp. 79–134 and 368–425; Foot, *Monastic Life*, pp. 75–137.
[5] Cambridge and Rollason, 'Pastoral Organisation', pp. 93–4; Foot, 'What was an Early Anglo-Saxon Monastery?', p. 50, and *Monastic Life*, pp. 77 and 283–336; Thacker, 'Monks, Preaching and Pastoral Care'; Aston, *Monasteries*, p. 48.

goes so far as to specifically, but subtly, separate his discussion of those minsters which were founded as a part of the conversion effort from that of those which were founded later, as the newly established Church was consolidated.[6] This book is concerned only with the former class of sites, but the traditional usage of minster is felt to be too general to be helpfully employed here, so, following the example of Stuart Rigold, the term 'missionary station' is instead used to describe those ecclesiastical sites which were founded during the initial wave of the conversion.[7]

In attempting to identify such missionary stations the first sites to be considered here are the ruinous Roman enclosures which were reoccupied by the newly arrived churchmen, who put the ruins to ecclesiastical use. Such enclosures were not the only sites deemed to be suitable for this purpose and a second tranche of archaeological evidence is derived from other pre-existing fortified enclosures which were similarly reoccupied. In the absence of an appropriate ready-made enclosure, a suitably delimited topographical setting was chosen instead for such missionary activity, most often a peninsula or riverine island, and these are considered in the final part of this chapter.

The reuse of Roman enclosures

The evidence for the establishment of the East Anglian bishopric was examined in the previous chapter, beginning with Sigeberht's gift of the elusive site of *Dommoc* to Bishop Felix *c.* AD 630/1.[8] As we have seen, there is much good evidence to suggest that *Dommoc* lay within the Roman fort at Walton Castle, which stood on the coast at Felixstowe, the maritime gateway to the Wuffingas' heartland in south-east Suffolk (Fig. 6). Unfortunately archaeological investigation of Walton Castle is not possible, as the fort was destroyed by the sea in the eighteenth century, but seventeenth-century records describe a narrow rectangular fort with round corner-bastions.[9] As was discussed in the previous chapter, there is documentary evidence to suggest that a pre-Conquest church stood inside the fort and that this church survived the construction of Roger Bigod's eleventh-century castle before being relocated in the twelfth century.[10] The loss of Walton Castle to the elements is undoubtedly one of the region's greatest archaeological tragedies, for it was clearly a site of great significance to the establishment of Christianity in the region, but its loss does not mean that nothing can be inferred about the site.

The fact that the bishopric should have been founded within the walls of a Roman fort is particularly telling, for it is part of a wider pattern of the reuse of Roman enclosures for ecclesiastical purposes that is seen across Britain. The Roman withdrawal from Britain in the early fifth century did not result in the sweeping-away of the existing Roman infrastructure and the Anglo-Saxon landscape

---

[6] Blair, 'Anglo-Saxon Minsters', p. 231, 'Ecclesiastical Organization', pp. 206–9, and *The Church in Anglo-Saxon Society*, pp. 65–73.

[7] Rigold, '*Litus Romanum*'.

[8] *HE*, ii, 15.

[9] Fox, 'Romano-British Suffolk', pp. 287–91; Fairclough and Plunkett, 'Drawings of Walton Castle', pp. 419–26.

[10] Davison, 'History of Walton Priory', pp. 142–3; Fairclough and Plunkett, 'Drawings of Walton Castle', pp. 425 and 451–2.

contained the remains of numerous Roman towns, villas, settlements and roads. Many of these structures were old even at the end of the Roman period and by the seventh century many would have been in a poor condition, if not entirely ruinous.[11] Dilapidated Roman masonry buildings, sometimes of immense size, would have been particularly awe-inspiring during the Early Saxon period, which was characterised by modest timber architecture; small wonder, then, that later Anglo-Saxon poets referred to such ruins as *enta geweorc*, 'the work of giants'.[12]

In Britain associations between early ecclesiastical sites and Roman ruins have long been recognised, although it was not until the 1980s that they began to be studied in a systematic fashion.[13] Links between Roman sites and early ecclesiastical foundations are also commonplace in Continental Europe, particularly Gaul and Italy, although in many instances these European sites were continuously occupied from the Roman period onwards.[14] By contrast, within much of lowland England there was a distinct hiatus between the end of Roman occupation and the beginning of ecclesiastical reoccupation, although greater continuity in the reuse of Roman sites for burials can be found in the west of England.[15] But why should ruinous Roman sites have been considered by the early ecclesiastics to be such advantageous locations?

One traditionally cited explanation for this association is the ready source of quarried stone that Roman buildings provided for the construction of new churches.[16] Across the country there are many examples of churches which contain reused Roman building materials, including several which are clearly Anglo-Saxon foundations, and once churches began to be built of stone Roman sites were quarried for their raw materials, but this secondary use has somewhat muddied the water. Yet, while the desirability of a convenient source of building material may well have been a factor in the siting of churches in some parts of lowland England, especially those where good building stone was scarce, it was clearly not the case in East Anglia. All of the East Anglian evidence — both archaeological and architectural — indicates that the building of stone churches did not begin in earnest in the region until at least the Late Saxon period, meaning that for some 400 years East Anglian church-builders effectively had no need of quarried stone.[17] A much more plausible explanation for the association between Roman ruins and early churches is to be found not in pragmatic considerations of building materials, but in the symbolic connotations carried in the seventh century by all things Roman.

By the seventh century the Church had come to regard itself as the natural successor to the Imperial Roman state, in both actual and metaphorical senses, and Pope Gregory appears to have approached the conversion of the English not only as the evangelisation of a new people but also as the spiritual reclamation of a lost Roman province.[18] This

---

[11] Dark and Dark, *Landscape*, pp. 135–47.

[12] Jack, *Beowulf*, lines 1679, 2717 and 2774; Bradley, *Anglo-Saxon Poetry*, 'The Ruin', line 2.

[13] Rigold, '*Litus Romanum*'; Rodwell and Rodwell, *Historic Churches*; Morris and Roxan, 'Churches on Roman sites'; Morris, *The Church*, pp. 40–45; Rodwell, 'Churches in the Landscape'; Blair, 'Anglo-Saxon Minsters', pp. 235–46; Bell, 'Churches on Roman Buildings' and *Religious Reuse*.

[14] e.g. James, 'Archaeology'; Percival, 'Villas and Monasteries'; Knight, *End of Antiquity*.

[15] Dark, *Civitas to Kingdom*; Bell, *Religious Reuse*, pp. 38–68.

[16] Morris, *The Church in British Archaeology*, pp. 43–5; Eaton, *Plundering the Past*, pp. 10–35.

[17] Taylor and Taylor, *Anglo-Saxon Architecture*, passim; Hoggett, 'Changing Beliefs', pp. 141–53.

[18] Bell, *Religious Reuse*, pp. 26–7.

sentiment was reinforced by Gregory's letter to Augustine of AD 601, in which he set out a vision of a Christianised England heavily based on the administrative structure of Late Roman Britain: archbishoprics were to be established in London and York, the capitals of *Britannia Superior* and *Britannia Inferior* respectively, while additional bishoprics were to be founded in accordance with the network of regional *civitas* capitals which had administered Roman Britain.[19] Such notions of *romanitas* — the desire for the ideals of Roman culture — were so ingrained that on their arrival in Britain the missionaries of the Roman church would have not only recognised the extant remains of Roman buildings for what they once had been, but also considered them to be extremely appropriate sites to host new ecclesiastical foundations.[20]

As is explored more fully in the next chapter, this desire for *romanitas* and, by association, Christianity was expressed strongly in the seventh-century burial record via the use of Classically influenced costumes and jewellery (below, pp. 104–8), but it was also made manifest in the landscape. Consequently, from the mid-seventh century strong intellectual associations were made between Roman sites and Christianity, a concept which not only resulted in the missionaries of the Roman church being drawn to such sites but was also widely disseminated as a result of these missionaries' subsequent actions.[21] Doubtless as a result of specific requests from missionaries of the Roman church, many ruinous Roman forts became the subject of royal gifts so that the sites might be reoccupied and put to ecclesiastical use: alongside the gift of *Dommoc* to Felix other regional examples recorded by Bede include the gift of the fort at Bradwell-on-Sea to Cedd by the king of Essex.[22] Nationwide, more than forty-six early ecclesiastical sites, many of them foundations directly attributable to missionaries of the Roman church, are associated with Roman forts or enclosures. Almost all of the Saxon Shore forts were reused in this manner, as well as a considerable number of the forts which line Hadrian's Wall, as well as those elsewhere.[23]

In every case, the existence of the walled enclosure itself seems to have been of greatest importance to the occupiers, rather than the presence of any particular building within it. These enclosures were not used for defensive purposes — indeed, many would not have been defensible by the seventh century — but the walls served to mark the boundary between the secular exterior world and the religious precinct enclosed within, while simultaneously providing a strong symbolic link with the Roman past.[24] They thus served to focus the attention of both the secular and religious populations, as well as being a defined religious social space, and therefore are also in accordance with the tenets of the framework propounded by cognitive archaeologists for recognising religiously motivated behaviour in the material record (see pp. 11–13).[25]

---

[19] Martyn, *Letters of Gregory*, 11.39.
[20] Blair, 'Minster Churches in the Landscape', p. 44, and 'Anglo-Saxon Minsters', pp. 235–46.
[21] Bell, 'Churches on Roman Buildings', pp. 5–8; Blair, *The Church in Anglo-Saxon Society*, pp. 16–22; Brown, *Life of St. Fursey*, pp. 18–19.
[22] *HE*, iii, 22.
[23] Rigold, '*Litus Romanum*'; Bell, 'Churches on Roman Buildings', pp. 14–15.
[24] Blair, 'Minster Churches in the Landscape', p. 46, and 'Anglo-Saxon Minsters', pp. 235–41; Bell, 'Churches on Roman Buildings', pp. 15–16; Foot, *Monastic Life*, pp. 96–106.
[25] Renfrew, *Archaeology of Cult*, pp. 18–19; Renfrew and Bahn, *Archaeology: Theories, Methods and Practice*, pp. 416–17.

It is clear that many of East Anglia's Roman buildings, having fallen out of use, remained abandoned until they were put to ecclesiastical use in the seventh century. Although not all instances of this reuse are documented, many can be materially demonstrated to have been an active part of the evangelisation of East Anglia. Within the region the predominant type of site reused in this fashion was the walled fort, of which coastal examples existed at Walton Castle, Burgh Castle, Caister-on-Sea and Brancaster. All these sites would have been attractive to seventh-century ecclesiastics and each can be shown to be relevant to this study. The walled Roman town at Caistor St Edmund (*Venta Icenorum*) is a related site, albeit of a different character and greater scale, and it is considered later in this chapter.

Burgh Castle

As was noted in the previous chapter (pp. 44–6), although most authors identify Burgh Castle as the site of *Cnobheresburg*, the site given to the Irish missionary Fursa by Sigebeorht in the AD 630s,[26] this identification is not easily supported by the historical evidence; but this does not mean that the site of Burgh Castle did not play an important role in the East Anglian conversion.

The late-third-century fort at Burgh Castle is situated in a strategic location on the banks of the river Waveney; during the Roman period it stood on the southern side of the Great Estuary, an area of tidal waters at the confluence of the rivers Bure, Yare and Waveney (Figs 2 and 6; Plate 2).[27] Today the fort's walls and external bastions survive on three sides; the western wall collapsed into the river shortly after the end of the Roman period. The site was reoccupied during the Middle Saxon period and after the Norman Conquest a castle motte was constructed in the south-western corner of the fort (Fig. 8A). The motte was ploughed flat only in 1837.[28] To date there has been a relatively limited degree of investigation at the fort. A series of small trenches was dug along the western perimeter in 1850 and 1855, and a series of small excavations was conducted inside the walls by Charles Green between 1958 and 1961 (Fig. 8B).[29] In total, less than a quarter of the interior of the fort has been excavated. In a more non-invasive vein, an aerial photographic analysis conducted by the Norfolk National Mapping Programme has identified the cropmarks of a number of buildings within the walls as well as identifying traces of the settlement which surrounded the fort.[30]

Like many people, Charles Green firmly believed Burgh Castle to be the site of *Cnobheresburg* and confidently expected his excavations to discover the remains of Fursa's monastery. Indeed, so strong was his conviction that in the excavation records some layers were simply labelled 'Fursey'.[31] The circular arguments inherent in Green's approach are plain to see, but, Fursa aside, his excavations *did* produce evidence for a significant phase of Middle Saxon occupation at the site. The trenches in the north-eastern corner of the fort produced nearly 300 sherds of Middle Saxon

[26] *HE*, iii, 19.
[27] Pearson, *Construction of the Saxon Shore Forts*, pp. 38–40; Gurney, *Outposts of the Roman Empire*, pp. 12–13; Albone *et al.*, 'Archaeology of Norfolk's Coastal Zone', pp. 102–3.
[28] Johnson, *Burgh Castle*, pp. 43–5, 118–20.
[29] Harrod, 'Excavations'; Johnson, *Burgh Castle*.
[30] Albone *et al.*, 'Archaeology of Norfolk's Coastal Zone', pp. 107–8.
[31] Johnson, *Burgh Castle*, pp. 7–8.

Plate 2: An aerial view of Burgh Castle from the south-west, 20 June 1990, showing the walls of the Roman fort (foreground) and the parish church (top left). TG4704/AJD/GBB1 (Derek Edwards). © *NMAS*

Ipswich ware, very few of which were associated with cut features. In these same trenches Green identified a number of oval structures of varying size which he took to be the foundations of Middle Saxon huts, but in his analysis of the excavations Johnson questions whether these ovals survived to the extent which Green suggested or, indeed, whether they had actually existed at all.[32] Certainly, a sub-circular plan would render these buildings unlike any known Middle Saxon buildings, all of the excavated examples of which are rectangular.[33] Given the depth of the plough damage within the fort's walls it seems highly unlikely that any Middle Saxon features would have survived in this area, suggesting that whatever these oval features might have been, they were not Middle Saxon.

[32] *Ibid.*, pp. 37–9.
[33] Rahtz, 'Buildings and Rural Settlement'; James *et al.*, 'Early Medieval Building Tradition'; Marshall and Marshall, 'Survey and Analysis' and 'Differentiation, Change and Continuity'.

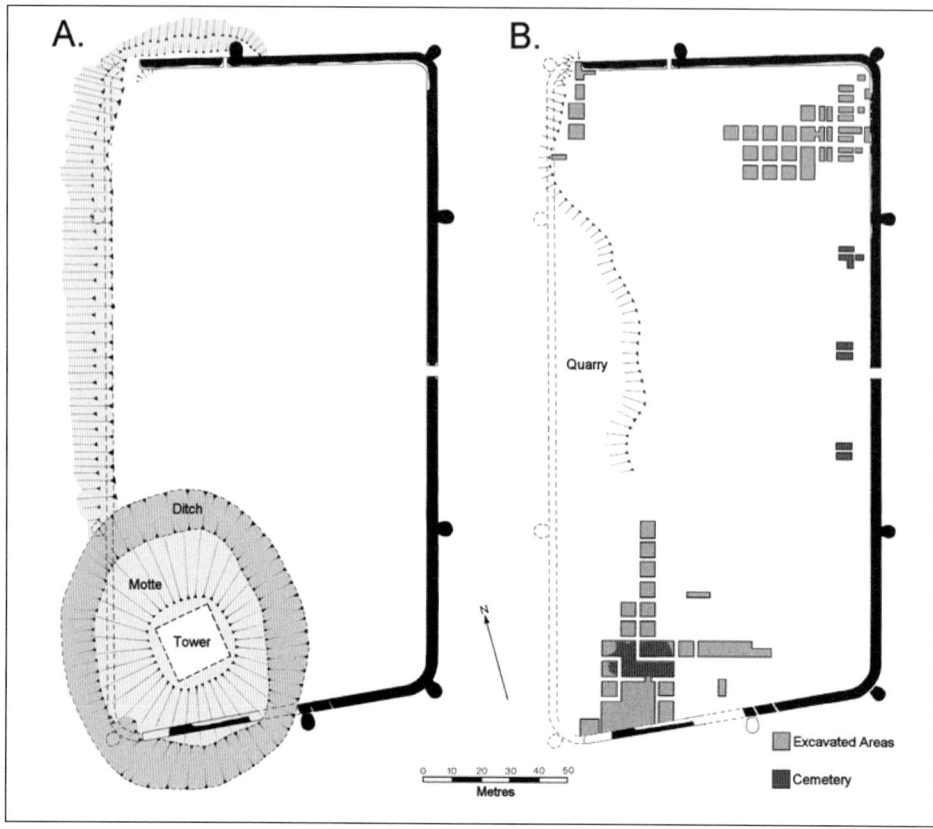

Fig. 8: Plans of Burgh Castle showing (A) the Norman motte and (B) the locations of Green's trenches, highlighting the area of the cemetery (after Johnson, *Burgh Castle*, figs 2, 20 and 29). © *NMAS*

The only area of the site in which Middle Saxon features were found *in situ* was in the south-western corner of the fort, where the medieval motte had stood and the depth of overlying soil was consequently greater. Here the remains of an extensive cemetery were discovered (Fig. 9), although the original ground surface from which the graves had been cut and several higher layers of burials had clearly been destroyed by ploughing.[34] Excavations further to the north revealed no trace of burials, suggesting that the northern extent of the cemetery was reached, but the burials apparently continued beyond the eastern and western extents of the excavated trenches. The southern extent of the cemetery was definitely reached, as it was delineated by the line of a broadly west–east Roman wall.

The cemetery clearly post-dated the Roman layers and was firmly sealed beneath the eleventh-century motte. Three radiocarbon dates from human skeletal remains suggested that the cemetery was begun in the early seventh century and continued in use into the Late Saxon period.[35] The excavated cemetery comprised 163 graves

---

[34] Johnson, *Burgh Castle*, pp. 55–60.
[35] *Ibid.*, pp. 111–12; Jordan *et al.*, *Radiocarbon Dates*, pp. 27–8.

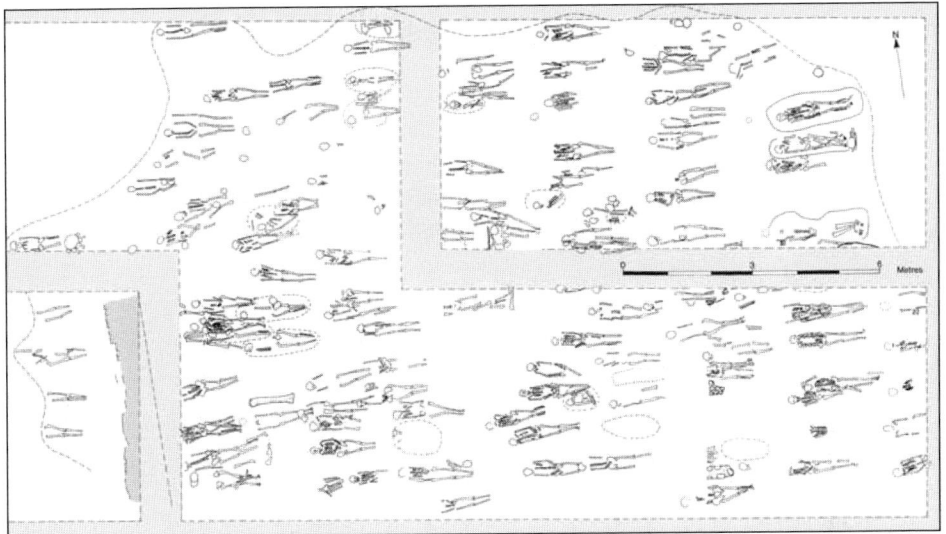

Fig. 9: Plan of the Burgh Castle cemetery (after Johnson, *Burgh Castle*, fig. 24). © *NMAS*

and much disarticulated bone which represented a mixture of males and females ranging in age from infancy to old age.[36] All of the burials were laid on their backs (supine), aligned west–east and arranged into rough north–south rows. In places there was evidence for later burials having been dug through earlier ones, suggesting that the cemetery lay within a confined area and was used over a long period of time. On this basis the cemetery at Burgh Castle was clearly Christian, a conclusion which has sparked much speculation about the presumed whereabouts of the associated church. Such discussions are largely superfluous, however, for it seems most likely that any trace of an associated Middle Saxon church, or indeed any other Middle Saxon building, has long since been ploughed away.[37]

Given that the Middle and Late Saxon religious focus lay within the fort it is notable that the present parish church at Burgh Castle stands approximately 250m north-east of the fort (Plate 2). This church comprises a nave, chancel and Romanesque round western tower, to which a northern aisle and vestry were added in the mid-nineteenth century.[38] In 1993–4 a small archaeological excavation immediately to the south of the churchyard revealed several Romano-British and Late Saxon agricultural ditches.[39] No evidence for any Middle Saxon activity was found near the church, which, combined with the agricultural nature of the underlying Late Saxon evidence and the date of the tower, suggests that the church might have been relocated to its present site in the early Norman period, conceivably when the fort was converted into a motte and bailey castle — a sequence not dissimilar to that witnessed at Walton Castle.

While the historical evidence suggests that Burgh Castle was not the site of

---

[36] Anderson and Birkett, 'Human Skeletal Remains'.
[37] Johnson, *Burgh Castle*, pp. 48–50.
[38] Pevsner, *Suffolk*, pp. 128–9; NHER 10500.
[39] Wallis, 'Excavations at Church Loke'.

Cnobheresburg, the limited archaeological excavations that have taken place within the fort indicate that the interior of the fort was host to a significant amount of early Christian missionary activity. This fits closely the patterns observed elsewhere in the country and, indeed, within the East Anglian region.

Caister-on-Sea

A similar sequence of Middle Saxon reoccupation occurred at the Roman fort of Caister-on-Sea, situated some 9km to the north-east of Burgh Castle on the opposite side of the Great Estuary (Figs. 2 and 6). The fort at Caister, which was built in the early third century AD, was approximately 400m square and comprised an earthen rampart, a stone wall and an outer defensive ditch. The walls of the fort were still standing in the seventeenth century, although they appear to have been demolished by the eighteenth century and much of the site now lies beneath residential buildings (Fig. 10).[40]

Since the 1930s a number of small- and medium-scale excavations have been conducted in and around the site of the fort, many of them in response to the threat posed by development, but despite this large parts of the fort's interior remain unexplored (Fig. 10). Excavation has revealed two ranges of Roman buildings, the southern gatehouse and a stretch of interior road, and demonstrated that the fort fell out of use in the last decades of the fourth century AD. The investigations also demonstrated that the overlying Anglo-Saxon archaeology had been greatly disturbed and, although large quantities of Ipswich ware and a number of *sceattas*

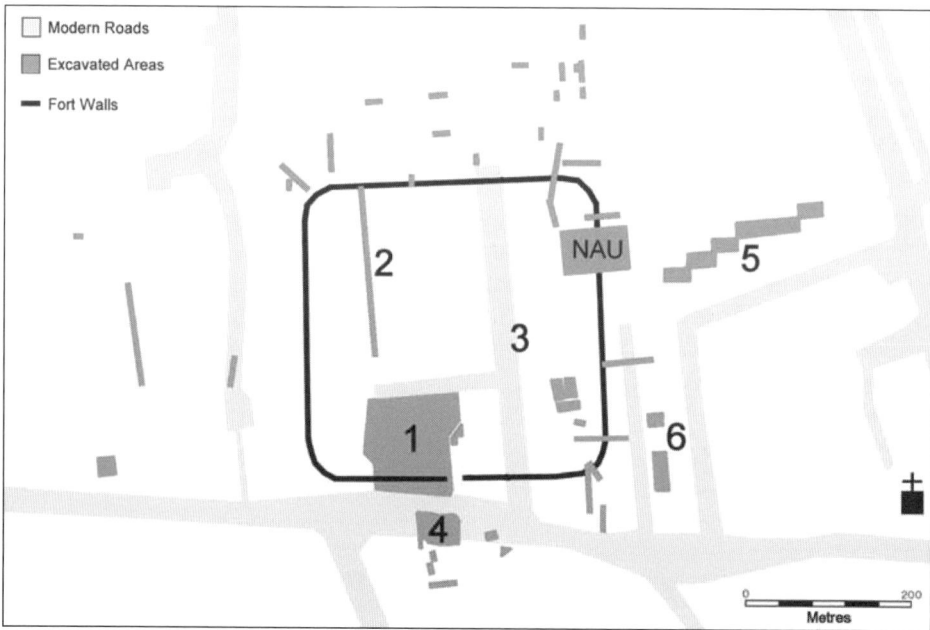

Fig. 10: Caister-on-Sea excavation plan, showing the line of the Roman walls and the excavations in and around the fort. Green's trenches are numbered; only Area 1 is now devoid of housing (after Darling with Gurney, *Caister-on-Sea*, fig. 5). © *NMAS*

[40] Darling with Gurney, *Caister-on-Sea*, pp. 1, 8–15.

were discovered, very little Anglo-Saxon settlement evidence survived intact.[41] The excavations did, however, reveal evidence for two *in situ* Middle Saxon inhumation cemeteries, one inside the fort and one immediately outside it to the south.[42]

Rumbelow first recognised the remains of an inhumation cemetery during excavations in the north-eastern quadrant of the fort in 1935.[43] From Rumbelow's report it would appear that 50–100 burials of men, women and children were discovered, all of them unfurnished, orientated west–east and laid in broad rows, like those at Burgh Castle. In places there were apparently several layers of burials, which occasionally intercut. Unfortunately no plans were made of this area of the cemetery, but the burials did not apparently continue far to the west. Charles Green's excavations at Caister in the 1950s (numbered 1–6 in Fig. 10) revealed two isolated Middle Saxon burials located towards the centre of the fort; and three additional burials were discovered in the north-eastern corner in the 1960s.[44] Additional archaeological excavations conducted in 2006 revealed further inhumations within the north-eastern quadrant of the fort (Fig. 10).[45]

Outside the fort, several west–east inhumations were discovered immediately to the south in 1932. More burials were found further south again in 1946–7 and in 1954 a trench revealed at least 147 inhumations, again all unfurnished, laid west–east and with areas of dense intercutting (Fig. 10, Area 4, and Fig. 11).[46] The skeletons from the cemetery comprised infants and adults both male and female.[47] It is thought that the northern and western extents of the cemetery were reached during the excavation, but the distribution of the other discoveries suggests the existence of a substantial cemetery to the south of the fort; estimates of the number of individual burials within this cemetery range from hundreds to thousands.[48]

It is clear from the archaeological evidence that both the intramural and extramural cemeteries at Caister-on-Sea were of Middle Saxon origin and similar in character. The lack of recorded details for the cemetery discovered in the north-eastern corner of the fort means that interpretation can only be speculative, however. In the light of evidence from this and other sites, it seems likely that the intramural cemetery had its origins in the seventh century, at the point when the ruined fort was presumably first reoccupied and put to ecclesiastical use. This cemetery seems to have continued into the Late Saxon period before falling out of use.

We can be more certain about the extramural cemetery, to which Darling and Gurney attribute a start date of *c.* AD 720 on the strength of the artefacts associated with some of the burials.[49] This cemetery also continued to be used into the Late Saxon period. If the intramural cemetery was a part of the original refoundation of the fort it would seem that the extramural cemetery was founded to accommodate

[41] *Ibid.*, pp. 37–45; Dallas, 'Middle and Late Saxon Pottery'; Sherlock, 'Post-Roman Coins'.
[42] Darling with Gurney, *Caister-on-Sea*, p. 37.
[43] Rumbelow, 'Finds on a Roman Site', pp. 180–82.
[44] *Ibid.*; Darling with Gurney, *Caister-on-Sea*, p. 45.
[45] Crawley, 'Archaeological Excavation and Watching Brief at Uplands, Caister-on-Sea'.
[46] Darling with Gurney, *Caister-on-Sea*, pp. 45–61.
[47] Anderson, 'Human Skeletal Remains'.
[48] Darling with Gurney, *Caister-on-Sea*, p. 45.
[49] *Ibid.*, p. 252.

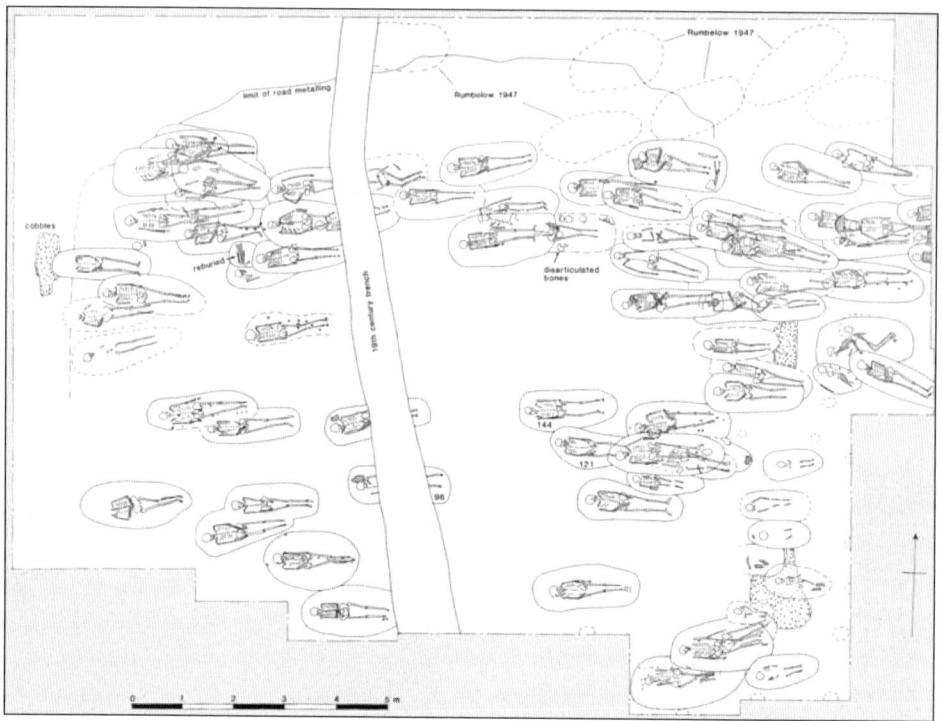

Fig. 11: Plan of the extramural cemetery at Caister-on-Sea, located within Green's Area 4 (after Gurney with Darling, *Caister-on-Sea*, fig. 26). © *NMAS*

the increasing numbers of burials which the site must have attracted as its influence grew. Certainly, the number of burials outside the fort suggests that this was the more regularly used cemetery, perhaps indicating that the right to be buried in the intramural cemetery became more exclusive over time.

Rather than being situated within the walls of the fort, the medieval church at Caister-on-Sea stands some 300m to the east (Fig. 10). The fabric of the church was heavily restored in the late nineteenth century, but traces of thirteenth- and fourteenth-century masonry survive.[50] No trace of Middle or Late Saxon activity has been discovered on the site, indicating that the church was a later foundation.[51] Unlike at Walton Castle and Burgh Castle, there was no Norman occupation of Caister fort which might have precipitated the relocation of an intramural church, yet the fact that the church was founded approximately 300m from the eastern wall of the fort might be significant. As was the case at Burgh Castle, it is clear that the Roman enclosure at Caister-on-Sea played host to Christian occupation during the conversion period. The discovery of two cemeteries — one intramural, one extramural — provides us with an insight into the way in which the initial religious focus might have expanded over time as its zone of influence grew.

[50] Pevsner and Wilson, *Norfolk I*, pp. 424–6.
[51] NHER 8683.

Plate 3: An aerial view of the Brancaster Roman fort from the south, 24 June 1976, showing the cropmarks of the walls. TF7844/AGY/AER4 (Derek Edwards). © *NMAS*

Brancaster

The Roman shore fort at Brancaster is situated on the north Norfolk coast. The fort was built in the second quarter of the third century and was roughly 200m square, with a rampart, corner turrets and a large external ditch (Fig. 6).[52] In the seventeenth century the walls were recorded as standing twelve feet high, but much of the masonry was removed and reused in the mid-eighteenth century.[53] Today the fort survives as an earthwork and a particularly spectacular series of cropmarks on the eastern edge of the village of Brancaster (Plate 3). The parish church lies about a kilometre to the west of the site.

[52] Cunliffe, 'The Saxon Shore'.
[53] Rose, 'A Note on the Demolition of the Walls'.

To date very little excavation has taken place within the fort, although the north-eastern corner turret was investigated in 1846, a series of cuttings was made across the western defences in 1935, and a number of surface finds have been made in and around the area of the fort.[54] Aerial photography has revealed something of the layout of the fort and a planned *vicus* surrounding the site.[55] In the 1970s two excavations were conducted within the western part of the *vicus*, revealing evidence for Roman settlement.[56]

The fort at Brancaster is unusual in its lack of evidence for seventh-century Christian reoccupation, for, given the patterns discussed above, one would expect the site to have been the focus of some kind of ecclesiastical institution in the immediate aftermath of the conversion.[57] The lack of large-scale archaeological investigation is, therefore, frustrating, but there are a number of incidental details which suggest that evidence for Middle Saxon occupation at Brancaster may yet be found. The excavation of a sherd of imported eighth-century Tating ware from the western *vicus* and the recovery of a piece of Middle Saxon metalwork from the vicinity of the fort both hint at some kind of higher-status occupation in the vicinity during the Middle Saxon period.[58] More significantly, Edwards and Green refer to a scatter of human remains discovered at the western wall of the fort, which they suggested might be the ploughed-out remains of later burials.[59] Given the nature of the other sites discussed here, these pieces of evidence provide a tantalising indication that Brancaster, too, was a focus of Christian activity, including burial, from the seventh century onwards. One strongly suspects that further archaeological investigation of the fort's interior would reveal evidence of early Christian occupation akin to that at Burgh Castle or Caister-on-Sea.

Caistor St Edmund

Venta Icenorum, the Roman town at Caistor St Edmund, is on a larger scale than those sites discussed thus far. It was situated to the east of the River Tas and has its origins in the mid-first century AD, when its street-grid was first established (Fig. 12). Subsequent decades and centuries saw the establishment of a series of public buildings and civic amenities, including a forum, a bath complex, an amphitheatre, a market, temples, workshops and houses.[60] *Venta Icenorum* was the administrative *civitas* capital of East Anglia, the region occupied by the Iron Age Iceni, and was therefore part of a wider network of similar towns across Roman Britain.[61] Like many other Roman towns, *Venta Icenorum* was walled during the late third century, reducing the area of the town by half and providing defences which in places were 7m high, 4m thick and fronted by a ditch 24m wide (Plate 4).[62]

---

[54] Warner, 'Notices of the Original Structure', pp. 11–15; St Joseph, 'The Roman Fort'; Green and Gregory, 'Surface Finds'.

[55] Edwards and Green, 'Saxon Shore Fort'; Albone *et al.*, 'Archaeology of Norfolk's Coastal Zone', pp. 104–6.

[56] Hinchcliffe with Green, *Excavations at Brancaster*.

[57] Rigold, '*Litus Romanum*'.

[58] Hodges, 'An Unusual (?) Tating Ware Vessel'; NHER 1003.

[59] Edwards and Green, 'Saxon Shore Fort', pp. 25–9.

[60] Wacher, *Towns*, pp. 227–38; Davies, *Venta Icenorum*, pp. 13–22.

[61] Wacher, *Towns*, pp. 226–88.

[62] Wacher, *Roman Britain*, pp. 95–102; Davies, *Venta Icenorum*, pp. 23–5.

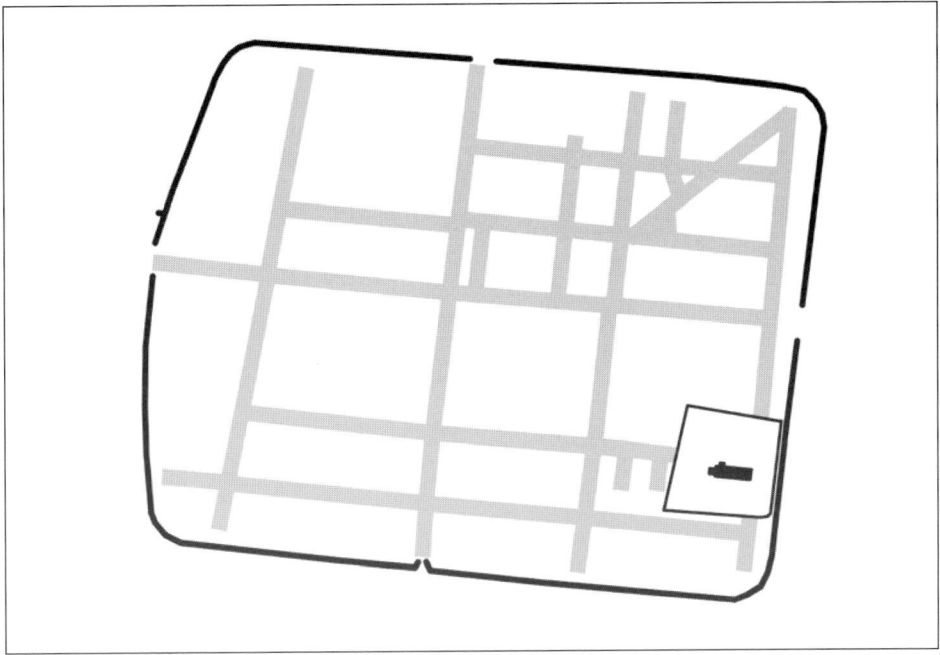

Fig. 12: The street-plan of Roman *Venta Icenorum* and the medieval parish church at 1:5,000.

Plate 4: An aerial view of *Venta Icenorum* from the south-west, showing the parish church (right) and cropmarks of the Roman street-plan. TG2303/AQC/HYY14 (Derek Edwards). © *NMAS*

Unlike other *civitas* capitals, *Venta Icenorum* did not become the medieval county town, Anglo-Saxon Norwich having superseded it, so the defences survive largely intact and, barring plough damage and some small-scale excavations, much of the site remains undisturbed.[63] As a consequence aerial photography has proved particularly rewarding, cropmarks and parchmarks revealing much of the street plan and individual buildings; at the time of writing the town's environs are the subject of an aerial photographic assessment being undertaken by the Norfolk National Mapping Programme, the preliminary results of which have already greatly increased our understanding of the landscape setting of the town.[64] Geophysical survey has proved equally rewarding and an extensive magnetometer survey of the interior of the town and its environs conducted in 2006/7 revealed a considerable amount of detail regarding the street plan and associated Roman buildings, as well as providing glimpses of possible pre- and post-Roman features.[65]

Like many of the sites discussed in this chapter, *Venta Icenorum* was a walled Roman enclosure, albeit on a large scale. In the seventh century it would doubtless also have attracted the attention of newly arrived Christian missionaries, all the more so if any administrative capacity or residual occupation remained at the site. The fact that some degree of occupation of the town continued into the Anglo-Saxon period is attested by the presence of two Early Saxon cemeteries on the hillsides overlooking the town,[66] while a dense spread of Middle Saxon metalwork has been located immediately to the west of the walled town and a substantial spread of Ipswich ware has been found immediately to its north.[67]

In the light of the preceding discussion it should come as no surprise that the parish church is sited within the walls of the Roman town, exactly where we would expect to find a church founded as a part of the missionary process (Plate 4). The present fabric of the church is largely thirteenth- to fifteenth-century, although traces of Late Saxon architecture have been identified. Comment has often been passed on the neatness with which the church's location and alignment complement the Roman street-grid, indicating that it was founded while these features were still visible and perhaps suggesting the reuse of a Roman building in the first instance.[68] If the church at Caistor St Edmund *is* another ecclesiastical site founded as a part of the conversion process, then it should also have had a concomitant cemetery of Burgh Castle/Caister-on-Sea type.

In 2009, as the final draft of this book was being prepared, an archaeological evaluation was conducted within the churchyard at Caistor St Edmund, presenting a rare opportunity to test some of the hypotheses developed here. During this evaluation residual sherds of Ipswich ware and other Anglo-Saxon pottery were recovered, while a trench excavated immediately adjacent to the blocked southern doorway of the nave revealed a charnel deposit, apparently disturbed during the

---

[63] Frere, 'The Forum'.

[64] Wilson, 'Air-Photography'; Bales *et al.*, 'Norwich, Thetford and A11 Corridor'.

[65] Bowden and Bescoby, 'The Plan of *Venta Icenorum*'.

[66] Myres and Green, *Anglo-Saxon Cemeteries*, pp. 31–4; Wacher, *Towns*, p. 238; Davies, *Venta Icenorum*, p. 26.

[67] Bellinger and Sims, 'Caistor St Edmund Fieldwalking Project'; Percival, 'Caistor St Edmund Metal-Detector Survey'; Pestell, 'The Afterlife of "Productive" Sites', pp. 130–31.

[68] NHER 1860; Rodwell, 'Churches in the Landscape', pp. 9–10; Davies, *Venta Icenorum*, p. 27.

construction of the nave, which the excavator believes might relate to an earlier, potentially Middle Saxon phase of the churchyard.[69] The full publication of the results of this evaluation, along with the relevant radiocarbon dates, is eagerly awaited.

The landscape setting of *Venta Icenorum* and the nature of the Anglo-Saxon funerary landscape within which it sits are explored in Chapter 5 (pp. 125–7); now, though, the focus of this chapter broadens to include other, non-Roman, enclosures that were similarly reoccupied and put to missionary use.

The reuse of earthwork enclosures

In addition to the Roman enclosures discussed above, other types of ready-made enclosure, those dating to the Iron Age in particular, were also reoccupied and put to ecclesiastical use during the conversion period.[70]

Burgh

The Iron Age enclosure at Burgh in south-east Suffolk fits well with the patterns discussed in this chapter (Fig. 13). In addition to its Iron Age occupation, excavations conducted throughout the twentieth century within the double-ditched earthwork enclosure revealed that it had contained a substantial villa complex and continued to be occupied throughout the Roman period.[71] As a result of this occupation, Tyler Bell included Burgh in his list of Roman enclosures reused for the sites of early churches, but the site has been classified separately here because the enclosure itself comprised an Iron Age earthwork, although it is not clear to what extent the Roman remains were still visible in the seventh century.[72]

The parish church of St Botolph, which is situated within the earthwork at Burgh, was recorded at Domesday and is commonly thought to have been founded in the tenth century as a chapel to temporarily house the remains of St Botolph once they had been removed from his minster at Iken (above, pp. 47–50).[73] However, it seems unlikely that Botolph's remains should have rested at a spot which was not already a site of some religious significance and at which there was not already a suitable structure to house them. Surprisingly, the excavations within the enclosure revealed very little evidence for Middle Saxon activity, and it is unfortunate that it was not possible to fieldwalk any land in the vicinity of the parish church as part of the Deben Valley survey (see Chapter 5, pp. 153–51).[74] Despite the lack of material evidence, the landscape context of the church strongly suggests an early-seventh-century missionary origin, akin to that at those sites discussed above.

The Burgh earthwork enclosure lies approximately at the centre of a block of land comprising the parishes of Burgh, Clopton, Grundisburgh and Otley, through which flows the River Lark (Fig. 14). It has been suggested that these four parishes

---

[69] Percival, 'Archaeological Evaluation at Caistor St Edmund'; I am grateful to Will Bowden and John Percival for providing me with a copy of their results.

[70] Blair, 'Anglo-Saxon Minsters', pp. 227–35; Foot, *Monastic Life*, pp. 96–106.

[71] Martin, *Burgh*, pp. 68–74.

[72] Bell, *Religious Reuse*, p. 198, fig. 55.

[73] LDB f.400v; West *et al.*, 'Iken'; Stevenson, 'St Botolph', pp. 43–5; Martin, *Burgh*, pp. 74–6.

[74] Martin, *Burgh*, pp. 74–6.

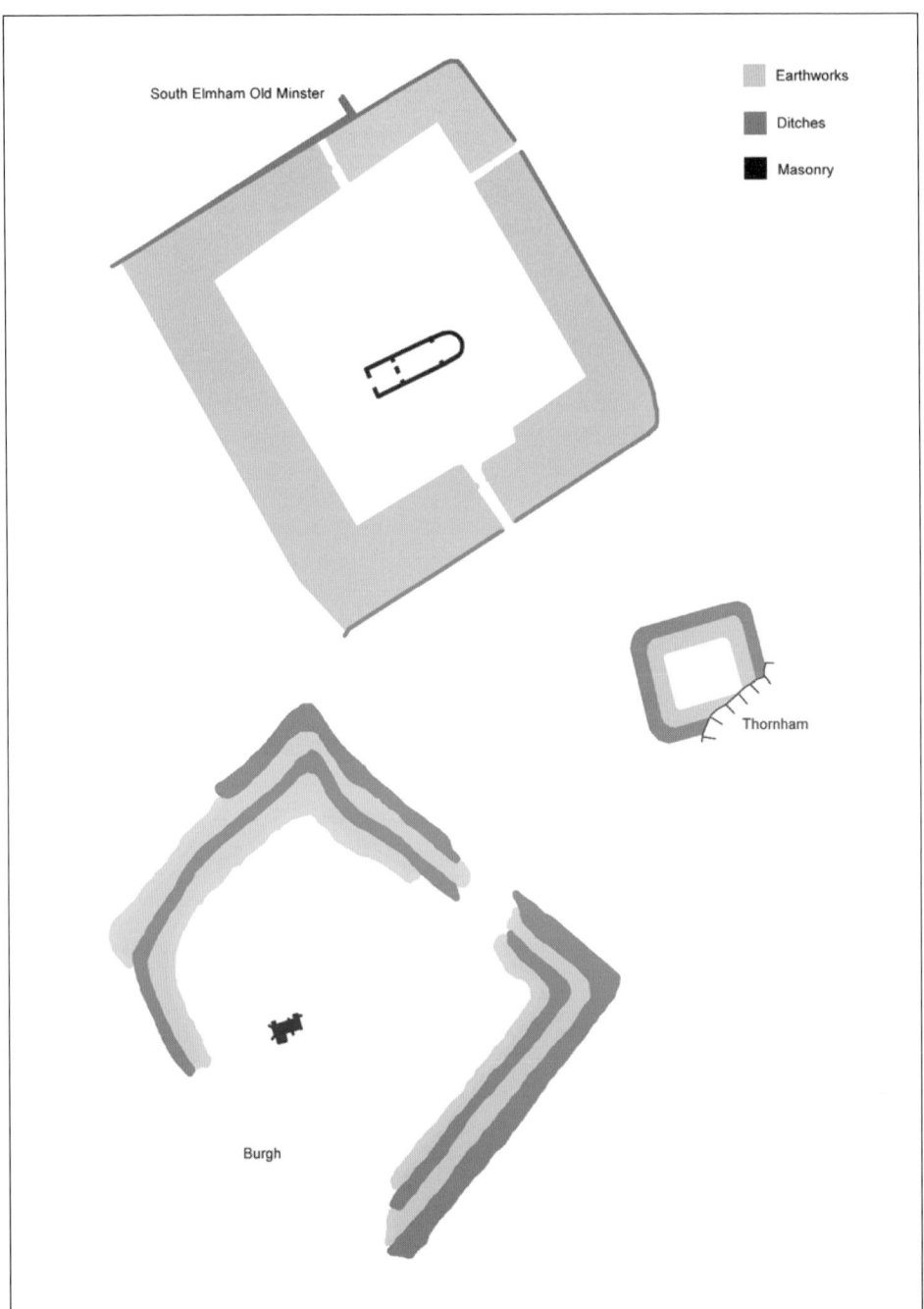

Fig. 13: Comparative plans of the earthwork enclosures at Thornham, South Elmham Old Minster and Burgh at 1:5,000.

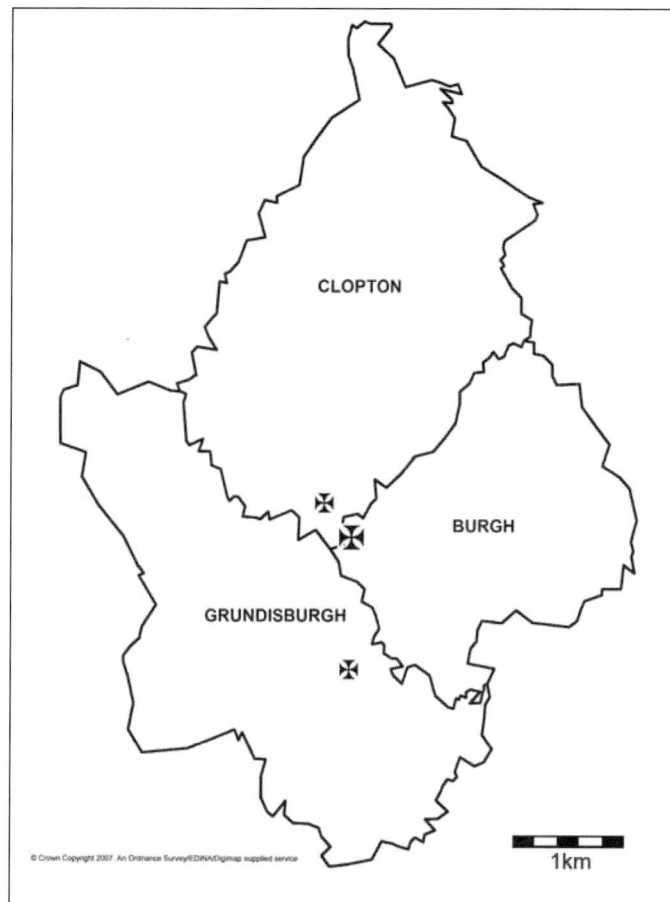

Fig. 14: The parishes
of Burgh,
Grundisburgh and
Clopton, showing the
relative locations of
the parish churches.

formed a Middle Saxon estate centred on the enclosure at Burgh, an estate which
had already begun to fragment during the Middle Saxon period.[75] Such an early
fragmentation would explain why fieldwalking revealed a substantial concentration
of Ipswich ware around Clopton church, some 400m to the north of the enclosure,
and a similar scatter around Grundisburgh church, a kilometre to the south. This
might also explain the lack of Middle Saxon material within the enclosure itself, for
the religious focus may have already been founded and relocated by the time that
Ipswich ware began to be used in earnest in the second half of the seventh century.

Tasburgh

A similar example of a reused non-Roman enclosure is to be found in the south
Norfolk parish of Tasburgh, where the parish church is sited within a hilltop
earthwork enclosure (Plate 5). The Tasburgh enclosure is broadly oval and
comprises a single bank and ditch, the northern section of which has been modified

[75] Martin, *Burgh*, pp. 74–6.

Plate 5: An aerial view of Tasburgh fort from the north, 27 April 1984, showing the earthworks of the enclosure (foreground) and the parish church (background). TM1996/N/AXA11 (Derek Edwards). © *NMAS*

and now forms a straight edge. The southern quarter of the site has been developed and contains a number of buildings, among them the parish church.[76] The enclosure is assumed to be Iron Age, largely on stylistic grounds, as limited excavations have failed to produce any definite dating evidence and few Iron Age surface finds have been made. Excavations in the 1970s uncovered several sherds of Late Saxon Thetford-type ware sealed beneath a raised bank of sand and dumped flints, which led some to conclude that the entire enclosure was Late Saxon.[77] However, the excavators were of the opinion that this bank was an addition to the original rampart and that its Late Saxon date did not call into question the presumed Iron Age date of the enclosure.[78]

Further excavations in the vicinity of Tasburgh church revealed 135 sherds of Ipswich ware, a particularly high number given the limited area investigated, suggesting that there was a strong Middle Saxon presence in the southern part of the enclosure. Large quantities of Late Saxon pottery and the foundations of a Late Saxon timber building were also excavated, indicating that the original Middle Saxon focus continued to develop into the Late Saxon period, after which time the settlement began to drift away from the church.[79] The church itself has a round tower and exhibits typical eleventh-century architectural features, but its location within the earthwork enclosure, combined with the pottery evidence, strongly suggests that it might be a seventh-century foundation of the kind discussed so far.

[76] Rogerson and Lawson, 'Earthwork Enclosure', pp. 31–5.
[77] NHER 2258.
[78] Rogerson and Lawson, 'Earthwork Enclosure', pp. 37–44.
[79] *Ibid.*, pp. 57–8.

On the strength of the material evidence discovered in their vicinities, but more particularly on the evidence of their being situated within ancient enclosures, the churches at Tasburgh and, more conjecturally, Burgh can both be argued to have been seventh-century foundations. The names of both sites also support the idea of their having been early ecclesiastical foundations for, as John Blair has observed, in many cases the *burg* place-name element was used as a vernacular synonym for *mynster*.[80] The deliberate location of both churches within pre-existing Iron Age earthwork enclosures is suggestive of their being founded in accordance with the early Christian ethos discussed above, specifically the desire to reoccupy an already enclosed area which could demark the boundary between secular and sacred spaces.[81] Admittedly not every extant Iron Age enclosure was reoccupied in this fashion, but Burgh had the added attraction of having hosted a significant degree of Roman activity,[82] while Tasburgh, despite having no significant Roman remains, is situated in the same river valley as the Roman town of *Venta Icenorum*, which lies some 7km to the north.[83]

The occupation of 'natural' enclosures

Pre-existing prehistoric and Roman enclosures were not the only topographic features which proved attractive to early ecclesiastics. Across the country many important Anglo-Saxon churches were founded on the summits or shoulders of low hills, on promontories or on islands in marshy floodplains, as indeed were many of their Gaulish or Germanic counterparts.[84] Such sites, at once both topographically separated from the surrounding world and yet fully integrated into the major riverine routes of communication, were ideally suited to the purposes of those who were seeking to combine a traditional life of religious devotion with the pro-active conversion of the surrounding population.[85] A number of East Anglian religious foundations exhibit this type of topographic isolation, suggesting, in conjunction with other evidence, that they were particularly early foundations which may have played an active role in the conversion.

Iken

The historical evidence for the foundation of Botolph's minster at *Icanho*, recorded in the Anglo-Saxon Chronicle for the year AD 653, was discussed in the previous chapter (pp. 47–50). *Icanho* has been firmly identified with Iken, in south-east Suffolk, and Iken church is situated on a spur of land which projects into the river, as the *-ho* place-name element suggests that it should (Plate 6).[86] In this instance the Middle Saxon foundation date of the building was confirmed by

---

[80] Blair, 'Anglo-Saxon Minsters', p. 239, and *The Church in Anglo-Saxon Society*, p. 250.
[81] Blair, 'Anglo-Saxon Minsters', pp. 231–46.
[82] Bell, 'Churches on Roman Buildings', pp. 5–8, and *Religious Reuse*, pp. 16–22.
[83] Rogerson and Lawson, 'Earthwork Enclosure', p. 57.
[84] Blair, 'Anglo-Saxon Minsters', pp. 227–31; Pestell, *Landscapes of Monastic Foundation*, pp. 52–6; Foot, *Monastic Life*, pp. 96–106.
[85] Cambridge and Rollason, 'Pastoral Organisation', pp. 93–4; Foot, 'What was an Early Anglo-Saxon Monastery?', p. 50; Aston, *Monasteries*, p. 48.
[86] Smith, *English Place-name Elements*, p. 356.

Plate 6: Iken church, probably the site of Botolph's minster, standing on its peninsula in the Alde estuary (author's photograph).

excavations inside and outside the church, which, as well as revealing the Norman masonry church, also produced sherds of Ipswich ware and identified the clay-filled foundation trenches of an earlier timber church built on a slightly different alignment to the later structure.[87]

Burrow Hill

A similarly isolated topographic situation was exploited at Burrow Hill, Butley, some 10km south of Iken (Fig. 1). The site's medieval name, *Insula de Burgh*, shares an element with the other 'burgh' sites discussed here and also indicates that the hilltop was once an island in the river valley, cut off from dry land by tidal mudflats over which an artificial causeway was constructed during the Anglo-Saxon or early medieval period.[88] An archaeological excavation conducted at Burrow Hill in 1978–81 revealed Middle Saxon settlement evidence, an unusually high quantity of metalwork and a substantial cemetery containing over 200 inhumations.[89] In her discussion of the site, the excavator emphasised the defensive nature of the island and stressed its strategic importance, but its *burgh* place-name, island location and Middle Saxon Christian cemetery are all strong indicators that its closest parallels are the other religious sites discussed here.[90] Burrow Hill fell out of use during the

---

[87] West *et al.*, 'Iken'.
[88] Fenwick, 'Insula de Burgh', pp. 35–7.
[89] *Ibid.*, pp. 37–40.
[90] *Ibid.*, pp. 40–41.

Anglo-Saxon period, perhaps as a result of Viking predations, and consequently the site never acquired a masonry church; indeed, the hilltop was not reoccupied until an unrelated Augustinian priory was founded there in the late twelfth century.[91] That the excavation of the site has yet to be published in anything more than an interim form and that the hilltop has now been quarried away are both sources of frustration, for the site would surely have provided much evidence of great relevance to this discussion.

Wormegay

Wormegay, a sandy island in the Nar valley, was fieldwalked as a part of the Fenland Project (see Chapter 5, pp. 156–7). This fieldwork revealed a substantial Ipswich ware scatter covering more than a hectare of ground adjacent to the church, which stands on the southern side of the island (see Fig. 35).[92] Subsequent metal-detecting has revealed an array of Middle Saxon artefacts within the same area.[93] The presence of relatively few sherds of Thetford-type ware in the scatter indicates that the settlement at Wormegay had already begun to drift away from the church by the Late Saxon period and that the church must have already been founded by that date. The site at Wormegay is relevant to this discussion for two reasons: as another example of the topographically isolated ecclesiastical sites discussed here; and as an illustration of the way in which the horizontal stratigraphy of surface scatters might be used to chart the development of the conversion period landscape, a method discussed in more detail in Chapter 5 (pp. 146–71).

Bawsey

Another site relevant to this discussion is located on a peninsula in the Gaywood valley at Bawsey, west Norfolk (Fig. 1). Although the site now lies several miles inland, during the Middle Saxon period it was surrounded by water on three sides and defined by a substantial ditch, which is now clearly visible as a cropmark on aerial photographs (Plate 7).[94] On the crest of a slight hill stands the ruined church of St James, which exhibits high-quality Romanesque architecture and obscures any earlier building phases.[95] Metal-detecting in this area has revealed material dating from the seventh century to the medieval period and there are also substantial scatters of Ipswich ware and Thetford-type ware covering much of the hilltop.[96] Geophysical surveys and evaluation excavations conducted at the site as a part of *Time Team Live* in 1998 revealed further evidence for intensive Middle and Late Saxon occupation, much of it industrial or agricultural in nature, as well as burials in the vicinity of the church, the earliest of which has been radiocarbon dated to the Middle Saxon period.[97] The Anglo-Saxon site at Bawsey has provoked much discussion, not least about how best the site should be categorised, but for the

---

[91] Pestell, 'The Afterlife of "Productive" Sites', p. 133.
[92] Silvester, *Fenland Project 3*, pp. 143–50.
[93] Rogerson, 'Six Middle Anglo-Saxon Sites', pp. 119–20.
[94] *Ibid.*, pp. 112–14.
[95] Batcock, *Ruined and Disused Churches*, pp. 114–16.
[96] Webster and Backhouse, *The Making of England*, pp. 231–2; Rogerson, 'Six Middle Anglo-Saxon Sites', pp. 112–14.
[97] Taylor, *Time Team*, pp. 67–73; Blair, *The Church in Anglo-Saxon Society*, p. 210, n. 120.

Plate 7: An aerial view of Bawsey from the west, 17 July 1989, showing the ruined church (top) and the cropmarks of the Anglo-Saxon enclosure. TF6620/AH/DNQ4 (Derek Edwards). © *NMAS*

purposes of this discussion it is enough to note that the site's topography and material culture conform to the criteria for identifying potential missionary foundations outlined thus far in this chapter.[98]

Brandon

Finally, the Middle Saxon site at Brandon is similarly located on an island in a river valley which is linked to the mainland by a causeway.[99] After the discovery of the famous gold plaque bearing the image of John the Evangelist (Plate 8) — in itself a clear indication that high-status religious activities were taking place at the site —

[98] Rogerson, 'Six Middle Anglo-Saxon Sites', pp. 112–14; Pestell, *Landscapes of Monastic Foundation*, pp. 31–3; Hutcheson, 'Origins of King's Lynn'.
[99] Carr *et al.*, 'Middle-Saxon Settlement at Staunch Meadow'.

Plate 8: The gold plaque depicting Saint John the Evangelist discovered at Brandon. © *Trustees of the British Museum*

large-scale excavation of the site was undertaken between 1979 and 1988. The results of these excavations demonstrated that it was perfectly possible for the ecclesiastical elements of a Middle Saxon settlement — in this case a timber church and two Christian cemeteries — to be fully integrated into the normal workings of a settlement which also engaged in river-borne trade, arable and pastoral agriculture, and light industry.[100] Indeed, sites such as Brandon and Bawsey have both caused much debate among those who have sought to categorise them, being neither wholly secular or wholly ecclesiastical in their character.[101] On the strength of the emerging evidence it would seem that many Middle Saxon sites performed a multiplicity of functions.[102]

The remains excavated at Brandon include the most complete example of a Middle Saxon timber church excavated so far in East Anglia (Plate 9).[103] At its greatest extent the church was a three-cell structure with a total length of approximately 25m. In its first phase it comprised a nave measuring 14m by 6.5m with an adjoining chancel of 5m by 4.3m. The chancel contained an isolated burial which had been disturbed by a later feature, and the remains of a structure at the eastern end of the nave have been interpreted as an altar. The walls were constructed from posts and planks set vertically in foundation trenches and the nave had opposing doors in the centre of each long side. A smaller door entered the chancel from the south. A third, western, cell, measuring 5.5m by 4.3m, appears to have

---

[100] Carr *et al.*, 'Middle-Saxon Settlement at Staunch Meadow', p. 375.
[101] e.g. Andrews, 'Middle Saxon Norfolk'; Aston, *Monasteries*, pp. 48–54; Pestell, *Landscapes of Monastic Foundation*, pp. 22–7; Hutcheson, 'Origins of King's Lynn'.
[102] e.g. Pestell, *Landscape of Monastic Foundation*, pp. 22–7; Foot, *Monastic Life*, pp. 186–248; Blair, *The Church in Anglo-Saxon Society*, pp. 204–12.
[103] Carr *et al.*, 'Middle-Saxon Settlement at Staunch Meadow'.

Plate 9: The excavated Middle Saxon church at Brandon, looking east. *Reproduced by kind permission of SCCAS.*

been added during a second phase of Middle Saxon building and was also entered via a southern doorway. The function of this third cell remains unknown, but it could have been a baptistery or even the base of a small tower.[104]

A contemporary inhumation cemetery was excavated to the south-east of the church. It comprised at least 220 inhumations of mixed age and sex, some of which had been buried in coffins.[105] This cemetery appears to have fallen out of use at the

[104] Carr *et al.*, 'Middle-Saxon Settlement at Staunch Meadow', p. 374.
[105] Anderson, 'Human Skeletal Remains'.

same time as a third phase of building saw the removal of the chancel and the replacement of the nave and the western cell with a building of similar size in broadly the same position. It is likely that both the church and cemetery ceased to function at this point and were presumably refounded to the north of the site, where a second, later, cemetery was partially excavated.[106]

That the Anglo-Saxon features at Brandon remained undisturbed and were able to be excavated is entirely due to the fact the medieval town developed at a slight remove to the south of the site.[107] Had this not occurred, these important Anglo-Saxon features would have been destroyed or remained sealed beneath the later settlement. The implications that this observation has for our understanding of the landscape of the conversion are explored more fully in Chapter 5.

'*Productive*' sites

Many of the sites discussed in this chapter are also linked by their being labelled so-called 'productive' sites, a term coined by numismatists in the 1980s to describe sites at which unusually large quantities of Middle Saxon coins and metalwork had been discovered, usually via metal-detecting.[108] There is now, however, a general consensus among many scholars that the term is unsatisfactory and has unhelpful connotations. In particular, fieldwork is increasingly demonstrating that the 'productive' sites were not an homogenous group and that they have little in common besides the discovery of metalwork.[109]

While the diversity of the 'productive' sites is clear, their individual functions are not so easily ascertained and have been much debated during the last twenty years.[110] Julian Richards is of the opinion that some 'productive' sites are simply settlements discovered via metal-detected finds instead of the more traditional methods of fieldwalking and excavation.[111] Another perspective is offered by Katharina Ulmschneider, who identifies many 'productive' sites as having been the sites of seasonal fairs or more permanent trading posts, largely on the basis of the number of coins discovered.[112] Of greater relevance to the sites discussed here is Tim Pestell's highlighting of the ecclesiastical and monastic elements of some 'productive' sites. Many sites, he argues, were important religious institutions during their Middle Saxon heyday and some continued to be so during their Late Saxon and medieval 'afterlives'.[113] Some 'productive' sites demonstrate elements of all of the types of site outlined here and there is no practicable reason why any one site should not fall into

---

[106] Carr *et al.*, 'Middle-Saxon Settlement at Staunch Meadow', pp. 374–7.
[107] *Ibid.*
[108] Rogerson, 'Six Middle Anglo-Saxon Sites'; Newman, 'Exceptional Finds'; Pestell and Ulmschneider, *Markets in Early Medieval Europe*, p. 2.
[109] e.g. Andrews, 'Middle Saxon Norfolk'; Richards, 'What's so Special about "Productive Sites"?'; Whyman, 'Emporia'; Pestell, *Landscapes of Monastic Foundation*, pp. 31–6.
[110] Pestell and Ulmschneider, *Markets in Early Medieval Europe*.
[111] Richards, 'What's so Special about "Productive Sites"?'.
[112] Ulmschneider, 'Archaeology, History and the Isle of Wight'; *Markets, Minsters and Metal-Detectors*; 'Settlement, Economy and the "Productive" Site'; and 'Central Places and Metal-Detector Finds'; Hutcheson, 'Origins of King's Lynn'.
[113] Pestell, 'An Analysis of Monastic Foundation'; 'The Afterlife of "Productive" Sites'; *Landscapes of Monastic Foundation*, pp. 31–6.

several categories. Indeed, several of the sites discussed so far, particularly Brandon, show signs of having performed a number of different roles simultaneously.[114] Brandon also benefits, however, from having been subjected to large-scale excavation, and further excavations at other 'productive' sites would doubtless be illuminating.

Conclusions

It is clear that a number of the region's walled Roman enclosures played an significant role in the evangelisation of East Anglia, as indeed such sites did in many other parts of the country.[115] There is compelling evidence that the Roman fort at Walton Castle became the site of the episcopal see, from which the authority of the bishop radiated across the region. Further north, the pair of forts which flanked the Great Estuary at Burgh Castle and Caister-on-Sea each became the focus of a Middle Saxon Christian community, the archaeological evidence for which is unequivocal, albeit heavily disturbed. Still further north, the Roman fort at Brancaster may also have been the focus of such a community. Once these enclosures had been reoccupied they became missionary stations from which the holy men could begin their work within the local population. The success of this work is difficult to measure, except in general terms, but a good indication of the degree of success enjoyed by early missionaries is provided by the extent of the Christian cemeteries associated with the sites described above. Excavations at Burgh Castle revealed a cemetery containing several hundred burials and it is probable that many more have been lost to ploughing. The intramural cemetery at Caister-on-Sea was perhaps of a similar size to that at Burgh Castle, while the extramural cemetery was apparently much larger. At Brancaster, ploughed-up human bone might suggest the presence of a similar cemetery, and it can be assumed that one or more Christian cemeteries formed part of the episcopal complex at Walton Castle. From the sheer quantity of burials discovered, particularly at Caister-on-Sea, it would seem that each missionary station had a zone of influence which extended far beyond its walls, with many individuals from the surrounding area being buried within or close to the fort. This interpretation is supported by the fact that all the excavated cemeteries have contained a mixture of males and females ranging from infancy to old age, indicating that the cemeteries catered for whole communities rather than one exclusive section of society.

Although no traces of any Anglo-Saxon churches have been found in association with any of these intramural cemeteries, something of the kind must surely have once existed and their absence may be explained by the organic nature of the original structures and the post-depositional disturbance that occurred at each site. In many parts of the country these early churches were either built of stone from an early date, so leaving material evidence for their existence, or continued to develop on the same site into the medieval period.[116] In East Anglia, however, with the possible exception of *Venta Icenorum*, the medieval church was subsequently built outside the fort. At Walton Castle there is historical evidence for the survival of the church until the Norman Conquest, but the disruption of the dioceses caused by the

---

[114] Pestell and Ulmschneider, *Markets in Early Medieval Europe*, pp. 5–9.
[115] Bell, 'Churches on Roman Buildings' and *Religious Reuse*.
[116] Bell, *Religious Reuse*, pp. 69–127.

tenth-century Viking incursions and the fact that only the later diocese of Elmham was refounded indicate that whatever remained at *Dommoc* had diminished greatly since its seventh-century heyday. Similarly, both Burgh Castle and Caister-on-Sea appear to have floundered in the Late Saxon period and it is possible that they too fell victim to the Vikings, either directly or via precautionary measures taken against attack from the sea. Certainly, all of the sites discussed here, Brancaster included, are in coastal positions and thus were very vulnerable to such incursions.

Roman sites, and the *romanitas* with which they were imbued, were clearly attractive to the first wave of Christian missionaries, but that is not to say that they were occupied to the exclusion of all other sites. In many cases the Roman sites are only the most archaeologically obvious form of sites which could have been employed in this manner and also happen to be sites which have attracted more archaeological attention. Many other sites were also either converted to a Christian purpose or founded anew during the course of the conversion, such as those sites discussed above which occupied prehistoric earthwork enclosures and those which utilised plateaux, promontories and riverine islands to achieve topographic isolation.

As 'productive' sites are largely identified from metal-detected finds they are particularly numerous in Norfolk and Suffolk, where the reporting of metal-detected material has been encouraged since the 1970s. Of the Roman sites argued here to have been reoccupied as a part of the conversion process, both Burgh Castle and Caister-on-Sea have earned the 'productive' epithet on the basis of the metalwork recovered during their excavations. The Roman town and 'productive' site of *Venta Icenorum* likewise falls into this category, and one must assume that, had it not been washed away, Walton Castle would have produced a similar array of Middle Saxon evidence.

The reused Iron Age enclosures at Burgh and Tasburgh are not considered to be 'productive', but a number of the Middle Saxon sites situated on peninsulas or islands are. Given the small size of the excavated area, the site at Burrow Hill was particularly 'productive', although this is probably because a metal-detector was routinely used to scan deposits throughout the excavation.[117] The scale of the excavations at Brandon meant that a large quantity of finds was discovered, some of them particularly rich. To date, Bawsey has only been partially excavated and the bulk of its metalwork is the result of metal-detecting over many years; this is also the case at Wormegay.[118]

The diversity of 'productive' sites is demonstrated by the facts that not all of the religious sites identified thus far might be classed as 'productive' and that there are other 'productive' sites which are clearly neither ecclesiastical nor monastic in their nature.[119] Therefore, although the issue of 'productive' sites is relevant to the study of early ecclesiastical sites, it, like the topographical associations of various sites, is not applicable in every instance. In fact, the only common feature linking all of the sites discussed thus is the presence of Christian burials, and it is to the subject of funerary rites and the evidence for religious conversion which can be gleaned from them that we now turn.

---

[117] Fenwick, 'Insula de Burgh', p. 37.
[118] Rogerson, 'Six Middle Anglo-Saxon Sites', pp. 112–14, 119–20.
[119] e.g. Silvester, 'West Walton'; Andrews, 'Middle Saxon Norfolk'; Rogerson, 'Six Middle Anglo-Saxon Sites'; Newman, 'Exceptional Finds'.

4

Burial and Belief

Burial evidence has often been employed in discussions of Anglo-Saxon religion, although there is a distinct bias towards the better-preserved and archaeologically more visible burials of the Early Saxon period.[1] At the same time, the widespread reliance on historical sources in studying the conversion has given rise to the belief that burial evidence has little to contribute to the debate. As we have seen, the historical evidence for conversion-period East Anglia is particularly sparse, but even on a national scale the historical record has little to say about the early Church's attitude towards burial.[2] However, although the historical record is quiet on the subject, the burial record itself is very rich and we are fortunate in that we are able to study funerary material from before, during and after the conversion period. John Blair is firmly of the opinion that 'burial practice offers our best hope of glimpsing religious attitudes among ordinary laity in the "age of conversion"',[3] and the East Anglian archaeological record clearly demonstrates that significant changes in burial practice occurred at the time of the conversion. These changes require explanation. In particular, inhumation was practised alongside cremation during the Early Saxon period, but by the mid-seventh century inhumation had become the sole burial rite. Furthermore, it is clear that the details of the inhumation rite changed considerably over time, particularly regarding the nature, quality and quantity of grave-goods deposited with the corpse.

Excavated Christian burials have demonstrated that unfurnished, supine, west–east burial was, and continues to be, the norm for Christian burial practice.[4] With regard to recognising the conversion in the burial record, a simple model has developed in which Christianity was introduced and burial rites were immediately transformed from those of the Early Saxon period — characterised by the use of cremation and the deposition of Germanic grave-goods — to those in the Christian mould of the medieval period.[5] In particular, studies have focused on the transition from furnished to unfurnished burial and the increasingly regular adoption of a west–east orientation, both criteria recently described in print as being among 'the

---

[1] e.g. Owen, *Rites and Religions*, pp. 67–125; Wilson, *Anglo-Saxon Paganism*, pp. 67–172; Arnold, *Archaeology of the Early Anglo-Saxon Kingdoms*, pp. 149–75; Taylor, *Burial Practice*, pp. 139–43.
[2] Wilson, *Anglo-Saxon Paganism*, pp. 67–9; Hadley, *Death in Medieval England*, p. 92; Morris, *Church in British Archaeology*, p. 50; Foot, *Monastic Life*, pp. 312–18.
[3] Blair, *The Church in Anglo-Saxon Society*, p. 245.
[4] e.g. Rahtz, 'Grave Orientation'; Rodwell, *Archaeology of Churches*, pp. 161–96; Gilchrist and Sloane, *Requiem*, pp. 130–83.
[5] Reviewed in Geake, *The Use of Grave-Goods*, pp. 1–3; Taylor, *Burial Practices*.

earliest tangible signs of the new religion in the archaeological record'.[6] Although such interpretations persist, they have been demonstrated to be overly simplistic and increasingly found not to fit the available evidence, but that does not mean that such approaches are futile or doomed to failure.

This chapter considers the degree to which burial evidence can be used to chart the conversion of East Anglia.[7] In the light of the ongoing debates summarised here, particular attention is paid to the cessation of cremation and the emergence during the Middle Saxon period of the main characteristics of the Christian burial rite: the inhumation of the dead without grave-goods and a west–east burial alignment. First, though, it is necessary to examine briefly the nature of the archaeological burial record of Anglo-Saxon East Anglia.

The Anglo-Saxon cemeteries of East Anglia

In March 2005 the Norfolk Historic Environment Record (NHER) contained records of 141 Early and Middle Saxon cemeteries, of which 135 could be accurately located, while the Suffolk Historic Environment Record (SHER) contained records of 75 cemeteries, of which 72 could be accurately located (Fig. 15). No two cemeteries are alike, but cemeteries may be analysed by the burial rites practised, by the number of burials and by period. In their 1973 gazetteer of East Anglian cemetery sites Myres and Green used burial rites and the number of burials to allocate cemeteries to one of five categories: 'predominantly inhumation cemetery', 'predominantly cremation cemetery', 'mixed cemetery', 'inhumation burials up to three in number' and 'cremation burials up to three in number'.[8] The analyses which underpin this chapter also employed Myres and Green's categories, and when these categories are plotted on a distribution map several trends become apparent (Fig. 16).

An attempt was made to calculate the minimum number of cremations and inhumations from each cemetery.[9] Of course, we have no way of knowing the number of burials which remain undiscovered and must assume that our figures are vastly under-representative. Metal-detected cemeteries also create difficulties because it is impossible to know how many burials they represent. For the purposes of this analysis each metal-detected cemetery was assumed to contain twenty burials, the average number of burials from all of the region's excavated sites. Following these assumptions, the total minimum number of burials from East Anglia is 9,992, of which 5,920 are cremations and 4,098 are inhumations, a ratio of approximately 3:2.

Of the 5,920 recorded cremations, Norfolk accounts for 5,077 (86 per cent) and Suffolk accounts for 843 (14 per cent). Despite this disparity, the percentages of each county's cemeteries with up to three cremations are broadly similar and both are low, reflecting the fact that cremations are most often found in large quantities. As Figure 16 clearly illustrates, the vast majority of the cremation cemeteries are in Norfolk, with only a handful of sites in north Suffolk. Of the 4,098 recorded

---

[6] MacGregor, 'Seventh-Century Pectoral Cross', p. 221.
[7] See also Hoggett, 'Charting Conversion'.
[8] Myres and Green, *Anglo-Saxon Cemeteries*, pp. 258–62.
[9] For the complete data set see Hoggett, 'Changing Beliefs', pp. 411–18.

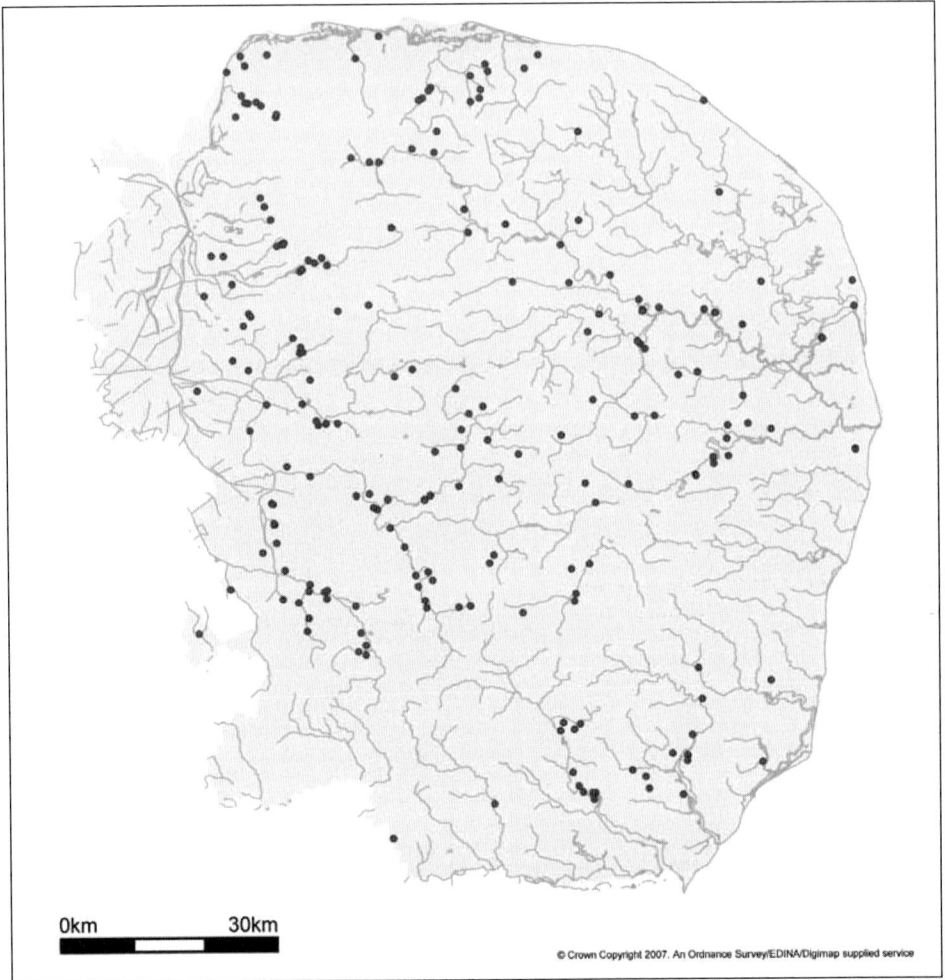

Fig. 15: The Anglo-Saxon cemeteries of Norfolk and Suffolk, plotted against the modern river network.

inhumations, Norfolk accounts for 2,062 and Suffolk accounts for 2,036, a near-even split. These burials and cemeteries are widely distributed throughout both counties, but exhibit a denser concentration in west Norfolk and west Suffolk, and a much higher percentage of Suffolk sites are cemeteries with up to three inhumations (Fig. 16). It would appear that inhumation was practised uniformly throughout Norfolk and Suffolk, but when one considers the number of Norfolk cemeteries which result from metal-detecting the Suffolk figures take on particular significance. In all likelihood, were an equivalent amount of metal-detecting to be undertaken in Suffolk, the number of inhumation cemeteries in the southern half of the region would far outstrip that of the northern half.

Suffolk also has a slightly higher proportion of mixed-rite cemeteries than Norfolk; the majority of the mixed-rite sites are distributed throughout south-west Norfolk and north-west Suffolk, in the area to the north of the Lark–Gipping river corridor, although there are additional clusters of sites in east Norfolk and south-east Suffolk

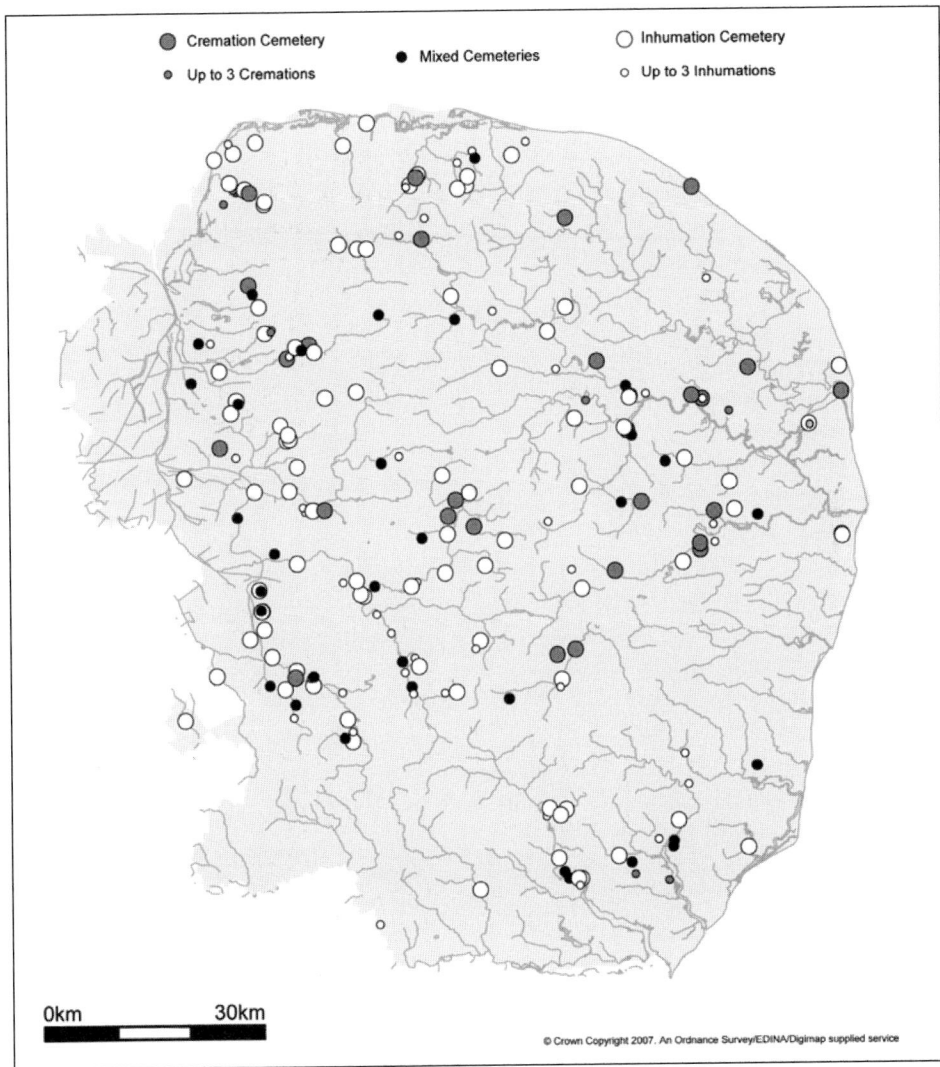

Fig. 16: The distribution of Anglo-Saxon cemeteries by burial rite, plotted against the modern river network.

(Fig. 16). This distribution appears to mark the broad boundary between the cremation-dominated area of Norfolk and north Suffolk and the inhumation-dominated areas to the south. A greater insight into the nature of this boundary is obtained by examining the ratios between cremations and inhumations in these mixed-rite cemeteries. Of the thirty-six sites shown in Figure 17, fifteen demonstrate an even division between burial rites, suggesting that no one rite was dominant. Twelve sites show a bias towards cremation, and the majority of these sites lie in Norfolk, with two examples in west Suffolk and one at Sutton Hoo, while the nine sites that show a bias towards inhumation all lie, with the exception of two sites in Norfolk, in west or south-east Suffolk, thus reinforcing the conclusion that cremation was prevalent in northern East Anglia and the area in which it was practised was tightly defined.

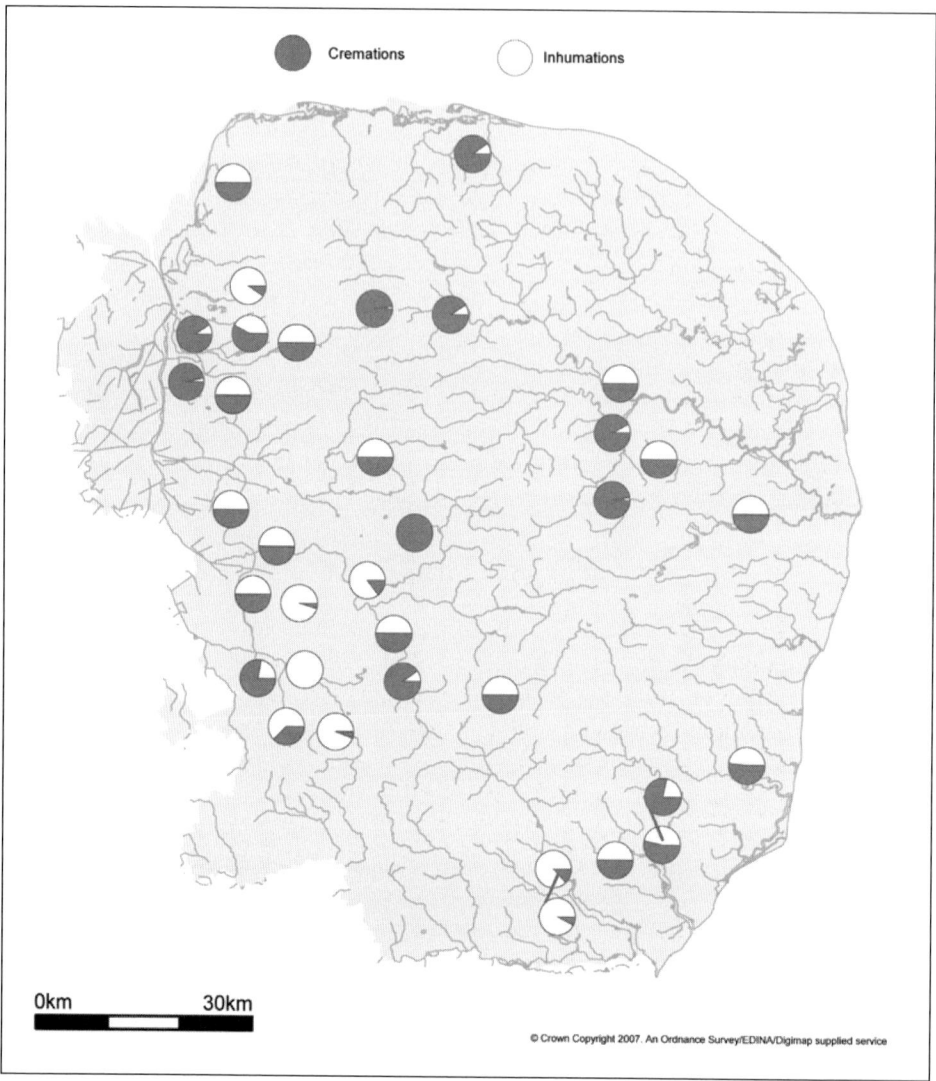

Fig. 17: The ratio of cremations to inhumations in mixed-rite cemeteries, plotted against the modern river network.

Cemeteries can also be classified chronologically. The NHER and SHER use the periods Early Saxon (AD 450–650) or Middle Saxon (AD 651–850), an artificial divide as the burial sequence flows seamlessly through both periods, although changes in burial practice are apparent throughout. All the cremation cemeteries and isolated cremations are Early Saxon, as are all thirty-five mixed-rite cemeteries. Of the isolated inhumations, forty-two of the forty-five (93 per cent) examples are Early Saxon, along with seventy-three of the ninety-six (76 per cent) inhumation cemeteries. In total there are 189 Early Saxon cemeteries and 27 Middle Saxon cemeteries in Norfolk and Suffolk.

There are a number of possible reasons for the heavy bias towards Early Saxon cemeteries. First, the grave-goods and other artefacts which accompany many Early Saxon burials are robust and highly visible, whereas the bones themselves survive poorly in acidic soils. This allows furnished burials to be actively metal-detected in addition to their being found accidentally and, more importantly, allows them to be dated with certainty to the Early Saxon period. By contrast, unfurnished Early and Middle Saxon burials cannot easily be detected and the lack of associated artefacts makes it difficult to ascribe a date to any discoveries. In many cases it is only through the use of radiocarbon dating that a Middle Saxon date may be confirmed. Thus many Middle Saxon burials have been identified in Ipswich because of the Suffolk archaeological authorities' policy of routinely dating human remains from the town. Another reason for the disparity lies in the relative accessibility of the landscape settings of Early and Middle Saxon cemeteries, an aspect that is considered at length in the next chapter; but now we turn to examine the archaeological evidence for individual burial rites.

The cremation rite

The archaeological potential of Anglo-Saxon cremations can be difficult to recognise and this had often led to the disposal of cremated material in the mistaken belief that nothing useful could be learnt from it.[10] Consequently, it was not until the 1930s that Anglo-Saxon cremations began to be studied in earnest.[11] In 1960 Wells published one of the first analyses of Anglo-Saxon cremated remains, based on material from Illington (Norfolk), in which he addressed both the demography of the cremated population and the technicalities of cremation itself.[12] More recently, McKinley's comprehensive analysis of the cremated material from Spong Hill has demonstrated the sheer quantity of information that can be recovered and provided a vivid insight into this often underestimated burial rite.[13] Cremation required a great many resources and considerable organisation and was, no doubt, a substantial and costly undertaking. As McKinley states, 'there is a considerable amount of unseen and unrecognised wealth in cremations, and to consider them the "poor man's" alternative to inhumation is to misunderstand them'.[14] This section discusses the cremation rite and examines what it can tell us about the beliefs of its practitioners.

Despite the thousands of excavated cremations, only a handful of possible cremation pyres have been discovered.[15] The first Anglo-Saxon example to be recorded in detail was found at Snape (Suffolk) and comprised burnt bone, charcoal, fragments of melted metal and several broken pots all preserved in a sixth-century

---

[10] Hills, 'Anglo-Saxon Cremation Cemeteries', p. 197.
[11] For the historiography of cremation see Williams, 'Remains of Pagan Saxondom?', pp. 47–57.
[12] Wells, 'A Study of Cremation'.
[13] McKinley, *Anglo-Saxon Cemetery at Spong Hill VIII*.
[14] *Ibid.*, p. 119.
[15] Genrich, 'A Remarkable Inhumation Grave', pp. 59–60; Lucy, *The Anglo-Saxon Way of Death*, p. 106.

soil.[16] Environmental evidence from among the cremated remains suggests that pyres comprised a timber frame filled with brushwood, which may have been of considerable size if more than one individual or a number of animals were to be cremated.[17] Pyres are by their very nature ephemeral features, but there is more to their scarcity than simple survival: their location is also a factor. That distinct locations were used for cremation pyres is suggested by urns from Spong Hill which contained intrusive bones, thought to have been collected accidentally after the reuse of a pyre site. However, as the overwhelming majority of the Spong Hill cremations did not contain intrusive bone, it must be assumed that either a fresh site was used for each cremation or the pyre site was usually well cleared.[18] That so few pyres have been discovered during the excavation of cemeteries indicates that the cremations themselves took place elsewhere, and the example at Snape appears to be exceptional. Significantly, no pyre sites have been found during the excavation of Early Saxon settlement sites either, and it would seem that the majority of cremations took place at sites which remain archaeologically elusive — perhaps near to settlements, but not situated within them.[19] An absence of cremation pyres from settlements may be explained as a minimising of the risk of fire, but it may also be a symptom of the separation of the living and the dead which characterised the settlements and cemeteries of the Early Saxon period (see below, pp. 119–21).

Despite the fragmentary nature of the cremated bone it is often possible to ascertain the age and sex of the deceased. The remains can also provide pathological evidence of disease or trauma, allowing something of the deceased's health and lifestyle to be reconstructed.[20] Analysis of the cremations from Spong Hill revealed that several urns contained the remains of more than one individual, a phenomenon also recognised among inhumations. In most cases multiple cremations comprise an adult and an infant, and such pairings are generally presumed to have been members of the same family.[21] Cremated remains also reveal a great deal about the treatment of the corpse. The differential burning of bones indicates that the corpse was laid on top of the pyre, while melted glass and bronze adhering to fragments of bone enable the reconstruction of the dress and posture of the corpse.[22] At Spong Hill, melted material was most often found on the skull, arm bones, hand bones and ribs, indicating jewellery worn on the head, neck, shoulders and wrists. This material had melted and cooled while remaining *in situ*, indicating that the body was laid on its back, occasionally with hands folded across the chest, and that the corpse was undisturbed once the pyre was lit.[23]

Excavated evidence suggests that 67 per cent of the cremations from Spong Hill,

---

[16] Carnegie and Filmer-Sankey, 'Saxon "Cremation Pyre"'; Filmer-Sankey and Pestell, *Snape*, pp. 252–5.

[17] McKinley, *Anglo-Saxon Cemetery at Spong Hill VIII*, pp. 82–4.

[18] *Ibid.*, pp. 82–3.

[19] Williams, 'Assembling the Dead', figs 5.6 and 5.7.

[20] Brothwell, *Digging Up Bones*, pp. 59–72 and 127–74; McKinley, *Anglo-Saxon Cemetery at Spong Hill VIII*, pp. 11–21; Mays, *Archaeology of Human Remains*, pp. 33–66 and 122–81.

[21] Wilson, *Anglo-Saxon Paganism*, pp. 132–4; McKinley, *Anglo-Saxon Cemetery at Spong Hill VIII*, pp. 100–102.

[22] Wells, 'A Study of Cremation', pp. 34–5; Welch, *Anglo-Saxon England*; McKinley, *Anglo-Saxon Cemetery at Spong Hill VIII*, pp. 83–4.

[23] McKinley, *Anglo-Saxon Cemetery at Spong Hill VIII*, pp. 83–4.

46 per cent of those from Caistor St Edmund, 34 per cent of those from Illington and 21 per cent of those from Lackford contained artefacts which had survived the heat of the pyre and were eventually buried.[24] These figures are broadly comparable to those for inhumation cemeteries, in which grave-goods are found in about half of all burials.[25] The vast majority of pyre-goods exhibit some evidence of burning, suggesting that the artefacts were placed on the pyre with the body, where they may have remained and been fully burnt or from which they may have fallen, thus being preserved intact.[26]

Melted metal and glass artefacts suggest that the corpse was fully clothed, perhaps in funerary costume. Other personal effects commonly found include finger rings, earrings, bone combs and toilet sets.[27] Analyses of correlations between pyre-goods and the sex of the deceased revealed that brooches, necklaces, spindle whorls, bronze rings, antler rings and ivory were all found with more females than males. Toilet sets, knife blades, antler/bone beads, worked antler and worked bone were all found with more males than females; bowls, buckets, glass vessels, gaming pieces, combs and iron rings were distributed evenly between the sexes.[28] Age appears to have been less significant than sex in the provision of pyre-goods, the same analyses suggesting that most types of pyre-good show little or no correlation with specific age groupings.[29] Overall, the provisioning of pyre-goods was 'partly age-linked, occasionally sex-linked, and subject to a great deal of variation between sites'.[30]

The possible religious connotations of pyre- and grave-goods are discussed with reference to both cremation and inhumations later in this chapter. Here it is sufficient to say that, while pyre-goods clearly reflect the social identity of the deceased, their presence also suggests a belief that the deceased would continue to need them after death. In assessing this 'need', a distinction should perhaps be drawn between those goods worn on the body and the deliberate inclusion of additional equipment or offerings. The latter encompasses caskets, bronze bowls and buckets, as well as pottery and glass vessels, which presumably contained provisions.[31] Offerings of food and drink are particularly suggestive of the individual being equipped for the future and are especially symbolic given that corpses have no need of food. Being organic, the nature of these offerings often remains obscure, but in some cases burnt nuts and cereal grains have been found, and a great many urns also contain cremated animal bone.[32]

---

[24] *Ibid.*, p. 86.
[25] Stoodley, *The Spindle and the Spear*, pp. 24–9.
[26] McKinley, *Anglo-Saxon Cemetery at Spong Hill VIII*, pp. 88–90; Hills, *Anglo-Saxon Cemetery at Spong Hill I*, pp. 23; Richards, *Significance of Form*, p. 78; Lucy, *The Anglo-Saxon Way of Death*, p. 108.
[27] Myres and Green, *Anglo-Saxon Cemeteries*, pp. 91–7 and 103–11; Hills, *Anglo-Saxon Cemetery at Spong Hill I*, pp. 25–9; McKinley, *Anglo-Saxon Cemetery at Spong Hill VIII*, p. 91; Williams, 'Material Culture'.
[28] Richards, *Significance of Form*, p. 126; McKinley, *Anglo-Saxon Cemetery at Spong Hill VIII*, pp. 88–92.
[29] McKinley, *Anglo-Saxon Cemetery at Spong Hill VIII*, p. 90; Richards, *Significance of Form*, p. 130.
[30] Lucy, *The Anglo-Saxon Way of Death*, p. 111.
[31] Myres and Green, *Anglo-Saxon Cemeteries*, pp. 77–113; Hills, *Anglo-Saxon Cemetery at Spong Hill I*, pp. 23–30.
[32] Murphy, 'Appendix II'; Lee, *Feasting the Dead*.

Again, Wells was among the first to note the presence of animal bone in the cremations at Illington, and its presence has since been widely recognised in a number of other cemeteries.[33] The use of animals in the cremation rite has been extensively discussed by Williams, who sees them as part of an overtly pagan, shamanistic 'ideology of transformation' involving the animals' ultimate destruction alongside and merging with the deceased individual.[34] At Spong Hill, 46 per cent of the cremations contained animal bone, often representing several different animals. Horses were found to be most numerous, followed by sheep/goats, pigs, cattle and dogs.[35] Cut marks were found on sheep/goat, cattle and pig bones, suggesting that these, at least, were butchered and presumably intended as food offerings. By contrast, horses and dogs were often cremated whole and were perhaps considered to be the personal possessions of the cremated individuals.[36] The Spong Hill remains suggest that more adult than child cremations, and more male cremations than female, contained animal remains.[37]

It would appear that the laying-out of the body with its pyre-goods was the most important part of the cremation process.[38] The death tableau was the point at which the greatest quantity of resources had been gathered in one place and were on display, along with the deceased individual, whose corpse would have been a powerfully symbolic object in itself.[39] When considered within the framework for the recognition of religiously motivated acts put forward by cognitive archaeologists, it is clear that the cremation pyre scores very highly, both as a focal point for the attention of the participants and also because of the funerary offerings being made (pp. 11–13).[40]

Once the pyre was lit the deceased, their pyre-goods and the pyre itself were all reduced to ashes in a prolonged and violent period of burning. Archaeologically we are unable to say much about what the burning was like, but something of the spectacle of cremation can be gleaned from the description of the hero's funeral at the end of *Beowulf*:

> The Geat people built a pyre for Beowulf,
> stacked and decked it until it stood foursquare,
> hung with helmets, heavy war-shields
> and shining armour, just as he had ordered.
> Then his warriors laid him in the middle of it,
> mourning a lord far-famed and beloved.

---

[33] Wells, 'A Study of Cremation', p. 37; Crabtree, 'Symbolic Role of Animals'; Williams, 'Ideology of Transformation' and 'Keeping the Dead at Arm's Length'; Bond, 'Cremated Animal Bone' and 'Burnt Offerings'.

[34] Williams, 'Ideology of Transformation', 'Death Warmed Up' and 'Keeping the Dead at Arm's Length'.

[35] Bond, 'Cremated Animal Bone', p. 121, and 'Burnt Offerings', pp. 78–9.

[36] Bond, 'Cremated Animal Bone' and 'Burnt Offerings', pp. 82–4.

[37] McKinley, *Anglo-Saxon Cemetery at Spong Hill VIII*, pp. 99–100; Richards, *Significance of Form*, pp. 128–34.

[38] Williams, 'Death Warmed Up', pp. 270–71.

[39] *Ibid.*

[40] Renfrew, *Archaeology of Cult*, pp. 18–19; Renfrew and Bahn, *Archaeology: Theories, Methods and Practice*, pp. 416–17.

On a height they kindled the hugest of all
funeral fires; fumes of woodsmoke
billowed darkly up, the blaze roared
and drowned out their weeping, wind died down
and flames wrought havoc in the hot bone-house,
burning it to the core. They were disconsolate
and wailed aloud for their lord's decease.[41]

The cremation pyre must have made a great impression on those who witnessed it, providing a veritable assault on the senses. We might expect a vigil of some kind to have been held while the burning occurred. Perhaps the ceremony took place at night, when it would look most dramatic, or possibly it occurred during the day, when the smoke would be visible for miles around. We can only imagine the sights, smells, sounds and intense heat that would have been experienced by the onlookers as the pyre burned.[42] Fortunately the archaeological evidence tells us a great deal more about what happened after the pyre had burnt out and cooled.

Charcoal is rarely found in cremation urns and the bone fragments are often particularly clean, indicating that the ashes were systematically removed.[43] Given the small size of some of the fragments this must have been a delicate and time-consuming job, which may have been achieved by winnowing or floating the ashes in water.[44] The difficulty of this task may explain the variation in the quantity of bone collected, which ranges from a few hundred to a few thousand grams per individual. The cremations from Spong Hill demonstrate that although all of the major parts of the body were represented, the remains were never collected in their entirety.[45] The fate of the rest of the pyre debris remains a mystery. We must assume either that it was disposed of in a way that left no archaeological trace or that it still remains to be discovered. The cremated remains that were collected were placed in a container, usually a pottery urn, but occasionally an organic container (Fig. 18).[46] There are also instances of bronze bowls being used as containers, which are discussed separately below (pp. 92–3).[47]

The urned cremation was ultimately taken to a cemetery, which may have been at some distance from the settlement, necessitating the expenditure of further resources to travel to the burial site.[48] The period of time that elapsed between the cremation ceremony and the final interment is unknowable, but could conceivably have been of quite some length, perhaps even months or years. Generally cremation urns were buried singly, although in a number of instances two or more urns appear to have been buried together. These urns often have similar shapes or decoration, and it is possible that they represent members of the same family buried together. Of course, urns buried together need not reflect the simultaneous death and cremation

---

[41] Heaney, *Beowulf*, lines 3137–49.
[42] See Williams, 'Death Warmed Up', although his account is not for the faint-hearted.
[43] Murphy, 'Appendix II'; Mays, *Archaeology of Human Bones*, p. 207.
[44] McKinley, 'Cremations', p. 73, and *Anglo-Saxon Cemetery at Spong Hill VIII*, pp. 85–6.
[45] McKinley, *Anglo-Saxon Cemetery at Spong Hill VIII*, pp. 85–91.
[46] Filmer-Sankey and Pestell, *Snape*, p. 250.
[47] Lucy, *The Anglo-Saxon Way of Death*, p. 115.
[48] Williams, 'Cemeteries as Central Places' and 'Assembling the Dead'.

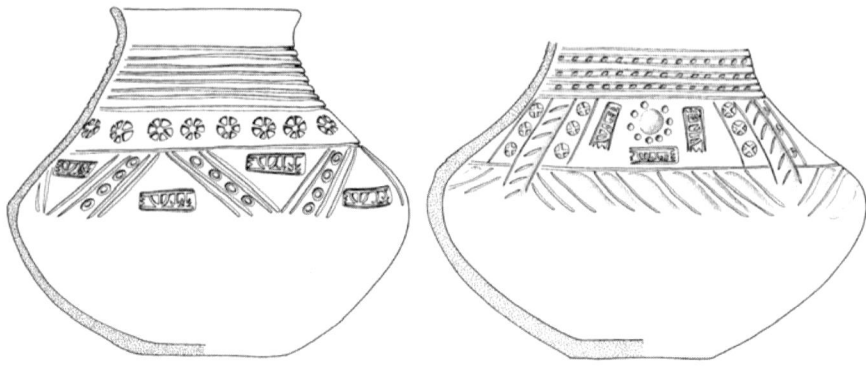

Fig. 18: Urns 1564 (left) and 1224 (right) from Spong Hill, both stamped with the runic name Tiw (reproduced from Hills, *Spong Hill I*, fig. 58). © *NMAS*

of their occupants, for it is perfectly possible that urns were curated above ground and only taken to the cemetery when a sufficient number of them had accrued to warrant the journey.[49]

Cremation vessels

Whereas cremated remains have suffered from a lack of academic interest, the opposite is true of the urns in which they are found.[50] Early Saxon pottery was handmade and domestic wares were simple, undecorated and poorly made, while funerary wares were well made and adorned with linear, bossed and/or stamped decoration.[51] The contrast between the two is so great that Myres found it 'sometimes difficult to believe that folk of the same culture and period were responsible for designing and making the complex and elaborately ornamented funerary Buckelurnen ['bossed urns'] on the one hand, and some of the shapeless and incompetent domestic bowls and cookpots on the other'.[52]

The widespread absence of funerary wares from domestic contexts strongly suggests that these wares were made deliberately for the purpose of burial and that display and prestige were important.[53] This is even more apparent when the decorative schemes employed on the urns are analysed. The design of every urn is unique and has the potential to differ greatly from its fellows, but despite this there is considerable repetition in the range of forms and decorative motifs employed, enabling common styles to be recognised and interpretative typologies to be developed.[54] This repetition suggests that the potters were working to a culturally defined template which dictated the form and appearance of cremation

---

[49] McKinley, *Anglo-Saxon Cemetery at Spong Hill VIII*, pp. 102–5.
[50] e.g. Myres, 'Some Anglo-Saxon Potters', *Anglo-Saxon Pottery* and *Corpus*.
[51] Dunning *et al.*, 'Anglo-Saxon Pottery'; Hurst, 'The Pottery', pp. 283 and 292–9; Kennett, *Anglo-Saxon Pottery*, pp. 7–14.
[52] Myres, *Anglo-Saxon Pottery*, p. 13.
[53] *Ibid.*, pp. 12–13; Hurst, 'The Pottery', pp. 292–9; Kennett, *Anglo-Saxon Pottery*, p. 7; West, *West Stow*, pp. 128–35.
[54] Myres, *Anglo-Saxon Pottery* and *Corpus*.

vessels. Furthermore, the existence of individual potters or workshops is suggested by the use of the same decorative stamps or groups of stamps, as well as similarities of form and design.[55]

Using data from cremation cemeteries throughout Anglo-Saxon England, Richards demonstrated that aspects of the form and decoration of Anglo-Saxon cremation urns were associated with the social identity of those whose remains they contained.[56] He found a close correlation between the age and sex of an individual and the size and shape of their urn: males tended to have taller and wider urns than females, while infants had the shortest urns and old adults the tallest.[57] The decorative schemes employed also had links to the contents of the urn, both in terms of grave-good assemblages and physical identity.[58] Richards concluded that each cremation urn was, to a greater or lesser extent, tailored to its occupant and recorded the identity of the deceased according to a set of symbolic rules.[59] The departed individual, having lost their personal identity, was afforded a symbolic identity by the decoration on the outside of their cremation urn in a manner akin to that of a headstone. Williams has described urns as a 'second body' for the cremated individual after the destruction of their first.[60]

Certain decorative motifs employed on cremation urns relate to pagan religious beliefs, the most commonly discussed examples being the swastika, the wyrm and the ↑-rune. Swastikas appear as both stamped and freehand decoration and are one of the symbols of the god Thunor, whose association with fire appears to be of particular relevance.[61] Likewise, the wyrm — the serpent or dragon traditionally the guardian of the burial mound and its treasure, and associated with the god Woden — is found in a variety of stylised forms.[62] Runes occur more rarely on cremation urns, but the use of the ↑-rune for the god Tiw is the most frequently found.[63] Three urns from Spong Hill were repeatedly stamped with Tiw's name, including the two urns illustrated here in Figure 18. The use of iconography to indicate the symbolic presence of the deities in question is a fundamental tenet of the framework propounded by cognitive archaeologists for recognising religiously motivated behaviour in the material record and it would appear to indicate such behaviour in this context (pp. 11–13).[64]

We are only able to identify the religious symbolism of these designs because of the complementary literary sources which are available to us. As Richards states, if the religious connotations of these three symbols can be identified 'it is likely that other aspects of the design [of urns] are also symbolic, although their meaning is no

---

[55] Myres, 'Some Anglo-Saxon Potters' and *Corpus*, pp. 68–83; Green *et al.*, 'The Illington/Lackford Workshop'.
[56] Richards, 'Funerary Symbolism'; *Significance of Form*; 'Style and Symbol'; and 'Anglo-Saxon Symbolism'.
[57] Richards, *Significance of Form*, pp. 134–48.
[58] *Ibid.*, pp. 157–91.
[59] *Ibid.*, pp. 193–210.
[60] Williams, 'Death Warmed Up', p. 282.
[61] Brown, 'Swastika Patterns'.
[62] Wilson, *Anglo-Saxon Paganism*, pp. 142–50.
[63] Myres, *Corpus*, pp. 66–7.
[64] Renfrew, *Archaeology of Cult*, pp. 18–19; Renfrew and Bahn, *Archaeology: Theories, Methods and Practice*, pp. 416–17.

longer understood, and their interpretation evades us'.[65] Richards thus makes the point that, although we are able to recognise many correlations and associations in the archaeological record, without a wider, usually literary, frame of reference we are often unable to ascribe religious or indeed any ideological significance to a particular feature or characteristic.

The chronology of cremation

The cremation rite was clearly one which called for the collection, display and destruction of substantial quantities of resources. Every stage of the process was demonstrably laden with religious significance, sometimes of great complexity, but how does this help us understand the East Anglian conversion? In this regard chronology is of fundamental importance, for if it can be demonstrated that cremation ceased to be practised before the reintroduction of Christianity to these shores then its cessation was clearly unrelated to the conversion. However, if the rite can be shown to have continued into the early seventh century then we must consider the possibility that its cessation may be related to the adoption of Christianity.

Unfortunately, as is so often the case, things are not as clear-cut as we would like them to be. Despite the enormous quantity of curated and published material, the precise dating of cremation is problematic and the rite's chronological end-date is rarely discussed in the literature.[66] This uncertainty is largely due to the vast majority of cremation urns now being devoid of their archaeological context and, more significantly, any associated finds that might allow them to be dated. To this day the main means of dating cremations remains the typology of urn styles developed by Myres from the 1930s onwards.[67] Although comprehensive, Myres' typology contained very few absolute dates and the largely stylistic nature of the work has been criticised for its assumption of linear and constant development over time.[68] Richards goes so far as to state of cremation urns that 'one might conclude that the material is undatable'.[69] Fortunately, the increasing number of cremations excavated under modern conditions is enabling more detailed dating to be achieved, both stratigraphically and by association. At Snape, for example, the excavators are confident that they have urned cremations which date from the early seventh century.[70] It is unlikely that these cremations were isolated cases and we can therefore assume that many other urned cremations must also date from this time.

While the use of pottery urns in the seventh century is still a subject of debate, most of the twenty-one known examples of cremations contained within various types of copper-alloy vessel are now dated to the late sixth and early seventh centuries. The use of such vessels in place of ceramic urns is interpreted as an indication of high status, as well as carrying connotations of hospitality and feasting.[71] There are twelve known East Anglian examples, discovered at Illington,

---

[65] Richards, *Significance of Form*, p. 41.
[66] e.g. Owen, *Rites and Religion*, pp. 85–95; Wilson, *Anglo-Saxon Paganism*, pp. 131–64; Lucy, *The Anglo-Saxon Way of Death*, pp. 104–22.
[67] Myres, *Anglo-Saxon Pottery* and *Corpus*.
[68] e.g. Hurst, 'The Pottery', pp. 294–9; Hills, 'The Archaeology of Anglo-Saxon England', pp. 324–6.
[69] Richards, *Significance of Form*, p. 25.
[70] Filmer-Sankey and Pestell, *Snape*, pp. 234–6.
[71] Carver and Fern, 'Seventh-Century Burial Rites', p. 289.

Brightwell Heath, Snape, the Sutton Hoo barrow cemetery and the Sutton Hoo Visitors' Centre cemetery.[72] To answer the question posed at the beginning of this section, the cremation rite can thus be demonstrated with some certainty to have continued into the seventh century and therefore its cessation can be demonstrated to be relevant to the study of the East Anglian conversion.

This brings us to what seem likely to be among the latest instances of cremation in the East Anglian burial record, the cremations at Sutton Hoo, which are dated to the first quarter of the seventh century.[73] That the cremation rite was enacted here is perhaps the most telling physical clue in ascertaining the relationship between the end of cremation and the acceptance of Christianity. Over a number of years Carver has promulgated the theory that the Sutton Hoo burial complex represents an overtly political statement of pagan defiance 'provoked by the perceived menace of a predatory Christian mission'.[74] In particular, he draws attention to the use of what he takes to be iconic pagan practices at the site: barrow burial, boat burial and cremation.[75] Anglo-Saxon barrow and boat burials are both very rare, and therefore can tell us little about the burial practices of the lower echelons of society, but cremation was widely practised at a grassroots level, arguably making it much more useful in charting the spread of the conversion. It is certainly telling that the last pagan kings of East Anglia should be among the last to practise cremation in the region.[76] Taking Carver's interpretation to its logical conclusion, it would appear that in the early seventh century cremation was seen as a totemic pagan rite and was flaunted at Sutton Hoo in an act of pagan defiance and resistance. The corollary of this is that the paganism which the rite symbolised must indeed have been under a perceived or direct threat from these 'predatory' Christian missionaries, and the episode is strongly suggestive of a Christian policy of eradicating cremation as a burial rite, albeit a policy that is unrecorded in early documents.

We saw in Chapter 1 that one of the means by which Christianity achieved its widespread success was through a deliberate policy of adoption and adaptation of local customs as it expanded into new territories.[77] Yet while this can be demonstrated to be true for many Early and Middle Saxon practices, of which more below, cremation appears to have been a burial practice which was simply not tolerated. Why, though, should the practice have been so deplorable to early Christians and its eradication have been so desirable? Many ethnographic parallels suggest that fire is seen as both a purifying force and a means of freeing the spirit of the deceased by destroying the body.[78] These interpretations have been echoed in an

---

[72] Dickinson and Speake, 'Seventh-Century Cremation'; Geake, 'When were Hanging Bowls Deposited?'; Davison, Green and Milligan, *Illington*; Reid-Moir, 'Excavation of Two Tumuli'; Filmer-Sankey and Pestell, *Snape*, pp. 250–55; Carver and Fern, 'Seventh-Century Burial Rites', pp. 285–7; Newman, 'Sutton Hoo', pp. 502–3.

[73] Carver and Fern, 'Seventh-Century Burial Rites'.

[74] Carver, *Sutton Hoo: Burial Ground of Kings*, p. 136.

[75] Carver, 'Kingship and Material Culture'; 'Conversion and Politics'; 'Boat-Burial in Britain'; *Sutton Hoo: Burial Ground of Kings*, pp. 134–6; and 'Burial as Poetry'; Carver and Fern, 'Seventh-Century Burial Rites', pp. 312–13.

[76] Carver, 'Kingship and Material Culture' and 'Conversion and Politics'.

[77] e.g. Carver, 'Conversion and Politics'; Urbańczyk, 'Christianisation' and 'Politics of Conversion'; Pluskowski and Patrick, 'How do you Pray to God?'.

[78] e.g. Bachelard, *Psychoanalysis of Fire*, pp. 99–109; Downes, 'Cremation'.

Anglo-Saxon context via Williams' 'ideology of transformation', in which cremation functioned as a mechanism through which the deceased was destroyed and transformed into a new ancestral form.[79] Such ideas would have been fundamentally at odds with the early Christian worldview and, although some ideologies and beliefs could be assimilated into the emerging doctrine, it would appear that the destruction of the body by fire and its transformation into something 'other' was simply not one of them.

Throughout the Christian West, early Christians continued the Jewish tradition of burial and actively supplanted cremation with inhumation.[80] At its most fundamental level the Christian opposition to cremation stems from the belief in corporeal resurrection on the Day of Judgement, a phenomenon for which the body of the deceased needed to be kept intact.[81] In Christian ideology the flames of the cremation pyre were equated with the fires of hell and the destruction of the corpse which cremation wrought was believed to prevent the chance of resurrection.[82] It is no coincidence that medieval heretics were burned alive, ensuring that the condemned had no body in the next life.[83] These beliefs were so strongly held that cremation remained anathema for Anglican Christians until the nineteenth century.[84] Similarly, it was not until 1963 that the Catholic church permitted cremation, although to this day the cremated remains cannot be scattered and must be kept together.[85]

Clearly the Christian opposition to cremation was the result of strongly ingrained doctrine regarding the mechanics of the resurrection. It can, therefore, be argued that the adoption of this doctrine may have accounted for the disappearance of cremation from the archaeological record in the early seventh century. With regard to recognising the conversion in the burial record it follows that any cemetery which contains cremations must represent a community which had yet to adopt Christianity in its entirety. Where they can be dated, these sites can be used to provide something of a *terminus post quem* for the localised adoption of Christianity. Obviously, the parts of the region to which this is applicable are limited to those areas where cremation was practised, which effectively means Norfolk and northern Suffolk. The fact that cremation should have ceased to be practised across such a large area in such a relatively short period during the early seventh century is strongly suggestive of the conversion to Christianity having been widespread at a local level from its earliest days. However, while the presence of cremation can be used to demonstrate the continued existence of pagan practices, its absence alone cannot be taken as conclusive proof of the adoption of Christianity, for cremation was only one of the pagan burial rites practised in the region, the other major rite being inhumation.

---

[79] Williams, 'Ideology of Transformation'; 'Death Warmed Up', 'Keeping the Dead at Arm's Length' and 'Animals, Ashes and Ancestors'.
[80] Prothero, *Purified by Fire*, p. 6.
[81] The anti-cremation arguments of the early Christian fathers are summarised by Meaney, 'Anglo-Saxon Pagan and Early Christian Attitudes', p. 238 n.4; see also Bullough, 'Burial, Community and Belief', p. 192; Gilchrist, 'Magic for the Dead?', p. 121.
[82] Ariès, *Hour of Our Death*, pp. 31–2.
[83] *Ibid.*; Bynum, *Resurrection of the Body*.
[84] Parsons, *Committed to the Cleansing Flame*, pp. 15–58.
[85] Cremation Society of Great Britain, *History of Modern Cremation*; Parsons, *Committed to the Cleansing Flame*, p. 227.

The inhumation rite

Although the Anglo-Saxon inhumation rite has been the traditional focus of interest, not all types of inhumation have received equal attention. Early Saxon inhumations have been studied at great length, largely because of the visibility (and desirability) of their associated metalwork; while the unfurnished inhumations of both the Early and Middle Saxon periods are often poorly preserved and, consequently, have not been extensively studied. The resulting synthetic literature therefore fails to address adequately the ways in which the inhumation rite changed during the period of the conversion, discussion tending to tail off with the end of furnished burials in the seventh century.[86]

Inhumation was practised alongside cremation during the Early Saxon period and eventually became the sole burial rite under Christianity, remaining so until the widespread reintroduction of cremation in the nineteenth century.[87] Inhumation is traditionally said to provide the key to identifying the conversion in the burial record, for, although it continued to be practised throughout the conversion period, the nature of the rite changed considerably during that period.[88] Particular attention has been paid to changes in the deposition of grave-goods and the increasingly regular adoption of a west–east alignment for the burial. This section considers the evidence for Early and Middle Saxon inhumation in East Anglia and evaluates its usefulness in charting the progress of the conversion.

In comparison with cremation, the Anglo-Saxon inhumation rite was relatively simple. After the death of an individual, the corpse was prepared, taken to a cemetery, laid out in a grave and buried. Inhumations are much more susceptible to decay than cremations and their material remains vary greatly in quantity and quality. Poor bone preservation is a serious problem in East Anglia and a number of the region's inhumation cemeteries situated in areas of acidic soils have suffered greatly.[89] Fortunately, the corpse was often not the only object deposited in a grave; the widespread practice of furnishing burials resulted in many artefacts of different materials also being deposited. Although organic artefacts may be completely destroyed, inorganic artefacts survive well in the burial environment and, indeed, are often the only elements which do survive.[90] In some circumstances metal artefacts may indicate the former presence of organic materials: for example, fixtures and fittings may indicate the shapes of boxes or furniture and metallic corrosion products may preserve adjacent organic material either as a pseudomorph or a cast.[91] In exceptional circumstances wooden objects or artefacts such as mattresses, mats, cushions, biers and coffins may be preserved as soil stains.[92]

---

[86] e.g. Owen, *Rites and Religion*, pp. 67–76; Wilson, *Anglo-Saxon Paganism*, pp. 67–130; Lucy, *The Anglo-Saxon Way of Death*, pp. 65–103.

[87] Parsons, *Committed to the Cleansing Flame*, pp. 15–58.

[88] Hadley, *Death in Medieval England*, p. 92.

[89] Wade, 'Anglo-Saxon and Medieval', p. 48.

[90] Hodges, *Artifacts*, pp. 64–98; Cronyn, *Elements of Archaeological Conservation*, pp. 176–237; Leahy, *Anglo-Saxon Crafts*, pp. 135–56.

[91] e.g. Crowfoot, 'The Textiles'; Härke, 'Anglo-Saxon Laminated Shields'; Hills *et al.*, *Anglo-Saxon Cemetery at Spong Hill III*, pp. 37–8.

[92] e.g. Filmer-Sankey and Pestell, *Snape*; Penn, *Excavations on the Norwich Southern Bypass*; Green and Rogerson, *Anglo-Saxon Cemetery at Bergh Apton*; Hills *et al.*, *Anglo-Saxon Cemetery at Spong Hill III*.

Not all graves were furnished: during the Early Saxon period approximately half of all graves were unfurnished or at the very least were furnished with grave-goods which left no archaeological trace. At sites where bone preservation is good these unfurnished burials are at least recognisable, but at sites where bone preservation is poor unfurnished burials appear as empty graves. As is examined further below, during the Middle Saxon period the deposition of grave-goods waned, meaning that Middle Saxon cemeteries can be recognised in areas of good bone preservation but may simply appear as a series of empty graves where they lie in areas of acidic soils. While such diverse degrees of preservation can make comparisons of cemeteries difficult, the advantage in studying inhumations over cremations is the amount of information that can be recovered about the deceased and the nature of their burial. Provided that bone preservation is good enough, we are able to infer something of the age, sex, health and lifestyle of the inhumed, allowing links between sex, age and burial practice to be explored.[93]

Early Saxon inhumations were laid out in a variety of positions: supine, prone or on one side or the other. The legs may be straight, crossed, flexed, crouched or contracted. Likewise, the arms may be laid by the sides, crossed across the pelvis or chest, or any combination of the above. However, despite the potential for great variability, the dominant burial position in Early Saxon cemeteries was extended supine: that is, the corpse laid out flat on its back.[94] Middle Saxon inhumations were also almost exclusively extended supine, suggesting that the prevailing tradition continued, but this position was more strictly enforced. This is also the position in which the body can be viewed most easily from the grave-side, highlighting the importance to the funerary process of viewing the burial tableau (of which more below).

While individual burial was the dominant rite, the burial of two or more individuals in the same grave was a widespread but rarely practised Early Saxon phenomenon; multiple burials are not a common feature of Middle Saxon cemeteries.[95] Where it did occur, in the vast majority of cases the individuals were inhumed contemporaneously and were laid side by side. Combinations of an adult and child are often interpreted as parent and offspring, while male and female combinations are often interpreted as husband and wife. Same sex pairings are also known and a familial relationship is most often suggested, although homosexuality should not be ruled out. In addition, the individuals may have been linked by any number of factors of which we remain unaware: lifestyle, profession, religion, ethnicity or even a shared death.[96] Beyond the fact that two individuals were buried together, these burials do not appear to have received special treatment: although obviously bigger than their single counterparts, the graves themselves do not display any exceptional characteristics and the range of grave-goods provided does not tend to differ from those of single burials,

---

[93] Brothwell, *Digging Up Bones*, pp. 59–72; McKinley, *Anglo-Saxon Cemetery at Spong Hill VIII*, pp. 11–21; Mays, *Archaeology of Human Bones*, pp. 33–66; Crawford, 'When do Anglo-Saxon Children Count?' and 'Children, Death and the Afterlife'; Lucy, 'Housewives, Warriors and Slaves?'; Stoodley, *The Spindle and the Spear* and 'From the Cradle to the Grave'.
[94] Lucy, *The Anglo-Saxon Way of Death*, pp. 78–81; Brush, 'Adorning the Dead', p. 221.
[95] Stoodley, 'Multiple Burials', pp. 103–5.
[96] *Ibid.*, pp. 112–14.

suggesting that pragmatism was often the governing factor behind multiple burials.[97] The evidence provided by multiple inhumations may help in the interpretation of multiple cremations, where similar pairings have been identified.

The treatment afforded to the corpse exhibited slight changes between the Early and Middle Saxon periods. The Early Saxon preference for extended supine burial became a uniformly applied practice in the Middle Saxon period, and the already minimal occurrences of multiple burials appear to have been largely phased out. Unfortunately, neither of these characteristics can be said to be definite indicators of changing religious beliefs because neither represented the introduction of a new practice. But can a greater insight into the conversion process be gleaned from the most regularly discussed characteristic of Anglo-Saxon graves, burial alignment?

Burial alignment

Studies of medieval and post-medieval Christian burials demonstrate that supine west–east burial was and is the norm.[98] It is generally accepted that the head was placed to the west so that were the dead to sit up in their graves they would be facing the east.[99] Despite being so ingrained in Christian practice, the reason for the adoption of this orientation appears to have been largely forgotten, although liturgical explanations have been offered for the Christian desire to face the east since at least the twelfth century.[100] Foremost among these explanations is that recorded by John Mirk in the fifteenth century, that Christ will return from the east on the Day of Judgement and the dead will rise towards him.[101]

Regarding the study of conversion, it does not follow that because all Christian burials are aligned west–east all such burials must be Christian. Examples of west–east burials occur in many demonstrably non-Christian contexts around the world and from throughout history. Although theology is used to explain the Christian adoption of a west–east alignment, many of the non-Christian examples have been explained as being aligned on the sunrise and/or sunset.[102] That the rising and, perhaps more significantly, the setting of the sun should become linked with death is not so surprising when one considers how fundamentally important it is to life, and we should certainly consider the possibility that the adoption of the west–east burial alignment is another instance of Christianity acquiring an already widespread practice and finding its own justification for the practice.

Given that the position of sunrise and sunset changes throughout the year it has also been suggested that burial alignment could be used to infer the time of year at which burial occurred.[103] One of the first considerations of the subject was by Wells and Green, whose analysis of burial alignments from the cemeteries at Caister-on-

[97] *Ibid.*, pp. 114–21.
[98] e.g. Rahtz, 'Late Roman Cemeteries' and 'Grave Orientation'; Rodwell, *Archaeology of Churches*, pp. 161–96; Gilchrist and Sloane, *Requiem*, pp. 152–6.
[99] Dearmer, *Parson's Handbook*, p. 432; Rahtz, 'Grave Orientation'; Kendall, 'Study of Grave Orientation'; Brown, 'Grave Orientation'.
[100] Thurston, 'Christian Burial'; Rahtz, 'Grave Orientation'; Gilchrist and Sloane, *Requiem*, p. 152.
[101] Erbe, *Mirk's Festival*, p. 294; cf. Matthew 24:27.
[102] e.g. Ucko, 'Ethnography'; Rahtz, 'Grave Orientation', pp. 1–3.
[103] e.g. Wells and Green, 'Sunrise Dating'; Hawkes, 'Orientation at Finglesham'; Hill, *Whithorn and St Ninian*, pp. 253–5.

Sea and Burgh Castle demonstrated that the burials were aligned within a broad solar arc.[104] However, they discovered that if the burials were aligned on the position of the sunrise the vast majority of them occurred within three months of the year, indicating that the solar hypothesis cannot be supported at these sites and at the same time illustrating the deliberate and organised uniformity of the burial alignments within Christian cemeteries.[105]

The solar alignment argument was taken one stage further by Hawkes in her study of burial alignment at Finglesham (Kent).[106] She argued that the conversion could be identified in the site's burial record by comparing the differences in alignment between the sixth-century burials and the seventh-century burials. Although all of the burials were broadly aligned west–east, the former fell outside the solar arc, while the latter fell within it, suggesting to Hawkes that the population had become Christian by the seventh century and had begun aligning burials on the sunrise. While the solar element of this hypothesis might not be valid, the difference between the dated alignments suggests that some sort of reorganisation had taken place and may well indicate a more tightly regimented approach to burials in the seventh century.

Unfortunately, such conclusions cannot easily be drawn in East Anglia, for numerous examples of west–east burials occur in many demonstrably pre-Christian cemeteries. For example, at both of the Early Saxon cemeteries at Bergh Apton and Morning Thorpe the burials were regularly laid out and aligned west–east, and at Westgarth Gardens the alignment was broadly north-west–south-east.[107] However, this was not the case in all East Anglian cemeteries; at Oxborough most of the Early Saxon burials were aligned on the prehistoric barrow around which the cemetery clustered.[108]

With the exception of a handful of cemeteries, there is a degree of uniformity of west–east burial within the East Anglian burial record from both before and after the period of the conversion, which effectively rules out alignment as a possible indicator of changing beliefs. Clearly, the adoption of Christian burial practice within East Anglia did not necessitate the adoption of a new tradition of burial alignment in very many instances, although its justification and meaning may well have been redefined in line with the new ideology. However, while the adoption of a west–east alignment is of little use to us as a direct indicator of conversion, the Christian observance is so strict that we can at least say with some certainty that burials which were not aligned west–east are demonstrably not Christian.

Grave-goods

We now turn to examine the aspect of the Anglo-Saxon inhumation rite which is most commonly said to indicate religious conversion, the changing use of grave-goods. Since the earliest days of archaeology authors have commented on the possible explanations for the provision of both pyre- and grave-goods, phenomena

---

[104] Wells and Green, 'Sunrise Dating'.
[105] Gilchrist and Sloane, *Requiem*, p. 49.
[106] Hawkes, 'Orientation at Finglesham' and 'Archaeology of Conversion'.
[107] Green and Rogerson, *Anglo-Saxon Cemetery at Bergh Apton*, p. 4; Green *et al.*, *Anglo-Saxon Cemetery at Morning Thorpe*, pp. 10–11; West, *Anglo-Saxon Cemetery*, pp. 7–8.
[108] Penn, *Anglo-Saxon Cemetery at Oxborough*, pp. 24–5.

found in many world cultures throughout history and prehistory.[109] Ucko famously offered a number of explanations drawn from ethnographic parallels for the use of grave-goods: they may have been items possessed by the deceased; they may be mourners' gifts to the departed; they may be provided to prevent the dead from returning to the world of the living; or they may be included as reminders of a person's deeds or character.[110] Yet, despite these alternatives, the most widely accepted explanation is that the deceased was being equipped for an afterlife in which it was believed that the provided artefacts would prove useful.[111] On a more theoretical footing, the provision of grave-goods also falls into the category of 'participation and offering' identified by cognitive archaeologists as a potential material indication of religiously motivated behaviour (pp. 11–13).[112]

Studies of Anglo-Saxon grave-goods have traditionally focused on individual classes of artefact, resulting in a series of chronological typologies which do not always agree, but the increasing use of statistical methods such as correspondence analysis enables artefacts to be more easily studied in combination and more coherent chronologies produced.[113] In addition to providing a chronological framework, the interpretation of grave-goods has addressed issues ranging from the purely technological to the socio-economic.[114]

To date, very few scholars have addressed the religious significance of Anglo-Saxon grave-goods, for it has become very fashionable, in British archaeology at least, to brand such approaches naive and instead to focus exclusively on social factors.[115] Notable exceptions are Williams, whose work on the religious meaning of cremation and pyre-goods has spilled over into inhumations and grave-goods, and Crawford, whose recent papers hopefully mark the start of a resurgence of interest in the religious significance of grave-goods.[116] Continental and Scandinavian scholars have taken a much more enlightened approach to the subject, and religious interpretations of grave-goods are more widely accepted; the lack of penetration of these ideas into British archaeology might be explained in part by the fact that few of the relevant articles have been published in English.[117]

Grave-goods are relevant to the study of the conversion of East Anglia for a number of reasons. First, the vast majority of our evidence for the Early Saxon period comprises grave-goods and a method of utilising this evidence must be

---

[109] Bahn, *Tombs, Graves and Mummies*; Allan, *Archaeology of the Afterlife*.

[110] Ucko, 'Ethnography', pp. 264–5.

[111] e.g. Lubbock, *Pre-Historic Times*, p. 133; Wilson, *Archaeology of Anglo-Saxon England*, p. 3; Parker Pearson, *Archaeology of Death*, pp. 7–11; Taylor, *Burial Practice*, pp. 23–4.

[112] Renfrew, *Archaeology of Cult*, pp. 18–19; Renfrew and Bahn, *Archaeology: Theories, Methods and Practice*, pp. 416–17.

[113] Jensen and Høilund Nielsen, 'Burial Data'; Høilund Nielsen, 'The Schism'; Brugmann, 'The Role of Continental Artefact Types'; Hines, 'Sixth-Century Transition'.

[114] Leahy, *Anglo-Saxon Crafts*; Huggett, 'Imported Grave Goods'; Welch, 'Cross-Channel Contacts'; Arnold, 'Wealth and Social Structure'; Pader, 'Material Symbolism' and *Symbolism*; Geake, *The Use of Grave-Goods*; Høilund Nielsen, 'From Society to Burial'; Ravn, 'Theoretical and Methodological Approaches' and *Death Ritual*.

[115] Hadley, 'Equality, Humanity and Non-Materialism', p. 150.

[116] Williams, 'Material Culture'; 'Artefacts in Early Medieval Graves'; and 'Keeping the Dead at Arm's Length'; Crawford, 'Anglo-Saxon Women' and 'Votive Deposition'; Dunn, *Christianization of the Anglo-Saxons*, pp. 191–3.

[117] Schülke, 'On Christianization', pp. 85–93; Rundkvist, 'Early Medieval Burial Studies', pp. 47–8.

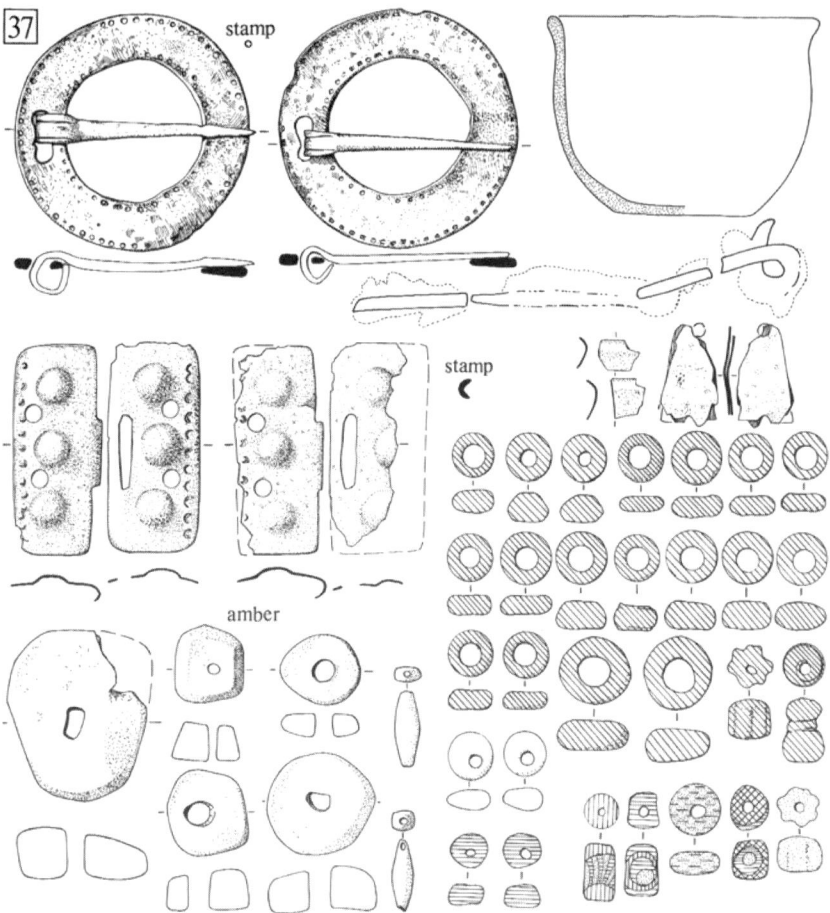

Fig. 19: A typical jewellery assemblage, from Spong Hill Grave 37 (after Hills, Penn and Rickett, *Spong Hill III*, fig. 90). © *NMAS*

developed. Secondly, the nature of grave-goods and the composition of the burial assemblage changed during the Anglo-Saxon period and these changes need to be explained. Finally, the practice of furnishing burials is traditionally considered to have been a pagan rite which was phased out under Christianity, although, as will be seen, this was not the case.

While the religious significance of grave-goods is emphasised here, there is no denying that burial assemblages were highly structured and symbolically reflected the social identity of the deceased. This was achieved through both the dress of the individual, including grave-goods worn on the body, and the inclusion in the grave of additional items of equipment or provisions. It is therefore prudent briefly to examine the nature of the symbolic language employed in the structured deposition of grave-goods before its relevance to the study of religious conversion is considered.

Grave-good assemblages have been studied in considerable detail and are particularly suited to statistical analysis to determine underlying patterns in their deposition.[118] It is clear that there were several ways of adorning the dead and that some were deemed more appropriate for particular individuals than others. Lucy identified four distinct types of Early Saxon burial assemblage: dress fittings, jewellery or ornamentation; weapons; goods other than jewellery and weapons; and no surviving artefacts.[119] As to the relative quantities of each type of burial assemblage, approximately half of all burials contained 'other goods' or fell into the 'no surviving artefacts' category. The remaining burials were divided between the 'jewellery' and 'weaponry' categories at a ratio of approximately 4:1.[120] These patterns have been generally recognised across Early Saxon England, although detailed studies have not been made of every region.[121]

Lucy's jewellery assemblages are almost exclusively associated with female burials (Fig. 19). It would therefore appear that women in the fifth, sixth and early seventh centuries were buried in their clothes and often adorned with personal jewellery.[122] It is worth noting that the vast majority of the typically female grave-goods are dress-related, being artefacts that were worn on the body either as elements of costume or as belt equipment. Additional equipment and tools do not seem to have been placed in female graves very frequently. Weapon burials have long been recognised as having a strong male association (Fig. 20).[123] Male burials contain fewer clothing-related artefacts, but textile impressions, occasional cloak-brooches and belt fittings all suggest that men, too, were buried clothed. Personal jewellery is rare in male burials, but occasionally finger rings or a decorative bead from the pommel of a sword are present.[124] The contrast with female burial assemblages is striking, for the vast majority of male grave-goods comprises additional equipment and tools added to the grave, rather than costume-related artefacts.

Lucy's third category, burials containing non-gender-specific grave-goods (Fig. 21), and her fourth group, burials containing no surviving artefacts, clearly indicate that biological sex was not the sole factor in the structuring of grave-good assemblages. There is no reason why these 'neutral' assemblages should not have been as symbolic as the other assemblages, but as the grave-goods included show no correlation with the sex or age of the inhumed, other aspects of social identity which we are less able to infer from the archaeological record must also have played a role.[125]

---

[118] e.g. Pader, *Symbolism*; Lucy, 'Housewives, Warriors and Slaves?' and *Early Anglo-Saxon Cemeteries of East Yorkshire*; Stoodley, *The Spindle and the Spear* and 'From the Cradle to the Grave'.

[119] Lucy, 'Housewives, Warriors and Slaves?', p. 157, *Early Anglo-Saxon Cemeteries of East Yorkshire*, p. 41, and *The Anglo-Saxon Way of Death*, p. 87.

[120] Lucy, 'Housewives, Warriors and Slaves?' and *Early Anglo-Saxon Cemeteries of East Yorkshire*, p. 41.

[121] e.g. Pader, *Symbolism*, Härke, 'Early Saxon Weapon Burials'; Brush, 'Adorning the Dead'; Stoodley, *The Spindle and the Spear*; Hadley, *Death in Medieval England.*; Penn and Brugmann, *Aspects of Anglo-Saxon Inhumation Burial.*

[122] Owen-Crocker, *Dress in Anglo-Saxon England*, pp. 28–57; Stoodley, *The Spindle and the Spear*, pp. 33–5; Stoodley, *The Spindle and the Spear*, pp. 30–33.

[123] Härke, 'Early Saxon Weapon Burials'; 'Knives in Early Saxon Burials'; '"Warrior Graves"?'; 'Changing Symbols'; 'Material Culture as Myth'; and 'Circulation of Weapons'.

[124] Owen-Crocker, *Dress in Anglo-Saxon England*, pp. 65–84; Stoodley, *The Spindle and the Spear*, pp. 29–33.

[125] Lucy, 'Housewives, Warriors and Slaves?', p. 157, *Early Anglo-Saxon Cemeteries of East Yorkshire*, p. 41, and *The Anglo-Saxon Way of Death*, p. 87.

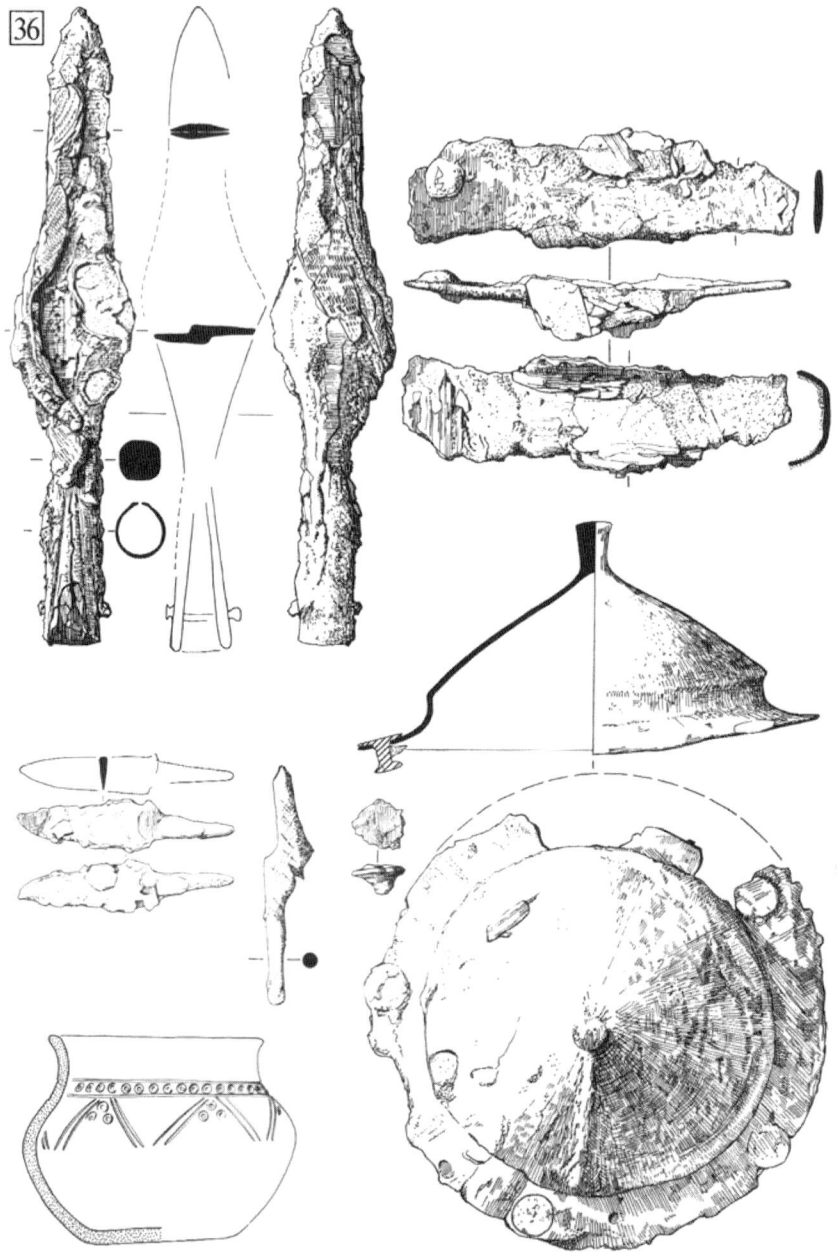

Fig. 20: A typical weaponry assemblage, from Spong Hill Grave 36 (after Hills, Penn and Rickett, *Spong Hill III*, fig. 89). © *NMAS*

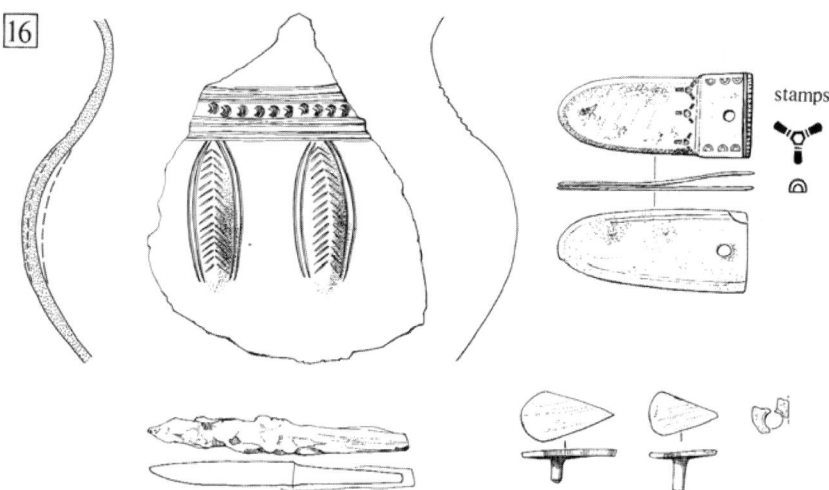

Fig. 21: A neutral assemblage, from Spong Hill Grave 16 (after Hills, Penn and Rickett, *Spong Hill III*, fig. 76). © *NMAS*

The age of the deceased was clearly a factor in the structuring of grave-goods and a series of age-related thresholds has been identified at which the composition of the burial assemblage changed. This suggests that the various stages of the Early Saxon lifecycle were of great importance and that they were symbolically marked in both life and death. Stoodley observed that the majority of excavated cemeteries contained no infant burials and that, at those sites which did, they were often found in double burials with an adult.[126] It was not until the age of 2–3 years that child burials began to be treated like those of adults — that is, with individual graves and grave-good assemblages which mirror adult assemblages.[127] Both 'male' and 'female' burial assemblages underwent a second change at around 10–14 years, coinciding with the onset of puberty, when the range of grave-goods employed increased; it would appear that this biological milestone was marked materially.[128] It was not until the late teens that the full burial rite described by Lucy began to be practised. As this last threshold does not coincide with any major physiological changes, it must represent a culturally defined stage of the lifecycle.[129] In late maturity both weapon and jewellery assemblages exhibited further changes: the number of weapons deposited declined and their types changed, and certain aspects of the jewellery assemblage also ceased to be deposited. Again, these changes may reflect the individual's changing social status, perhaps marking the end of their being a warrior or being capable of giving birth.[130]

[126] Stoodley, 'From the Cradle to the Grave', pp. 458–9; cf. Buckberry, 'Missing, Presumed Buried'.
[127] Stoodley, 'From the Cradle to the Grave', pp. 459–62.
[128] *Ibid.*, pp. 461–2; Crawford, 'When do Anglo-Saxon Children Count?'; 'Children, Death and the Afterlife'; *Childhood in Anglo-Saxon England*; and 'Children, Grave Goods and Social Status'.
[129] Stoodley, 'From the Cradle to the Grave', pp. 461–5.
[130] Stoodley, 'Multiple Burials', pp. 461–5.

The distinct types of burial assemblage and the trends and thresholds identified in their use are indicative of biologically and culturally defined practices which, in some cases, reflected aspects of both the age and sex of the deceased. Yet age and sex alone do not explain all the patterns that we see in the burial record and there must have been a great many other factors at work of which we remain unaware. The patterns discussed here primarily apply to the Early Saxon burials of the fifth, sixth and early seventh centuries and have been included here because it is only by understanding the norm in the Early Saxon period that the changes in the inhumation rite that occurred during the seventh century can be fully appreciated.

The 'Final Phase': grave-goods

Grave-good assemblages were highly structured and symbolically expressed a number of different messages, some pertaining to the sex and age of the deceased, but is this of any use when trying to recognise the conversion in the burial record? It is a commonly held belief that the conversion was responsible for the demise of the practice of burying grave-goods, but grave-goods continued to be employed until the first half of the eighth century, at least a century after the main period of conversion. Geake places the end of the grave-good tradition at AD 720–30 and notes that it occurred suddenly among all types of artefact, with little or no evidence to suggest that some types were abandoned before others.[131] Clearly, then, the end of the grave-good tradition cannot be related to the initial period of conversion, although its end is probably related to the subsequent development of churchyard burial and the associated institutions.[132] Even if this were not the case, the simple criterion 'furnished/unfurnished' could not be used as an indicator of conversion, because, as we have seen, approximately half of Early Saxon burials were unfurnished or furnished with artefacts which leave no archaeological trace.[133] However, although both pagan and Christian burials might contain grave-goods this does not mean that grave-goods cannot be employed in the study of the conversion, for there are a number of ways in which they prove to be illuminating.

It has often been observed that there are three distinct phases in the development of the inhumation rite: pagan inhumation, Christian inhumation, and a transitional phase between the two, which straddles the period *c.* AD 600–800 and has come to be known as the 'Final Phase'.[134] The existence of this transitional phase has long been recognised, with Lethbridge's excavations at Burwell and Shudy Camps (Cambridgeshire) in the 1930s providing the stimulus for Leeds' initial description of the material evidence for the 'Final Phase'.[135] Originally, Leeds was referring to the final phases of Early Saxon furnished burial, but the term 'Final Phase' has since become synonymous with a wider model of conversion and cemetery

---

[131] Geake, *The Use of Grave-Goods*, p. 125; Hadley, *Death in Medieval England*, pp. 96–7.
[132] e.g. Evison, 'An Anglo-Saxon Cemetery'; Hyslop, 'Two Anglo-Saxon Cemeteries'; Meaney and Hawkes, *Two Anglo Saxon Cemeteries*; Carver, 'Kingship and Material Culture'; Boddington, 'Models of Burial'.
[133] e.g. Filmer-Sankey and Pestell, *Snape*; Penn, *Excavations on the Norwich Southern Bypass*.
[134] Reviewed in Geake, *The Use of Grave-Goods*, pp. 1–6.
[135] Lethbridge, *Recent Excavations* and *A Cemetery at Shudy Camps*; Leeds, *Early Anglo-Saxon Art*, pp. 98–114.

development.[136] This model is discussed more fully in the following chapter, where its relevance to the study of settlements and cemeteries is addressed (pp. 121–30); here we focus on the grave-goods of the 'Final Phase' and in particular on the distinct differences between the burial assemblages of the fifth and sixth centuries and those of the seventh and early eighth centuries.

Many of the sex- and age-related patterns in grave-good assemblages discussed above remained constant, with regional variation, throughout the majority of the Early Saxon period.[137] However, during the early seventh century, while some classes of artefact continued to be deposited, the use of many of the diagnostic grave-good types ceased abruptly, to be replaced by grave-goods of a markedly different character (Fig. 22).[138] Whereas approximately half of all Early Saxon burials were furnished, during the 'Final Phase' the proportion of unfurnished burials in cemeteries rose considerably. Most burials that contained grave-goods were poorly furnished, usually only with a knife, while those very few burials which were properly furnished were furnished richly and tended to be those of females.[139] In general, while costume-related grave-goods continued to be deposited, there was a marked drop-off in the deposition of additional equipment and foodstuffs with the body, suggesting that the religious and ideological reasons which had previously governed their deposition — that is, that individuals were being equipped for an afterlife — had changed.

Within this smaller number of furnished graves sex and age continued to be signalled, but in new ways. The nature of the non-sex-specific assemblages changed: for example, glass vessels became less popular, bronze bowls became more popular, and new designs of combs and buckles were introduced.[140] From their mid-sixth-century peak, the proportion and frequency of weapon burials declined steadily until they ceased completely at the end of the seventh century.[141] The same types and combinations of weapons continued to be deposited, although some of the seventh-century weapons showed a Frankish influence.[142] The weapon rite appears to have been one of the few Early Saxon burial practices which continued unchanged into the 'Final Phase', albeit in a greatly reduced form. Aside from the few weapon burials, 'Final Phase' burials of both men and boys are archaeologically invisible.[143]

The greatest changes in the grave-goods of the 'Final Phase' were exhibited in the female jewellery assemblages: the major Germanic brooch types of the sixth century stopped being used 'almost overnight',[144] as did long strings of beads and many of the girdle items which typified the earlier assemblages. These were replaced by

---

[136] e.g. Evison, 'An Anglo-Saxon Cemetery'; Hyslop, 'Two Anglo-Saxon Cemeteries'; Meaney and Hawkes, *Two Anglo Saxon Cemeteries*; Faull, 'Location and Relationship'; Morris, *The Church in British Archaeology*, pp. 49–62; Boddington, 'Models of Burial'; Crawford, 'Anglo-Saxon Women' and 'Votive Deposition'.

[137] Lucy, *The Anglo-Saxon Way of Death*.

[138] Hyslop, 'Two Anglo-Saxon Cemeteries'; Geake, *The Use of Grave-Goods*, pp. 107–22, and 'Invisible Kingdoms'; Hines, 'Sixth-Century Transition'.

[139] Boddington, 'Models of Burial'; Geake, *The Use of Grave-Goods*, pp. 126–7.

[140] Geake, 'Invisible Kingdoms', pp. 203–4.

[141] Härke, '"Warrior Graves"?', pp. 28–31.

[142] Geake, *The Use of Grave-Goods*, pp. 116–17.

[143] *Ibid.*, pp. 128–9.

[144] Geake, 'Invisible Kingdoms', p. 204.

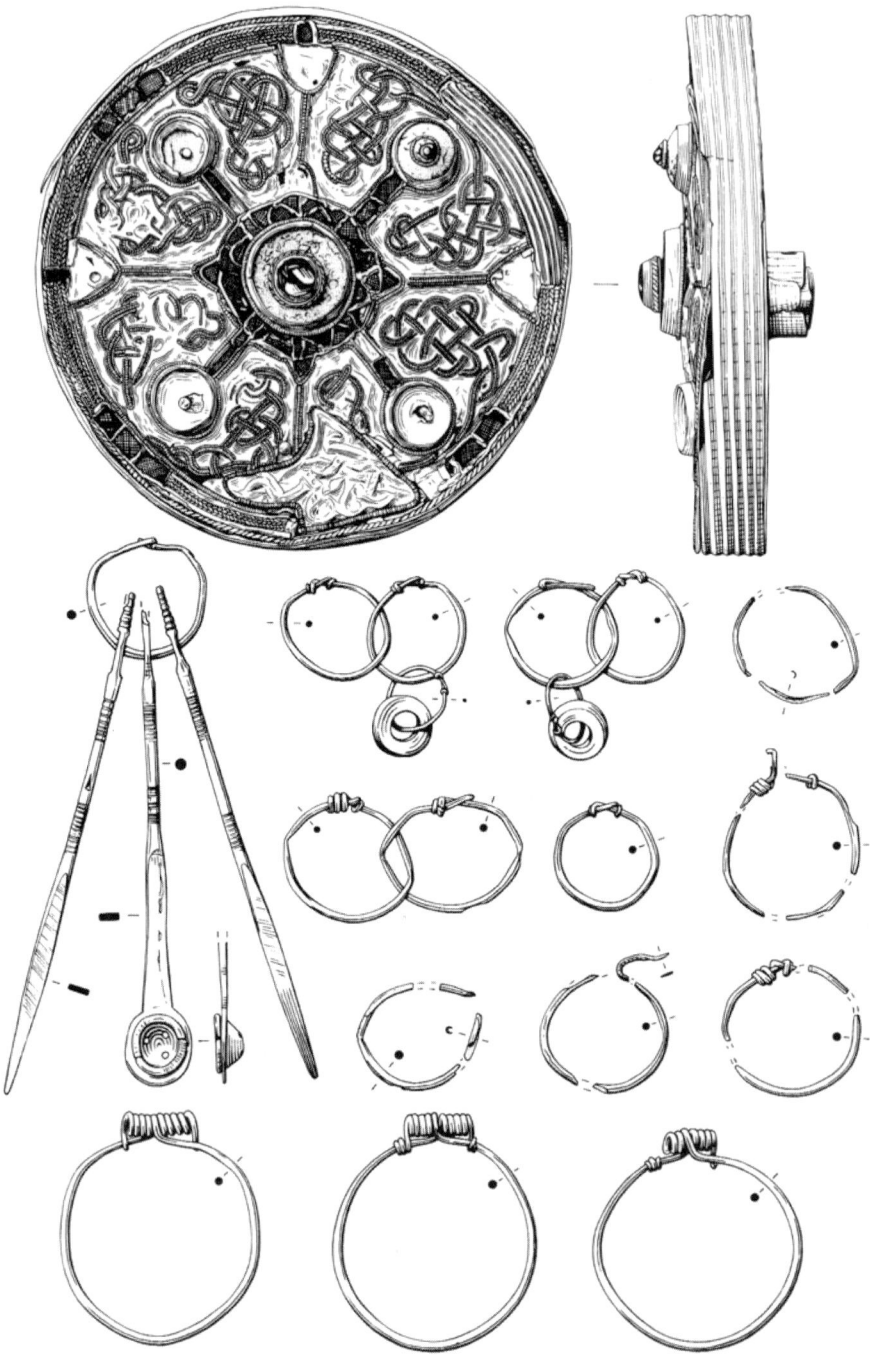

Fig. 22: Selected elements of a typical 'Final Phase' burial assemblage, from Harford Farm Grave 11 (reproduced from Penn, *Harford Farm*, figs 84 and 85). © *NMAS*

classically influenced single disc brooches, single pins and pairs of pins linked by chains, new types of necklaces with pendants and new types of girdle item, including iron latch-lifters, spoons, toilet sets, bags and 'workboxes'.[145] In addition, the burials of girls, which in the Early Saxon period contained only limited ranges of grave-goods, were instead furnished with the full array of adult female accoutrements.[146]

It would appear that the biological and cultural stages of the lifecycle that were so clearly signalled during the Early Saxon period changed during the 'Final Phase'. Instead of marking a number of distinct stages, the uniformity of the grave-goods for young and old alike suggests that a single social status was being signalled, one which had its origins early in life. Crawford has argued that Christian baptism was the earliest milestone in the lives of these seventh- and eighth-century individuals, lending support to the wider argument that many of the characteristics of the 'Final Phase' were influenced by the Church.[147]

Traditionally, the grave-goods of the 'Final Phase' were considered to be Frankish and their occurrence throughout Anglo-Saxon England was ascribed to their diffusion from Kent.[148] However, the lack of Frankish parallels for many of the new types of grave-goods suggested to Geake that this Kentish/Frankish model was wrong and that instead the inspiration behind the fashions of the 'Final Phase' could be found further afield, in the Roman and later Byzantine world.[149] Others, such as Marzinzik, have argued that even this Romano-Byzantine influence was the result of acculturation via the Franks, but Geake refutes this and suggests a more direct conduit in the form of the Christian mission itself.[150]

Geake stops short of suggesting that the Church was the ultimate cause of the 'Final Phase', describing it only as the mechanism by which the 'Final Phase' was brought about. She cites instead the rise of kingship as being the cause, arguing that the desire of emerging Anglo-Saxon kings to legitimise their position led to the use of Romano-Byzantine artefacts in an attempt to recall the days when Britain had been a part of the Roman Empire.[151] Yet this interpretation of events is at odds with much of the data which Geake presents and other writers, such as Crawford, have been more certain in concluding that Christianity was the principal factor responsible for the widespread adoption and use of Romano-Byzantine artefacts.[152] This interpretation dovetails much more neatly with the idea explored in the previous chapter that *romanitas* was propagated directly by the arrival of the Christian mission and the subsequent spread of Mediterranean ecclesiastics throughout Anglo-Saxon England (pp. 53–6). These ideas were also developed indirectly via the desire for *romanitas* instilled by the increasing authority of the

---

[145] Owen-Crocker, *Dress in Anglo-Saxon England*, pp. 107–29; Geake, *The Use of Grave-Goods*, 'Invisible Kingdoms' and 'Persistent Problems'.

[146] Geake, *The Use of Grave-Goods*, pp. 128–9.

[147] Crawford, 'Children, Death and the Afterlife', 'Anglo-Saxon Women' and 'Votive Deposition'.

[148] e.g. Leeds, *Early Anglo-Saxon Art*; Hyslop, 'Two Anglo-Saxon Cemeteries'; Meaney and Hawkes, *Two Anglo Saxon Cemeteries*.

[149] Geake, *The Use of Grave-Goods* and 'Invisible Kingdoms'.

[150] Marzinzik, *Early Anglo-Saxon Belt Buckles*, pp. 85–6; Geake, *The Use of Grave-Goods*, pp. 121–2.

[151] Geake, *The Use of Grave-Goods*, p. 133, and 'Invisible Kingdoms', pp. 209–12.

[152] Crawford, 'Anglo-Saxon Women' and 'Votive Deposition'; Hoggett, 'Charting Conversion'; Dunn, *Christianization of the Anglo-Saxons*, pp. 191–3.

Church at a popular level in seventh-century society — seemingly a much more likely conduit for this Romano-Byzantine influence.[153]

The uniformity of 'Final Phase' burial assemblages across the kingdoms of Anglo-Saxon England has often been the subject of comment.[154] Geake ascribes this uniformity to the near-contemporaneous development of kingship in each of the kingdoms of the Heptarchy, with each kingdom independently choosing to focus on Romano-Byzantine material in the manner of convergent evolution.[155] Yet, while the kingdoms remained independent political entities, albeit often linked by intermarriage, the Church was an overarching entity capable of planting and promoting its ideas across secular political boundaries. Therefore, a much more convincing explanation for the uniformity of the 'Final Phase' assemblages might be found in the teachings of the Church as it spread throughout the Anglo-Saxon kingdoms. In this regard, it is particularly telling that the areas of Anglo-Saxon England to have been converted last — Sussex and the Isle of Wight — are also the areas which have the fewest 'Final Phase' burials.[156] While the motivating forces behind the changing burial assemblages of the 'Final Phase' thus remain a matter of debate, there are some seventh-century artefacts which do nevertheless display a clear Christian influence.

Christian iconography

The inherent difficulties in interpreting pagan religious symbols in the archaeological record have already been alluded to in the context of deciphering the decorative schemes employed on cremation urns (pp. 90–2). There it was also noted that the use of iconography is a key part of the framework for the recognition of religiously motivated behaviour in the material record propounded by cognitive archaeologists.[157] The Christian cross is an easily recognised symbol and its presence on artefacts from seventh-century graves might be taken to be an indication of the spread of Christian beliefs.[158] However, the cross it is also a very common decorative motif more generally, and may be found on many demonstrably non-Christian artefacts; context, therefore, is all-important. There are, on this basis, a number of artefacts discovered in the East Anglian graves for which Christian connotations can be argued.

Some of the most frequently discussed examples of possible Christian iconography are the ten silver bowls and two spoons from the Mound 1 ship burial at Sutton Hoo.[159] These bowls are decorated with equal-armed crosses, although

---

[153] Geake, *The Use of Grave-Goods*, pp. 121–2 and 132–3, and 'Invisible Kingdoms', pp. 209–12; Bell, 'Churches on Roman Buildings', pp. 5–8, and *Religious Reuse*, pp. 16–22.
[154] Boddington, 'Models of Burial'; Geake, 'Invisible Kingdoms'; Crawford, 'Anglo-Saxon Women' and 'Votive Deposition'.
[155] Geake, 'Invisible Kingdoms'.
[156] *Ibid.*, p. 214.
[157] Renfrew, *Archaeology of Cult*, pp. 18–19; Renfrew and Bahn, *Archaeology: Theories, Methods and Practice*, pp. 416–17.
[158] Crawford, 'Anglo-Saxon Women' and 'Votive Deposition'.
[159] e.g. Hawkes, 'Archaeology of Conversion', p. 48; Webster and Backhouse, *The Making of England*, p. 32; Werner, 'A Review of *The Sutton Hoo Ship Burial*'; Evans, *Sutton Hoo*, pp. 59–63; Arnold, *Archaeology of the Early Anglo-Saxon Kingdoms*, pp. 167–8.

this in itself does not automatically indicate that they had Christian connotations. The spoons are of identical form and bear respectively the Greek inscriptions 'Saulos' and 'Paulos', names thought to be a reference to St Paul's conversion on the road to Damascus.[160] Although it is possible that 'Saulos' is actually a failed attempt at rendering 'Paulos' (the Greek characters are very similar), the spoons are often interpreted as having been a baptismal gift to the individual buried under Mound 1. This arguably strengthens the suggestion that Mound 1 was indeed Rædwald's grave, the king having been baptised in Kent *c*. AD 604 and having subsequently renounced his new faith (above, pp. 28–30). Again, context is important, for although the spoons themselves might be Christian artefacts, they are deposited in what was in every other respect an overtly pagan funerary display.[161] To those who constructed the burial tableau, most of whom may not have been able to read the Greek inscriptions, these spoons may have had as much significance as bullion as they did as Christian artefacts.[162]

There are other artefacts from seventh-century graves that speak more clearly of Christianity, especially when they are found in combination with artefacts bearing the same imagery. Two coins discovered at the head end of the particularly well-furnished Grave 18 in the 'Final Phase' cemetery at Harford Farm (Norfolk) may have been placed on the deceased's eyes, perhaps as a form of 'Charon's obol'.[163] Both coins are Series B *sceattas* dating from the last two decades of the seventh century and, significantly, they bear the image of a dove sat atop a cross on their reverse.[164] This design has biblical origins, the dove representing the Christian soul, and the deliberate inclusion of the coins in the burial suggests that Christian beliefs were being signalled.[165] Similarly, a single cross-bearing Series B *sceat* dating from AD 690–700 was discovered near the head of the female individual buried in Grave 93 at Boss Hall (Suffolk), a grave which also contained, deposited in a leather pouch near the corpse's head, a number of other artefacts which arguably employed Christian iconography to a greater or lesser degree. Foremost among these artefacts was a gold and garnet composite disc-brooch, probably manufactured in the middle two decades of the seventh century, the design of which comprises a splayed, equal-armed cross in gold set against a background of cloisonné garnets (Fig. 23).[166] Other potentially Christian artefacts from the grave included two gold pendants depicting equal-armed crosses in gold filigree and a gold *solidus* of Sigeberht III (AD 639–56), which had been mounted as a pendant in such a way that the cross motif on the reverse of the coin might be displayed by the wearer (Fig. 23).[167]

The artefacts from Boss Hall are by no means unique in the East Anglian archaeological record. A similar composite disc brooch bearing a garnet linear cross with bossed ends set against a gold background was recovered from Grave 11 in the

[160] Acts 9: 1–31.
[161] Carver, 'Burial as Poetry' and *Sutton Hoo: A Seventh-Century Princely Burial Ground*, pp. 153–99.
[162] Evans, *Sutton Hoo*, p. 63.
[163] Geake, *The Use of Grave-Goods*, p. 32; Gannon, *Iconography*, p. 9.
[164] Penn, *Excavations on the Norwich Southern Bypass*, pp. 18–19, 75–6 and Plate XXII.
[165] Abramson, *Sceattas*, p. 49.
[166] Scull, *Early Medieval Cemeteries*, pp. 16–18, 43–4 and 114; cf. Avent, *Anglo-Saxon Garnet Inlaid Disc*, p. 64.
[167] Scull, *Early Medieval Cemeteries*, pp. 16–18 and 43–4.

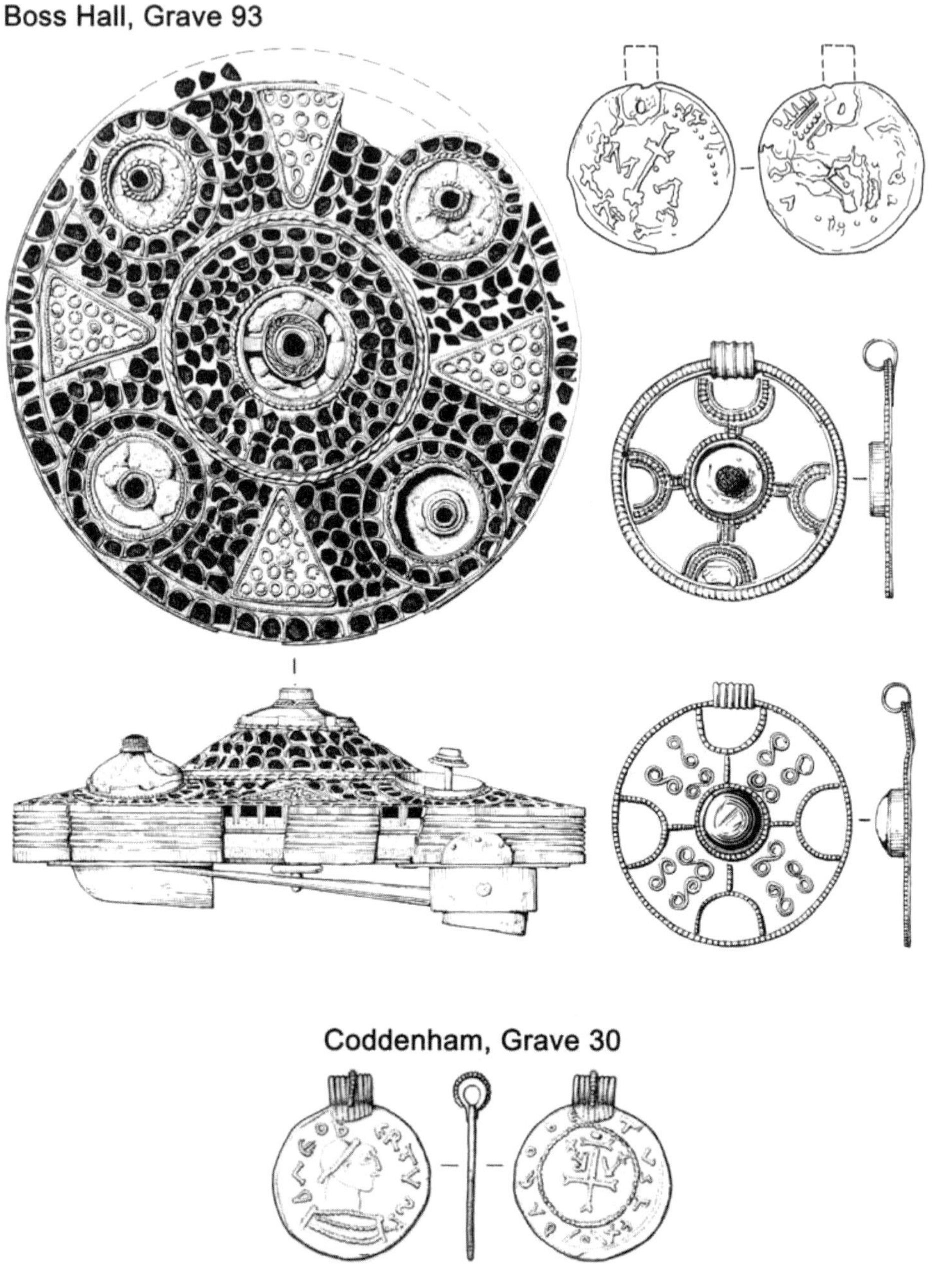

Boss Hall, Grave 93

Coddenham, Grave 30

Fig. 23: Artefacts exhibiting Christian iconography from Boss Hall Grave 93 and Coddenham Grave 30 (after Scull, *Early Medieval (Late 5th–Early 8th Centuries AD) Cemeteries*, figs 2.20 and 2.21 (© SMA); Penn, *Anglo-Saxon Cemetery at Shrublands*, fig. 100 (© SCCAS)).

'Final Phase' cemetery at Harford Farm, where it is thought to have been deposited in the later seventh century (Fig. 22).[168] Further parallels can be found in the three series B *sceattas* which were discovered in association with a high-status seventh-century bed burial in Grave 30 at Shrublands Quarry, Coddenham (Suffolk). This burial assemblage also contained a gold pendant which utilised a *solidus* of Dagobert I (AD 629–39), again mounted in such a way as to display the cross motif on its reverse (Fig. 23), and three large amethyst beads, which may also be read as a Christian symbol, amethysts being associated with the colour of heaven.[169] Among the grave-goods at the Ipswich Buttermarket cemetery were, in Grave 1356, a Kentish *tremissis* adorned on its reverse with a plain Latin cross and a second contemporary forgery of the same, and, in Grave 4275, two similar forgeries, both of which had been mounted as pendants and each of which had a cross and a possible Chi-Rho on their obverse.[170]

It is significant that many of the coins found in seventh-century burials are those bearing crosses, especially when they are found in association with other artefacts bearing Christian imagery.[171] We can be more certain about the Christian symbolism inherent in artefacts such as the seventh-century necklace discovered in Grave 11 of the 'Final Phase' cemetery at Carlton Colville (Suffolk). This necklace comprised a series of silver pendants flanking a silver-sheet cross (Fig. 27) and is an object that has parallels in several other seventh-century cemeteries across lowland England, including a very high-status burial which is probably associated with the late-seventh-century monastery at Ely.[172] Although none of these artefacts can unequivocally be demonstrated to be examples of Christian iconography they all form part of a growing corpus of material which strongly suggests that early Christians regularly employed the iconography of the cross to express their faith, both in their daily apparel and, by extension, in their funerary dress.[173] That said, there is one class of artefact which is incontrovertibly of Christian significance: pectoral crosses.

Pectoral crosses are considered to be among the earliest overtly Christian artefacts in the archaeological record. Two East Anglian examples, the Ixworth Cross and the Wilton Cross, from Suffolk and Norfolk respectively, came to light in the nineteenth century.[174] The Ixworth Cross, named after the parish in which its nineteenth-century owner lived, was purchased in 1856 as a part of a group of objects reportedly discovered in a gravel pit in the neighbouring parish of Stanton, although the exact findspot is not known.[175] The cross was said to have been found with twenty-four staple-like iron objects and the broken front plate of a gold disc brooch from which the gems had been removed, all of which would seem to indicate

---

[168] Penn, *Excavations on the Norwich Southern Bypass*, pp. 45–9.

[169] Penn, *Anglo-Saxon Cemetery at Shrubland Hall Quarry*; Scull, *Early Medieval Cemeteries*, p. 101; Watkins, 'Anglo-Saxon Grave Mystery', p. 42.

[170] Scull, *Early Medieval Cemeteries*, pp. 140–41, 152–4 and 241–2.

[171] I am grateful to John Newman for bringing this to my attention.

[172] Lucy *et al.*, *Anglo-Saxon Settlement and Cemetery*, pp. 385–416; Lucy *et al.*, 'The Burial of a Princess?', pp. 120–22.

[173] Crawford, 'Anglo-Saxon Women' and 'Votive Deposition'; Scull, *Early Medieval Cemeteries*, p. 90.

[174] MacGregor, 'Seventh-Century Pectoral Cross'.

[175] SHER STN Misc.

Pendant cross from Wilton, Norfolk.   British Museum
Width across arms 4.4 cm.

Pendant cross from Ixworth, Suffolk.   Ashmolean Museum
Width across arms 3.9 cm.

Plate 10: Both sides of the seventh-century Wilton and Ixworth crosses. Reproduced from *The Antiquaries Journal* XVII, No. 3 (July 1937) by kind permission of the Society of Antiquaries of London, copyright reserved.

the richly furnished burial of a high-status woman.[176] It has four equally flared arms, is in the cloisonné style, inset with garnets, and is suspended from a barrel-shaped loop; the rear shows traces of an ancient repair (Plate 10). It dates from the mid-seventh century.[177]

Similarly, the Wilton Cross was discovered by gravel diggers in the Norfolk parish of Wilton in the early 1850s.[178] The exact location and context of the discovery were unrecorded, but the similarities between it and the Ixworth Cross suggest that this cross too furnished an inhumation. The Wilton Cross is also in the cloisonné style, inset with garnets, and has three flared arms, the fourth ending in a bi-conical loop (Plate 10). The central roundel holds a gold *solidus* of the Byzantine Emperor Heraclius, which dates from between AD 613 and 630.[179] The reverse of this coin, which bears the image of the cross, set atop four steps representing the hill of Golgotha, is displayed. The coin is actually displayed upside-down, perhaps so that the cross on it appeared the right way up to the wearer, although the fact that the hidden obverse of the coin was set the correct way up suggests that the maker did not realise that the obverse and reverse of the coin were misaligned and did not fully appreciate the significance of the steps. The Wilton cross also dates from the mid-seventh century.[180]

Both crosses have close stylistic affinities to several items of cloisonné jewellery recovered from the Sutton Hoo ship burial and all these objects were probably made in the same East Anglian workshop during the first half of the seventh century, demonstrating a remarkable degree of continuity in the manufacture of pagan and Christian items.[181] That two such pieces should have come to light, despite the laws of diminishing returns which govern the archaeological record, must surely be an indication that several crosses of the type must have been in circulation; indeed, another example, seemingly from the same workshop, was discovered as far afield as Holderness (East Yorkshire).[182] Many others may still be awaiting discovery.

That the two crosses can be linked to the workshop which produced the royal regalia of the pagan kings of East Anglia raises interesting questions about the status of the crosses' owners and the means by which they acquired the objects. The general consensus is that such pectoral crosses were worn by the women of upper-class families and were ultimately used to furnish their burials.[183] However, a close parallel for the two East Anglian crosses (although the product of a Northumbrian workshop) is the pectoral cross of St Cuthbert, found *in situ* when his coffin was opened in Durham cathedral in 1827.[184] In life Cuthbert had been bishop of Lindisfarne, so the assumption that pectoral crosses are an ornament of secular females arguably underplays their potential significance. The Wilton Cross is

---

[176] Speake, *A Saxon Bed Burial*; West, *Corpus*, p. 96.
[177] Webster and Backhouse, The Making of England, pp. 26–7.
[178] Chester, 'Notice of a Gold Cross'.
[179] Webster and Backhouse, *The Making of England*, pp. 27–8.
[180] *Ibid.*
[181] *Ibid.*, p. 28.
[182] MacGregor, 'Seventh-Century Pectoral Cross', pp. 220–21.
[183] e.g. Hawkes, 'Archaeology of Conversion', p. 49; Geake, *The Use of Grave-Goods*, p. 179; Crawford, 'Anglo-Saxon Women', p. 2.
[184] Bruce-Mitford, *Aspects of Anglo-Saxon Archaeology*, pp. 294–5; Campbell, *The Anglo-Saxons*, pp. 80–81.

essentially without provenance, and the circumstances and associations of the Ixworth Cross are by no means certain; artefacts having been purchased together does not necessarily indicate that they were found together. Could not both the Ixworth and Wilton crosses have been worn by seventh-century East Anglian ecclesiastics of a similar standing to Cuthbert? This is certainly a valid inference and the clear links with the Sutton Hoo workshop seem to indicate that the ecclesiastics who wore these crosses enjoyed royal patronage. It is frustrating that the provenances of the two crosses are not better known, for we may have missed out on a chance to discover an 'East Anglian Cuthbert' (or perhaps even two of them). Nevertheless, these two artefacts are at the least a testament to the strong Christian ethos that gripped the region in the mid-seventh century. Of course, we must not forget that these are only the artefacts which have survived to be found; we have no way of knowing the extent to which wooden, textile or other organic artefacts may have been used to convey Christian iconography.

Conclusions

If, as Taylor believes, 'religious change … is particularly likely to be marked by radical shifts in burial practice', then it should be possible to identify the conversion in the archaeological record.[185] The burial record presents two main avenues of investigation — cremation and inhumation — each of which brings different aspects to the study of the conversion. Cremation was predominant in Norfolk and north Suffolk during the Early Saxon period and has been demonstrated to have been an archetypal pagan rite, laden with religious imagery and requiring a large outlay of resources. The cessation of cremation during the early seventh century is the most significant archaeological indicator of the conversion, as the Christian antithesis towards cremation and its use as a totemic pagan rite at Sutton Hoo testify. The speed with which the rite was abandoned and the size of the region within which this abandonment took place suggest that the conversion process was quick and widespread at a grass-roots level. As a result, it can be confidently stated that cemeteries which contain cremations represent communities that had yet to be converted and an absence of cremation is a necessary criterion for any identification of a Christian cemetery. However, the absence of cremation from a cemetery does not automatically signal Christian burial, for there were many demonstrably pre-Christian cemeteries which did not feature cremation either.

Several aspects of the inhumation rite can also be used to chart the course of the East Anglian conversion. The increasingly regular adoption of a west–east alignment for burials is often cited as one such indicator, but within East Anglia a west–east alignment was particularly common among the inhumations of the Early Saxon period and there was little change in this practice over time. While it is true that a west–east orientation is a necessary criterion for identifying a Christian burial and that burials which are not orientated west–east are not Christian, the uniformity of this practice both before and after the period of the conversion effectively rules it out as an indicator of Christianisation.

---

[185] Taylor, *Burial Practice*, p. 15; cf. Dunn, *Christianization of the Anglo-Saxons*, pp. 191–3.

Unfurnished burial was practised to varying degrees throughout the Early and Middle Saxon periods and is in itself not a sound criterion for recognising conversion. However, the cessation of the practice of burying grave-goods is often cited as an indicator of conversion. The deposition of grave-goods did not cease completely until the early eighth century and therefore cannot have resulted from the adoption of Christianity, but grave-goods became rarer in the seventh century and there was a distinct change in their character, from a Germanic to a Romano-Byzantine influence, dubbed the 'Final Phase'. These changes clearly represent a radical alteration in wider spheres of influence and a growth of interest in *romanitas*, which can be identified with the arrival of the Church. It is not unreasonable to suggest that, while the presence of Germanic grave-goods signals a non-Christian burial, the presence of Romano-Byzantine grave-goods, some of them with strong Christian iconography, is an indication of a converted population. The changing composition of grave-good assemblages also indicates that there was a move away from the inclusion of grave-goods which we might interpret as equipment or provisions for the deceased, such as weaponry or food offerings. Instead, the majority of grave-good assemblages came to comprise dress fasteners and items of personal jewellery. This would seem to indicate that notions of equipping the deceased for an afterlife had changed.

The clearly defined biological and cultural stages of the Early Saxon lifestyle expressed via grave-goods also disappeared during the 'Final Phase', to be replaced by more uniform types of burial assemblages which were deemed suitable for all ages and which may have signified the Christian baptism of the deceased. All of these interpretations sit comfortably with the idea, discussed in Chapter 1 (pp. 16–19), of a conversion process which took on and adapted existing local practices, changing their character but not banning them outright, and ultimately resulted in a uniquely East Anglian form of Christianity. The changing burial practices discussed here conform with the tenets of the third 'Institution/Consolidation' phase of the conversion process proposed by Birkeli and Foote (Fig. 4), while Insoll's suggested subdivisions of that phase — Inclusion, Identification and Displacement — are also clearly identifiable in the patterns recognised here, particularly with regard to the 'Final Phase'.[186]

Despite some provisos, it has been possible to demonstrate that not only is the conversion visible in the burial record, it is represented in a number of different, but complementary, ways. The evidence suggests that the conversion of East Anglia occurred early in the first half of the seventh century and that it was a widespread affair, not merely the preserve of the upper classes. A final aspect of the funerary evidence — the landscape context of the cemeteries in which these burials were found — can also be used to chart the progress of the conversion, and this subject forms part of the following chapter.

---

[186] The structure of Birkeli's framework is explained in Lager, 'Runestones', p. 497; Foote, 'Historical Studies', p. 137; Insoll, 'Introduction'.

5

The Landscape of Conversion

Funerary evidence has more to offer than just the study of individual burial rites. While the foundation of missionary stations introduced a new type of site to the Middle Saxon landscape, in contrast the burial of the dead in archaeologically visible cemeteries occurred before, during and after the conversion. As is explored below, the conversion can be seen not just in burial rites but also in the changing landscape context of the cemeteries themselves. The locations chosen for the burial of the dead were not arbitrary and, although it may be difficult for us to identify all of the relevant criteria in the decision-making process, we are able to say something about the reasoning behind the siting of cemeteries. The contrasting types of site used for Early and Middle Saxon cemeteries and the differing relationships between cemeteries and settlements of those periods both suggest that the changes which occurred during the conversion period affected where the dead were placed in the landscape.

Whereas pre-Christian settlements and cemeteries remained separate landscape entities, under the influence of Christianity settlements and cemeteries converged to become a unified whole, providing us with a vivid material indication of the progress of the conversion. This chapter explores the ideological explanations for this convergence and examines the archaeological evidence from the period's execution cemeteries, which provide a material indication that several recognisable tenets of Christian doctrine were being enforced in the seventh century, including the notion of consecrated ground and the exclusion of criminals therefrom.

The integration of settlements and cemeteries was not the only seventh-century development in the choice of burial location. The central section of this chapter returns to the theme of the 'Final Phase' and examines the distinctive class of cemeteries that was established in tandem with the changing approach to the use of grave-goods discussed in the previous chapter. These cemeteries, of which there are a handful of excavated examples in the East Anglian region, were short-lived, and many had fallen out of use by the early eighth century, by which time, it would appear, the vast majority of burials were taking place in cemeteries located within settlements.

Although the integration of burial foci within settlements was a distinctive archaeological indicator of religious change, the establishment of those settlements resulted in the creation of fixed points in the landscape around which later occupation clustered. In many instances this has led to the archaeological evidence for these earlier phases becoming obscured or even destroyed by later development, making it difficult to study these phases directly. In an effort to address these problems, the final part of this chapter considers the usefulness of Anglo-Saxon artefacts found in churchyards and wider spreads of Anglo-Saxon material discovered adjacent to churches during fieldwalking surveys to the archaeological study of the conversion-period landscape.

Early Saxon cemeteries in the landscape

Somewhat surprisingly, given the amount of academic attention that both funerary remains and the Anglo-Saxon landscape have received, the landscape context of Anglo-Saxon cemeteries has been particularly poorly studied and is conspicuously absent from many otherwise comprehensive surveys.[1] A notable exception is to be found in Bonney's work on the relationship between cemeteries and administrative boundaries, although the validity of his studies has been questioned.[2] Nevertheless, it would seem that the place of cemeteries in the Anglo-Saxon landscape has rather fallen into the gap between burial studies and settlement studies.

Since the 1990s a number of scholars have attempted to rectify this situation: Lucy's analysis of the cemeteries of East Yorkshire marked the beginning of this trend and other regional studies have since been completed, including Chester-Kadwell's study of the Early Saxon cemeteries of Norfolk.[3] Individual themes have also been explored, in particular the reuse of prehistoric and Roman monuments as foci for Anglo-Saxon burials,[4] and geographical information system (GIS) software is increasingly being used to produce computerised models of cemetery locations in the Anglo-Saxon landscape.[5]

We have already seen that inhumation, cremation and mixed-rite cemeteries all existed in Early Saxon East Anglia and that they varied greatly in the number of burials which they contained. In 1979 Hills observed that such Early Saxon cemeteries were often to be found on higher ground, hilltops or terraces above river valleys (Fig. 15).[6] Of the relationship between cemeteries and settlements she stated that, while Early Saxon settlements and cemeteries might lie in close proximity, they remained separate entities, and she went on to explain that many cemeteries may have served large geographical areas containing numerous settlements.[7] Further work conducted during the subsequent three decades in

---

[1] e.g. Wilson, *Archaeology of Anglo-Saxon England*; Welch, *Anglo-Saxon England*; Halsall, *Early Medieval Cemeteries*; Arnold, *Archaeology of the Early Anglo-Saxon Kingdoms*; Hooke, *Landscape of Anglo-Saxon England*; Reynolds, *Later Anglo-Saxon England*.

[2] Bonney, 'Pagan Saxon Burials'; 'Early Boundaries in Wessex'; and 'Early Boundaries and Estates'; Goodier, 'The Formation of Boundaries'; Reynolds, 'Burials, Boundaries and Charters'; Draper, 'Roman Estates'.

[3] Lucy, *Early Anglo-Saxon Cemeteries of East Yorkshire* and 'Changing Burial Rites'; Hadley, *Death in Medieval England*; Semple, 'Burials and Political Boundaries'; Richardson, *Anglo-Saxon Cemeteries of Kent*; Chester-Kadwell, *Early Anglo-Saxon Communities*, pp. 91–145.

[4] e.g. Williams, 'Ancient Landscapes'; 'Monuments and the Past'; 'Placing the Dead'; and *Death and Memory*; Semple, 'A Fear of the Past' and 'Burials and Political Boundaries'; Bell, 'Churches on Roman Buildings' and *Religious Reuse*.

[5] Chester-Kadwell, 'Metal-Detector Finds in Context'; Brookes, 'Walking with Anglo-Saxons'.

[6] Hills, 'The Archaeology of Anglo-Saxon England', p. 310.

[7] *Ibid.*

various parts of the country has done little to challenge these observations, although some of the detail has been refined.[8]

Lucy was among the first to attempt to quantify and characterise the landscape setting of different types of Early Saxon cemetery.[9] Taking East Yorkshire as her study area, she identified a number of distinctive characteristics exhibited by Early Saxon cemeteries. Cremation cemeteries tended to lie more than 500m from water, be sited above the 50m contour line and lie at the top of south-west-facing slopes. Inhumation cemeteries also occurred in such locations, but were discovered in a variety of other locations as well and exhibited a particular association with gravel terraces above rivers. Larger cemeteries tended to lie mid-slope, while smaller sites were generally located at the tops and bottoms of slopes, and the reuse of existing monuments as burial foci was prevalent.[10] Lucy's observations are specific to East Yorkshire, but echo patterns observed in other regions. For example, Richardson's study of cemeteries in Kent recognised similar associations with the sloping ground of river valleys, hilltop locations and ancient routeways, the last of which was subsequently examined by Brookes.[11] The strong association between prehistoric monuments and Anglo-Saxon burials seen elsewhere was also noted by Richardson.[12]

The reuse of extant prehistoric monuments, particularly barrows, as foci for Early Saxon burials is a phenomenon which has long been recognised by those engaged in studying the earlier features, although it is only comparatively recently that Anglo-Saxon specialists have approached the subject.[13] Both Norfolk and Suffolk have a long history of 'hill-digging' — Norfolk's beginning in the fifteenth century, Suffolk's in the sixteenth — and several hundred of these sites are known to have been 'excavated', although it is unrealistic to expect that many, if any, of the sites discovered prior to the mid- to late eighteenth century were recorded.[14] The vast majority of the barrows concerned have proved to be Bronze Age, but several had secondary Anglo-Saxon burials focused around them. Those Anglo-Saxons who reused these burial sites were apparently aware of the great antiquity of the earthworks which dotted the landscape. The deliberate association of their dead with these monuments is best interpreted as an attempt on the part of the Anglo-Saxons to forge a direct link with the past, thereby legitimising authority and defining territory in the present.[15]

In Early Saxon East Anglia, Bronze Age round barrows were commonly reused

---

[8] e.g. Boddington, 'Models of Burial'; Newman, 'Sutton Hoo before Rædwald', pp. 31–4; West, 'The Early Anglo-Saxon Period'; Wade, 'The Later Anglo-Saxon Period'; Williams, 'Placing the Dead'; Lucy, *The Anglo-Saxon Way of Death*, p. 152; Penn, 'Early Saxon Settlement'; Rogerson, 'Middle Saxon Norfolk'; Zadora-Rio, 'The Making of Churchyards'.

[9] Lucy, *Early Anglo-Saxon Cemeteries of East Yorkshire*, pp. 76–101.

[10] *Ibid.*, pp. 79–87.

[11] Richardson, *Anglo-Saxon Cemeteries of Kent*, pp. 69–77; Brookes, 'Walking with Anglo-Saxons'.

[12] Richardson, *Anglo-Saxon Cemeteries of Kent*, pp. 74–5.

[13] Marsden, *The Early Barrow-Diggers*.

[14] Lawson *et al.*, *Barrows of East Anglia*, pp. 36–8 and 67–9.

[15] Lucy, 'The Significance of Mortuary Ritual'; Williams, 'Ancient Landscapes' and 'Monuments and the Past'.

as burial foci.[16] The region's cemeteries also conform to many of the other typical characteristics noted above.[17] Figure 15 clearly demonstrates the close correlation between major river valleys and Early Saxon cemetery sites of all types, a correlation which would be even more pronounced if minor tributaries had also been included on the Figure. Very few of the cemeteries are immediately adjacent to the rivers themselves; rather, they are set back from the water on the sloping sides of the valleys. In areas with land above 30m OD cemeteries are generally found clustered in the river valleys below the 30m contour line, while no cemeteries are to be found on land which is over 60m OD.

That the pattern of cemetery distribution should so closely mirror the river network should come as no great surprise, for the river valleys also accommodated in life those who would be buried in the cemeteries. It is the relationship between settlements and cemeteries, rather than the landscape context of cemeteries *per se*, that is of the greatest relevance when using evidence of wider landscape changes to chart the progress of the conversion.

Cemeteries and settlements

Hills' observation that Early Saxon cemeteries might lie in close proximity to Early Saxon settlements, yet remain separate entities in the landscape, can be shown to be broadly true in East Anglia. This relationship is a distinctive characteristic of the Early Saxon landscape.[18] Yet the ratio of settlements to cemeteries was not one-to-one — rather, it was one-to-many or many-to-one: any number of settlements and farmsteads might have contributed to the population of a single cemetery, while individuals from a single settlement might have been buried in any number of cemeteries.[19] Close proximity between an Early Saxon settlement and one or more cemeteries can be taken as an indication that there was a link between the two, but the distinctly separate characteristics of domestic and funerary pottery and metalwork assemblages make it difficult to prove such links materially.[20] Such avenues of investigation are not helped by the strong archaeological bias towards Early Saxon funerary material, meaning that we know of considerably more cemeteries than we do settlements.

An examination of the relationship between the well-excavated Early Saxon settlement at West Stow and contemporary local cemeteries is very revealing. The settlement was sited on a sandy rise to the north of the River Lark in west Suffolk and was extensively excavated between 1957 and 1972.[21] Excavations in the nineteenth century had already demonstrated that an inhumation cemetery containing some 100 graves lay approximately 350m to the north-east of the settlement. No plans of the cemetery were made, but all the burials were orientated

---

[16] Williams, 'Ancient Landscapes', pp. 19–20 and fig. 14; Lawson *et al.*, *Barrows of East Anglia*, pp. 26, 40–41 and 71.
[17] Chester-Kadwell, *Early Anglo-Saxon Communities*, pp. 91–145.
[18] Hills, 'The Archaeology of Anglo-Saxon England', p. 310; cf. Arnold, *Archaeology of the Early Anglo-Saxon Kingdoms*, p. 166; West, 'The Early Anglo-Saxon Period'; Penn, 'Early Saxon Settlement'.
[19] Williams, *Death and Memory*, p. 188.
[20] Chester-Kadwell, 'Metallic Taste'.
[21] West, *West Stow* and *West Stow Revisited*.

south-west–north-east and many of them were furnished; one was buried in a reused Roman stone coffin.[22] This cemetery was presumably closely linked to the settlement, but it was not the only cemetery accessible to the settlement's inhabitants. Two kilometres to the west lay an inhumation cemetery of at least 25 burials clustered around a Bronze Age barrow,[23] while metal-detecting a kilometre to the south of West Stow has revealed material indicative of another inhumation cemetery.[24] Furthermore, at Lackford, two kilometres south-west of West Stow, lay Suffolk's largest cremation cemetery, which was partially excavated by Lethbridge in 1947 and demonstrated to have contained at least 500 cremations and probably many more.[25] The inhabitants of West Stow clearly had a number of options available to them when the time came to dispose of their dead, as indeed would the inhabitants of the many other Early Saxon settlements and farmsteads elsewhere in the Lark valley and surrounding areas.[26]

Cemetery excavations far outweigh those of settlements and the fact that so few traces of settlement evidence are found in the vicinity of cemeteries only serves to reinforce the point that Early Saxon settlements and cemeteries were separate elements in the landscape. None of the region's extensively excavated Early Saxon cemeteries — Bergh Apton, Morning Thorpe, Caistor St Edmund and Oxborough (all Norfolk), and Snape, Lackford and Westgarth Gardens (all Suffolk) — has revealed any traces of adjacent settlement.[27] Similarly, large-scale excavations at Kilverstone (Norfolk) revealed evidence for an Early Saxon settlement comprising several sunken-featured buildings and post-built structures, with a small, but discrete, contemporary cemetery lying some 500m to the south.[28] At Spong Hill, a small number of Early Saxon structures were discovered lying immediately adjacent to, but distinct from, the cremation cemetery, although these structures were not extensively excavated and their precise function is unclear.[29]

The previous chapter demonstrated that it is very difficult to discover the criteria dictating which burial rites were considered appropriate for any given individual. Similar difficulties arise when we attempt to ascertain why a given individual was buried in any particular cemetery. The existence of single-rite cremation and inhumation cemeteries suggests that in some areas of East Anglia the choice of cemetery might be dictated by preferred burial rite, or that the choice of burial rite was dictated by the preferred cemetery, but the existence of a number of mixed-rite cemeteries indicates that this was not uniformly the case. The close proximity of a cemetery to a particular settlement would almost certainly have been a factor in the choice of burial location, particularly in the case of inhumation, which required the

---

[22] SHER WSW003; West, *West Stow*, pp. 64–9.
[23] SHER IKL026.
[24] SHER LKD045.
[25] SHER LKD001; Lethbridge, *A Cemetery at Lackford*.
[26] West, *West Stow*, pp. 155–9.
[27] Green and Rogerson, *Anglo-Saxon Cemetery at Bergh Apton*; Green *et al.*, *Anglo-Saxon Cemetery at Morning Thorpe*; Myres and Green, *Anglo-Saxon Cemeteries*; Penn, *Anglo-Saxon Cemetery at Oxborough*; Filmer-Sankey and Pestell, *Snape*; Lethbridge, *A Cemetery at Lackford*; West, *Anglo-Saxon Cemetery at Westgarth Gardens*; Penn and Brugmann, *Aspects of Anglo-Saxon Inhumation Burial*.
[28] Garrow *et al.*, *Excavations at Kilverstone*, pp. 170–201.
[29] Rickett, *Anglo-Saxon Cemetery at Spong Hill VII*, pp. 41–58 and 154–8.

transportation of the corpse to the site. Yet such considerations would be of lesser significance in the case of cremation cemeteries, which required only the urn to be transported to the site. In the case of large cremation cemeteries, such as Lackford and Spong Hill, the vast number of burials (several hundred and several thousand respectively) suggests that the cemeteries served large geographical areas containing numerous settlements and that people travelled some distance to bury their dead.[30]

*

Significant inroads have already been made, but clearly a great deal more work remains to be done investigating the landscape context of Early Saxon cemeteries in East Anglia. Yet from the examples examined here it is clear that the commonly held views on the types of landscape setting preferred for Early Saxon cemeteries — the sloping ground of river valleys and an association with prehistoric monuments in particular — are as applicable to East Anglia as they are to other regions. It is also clear from the few examples of excavated Early Saxon settlements and the numerous Early Saxon cemeteries that the two types of site were separate entities within the landscape, and deliberately so, although in some instances they were situated in close proximity. Such a separation conforms to the theory put forward by cognitive archaeologists that sites which are clearly designated in this fashion may be read as material indicators of religiously motivated acts, particularly when they also serve as a focus for funerary rituals (pp.11–13).[31]

Although we do not (and arguably cannot) fully understand the selection of any particular cemetery for the burial of an individual we are, in a similar fashion to the interpretations offered in the previous chapter, at least able to recognise patterns of behaviour and observe changes in those patterns which occurred over time. The effect that the conversion had on individual burial rites has already been considered, but the conversion can also be demonstrated to have had a dramatic effect on the landscape setting of cemeteries, particularly their relationship with settlements.

The 'Final Phase': cemeteries

We have seen that Middle Saxon burials are poorly understood compared with their Early Saxon counterparts. This is partly due to the relative archaeological invisibility of Middle Saxon burials, the vast majority of which were unfurnished and, therefore, unlike Early Saxon cemeteries, not easily located or dated. However, the relatively low number of discoveries is also due to the changes in the landscape setting of cemeteries which occurred during the Middle Saxon period, resulting in the vast majority of Middle Saxon cemeteries being obscured by later settlement features, in particular by later churchyards and churches.

When compared to the vast body of literature dedicated to Early Saxon burial rites, the burials of the Middle Saxon period have received very little attention and

---

[30] Hills, 'The Archaeology of Anglo-Saxon England', p. 310; McKinley, *Anglo-Saxon Cemetery at Spong Hill VIII*, pp. 66–71; Williams, 'Cemeteries as Central Places', pp. 343–6, and 'Assembling the Dead', p. 127.
[31] Renfrew, *Archaeology of Cult*, pp. 18–19; Renfrew and Bahn, *Archaeology: Theories, Methods and Practice*, pp. 416–17.

the transition from one state of affairs to the other has received even less. The exception are those cemeteries which contain 'Final Phase' burials of the kind examined here (pp. 104–8).[32] Since the 1950s the 'Final Phase' model has developed beyond the simple characterisation of the grave-goods found in burials dating from between *c.* AD 600–800 and has broadened to include a significant landscape aspect,[33] suggesting that artefactual changes — Romano-Byzantine-influenced stylistic changes and age-related patterning suggesting an adherence to the Christian lifecycle — were not the only way in which Christian influences were expressed. These cemeteries' relationships with earlier, contemporaneous and later cemeteries and settlements are particularly enlightening in this regard.

'Final Phase' cemeteries are generally seen as being the Christian successors of Early Saxon cemeteries, founded on fresh sites in the seventh century and each eventually being superseded by a churchyard located elsewhere.[34] Lethbridge was of the opinion that both of the cemeteries containing 'Final Phase' burials which he had excavated in Cambridgeshire — at Burwell and Shudy Camps — contained Christian burials, some of which were furnished.[35] He also concluded that both cemeteries had been founded towards the end of the main period of furnished Early Saxon inhumation and saw their foundation as an indication that Christians were being buried away from the sites of their pagan predecessors. This notion was subsequently developed by Hyslop, whose discussion of the relationship between the two cemeteries in Leighton Buzzard (Bedfordshire) included the first summation of the defining characteristics of 'Final Phase' cemeteries.[36]

In defining what constituted a 'Final Phase' cemetery, Hyslop stated that they did not contain burials which dated from before the seventh century and that they were founded as neighbouring Early Saxon cemeteries fell out of use.[37] This aspect of the model was subsequently explored in Meaney and Hawkes' discussion of the two Winnall cemeteries on the outskirts of Winchester (Hampshire) and has remained at the heart of the 'Final Phase' model ever since.[38] An additional landscape element of the 'Final Phase' model was introduced by Faull, whose analysis of the relationship between two cemeteries at Sancton (Yorkshire) included the observation that 'Final Phase' cemeteries were established closer to contemporary settlements than their Early Saxon counterparts.[39] This she attributed to the break-up of the larger territory served by the large cremation cemetery, 'Sancton I', and she suggested that the 'Final Phase' cemetery, 'Sancton II' had been founded in its stead, along with a number of similar, smaller cemeteries founded elsewhere.

The 'Final Phase' model has proved to be very popular and is widely accepted,

---

[32] Lethbridge, *Recent Excavations* and *A Cemetery at Shudy Camps*; Leeds, *Early Anglo-Saxon Art*, pp. 98–114.
[33] Boddington, 'Models of Burial'; Geake, *The Use of Grave-Goods*, pp. 1–6.
[34] The development of this model is summarised in Boddington, 'Models of Burial'; see also Taylor, *Burial Practice*, p. 165; Meaney, 'Anglo-Saxon Pagan and Christian Attitudes', pp. 240–41.
[35] Lethbridge, *Recent Excavations*, p. 48, and *A Cemetery at Shudy Camps*, pp. 27–9 and 48.
[36] Hyslop, 'Two Anglo-Saxon Cemeteries'.
[37] *Ibid.*, pp. 189–94.
[38] Meaney and Hawkes, *Two Anglo Saxon Cemeteries*, pp. 45–55.
[39] Faull, 'Location and Relationship', pp. 232–3.

but it is not without its critics.[40] Although there was undeniably a change in the nature of the grave-goods deposited during the seventh century, argued here to reflect the Christian beliefs of those using cemeteries, the notion of a linear development of cemetery types — an Early Saxon cemetery being succeeded by a 'Final Phase' cemetery which was replaced in turn by a churchyard — is more problematic.[41] This is not least because the total number of known 'Final Phase' inhumations falls far short of representing even a fraction of the seventh-century population, meaning that the vast majority of seventh-century burials remain unaccounted for.[42] Even factoring in the effects of poor preservation and the lack of secure dating evidence, the imbalance between the number of Early Saxon burials and the number of 'Final Phase' burials is so great as to suggest that 'Final Phase' burial was very much the exception rather than the rule. This is particularly true in East Anglia, where, despite the intensive work conducted by archaeologists and metal-detectorists alike, only a few stand-alone 'Final Phase' cemeteries have been discovered, including those at Thornham and Harford Farm in Norfolk, and at Coddenham, Carlton Colville and the Ipswich Buttermarket in Suffolk.[43] It is clear that the linear development propounded by the traditional 'Final Phase' model does not explain the seventh-century funerary landscape of East Anglia, raising questions, rather, about the location of the burials of the majority of the seventh-century population.

'Final Phase' landscapes

One of the few excavated examples of an East Anglian 'Final Phase' cemetery lies at Thornham, 6km west of the Roman fort at Brancaster on the north Norfolk coast (Figs 1 and 13). The cropmark of an enclosure was recognised at Thornham in 1948 and excavated during the 1950s, when it was found to be of mid-first-century date and to consist of an earthen rampart and external ditch.[44] Initially the site was thought to have been a Roman military signalling station, but the excavation showed the site to have been sparsely occupied during the Roman period and its precise function remains unclear.[45] The substantial earthworks of the rampart would doubtless still have been visible in the seventh century, when the site became the focus of an inhumation cemetery comprising at least twenty-four west–east inhumations arranged in rough rows. Thirteen of the graves were unfurnished and most of the others contained only belt buckles and knives. One individual was buried wearing a bronze bracelet, a variety of beads and possibly two chatelaines, one of which was adorned with a pierced hanging bowl escutcheon. The

---

[40] e.g. Morris, *The Church in British Archaeology*, pp. 53–9; Boddington, 'Models of Burial'.

[41] Taylor, *Burial Practice*, p. 165; Meaney, 'Anglo-Saxon Pagan and Early Christian Attitudes', pp. 240–41.

[42] Geake, 'Persistent Problems', pp. 144–8.

[43] Gregory and Gurney, *Excavations at Thornham*; Penn, *Excavations on the Norwich Southern Bypass*; Penn, *Anglo-Saxon Cemetery at Shrubland Hall Quarry*; Lucy et al., *Anglo-Saxon Settlement and Cemetery*; Scull, 'A Cemetery of the 7th and 8th Centuries' and *Early Medieval Cemeteries*, pp. 129–304.

[44] Gregory and Gurney, *Excavations at Thornham*, pp. 1–5.

[45] *Ibid.*, pp. 8 and 13; Albone et al., 'Archaeology of Norfolk's Coastal Zone', p. 74.

inhumations were distributed throughout the interior of the enclosure and were evenly spaced with no evidence of intercutting, and it would seem that the life-span of the cemetery was not particularly great. The landscape setting of the Thornham cemetery is somewhat reminiscent of the missionary stations discussed in Chapter 3, but the character of the burials clearly indicates that the reoccupation of the Thornham enclosure was not of the same character as that seen at Burgh Castle or Caister-on-Sea. The fact that a new cemetery was established in the seventh century indicates an abandonment of the Early Saxon cemeteries, by some of the population at least, and it is possible that the postulated Christian reoccupation of the fort at Brancaster was the stimulus for this change. Might the new cemetery have been founded within an earthwork enclosure under instructions from missionaries stationed at Brancaster?

At Coddenham excavation revealed fifty 'Final Phase' graves focused around a probable prehistoric barrow; many more burials had probably been lost to quarrying.[46] Most of the burials were unfurnished or sparsely furnished, but there was a handful of richly furnished graves, including three graves which appear to have had barrows raised over them and a woman buried on an iron-framed bed. The finds indicate a seventh- to early-eighth-century date for the cemetery, and the artefacts associated with the bed burial in particular convey a strong Christian symbolism (see above, p. 11). Bed burials are rare and are associated with the upper end of the social spectrum, although they are also thought to have links with the burial of invalids.[47]

It seems likely that the cemetery at Coddenham was related to the seventh-century 'productive' site identified some 600m to the north, from which over sixty coins and a range of other material have been recovered by metal-detecting.[48] Small-scale excavations at the site have also revealed evidence for sunken-featured buildings and a rectangular timber hall.[49] It is clear from the exceptionally high number of coins found that Coddenham was an important Middle Saxon settlement, although its 'productivity' did not extend much beyond AD 700. An element of this importance seems to have survived, however, as Domesday Book records a very complex arrangement of whole and partial churches in Coddenham shared between a number of landholders, an arrangement which indicates that Coddenham was host to an important minster church.[50]

At both Thornham and Coddenham it is clear that the 'Final Phase' lasted for only around a century. The observation arising from this — that 'Final Phase' cemeteries were relatively short-lived — is supported by important work at the 'Final Phase' Ipswich Buttermarket cemetery. Excavations here revealed that the cemetery was established on heathland at the edge of the proto-town probably early in the seventh century and apparently fell out of use in the latter years of that

[46] Penn, *Anglo-Saxon Cemetery at Shrubland Hall Quarry*.
[47] Hines, *Anglo-Saxon Cemetery at Edix Hill*, pp. 261–8; Penn, *Anglo-Saxon Cemetery at Shrubland Hall Quarry*.
[48] Newman, 'Exceptional Finds', pp. 103–6.
[49] Faulkner, *Hidden Treasure*, pp. 119–25.
[50] Newman, 'Exceptional Finds', pp. 103–6; Pestell, 'The Afterlife of "Productive" Sites', pp. 132–3; Blair, *The Church in Anglo-Saxon Society*, p. 399.

century, as the growing town expanded across the site. Traces of seventy-one burials were revealed, many of them heavily disturbed, of which approximately half were furnished with typically 'Final Phase' burial assemblages. Unlike many of the cemeteries discussed here, the interpretation of the Buttermarket cemetery benefits from the fact that a number of the inhumations have been subjected to a programme of high-precision radiocarbon dating, which when combined with more conventional artefactual dating and the *termini post quos* provided by a number of interred coins has clearly demonstrated how short-lived such 'Final Phase' cemeteries actually were.[51]

Further indications of the complex relationships between traditional Early Saxon cemeteries and their 'Final Phase' successors are provided by the archaeological evidence recovered from the Roman town of *Venta Icenorum* and its environs (Plate 4). As was discussed in Chapter 3, the Roman town fell out of use in the early fifth century, but the fact that the hillsides overlooking the town were host to a pair of Early Saxon cemeteries suggests that some kind of Early Saxon occupation continued in the vicinity (see pp. 64–7). On the hillside to the east lay a mixed-rite cemetery containing several hundred cremations and sixty inhumations, while on a hill to the north-west of the town lay a smaller cemetery containing over a hundred cremations.[52] Both cemeteries fell out of use in the early seventh century, in accordance with the now-familiar patterns, yet it is clear that this was not caused by the final abandonment of the town, as new, successor cemeteries were founded in their place.

The Harford Farm 'Final Phase' cemetery was sited on a spur of land overlooking *Venta Icenorum*, some 600m to the north-west of the town itself (Fig. 24). Doubtless this view was a factor in the choice of its location, as was the cluster of Bronze Age barrows around which groups of Anglo-Saxon inhumations were buried during the seventh and early eighth centuries. Two clusters of burials totalling forty-six inhumations were excavated at the site, all of them orientated west–east and the majority unfurnished or accompanied only by a buckle and a knife (Fig. 25). Four of the graves were lavishly furnished with typical 'Final Phase' burial assemblages, including Grave 11, which included a garnet-inlaid brooch (Fig. 22), and Grave 18, which included two *sceattas* bearing cross motifs and a cylindrical threadbox.[53]

It would seem that those inhumed at Harford Farm represent part of a Christian community that was focused on the Roman town, but these burials cannot represent the entire population and we must conclude that Harford Farm was not the only cemetery in the area. As was discussed in Chapter 3, the walled Roman town is likely to have been occupied by Christian missionaries during the seventh century and the present parish church's location within the Roman street-grid suggests that it was founded as a part of the missionary process. It seems highly likely that any Christian focus within the town would have had a concomitant cemetery of Burgh Castle/Caister-on-Sea type (traces of which were perhaps glimpsed in the 2009

[51] Scull, *Early Medieval Cemeteries*, pp. 256–70.
[52] Myres and Green, *Anglo-Saxon Cemeteries*, pp. 1–11, 209–10 and 234–9.
[53] Penn, *Excavations on the Norwich Southern Bypass*, pp. 1–4 and 96–101.

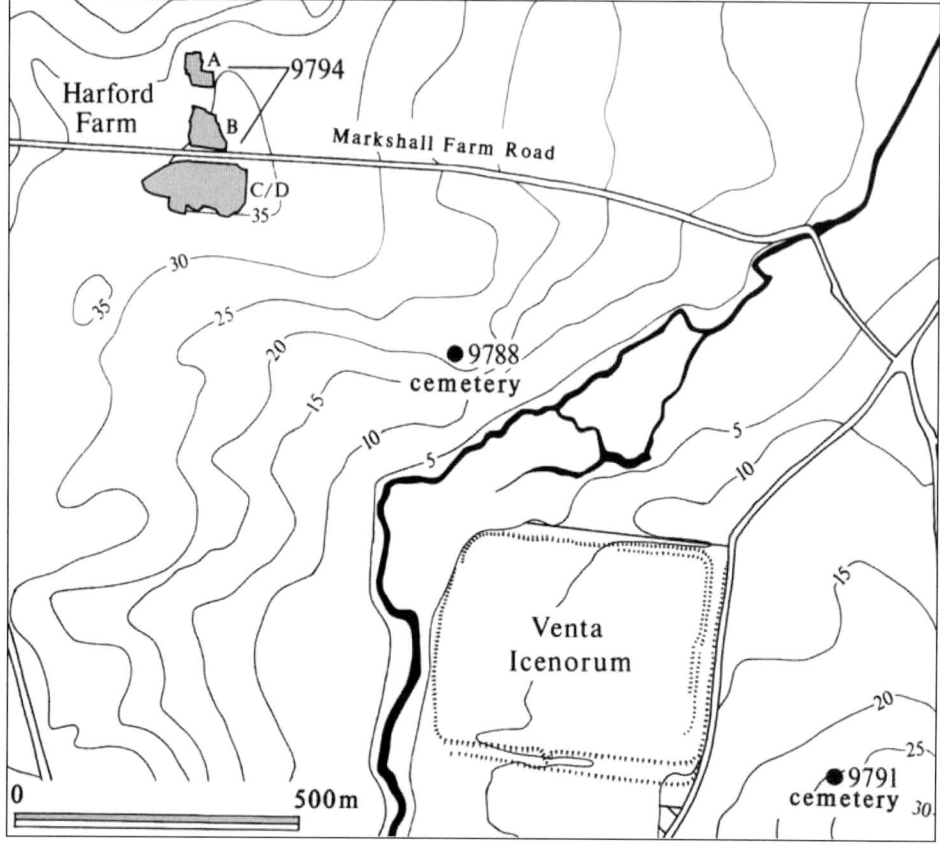

Fig. 24: Map showing the topographic relationship between the Harford Farm cemetery and the Roman town of *Venta Icenorum* (after Penn, *Harford Farm*, fig. 79, © *NMAS*).

archaeological evaluation in the churchyard)[54] which would presumably have accommodated that proportion of the population not buried in the 'Final Phase' cemetery at Harford Farm. It seems that both cemeteries were used simultaneously, but that the 'Final Phase' cemetery at Harford Farm was abandoned in the late seventh or early eighth century, while the churchyard inside the town continued to thrive and remains the local cemetery to this day.

One possible exception to the pattern of 'Final Phase' cemeteries having been founded in locations which had not previously served as cemeteries is the 'Final Phase' burial in Grave 93 at Boss Hall, Ipswich.[55] This burial is unusual in that it is a demonstrably late-seventh- or even early-eighth-century 'Final Phase' inhumation, furnished with a rich array of grave-goods, yet it was made on the site of a typical Early Saxon cemetery as much as a century after the cemetery had apparently fallen out of use. One possible explanation for this apparent anomaly is that further 'Final Phase' burials may lie outside the excavated area, thus leaving us with an unrepresentative picture of the isolated burial, while other possible interpretations

---

[54] Percival, 'Archaeological Evaluation at Caistor St Edmund'.
[55] Scull, *Early Medieval Cemeteries*, pp. 16–18.

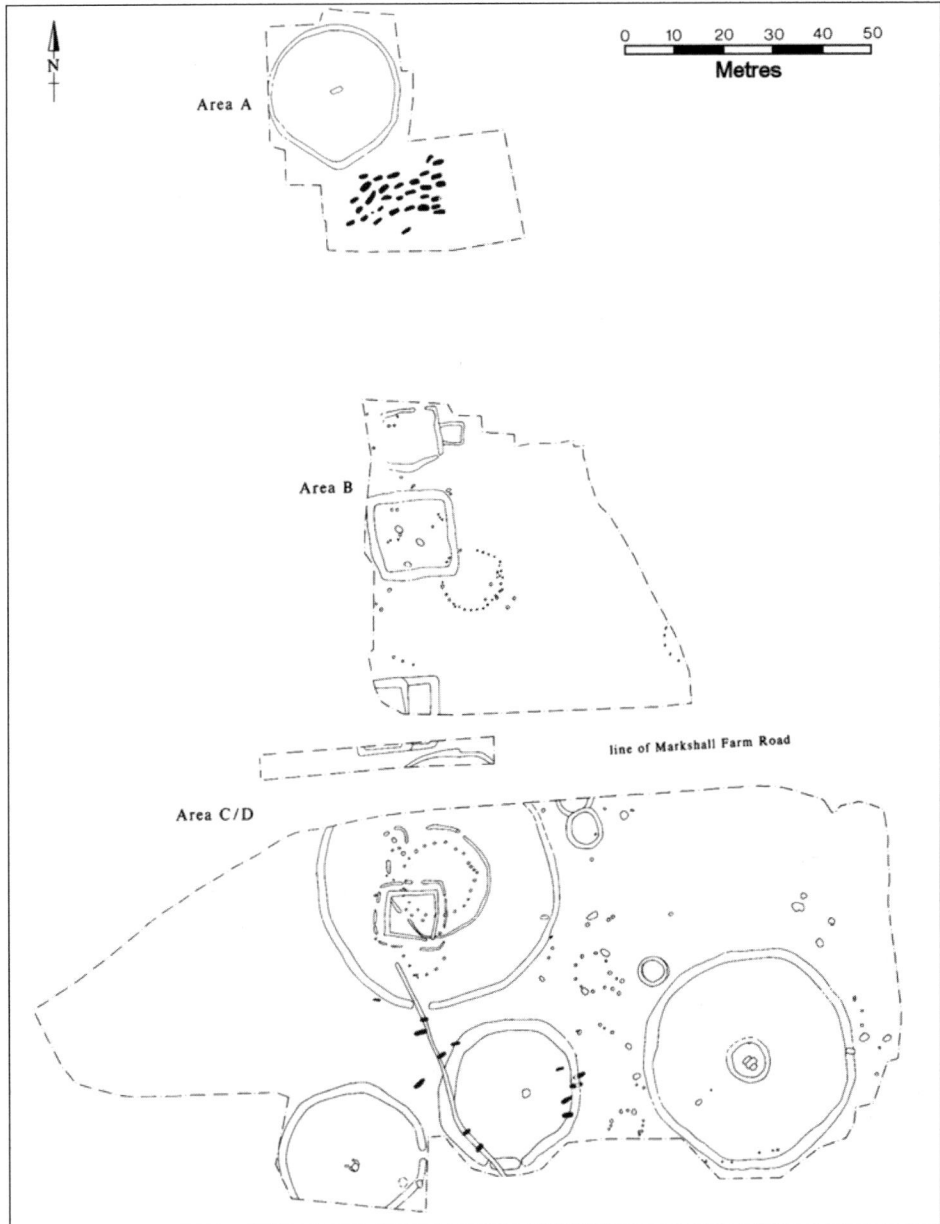

Fig. 25: Plan of the 'Final Phase' cemetery at Harford Farm, showing the two clusters of burials (after Penn, *Harford Farm*, fig. 3, © NMAS).

might include the inhumed individual's having had ancestral links with the cemetery or even the use of the burial — argued above to display strong Christian iconography (p. 109) — to sanctify the site of the earlier cemetery.[56]

---

[56] *Ibid.*, p. 127; Crawford, 'Votive Deposition', p. 95.

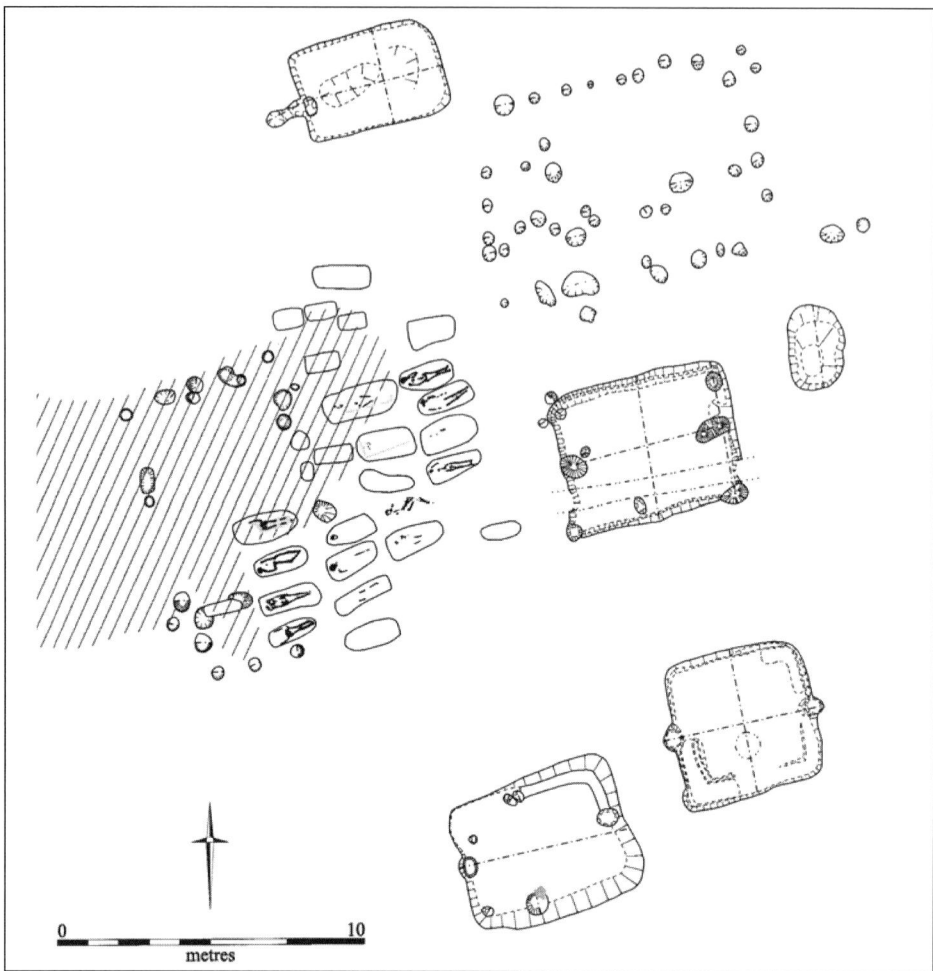

Fig. 26: Plan of the excavated cemetery and surrounding buildings at Carlton Colville (after Lucy *et al.*, *The Anglo-Saxon Settlement*, fig. 6.26, © CAU).

The landscape setting of the 'Final Phase' cemetery at Carlton Colville (Suffolk) is similarly unusual, for, unlike the other sites considered here, it lay at the heart of an Early to Middle Saxon settlement comprising a mixture of post-built and sunken-featured buildings spanning the sixth to late seventh or early eighth centuries. Stratigraphically, the cemetery is late in the occupation sequence and post-dated an earthfast rectangular timber building, although the burials were in turn overlain by a dark layer of occupation debris, suggesting that the settlement continued to be occupied, at least for a short period, beyond the lifespan of the cemetery. Therefore, at Carlton Colville we are presented with an Anglo-Saxon settlement which straddled the conversion period and from which we are able to infer a great deal about the material changes brought about by the conversion.

High-precision radiocarbon dating was also applied to the 'Final Phase' inhumations excavated at Carlton Colville, producing an equally short-lived

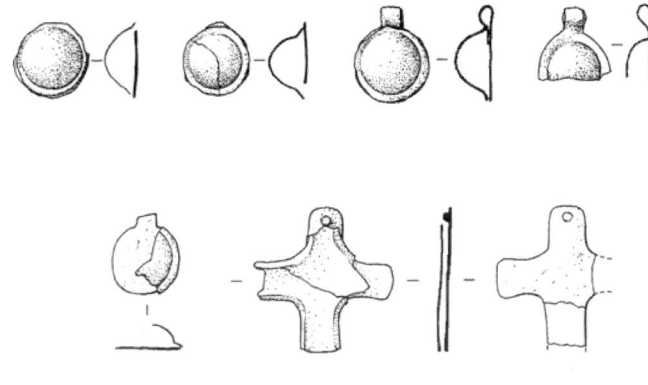

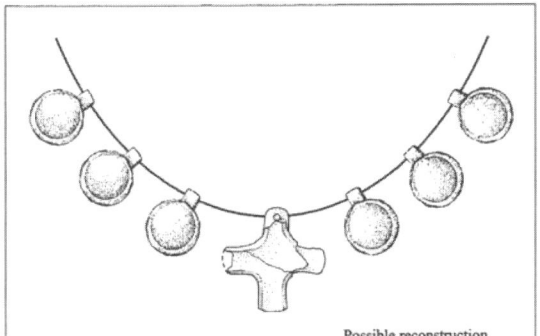

Fig. 27: The silver necklace from Grave 11, Carlton Colville (after Lucy *et al.*, *The Anglo-Saxon Settlement*, fig. 7.10, © CAU).

Possible reconstruction

seventh-century date-range for the burials. Twenty-nine west–east inhumations of both sexes and different ages were excavated at the site, ten of which were furnished with 'Final Phase' grave-goods (Fig. 26). Three of these burials were very richly furnished, including Grave 23, which contained a silver-gilt disc brooch with a red-garnet cross, and Grave 11, which contained a delicate necklace of hemispherical silver pendants flanking a silver-sheet cross (Fig. 27); the remainder of the furnished burials had very simple grave-goods, such as buckles and knives.[57] The cross is a particularly overt Christian artefact and the excavators consider it to be 'overwhelmingly likely' that the cemetery represents a Christian community.[58]

The relationship between Early Saxon settlements and cemeteries was discussed above, where it was observed that the two remained separate, although sometimes closely adjacent, landscape elements (pp. 119–21). This was apparently also the case during the majority of the Early Saxon period at Carlton Colville, as metal-detecting has revealed the presence of a furnished inhumation cemetery located several hundred metres to the south-west of the settlement.[59] It would seem that during the early decades of the seventh century this furnished inhumation cemetery fell out of

---

[57] Lucy *et al.*, *Anglo-Saxon Settlement and Cemetery*, pp. 385–416.
[58] *Ibid.*, pp. 419–20; cf. Lucy *et al.*, 'The Burial of a Princess?', pp. 120–22.
[59] Lucy *et al.*, *Anglo-Saxon Settlement and Cemetery*, pp. 7–12.

use and was superseded by the 'Final Phase' cemetery established within the settlement, which the artefactual evidence suggests was a Christian burial ground and which high-precision radiocarbon dating suggests was in use for perhaps as few as twenty years in the mid-seventh century.[60]

As we have seen, the landscape settings of most of the East Anglian 'Final Phase' cemeteries demonstrate that the Early Saxon separation of settlement and cemeteries continued to be practised, albeit with 'Final Phase' cemeteries being established on new sites. Clearly this was not the case at Carlton Colville, although there is evidence to suggest that some form of more conventionally placed 'Final Phase' burials may also have been associated with the settlement. In their analysis the excavators comment on the apparent lack of high-status male burials in the Carlton Colville assemblage and suggest that this element of the male population was buried in the vicinity of a high-status seventh-century barrow burial which eighteenth-century excavations suggest stood on the summit of Bloodmoor Hill, some 300m to the south of the settlement.[61] Further discussion here of the landscape setting of the Carlton Colville cemetery is held over until the next section, where the practice of integrating cemeteries into settlements is argued to be a characteristic of Christian burial practice and, therefore, a material indictor of conversion. Suffice it to say at this point that at Carlton Colville we are seeing a hybridised combination of 'Final Phase' Christian burial rites being employed in a landscape context more usually associated with unfurnished churchyard-type cemeteries.

✻

All the funerary evidence discussed thus far indicates that a widespread and near-contemporaneous abandonment of all kinds of Early Saxon cemetery occurred during the first half of the seventh century. The archaeological record suggests that this abandonment was coincident with the cessation of the cremation burial rite and occurred immediately before the adoption of the 'Final Phase' Romano-Byzantine grave-goods discussed above. In the previous chapter both the end of cremation and the beginning of the use of 'Final Phase' grave-goods were argued to be strong material indicators of conversion to Christianity and it follows, by extension, that the abandonment of the Early Saxon cemeteries and foundation of 'Final Phase' cemeteries can also be argued to be symptomatic of conversion having occurred. While the vast majority of 'Final Phase' cemeteries were apparently founded on virgin sites, there is growing evidence to suggest that there are much finer subtleties than hitherto appreciated to the traditional models of cemetery foundation, not least regarding the integration of burials and cemeteries into existing settlements. It is to this subject which we now turn.

Middle Saxon cemeteries in the landscape

Rather than following a simple linear course of development, it would appear that multiple Early Saxon cemeteries were superseded by a variety of Middle Saxon

[60] *Ibid.*, pp. 414–16.
[61] *Ibid.*, pp. 7–12 and 424; Newman, 'New Light on Old Finds'.

Christian cemeteries. As we have seen, in the minority of cases burials — some furnished with Romano-Byzantine style grave-goods — began to be made in 'Final Phase' cemeteries, the majority of which were located away from settlements, but these cemeteries account for only a small proportion of the population. A further proportion can be accounted for by the cemeteries at the missionary stations discussed in Chapter 3, all of which featured intramural inhumation cemeteries founded during the seventh century and, in the case of Caister, an extramural cemetery as well. Tellingly, the demographic profiles of these missionary cemeteries indicate that the inhumed populations comprised men and women, young and old alike.[62] Such profiles are representative of a normal population and it would thus appear that these missionary stations became the loci of burial for the inhabitants of their hinterlands during the seventh century.

Several examples of certain and probable missionary stations have been discussed thus far, and there were doubtless many other examples of which we remain archaeologically unaware, yet these sites alone cannot have accommodated all of the East Anglian dead who were not inhumed in 'Final Phase' cemeteries. How, and where, was the rest of the Christian population Middle Saxon East Anglia disposed of? The problem of the 'missing' seventh-century inhumations is one which has vexed scholars for many years and for which a number of explanations have been offered.[63] It is possible that the dead were simply disposed of in a manner which left little archaeological trace, such as excarnation or burial at sea, but there is nothing to suggest that either of these rites was practised in East Anglia and both rites would be at odds with Christian practice. On a more pragmatic note, the inherent difficulties in recognising and dating unfurnished seventh-century burials were alluded to in the previous chapter, the situation being made worse in regions of acidic soils where bone preservation is poor, and it is possible that many seventh-century burials have simply not survived or have gone unrecognised in the archaeological record. One example of just this kind of misidentification is the case of the 'Hunstanton Woman', an isolated skeleton which was thought to be prehistoric until radiocarbon dating revealed it to be Middle Saxon.[64]

While such possibilities remain valid, the archaeological record affords us a tantalising glimpse of a third class of seventh-century cemetery which may hold the key to the mystery of the missing Middle Saxons. Such sites are often referred to as 'churchyard-type' cemeteries or 'folk' cemeteries, and contain small numbers of west–east inhumations, the majority of which are unfurnished, although occasionally very simple grave-goods, such as knives or buckles, are present. Crucially, rather than being separate landscape elements, these cemeteries are thoroughly integrated into contemporary settlements. In their style these cemeteries resemble those associated with later churches, hence their name, but the original circumstances of their foundation are hard to ascertain archaeologically. Some may have been associated with churches from the outset, placing them into the same category as the unknown missionary churches discussed above, but there is growing

---

[62] Anderson and Birkett, 'Human Skeletal Remains'; Anderson, 'Human Skeletal Remains'.
[63] e.g. Geake, 'Persistent Problems', pp. 144–8; Meaney, 'Anglo-Saxon Pagan and Christian Attitudes', pp. 240–41; Blair, *The Church in Anglo-Saxon Society*, pp. 240–45.
[64] Hoare and Sweet, 'A Grave Error'.

evidence that many were founded without an attendant church, the cemetery itself effectively forming the early Christian focus for a settlement.[65]

Unfortunately our understanding of these churchyard-type cemeteries is marred by two linked factors, both of which are explored more fully below. First, the physical integration of these cemeteries into thriving settlements, indicative of substantial upheaval in the Middle Saxon landscape, makes such sites difficult to study archaeologically; and, secondly, the fact that many of these sites acquired attendant churches later in their histories makes it difficult to separate cemeteries and churches founded during the conversion period from foundations of later periods. The problem was neatly summarised by Audrey Meaney, who stated: 'one of the major problems in identifying the earliest of the English churchyard burials is that they are at the bottom of the sequence in a confined space that was used over and over again'.[66]

Settlements and cemeteries

One characteristic which unites all the excavated examples of Middle Saxon cemeteries, including missionary cemeteries and churchyard-type cemeteries, is the fact they were all firmly integrated into Middle Saxon settlements of some kind. This fusion of settlement and cemetery indicates that the separation of the two landscape elements which characterised the Early Saxon period had been superseded by an attitude which saw the dead being placed in the heart of the community, but from where did the impetus for this change of attitude come?

It has been recognised for a long time that a great restructuring of the East Anglian landscape occurred during the Middle Saxon period, not least the major dislocation of settlements, sometimes referred to as the 'Middle Saxon shuffle'.[67] The large quantities of archaeological data gathered in the region, particularly as a result of fieldwalking and metal-detecting, indicate that during the Middle Saxon period numerous transitory Early Saxon settlements coalesced into more permanent nucleated settlements, the locations of which are often indicated by the presence of Ipswich ware. A number of explanations for these changes have been suggested, primarily of an economic, social or environmental nature, and many commentators have attributed the fusion of cemeteries and settlements to these same factors.[68] However, it would seem that that the convergence of cemeteries and settlements was the result of independent factors and not just another characteristic of the Middle Saxon reorganisation of the landscape, because excavated examples of integrated cemeteries within settlements are known from both before and after the period of the 'Middle Saxon shuffle'.

The seventh-century 'Final Phase' cemetery excavated within the Early Saxon settlement at Carlton Colville (Suffolk) was discussed in the previous section, where

---

[65] Blair, *The Church in Anglo-Saxon Society*, pp. 228–45. [66] Meaney, 'Anglo-Saxon Pagan and Christian Attitudes', p. 240.

[67] Arnold and Wardle, 'Early Medieval Settlement Patterns'; Welch, 'Rural Settlement Patterns'; Hodges, *The Anglo-Saxon Achievement*, pp. 43–68; Moreland, 'Significance of Production'; Hamerow, 'Settlement Mobility' and *Early Medieval Settlements*, pp. 120–23.

[68] Andrews, 'Middle Saxon Norfolk'; Rogerson, 'Rural Settlement'; Hamerow, *Early Medieval Settlements*, p. 123; Williamson, *Shaping Medieval Landscapes*; Rippon, *Beyond the Medieval Village*, pp. 186–9.

the direct association of furnished 'Final Phase' burials and settlement was identified as being anomalous.[69] However, it is only the character of the burials which is anomalous in this context, for, as will become clearer, the deliberate integration of a seventh-century cemetery into a contemporary settlement is perfectly normal practice for this period. The excavated evidence suggests that the cemetery at Carlton Colville effectively became the focus of the later phases of the settlement, with timber buildings having been constructed around it. We are particularly fortunate in that the overtly Christian nature of some of the grave-goods allows us to unequivocally identify the cemetery as being Christian. Indeed, given the timescale for the East Anglian conversion established in Chapter 2, which attributes the first major wave of conversion proper to the reign of Sigeberht in the AD 630s, the cemetery at Carlton Colville must have been founded by one of the first generations of converts; the fact that Burgh Castle only lies some 10km to the north of the site may have been an influential factor in this.

The cemetery at Carlton Colville appears to have fallen out of use in the late seventh century, while the settlement itself appears to have continued in occupation into the early years of the eighth century, during which time a layer of detritus spread across the cemetery. The excavators have speculated that the cemetery and ultimately the settlement may have been abandoned in favour of burial and settlement around the site of Carlton Colville church, which may have been founded at around this date and is situated approximately a kilometre to the west of the site.[70]

Another example of burials made within an Early Saxon settlement was discovered at West Stow, although this was on a smaller scale than the cemetery at Carlton Colville and the burials are often overlooked in discussions of the site. The spatial relationships between the Early Saxon settlement, its adjacent cemetery and other cemeteries in the Lark valley were discussed above (pp. 119–20). The occupation of the site did not end there, however; large quantities of Ipswich ware and metalwork recovered from across the site demonstrate that settlement continued there well into the seventh century. The stratigraphic sequence demonstrates that in its last phases West Stow comprised only one hall and associated buildings, suggesting the presence of a single extended family, and it is therefore particularly significant that two west–east, unfurnished inhumations should have been discovered in the centre of the settlement.[71]

Helena Hamerow, one of the few scholars to have attempted a systematic study of human and animal burials within Early Saxon settlements, has interpreted the presence of these burials within the wider ideological sphere of 'Special Deposits'.[72] This is a term borrowed from prehistorians and in an Anglo-Saxon context is applied to deposits which display highly ritualised elements, often comprising whole or partial human or animal burials which have been deliberately and carefully placed into cut features. While in a general sense all burials might therefore be considered to be 'Special Deposits', comparisons with Carlton Colville and other seventh-century sites suggest that the two inhumations at West Stow should perhaps

---

[69] Lucy *et al.*, *Anglo-Saxon Settlement and Cemetery*, pp. 419–26.
[70] *Ibid.*, pp. 427–9.
[71] West, *West Stow*, pp. 58–9 and fig. 236, and *West Stow Revisited*.
[72] Hamerow, '"Special Deposits"', pp. 3–16.

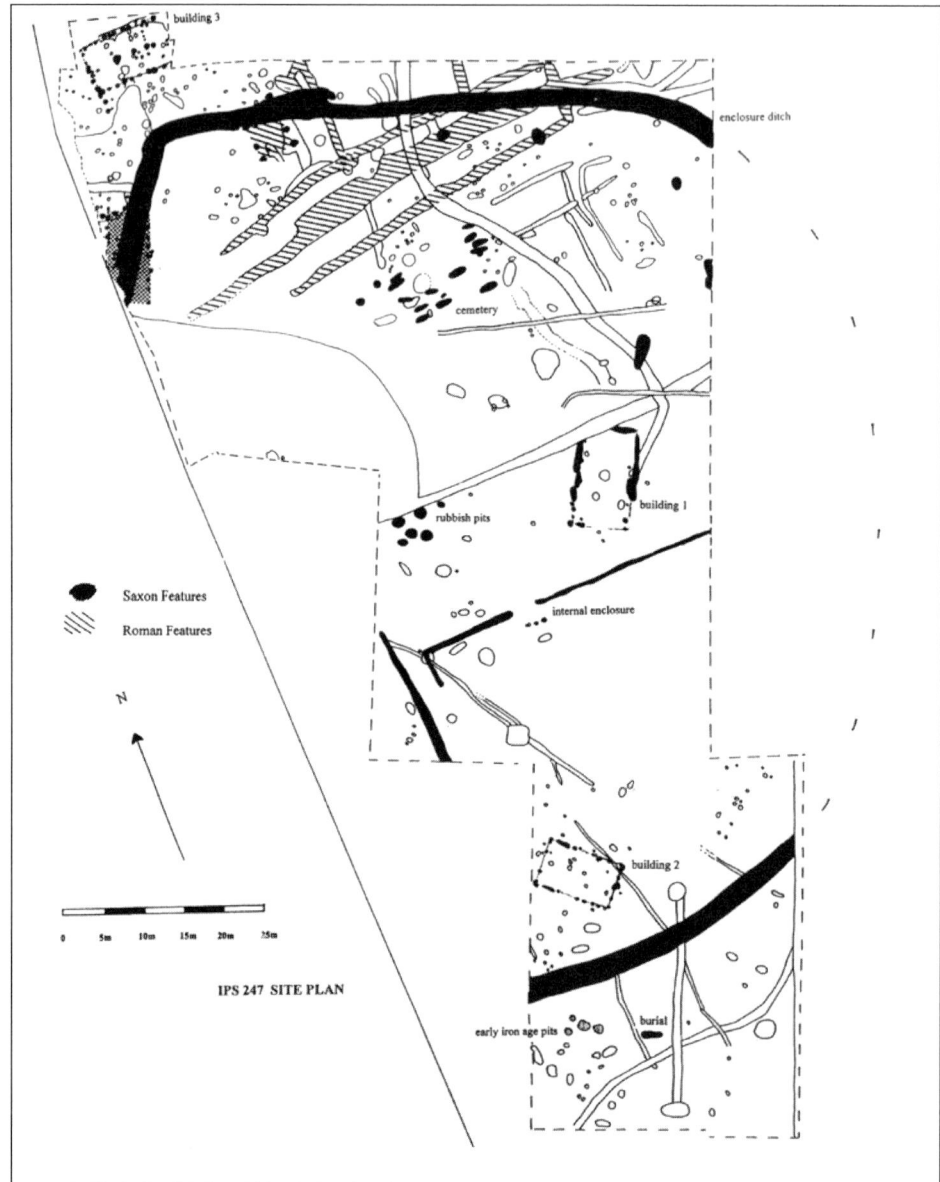

Fig. 28: Plan of the excavated features at the Whitehouse Industrial Estate, highlighting the Middle Saxon settlement features and cemetery. *Reproduced by kind permission of SCCAS.*

be interpreted more readily as early Christian burials made within the settlement during its latter phases of occupation. This would seem to suggest that the ideological change which saw the dead beginning to be interred within the defined area of a settlement had already begun to take hold before the settlement was finally abandoned, the small number of inhumations reflecting how short the period between the two events might have been. Carlton Colville and West Stow are both extensively excavated and analysed sites, and we should not be surprised if other

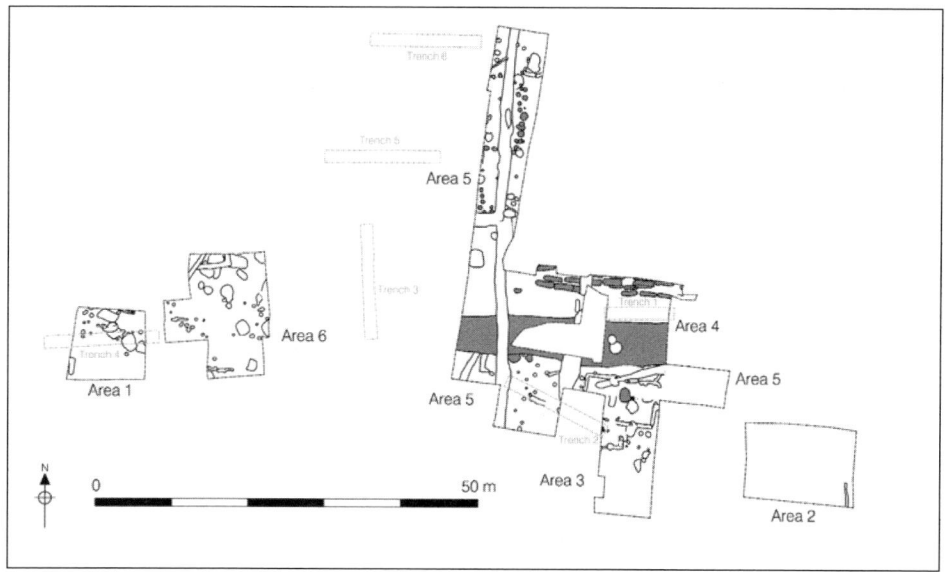

Fig. 29: Plan of the excavated features at Whissonsett, highlighting the Middle Saxon settlement features and cemetery. © *NAU Archaeology*

examples of seventh-century inhumations within long-established Early to Middle Saxon settlements come to light as further sites are excavated.

Another example of a cemetery integrated into a settlement, this time one of 'post-shuffle' Middle Saxon origins, was excavated at the Whitehouse Industrial Estate on the outskirts of Ipswich in the mid-1990s. Here the remains of a small Middle Saxon settlement measuring approximately 80m by 100m and situated within an enclosing ditch were revealed (Fig. 28).[73] The enclosure was divided by an internal ditch, the southern and northern halves each containing a rectangular timber building, although the northern half also contained a small inhumation cemetery of nineteen graves containing the remains of twenty-two adults and children. The burials were unfurnished, orientated west–east and were radiocarbon-dated to the Middle Saxon period. The layout of the graves suggests that there was a boundary to the cemetery, although no material trace of it survived. This small site appears to have thrived during the Middle Saxon period, but the enclosure ditch had evidently silted up by the Late Saxon period, when a post-hole building was erected over it, and the site appears to have fallen out of use shortly afterwards.

An archaeological evaluation conducted within the central Norfolk village of Whissonsett in 2004 revealed traces of a Middle Saxon settlement and cemetery located some 60m to the north-east of the parish church.[74] Subsequent excavation on the site revealed nineteen unfurnished west–east inhumations which marked the southern extent of a small inhumation cemetery now sealed beneath surrounding residential development (Fig. 29). The footings of two post-hole buildings lying to the north of the burials were also revealed, and both the settlement and cemetery

[73] Caruth, 'Ipswich, Hewlett Packard plc' and pers. comm.
[74] Mellor, 'Archaeological Evaluation'.

were contained within a large double-ditched enclosure, which was observed running east–west across the excavated area and seen to extend northwards.[75] Evaluations conducted to the north of the site in 2005 demonstrated that the Middle Saxon settlement did indeed extend in that direction.[76] The excavated areas clearly continued to be occupied into the Late Saxon period, although this occupation was of a sufficiently different character to suggest that by this period the focus of the settlement had already drifted southwards to the site of the parish church. This would seem to be confirmed by the discovery of the head of a Late Saxon interlace-decorated stone cross made in the churchyard in 1900.[77] The results from the various excavations at Whissonsett are currently being prepared for publication, but it is clear from the preliminary analyses that the site belongs to the category of integrated Middle Saxon settlements and cemeteries considered here.

A similar example of an integrated cemetery, albeit on a much larger scale, was discovered at Sedgeford in north-west Norfolk in the 1950s and became the focus of ongoing excavations in the late 1990s.[78] Here a slight westward shift in the location of the Late Saxon settlement has facilitated the large-scale excavation of the Middle Saxon phases of the settlement, including an inhumation cemetery of more than 200 unfurnished west–east burials arrayed on a hillside. Some of these burials were in coffins, but the majority appear to have been buried in shrouds, and the sometimes dense intercutting of burials and repacking of charnel around new burials indicate that the cemetery was used intensively for a substantial period of time (Plate 11). The footings of several timber buildings have been excavated in the vicinity of the cemetery, but none appears to have been an attendant church, suggesting that the cemetery itself was the Christian focus of the settlement. During the Late Saxon period the landscape setting of the cemetery was drastically altered by the damming of the adjacent river to create a *vivarium* and mill pond. The cemetery was closed at this point and the settlement was relocated to the opposite side of the river, some 150m to the west, where the present parish church and its churchyard became the focus of the medieval manorial centre.[79]

Other examples of Middle and Late Saxon churchyard-type cemeteries of varying sizes integrated into settlements have been excavated in East Anglia, such as at Wimbotsham (Norfolk), and also elsewhere in Anglo-Saxon England, including Yarnton (Oxfordshire) and Flixborough (Lincolnshire).[80] Further afield, Zadora-Rio has recently highlighted the increasing number of European excavations revealing small groups of burials within the confines of early medieval settlements, an occurrence which is widely represented in France, where there are few excavated settlements that do not contain such clusters of burials, as well as in Germany and the Netherlands.[81] Significantly, in many of these domestic and Continental

---

[75] Trimble and Hoggett, 'Archaeological Excavation at Church Close, Whissonsett'.
[76] *Ibid.*
[77] Collingwood, 'The Whissonsett Cross'.
[78] Cabot *et al.*, 'Sedgeford'.
[79] Hoggett, 'Origin and Early Development'.
[80] Watkins, 'Archaeological Strip, Map and Sample Excavation at Wimbotsham'; Reynolds, *Later Anglo-Saxon England*, p. 144; Hey, *Yarnton*, pp. 75–6, 163–5 and 320–21; Loveluck and Atkinson, *Flixborough*, pp. 113–24.
[81] Zadora-Rio, 'The Making of Churchyards', pp. 2–7.

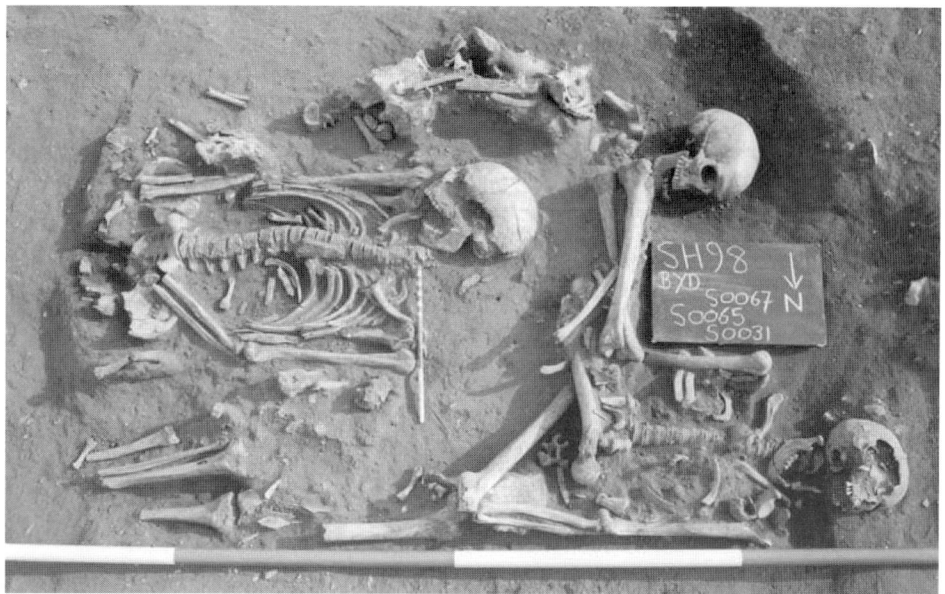

Plate 11: Intercutting inhumations S0067, S0065 and S0031 at Sedgeford. Note the repacking of the charnel around the central burial. © *SHARP*

examples it appears that the burial clusters were integrated into settlements without being linked to the construction of a church, although in many cases a church was later added to the cemetery. Zadora-Rio concludes that this choice of burial location 'does not in itself allow the evaluation of the level of Christianization among the population',[82] but, as has been demonstrated in the examples discussed thus far, the absence of a church does not mean that such an integration was not religiously motivated.[83] It has been argued here that the foundation of missionary stations and the establishment of several new classes of cemetery were intimately bound up with the abandonment of the old cemeteries and this abandonment has, by extension, also been argued to have been a direct result of the conversion to Christianity. It therefore follows that the coming together of cemeteries and settlements should be attributed to the same process of Christianisation.

The accommodation of the dead within the settlements of the living is a recognised characteristic of Christian practice throughout medieval Europe and is most commonly seen in the conjunction of a church and churchyard at the heart of a settlement. As we have seen, this is also evidenced in the archaeological record by the incorporation of overtly Christian inhumation cemeteries into Early and Middle Saxon settlements.[84] An explanation for this coming together of cemetery and settlement may be found in two main tenets of Christian belief about death and the afterlife: first, that the buried dead were awaiting resurrection on the Day of

---

[82] *Ibid.*, p. 18.
[83] cf. Butler, 'The Churchyard in Eastern England', pp. 383–5.
[84] e.g. Boddington, 'Models of Burial'; Thompson, *Dying and Death*, pp. 26–56; Daniell, *Death and Burial*, pp. 87–115; Blair, *The Church in Anglo-Saxon Society*, pp. 228–45.

Judgement, when their corpse and soul would be reunited; and, second, that the conduct of an individual in life governed the fate of an individual's soul after death.[85] We have already seen how the belief in preserving the integrity of the corpse might have played a role in the cession of cremation as a burial practice (see pp. 92–4); with the second tenet came the belief that the living could improve the prospects of the departed by ensuring that the dead received appropriate funerary treatment and intercessory prayers.[86] Arguably the integration of Christian dead into settlements was a physical reflection of the fact that under Christianity the dead remained an important part of the community and formed a focus of its worship.[87]

Within the confines of a settlement the areas given over to Christian cemeteries were clearly bounded spaces (evidenced by the dense intercutting of burials) where the dead safely awaited their resurrection, being at once both a part of the secular world and yet separated from it.[88] The earliest surviving Anglo-Saxon liturgical evidence for the consecration of Christian cemeteries, dating from the tenth century, describes how a cemetery could only be consecrated by a bishop in a ceremony involving the ritual demarcation and purification of the area to be used for burial, transforming it into a sacred space.[89] This date is relatively late to be directly applicable to the material evidence considered here, but Helen Gittos has argued convincingly that the homogeneity of the surviving sources suggests that they enshrined much older customs, included the exclusion of burials of the unbaptised, criminals and suicides from consecrated ground, and that these customs may have emerged in the late seventh century.[90] This conclusion would certainly seem to be supported by the East Anglian archaeological record, for, as we have seen, we are afforded tantalising material glimpses which suggest that nascent forms of some of these later practices might well have seventh-century origins. In this regard, the burial locations chosen for those who were excluded from such cemeteries are also of particular relevance.

Execution cemeteries

The landscape settings chosen for Middle and Late Saxon execution cemeteries emphasise the changing attitude towards what were considered to be appropriate locations for the dead in newly Christianised societies. So-called 'deviant' burials, characterised by the burial of individuals prone or exhibiting evidence for beheading, were prevalent throughout the Anglo-Saxon period and are interpreted as the burials of miscreants or outcasts to whom justice had been meted out, their shame being expressed and reinforced in the burial tableau.[91] Unlike some of the

---

[85] Hadley, *Death in Medieval England*, pp. 58–62; Dunn, *Christianization*, pp. 12–14 and 25.

[86] Ariès, *Hour of Our Death*, pp. 29–40; Geary, *Living with the Dead*, pp. 77–87; Binski, *Medieval Death*, pp. 24–7; Dunn, *Christianization*, pp. 21–4 and 168–86.

[87] Bullough, 'Burial, Community and Belief'; Penn, 'Early Church in Norfolk'; Gittos, 'Creating the Sacred'; Thompson, *Dying and Death*, pp. 170–206.

[88] Gittos, 'Creating the Sacred', p. 195.

[89] Thompson, *Dying and Death*, pp. 35–6; Gittos, 'Creating the Sacred', pp. 195–201; Blair, *The Church in Anglo-Saxon Society*, p. 463–71.

[90] Gittos, 'Creating the Sacred', pp. 195–201; Foot, *Monastic Life*, p. 313, n. 144.

[91] Hawkes and Wells, 'Crime and Punishment'; Reynolds, 'Rape of the Anglo-Saxon Women'; Hirst, 'Death and the Archaeologist'; Wilson, *Anglo-Saxon Paganism*, pp. 77–86 and 92–5; Reynolds, 'Definition and Ideology' and *Anglo-Saxon Deviant Burial Customs*, pp. 34–60.

burial rites discussed in the previous chapter, 'deviant' burials are found in both pre- and post-conversion contexts, suggesting that traditional practices continued, but the conversion period saw dramatic changes in the landscape settings chosen for such burials and the emergence of another new class of cemetery in the archaeological record, the execution cemetery.[92]

Many Early Saxon 'deviant' burials have been found within the same cemeteries as the more 'normal' burials discussed in the previous chapter, and it would seem that during the Early Saxon period the corpses of the deviant dead were accepted into the existing communal cemeteries, albeit with the employment of unusual burial practices.[93] East Anglian examples of Early Saxon deviant burials include the prone male burial in Grave 32 at Westgarth Gardens (Suffolk), the left hand of which had apparently been cut off before death, an action interpreted as a punishment.[94] Other prone burials have been excavated at Snape, Swaffham and Caistor St Edmund; at the last of these a decapitated burial was also found.[95] However, from the conversion period onwards such 'deviant' burials rarely appear in the communal Christian churchyard-type cemeteries discussed above; instead, they are discovered in isolated groups or in dedicated execution cemeteries.[96]

Reynolds has defined a series of characteristics by which Anglo-Saxon execution cemeteries might be recognised archaeologically: execution burials are often very shallow and randomly orientated, with little regard apparently shown for the treatment of the corpse; evidence for trauma, such as beheading or a broken neck, and for tied hands or feet are also common features of such burials. On a broader scale, the landscape settings of such cemeteries are also distinctive, with the majority of execution cemeteries being associated with ancient earthworks, particularly Bronze Age barrows, and lying in locations intervisible with major communication routes, where they presumably served as a warning to passers-by. Very often execution cemeteries were located on principal boundaries, especially hundredal boundaries, the physical liminality of such locations reflecting the social casting-out of the executed dead.[97]

East Anglian examples of execution cemeteries are known from the later phases of Sutton Hoo and also from South Acre (Norfolk). Two groups of execution burials were excavated at Sutton Hoo. The first cluster was grouped around one of the early-seventh-century barrows, Mound 5, and comprised sixteen burials, including three or possibly four prone burials and five decapitated individuals; one burial contained traces of a rope, thought to be the remains of a noose, around the neck. The second cluster of executions lay on the eastern edge of the cemetery and comprised twenty-three burials arrayed in two arcs around a group of post-holes interpreted as the site of a gallows. Four of these burials were prone, with signs of their hands having been tied; two individuals had been

---

[92] Reynolds, 'Definition and Ideology' and *Anglo-Saxon Deviant Burial Customs*, pp. 94–7.

[93] Reynolds, *Anglo-Saxon Deviant Burial Customs*, pp. 181–3 and 201–3.

[94] West, *Westgarth Gardens*, p. 28.

[95] Filmer-Sankey and Pestell, *Snape*, p. 94; Hills and Wade-Martins, 'The Anglo-Saxon Cemetery', p. 7; Myres and Green, *Anglo-Saxon Cemeteries*, pp. 226 and 230.

[96] Reynolds, *Anglo-Saxon Deviant Burial Customs*, pp. 97–151.

[97] Reynolds, 'Definition and Ideology', p. 37; *Later Anglo-Saxon England*, pp. 105–10; and *Anglo-Saxon Deviant Burial Customs*, pp. 151–79.

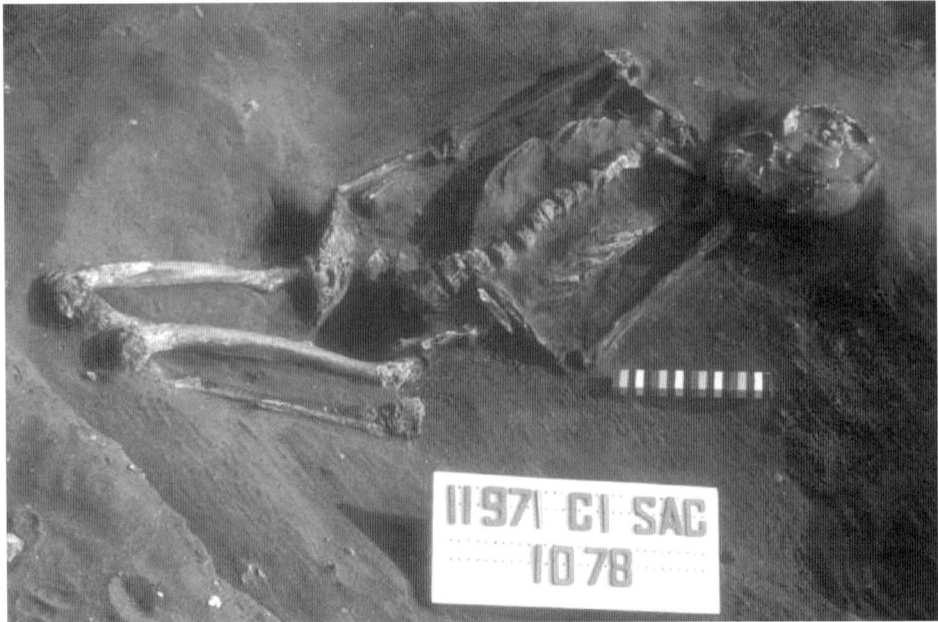

Plate 12: Execution burial SK1078 at South Acre. Note the legs bent under the body and the suggestion of tied hands. © *NMAS*

decapitated; and a third had a broken neck. Radiocarbon dating of both clusters indicated that the execution burials began in the seventh century and continued throughout the Middle and Late Saxon periods.[98]

At South Acre the excavation of a ploughed-out Bronze Age barrow revealed the shallow graves of a minimum of 119 individuals clustered primarily around the eastern side of the barrow. All the burials demonstrated a disregard to the laying out of the dead, many appearing to have been thrown unceremoniously into their graves (Plate 12); seven were prone burials. Many of the burials exhibited evidence for their hands and/or feet having been tied and at least eight individuals had been decapitated. The orientation of the graves was influenced by the presence of the ring-ditch. It is not known when the barrow was levelled, but it is assumed to have accommodated a gallows; the dense intercutting and heavy disturbance of earlier burials indicated that the cemetery was used sporadically over a long period, and radiocarbon dating returned dates for the burials which span the Anglo-Saxon period.[99]

As we have seen, the deliberate association of burials and cemeteries with Bronze Age barrows and other prehistoric earthworks was a potent, positive and symbolic statement during the Early Saxon period (pp. 118–19). It appears that during the conversion period barrows very quickly came to be regarded as unholy and liminal places with wholly negative connotations.[100] Felix's *Life of Guthlac*, a document

[98] Carver, *Sutton Hoo: Burial Ground of Kings?* pp. 137–43, and *Sutton Hoo: A Seventh-Century Princely Burial Ground*, pp. 315–59.
[99] Wymer, 'Excavation of a Ring-Ditch'.
[100] Williams, 'Ancient Landscapes' and 'Monuments and the Past'; Semple, 'Fear of the Past'.

which was probably composed in an East Anglian monastic house, tells how Guthlac chose a barrow for the site of his hermitage precisely because it was haunted by devils.[101] In later Anglo-Saxon literature barrows were written of as the abode of dragons, fiercely guarding their treasure, and were also associated with the supernatural — with goblins, elves and restless spirits. In short, in the Christian world-view barrows were places to be feared and therefore highly appropriate locations for executions and the burial of social outcasts, both as a physical symbol of their exclusion but also because the dead might be tormented further by the restless spirits which inhabited the barrows.[102]

Although the earliest surviving written law prohibiting the burial of certain classes of offender in consecrated ground dates from the first half of the tenth century, the evidence provided by the archaeological record would seem to suggest that a rudimentary form of this prohibition began in the seventh century, and presumably also extended to other classes of criminals, suicides and the unbaptised, although such individuals are much more difficult to identify materially. That social outcasts, some of whom were executed, should have been buried on the periphery of territories also reinforces the observation that the appropriate location for the revered dead during the Middle Saxon period was considered to be 'closer to home', in a cemetery that formed an integral part of a settlement.

*

Within the conversion-period funerary landscape of East Anglia were several types of Christian inhumation cemetery. First, there are the 'Final Phase' cemeteries, discussed in the previous section, which contain some burials adorned with Christian imagery; secondly, there the cemeteries established as part of the apparatus of Christian missionary stations and in which elements of the local population were buried; thirdly, there are the churchyard-type cemeteries founded, in the absence of suitable local missionary stations, within individual settlements, providing a Christian focus for the Middle Saxon community; finally, there are the execution cemeteries containing the burials of those excluded from the Christian burial practices that were increasingly becoming the norm.

The chronological gap between the end of furnished and 'Final Phase' burials and the recognised origins of churchyard burial has often been highlighted, although few commentators have offered an explanation for it or explained how the dead were disposed of during the period in question.[103] It would seem that the continued acceptance of this hiatus is largely due to the relative silence of the historical record on the subject of the early Church's attitude towards burial, yet despite this silence it is apparent from the archaeological record that even in the early years of the conversion the teachings of the church *did* have profound effects on burial practices

[101] Meaney, 'Felix's Life of St Guthlac' and 'Anglo-Saxon Pagan and Early Christian Attitudes', pp. 229–32; Roberts, *Guthlac of Crowland*, pp. 12–18.
[102] Semple, 'Fear of the Past', pp. 109–15; Reynolds, 'Definition and Ideology', p. 39.
[103] e.g. Morris, *The Church in British Archaeology*, pp. 49–62; Boddington, 'Models of Burial'; Geake, 'Persistent Problems', pp. 144–8; Gittos, 'Creating the Sacred'; Hadley, *Death in Medieval England*, pp. 17–29; Meaney, 'Anglo-Saxon Pagan and Christian Attitudes', pp. 240–41; Blair, *The Church in Anglo-Saxon Society*, pp. 240–45.

and funerary topography.[104] The previous chapter explored how the Christian belief in corporeal resurrection can be argued to have been instrumental in the cessation of cremation during the seventh century, while the effects of the adoption of Christian theology on other aspects of funerary practices, such as the changing locations of cemeteries, the relationship between the living and the dead, and the exclusion of 'deviants' from Christian cemeteries, has been examined here.

Many of the excavated examples of early Christian churchyard-type cemeteries described here are from sites where the later phases of the settlement were relocated or the settlement was abandoned, leaving the Middle Saxon phases undisturbed and free to be studied archaeologically. When this observation is considered alongside the demonstrable paucity of known seventh-century burials one is led to the inevitable conclusion that the vast majority of Christian Middle Saxon cemeteries must lie hidden beneath later settlements, and in particular beneath the later churches and churchyards which grew up around these initial Christian foci.[105] Thus not only is it difficult to bring archaeological methods to bear on the problem, but the disturbance caused during the subsequent 1,400 years would doubtless have disturbed much of this earlier material. However, there are some methodological approaches which can be employed to overcome such problems and these are explored in the final section of this chapter.

Studying church environs

Somewhat frustratingly, we are able to excavate and thus understand the origins of missionary stations and churchyard-type cemeteries only where the cemetery and possible attendant church eventually faltered or were relocated. The Roman forts at Burgh Castle and Caister-on-Sea and settlements such as Brandon, discussed in Chapter 3, are all examples where the later religious focus was relocated elsewhere, allowing the Middle Saxon layers to be excavated.[106] Similar circumstances resulted in the excavations at Sedgeford and the Whitehouse Industrial Estate.[107] By contrast, at sites such as Iken, Tasburgh and Caistor St Edmund, where the cemetery and possible attendant church continued to thrive and eventually came to function as the parish church, we are unable to study the earliest phases directly, except in the most limited fashion, because they are sealed beneath later buildings or have been badly disturbed by subsequent burials.[108]

In the absence of excavated evidence for an early foundation date, alternative indications of the possible Middle Saxon origins of a cemetery and church might more readily be found in the soil of the churchyard, disturbed from the underlying archaeological contexts by the continual digging of graves or the action of

[104] cf. Meaney, 'Anglo-Saxon Pagan and Christian Attitudes', p. 236; Geake, 'Control of Burial', p. 261.
[105] cf. Geake, 'Burial Practice', pp. 86–7; Newman, 'Sutton Hoo before Rædwald', p. 26; West, *Corpus*, p. 317.
[106] Johnson, *Burgh Castle*; Darling with Gurney, *Caister-on-Sea*; Carr *et al.*, 'Middle-Saxon Settlement at Staunch Meadow'.
[107] Cabot *et al.*, 'Sedgeford'; Hoggett, 'Origin and Early Development'; Caruth, 'Ipswich, Hewlett Packard plc'.
[108] Rogerson and Lawson, 'Earthwork Enclosure'; Percival, 'Archaeological Evaluation at Caistor St Edmund'.

burrowing animals. Of course, the recovery and recording of such evidence is not consistent, but the notion of broadening the search beyond the footprint of the church building itself is a sound one and its application is explored here.

Fortunately for this purpose, the East Anglian phenomena of common-edge drift and settlement desertion have resulted in a number of churches now standing in isolation, surrounded by arable land and ripe for archaeological investigation via fieldwalking.[109] The immediate environs of a large number of East Anglian churches have been investigated in this manner and the presence or absence of Middle Saxon Ipswich ware and Late Saxon Thetford-type ware can be used to draw conclusions about foundation dates. Such evidence is difficult to interpret with certainty, as many churches are associated with both Middle and Late Saxon artefact scatters, but when this class of evidence is combined with others, such as topography or associations with existing sites, a more comprehensive picture of the early Christian landscape emerges.

Anglo-Saxon finds from churchyards

Whereas the area beneath a church is sealed and reachable only via partial excavation of the interior of the building, the surrounding churchyard is at once both more accessible and considerably more disrupted. The use of the churchyard for burial will have disturbed any underlying archaeological deposits and the hope of finding *in situ* evidence for earlier structures or burials is minimal. However, the restrictions placed on the removal of soil from consecrated ground mean that any artefacts disturbed should at least have remained on site, where they can be discovered,[110] and where revealed they can be collected in a manner akin to finds recovered during fieldwalking or metal-detecting. Although we cannot always be sure exactly what type of features such artefacts might represent, they do at least provide an indication of activity on the site; in particular, Middle and Late Saxon artefacts might indicate activity that is contemporary with the foundation of the church or the Christian cemetery which may have preceded it.

By March 2005 the Norfolk and Suffolk HERs contained records of Early, Middle or Late Saxon material in 89 out of some 1,500 East Anglian churchyards (Fig. 30). The majority of this material is pottery, primarily Middle Saxon Ipswich ware and Late Saxon Thetford-type ware, although some metalwork has also been recovered. These artefacts are mainly surface finds, brought to light by burrowing animals or the constant redigging of graves, with the remaining finds being made at greater depth during the excavation of cable trenches, drains and occasionally in the bottom of freshly dug graves.

Significantly, only fifteen churchyards have produced Early Saxon finds. In most cases these were abraded sherds of probably domestic pottery, which is often difficult to distinguish from Iron Age pottery, perhaps meaning that the total number of sites might be even smaller. However, there have been some more notable Early Saxon discoveries, many of them of a funerary character: a small cremation urn, furnished with an iron knife and tweezers, was found during grave-digging at Waldringfield (Suffolk) in 1841,

---

[109] Williamson, *Origins of Norfolk*, pp. 167–71; *Shaping Medieval Landscapes*, pp. 91–101; and *England's Landscape: East Anglia*, pp. 51–6.
[110] Thompson, *Dying and Death*, pp. 172–6.

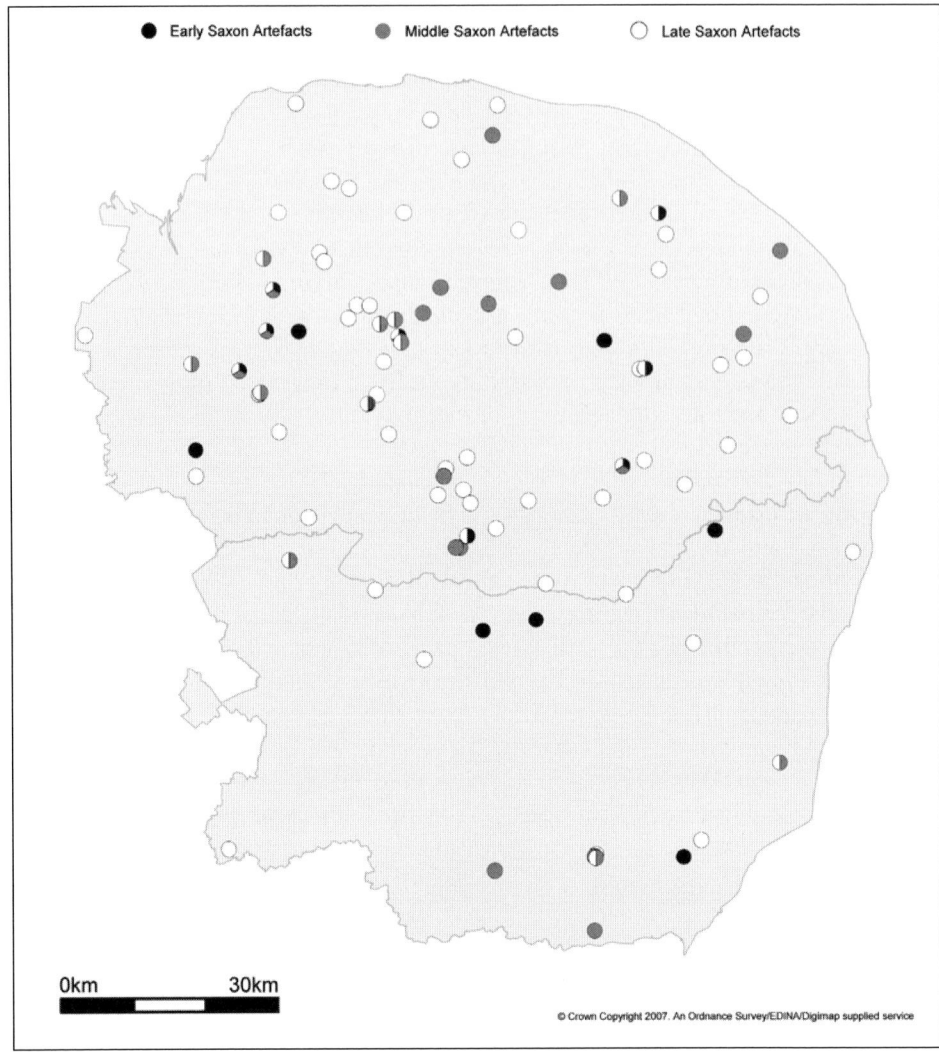

Fig. 30: The distribution of churchyards within which Early, Middle and Late Saxon artefacts have been discovered.

while in Norfolk a similar urn was discovered in Earsham churchyard in 1906.[111] Also in Norfolk, four or five cremation urns were unearthed in North Runcton churchyard in 1907, and a furnished inhumation, represented by an iron spearhead, a pin and an accessory vessel, was found in Hilgay churchyard in 1897.[112]

At first glance the discovery of cremations within a Christian churchyard seems significant, but on closer examination these discoveries can be demonstrated to be coincidental, as is the same in almost every similar case across lowland England.[113]

---

[111] SHER WLD001 and NHER 11110.
[112] NHER 3348 and 3369; NHER 4453.
[113] cf. Morris, *The Church in British Archaeology*, pp. 59–62; Blair, *The Church in Anglo-Saxon Society*, pp. 237–8.

We have seen that cremation was anathema to Christians and that cemeteries containing cremations were abandoned in the seventh century in favour of new cemeteries founded on distinctly separate sites, both factors which argue against any form of continuity of burial practice at these sites. An examination of the immediate surroundings of the three churchyards in question reveals that the Earsham urn was seemingly an outlier of a small cremation cemetery which clustered around several Bronze Age barrows lying to the north-east of the church, while the North Runcton urns also seem to have been outliers of a nearby mixed-rite cemetery. It is possible that this was also the case at Waldringfield. Finally, none of the three churchyards from which cremation urns have been recovered has produced any Middle or Late Saxon material, which, following arguments developed further below, would suggest that the churchyards in question might not have been established until the post-Conquest period, some 500 years or more later.

Of greater relevance to the search for cemeteries and churches that might have been founded during the Middle Saxon period are the twenty-eight churchyards from which Middle Saxon artefacts have been recovered. The majority of these artefacts are sherds of Ipswich ware, but several pieces of Middle Saxon metalwork have also been found: brooches and a strap-end were discovered by metal-detecting at Wangford (Suffolk), an equal-armed brooch was found at Congham (Norfolk), and a spectacular hoard of six silver brooches of exceptionally high quality was disturbed during grave-digging at Pentney (Norfolk).[114] The Pentney finds appear to have been deliberately deposited, with a deposition date thought to lie in the first half of the ninth century; it has been suggested that these objects were buried in the churchyard for safekeeping during the unrest precipitated by the Viking incursions and that they were subsequently forgotten or could not be reclaimed.[115]

Late Saxon artefacts have been recovered from seventy East Anglian churchyards. These are primarily sherds of Thetford-type wares, although Late Saxon coins have been discovered at Oxborough and South Pickenham (Norfolk), and Wangford and Laxfield (Suffolk).[116] Single Late Saxon finger rings have been recovered at Laxfield and Ixworth (Suffolk); a brooch was found at Shouldham (Norfolk), a strap-end at Little Hautbois (Norfolk), a pair of iron shears at Threxton (Norfolk) and the blade of an iron knife at Blofield (Norfolk).[117] It is possible that these stray artefacts, and the Middle Saxon items referred to above, represent dress fittings from buried individuals, for the presence of such items in burials is not unheard of; or they may, as seems more likely, simply represent stray losses which typify domestic assemblages of these dates.

An examination of the combinations of Early, Middle and Late Saxon artefacts recovered from churchyards is particularly revealing. Six churchyards produced only Early Saxon artefacts, of which three are accounted for by the urns discussed above, while a further four churchyards are recorded as containing only Early Saxon and Late Saxon finds. As with the urns, these combinations might represent the reoccupation after several centuries of a site previously inhabited during the Early

---

[114] SHER WNG016; NHER 3562 and 3941.
[115] Webster and Backhouse, *The Making of England*, pp. 229–31.
[116] NHER 2628 and 4717; SHER WNG016 and LXD032.
[117] SHER IXW010; NHER 4290, 7695, 4686 and 10265.

Saxon period. Combinations of Early and Middle Saxon artefacts have been reported from only five churchyards, and it is interesting that the same five have all produced Late Saxon finds as well. All five of these churches, however — which include Tasburgh and Pentney (pp. 69–71 and 145) — have been subjected to an unusually high degree of archaeological investigation.

Middle Saxon artefacts alone have been recovered from twelve churchyards and might indicate early foundations from which settlement has subsequently moved away. Sixteen churchyards have produced both Middle and Late Saxon material, meaning that either a Middle Saxon or a Late Saxon foundation date is possible. Fifty-one churchyards have produced only Late Saxon material, suggesting that these churchyards might be later foundations. While we must not attach too much significance to these figures, it is interesting that the totals and combinations of artefacts recovered broadly mirror what we know of the two waves of Anglo-Saxon church foundation: that is, a few Middle Saxon foundations followed by a larger second wave of Late Saxon foundations.[118] The interpretation and implications of these developmental sequences are discussed at greater length in the next section.

The conclusions which may be drawn from unsystematically collected stray finds such as these are limited; the presence or absence of such finds, while informative, is not necessarily representative of a wider pattern of occupation. One indication of the biased nature of this data set is the fact that many of the Norfolk discoveries result from site visits by Andrew Rogerson, one of only a few archaeologists who actively search for such artefacts; indeed, one of the churchyards from which Early, Middle and Late Saxon material has been produced — Fransham — lies in the parish which formed the subject of Rogerson's doctoral research.[119]

Despite these provisos, the discoveries from churchyards discussed here do at least provide a useful indication of Anglo-Saxon activity on a given site, particularly in developed areas where the churchyard remains the only available space with archaeological potential. Fortunately, the dispersed nature of the East Anglian settlement pattern and the changes — such as common-edge drift — which it underwent during the Late Saxon and medieval periods have resulted in numerous churches which are not now hemmed in by development.[120] Many churches, both in use and ruined, are surrounded by arable fields, and in many instances these fields have been systematically fieldwalked, producing significant quantities of data which we can use to infer something of the development of the Anglo-Saxon ecclesiastical landscape.

Pottery scatters around churches

In a region in which such a high percentage of land is given over to arable farming, fieldwalking has been demonstrated to be a particularly effective technique for investigating changing settlement patterns.[121] The potential of fieldwalking surveys to increase our understanding of the development of ecclesiastical sites during the

---

[118] Morris, *Churches in the Landscape*; Blair, *The Church in Anglo-Saxon Society*.

[119] Rogerson, 'Fransham'.

[120] Williamson, *Origins of Norfolk*, pp. 167–71; *Shaping Medieval Landscapes*, pp. 91–101; and *England's Landscape: East Anglia*, pp. 51–6.

[121] e.g. Wade-Martins, *Village Sites*; Silvester, *Fenland Project 3*, *Fenland Project 4*; Newman, 'Sutton Hoo before Rædwald' and 'Survey in the Deben Valley'.

Anglo-Saxon period has been appreciated since the 1960s, and anecdotal evidence for the association of Ipswich ware scatters with churches is widespread, yet the available data have yet to be fully synthesised.[122] Unlike the casual collection of stray finds from churchyards, fieldwalking of the areas surrounding churchyards provides a systematically recovered, and therefore much more comprehensive, data set from which to draw inferences. Also, unlike investigations of churchyards, which often realise no more than a single sherd of pottery, fieldwalking surveys have the added benefit of recovering large scatters of material and can therefore shed greater light on the landscape context of an individual churchyard.

In order to use fieldwalking to ascertain when a church or its churchyard-type cemetery precursor might have been founded we are again largely reliant on the presence of Ipswich ware and Thetford-type wares as indicators of Middle Saxon and Late Saxon activity respectively. If systematic surface collection reveals that either or both of these pottery types are present then we are able to infer something about the possible foundation date and development of the site. In addition, the spatial element of fieldwalking data means that we are also able to use horizontal stratigraphy to examine the relationship between the Middle Saxon and the Late Saxon phases of the settlement, especially where these show a marked difference in focus.

Put simply, if a churchyard is not surrounded by any Anglo-Saxon material we can conclude that it is likely to be a post-Conquest foundation. If a church is associated with a Late Saxon surface scatter, then we might suppose a Late Saxon foundation date. If both Late Saxon and Middle Saxon scatters surround the church then we might consider either a Late or a Middle Saxon foundation date, although following the arguments developed here a Middle Saxon foundation date for the churchyard-type cemetery, if not the church itself, would seem to be the more likely. Finally, if a church is surrounded only by a Middle Saxon scatter, then we can say with confidence that the church and churchyard were Middle Saxon foundations and that, although the church continued to be used into the Late Saxon period and beyond, by the Late Saxon period its associated settlement had already begun to drift away.

During the last forty years East Anglia has played host to a number of large-scale fieldwalking projects, some spanning many parishes, which have produced data enabling large tracts of landscape to be studied. There have also been a number of smaller-scale fieldwalking surveys which have examined individual parishes or small groups of parishes (Fig. 31). Many of these surveys have examined church environs and provide a vivid insight into the ecclesiastical development of the region.

THE LAUNDITCH HUNDRED SURVEY

Between 1967 and 1970 Peter Wade-Martins conducted an extensive campaign of fieldwalking and other fieldwork in the central Norfolk hundred of Launditch (Fig. 31).[123] He focused his researches on the areas of each parish which contained settlement and particularly on the sites of parish churches, and while this approach did not provide complete coverage of all the available land it did result in comparative

---

[122] e.g. Wade-Martins, *Village Sites*; Andrews, 'Middle Saxon Norfolk'; Rogerson, 'Rural Settlement'.
[123] Wade-Martins, 'Development of the Landscape'; *Excavations in North Elmham Park*; and *Village Sites*.

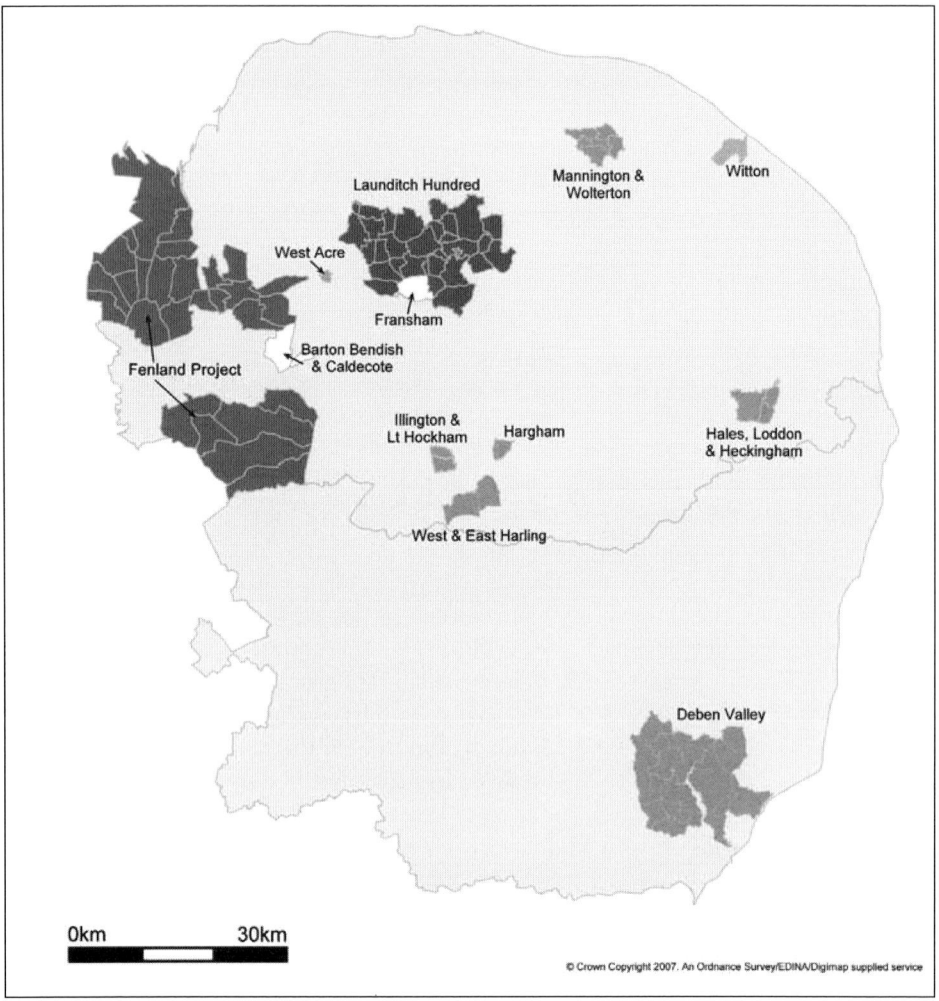

Fig. 31: The locations of the fieldwalking surveys discussed in the text.

data from around the churches of a group of adjoining parishes (Fig. 32).[124] Inevitably some of the parish churches within the hundred were too hemmed in by settlement to enable fieldwalking to take place, but in the thirty parishes which were examined the environs of only two churches could not be studied at all, while a limited degree of fieldwork near a further nine churches resulted in the recovery of no surface evidence. The environs of the remaining nineteen parish churches revealed surface evidence which enabled something of their history to be ascertained.

Four of the churches in the Launditch Hundred — East Bilney, Brisley, Gressenhall and Beeston — were associated only with medieval pottery scatters, indicating that they are likely to have been post-Conquest foundations.[125] These

[124] Wade-Martins, *Village Sites*, pp. 3–7.
[125] Wade-Martins, 'Development of the Landscape', pp. 209–27, and *Village Sites*, pp. 19–23.

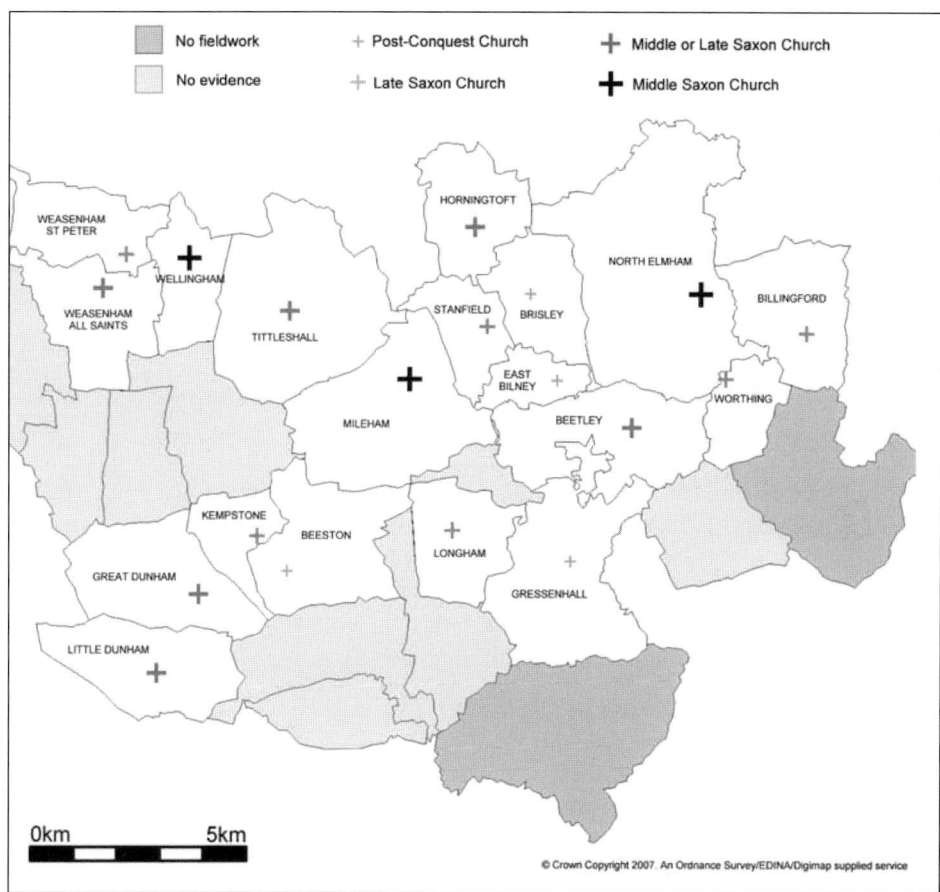

Fig. 32: The foundation dates of the parish churches in Launditch Hundred, as inferred from surrounding Middle and Late Saxon pottery scatters.

conclusions are supported by the other available evidence: for example, the church at East Bilney was first recorded in 1254 and stands within an oval enclosure some 800m long thought by Wade-Martins to represent the pale of a medieval deer park.[126] Similarly, Brisley was not recorded in Domesday Book, at which time it is believed to have still been a part of neighbouring Elmham, and the first known reference to it dates from 1100 × 07.[127]

Six Launditch churches — Kempstone, Longham, Stanfield, Weasenham St Peter, Worthing and Billingford — were surrounded by surface scatters that included Late Saxon Thetford-type wares but not Middle Saxon Ipswich ware, suggesting that they were Late Saxon foundations.[128] Again, these interpretations are supported by additional evidence. At Kempstone, for example, the Late Saxon settlement was focused around the site of the church, but during the medieval period the settlement

---

[126] Wade-Martins, *Village Sites*, pp. 19–20.
[127] *Ibid.*, pp. 21–3.
[128] Wade-Martins, 'Development of the Landscape', pp. 209–27, and *Village Sites*, pp. 19–23.

drifted south-west towards the edge of Kempston Green.[129] Similarly, at Worthing the Late Saxon settlement surrounded the church, with the medieval settlement drifting first to the south-east and eventually relocating some 500m to the north-east of the church during the post-medieval period.[130] In Longham it is clear from a nearby scatter of Ipswich ware that the Middle Saxon settlement focus lay some 100m to the south-east and that the settlement expanded during the Late Saxon period before the church was founded (Fig. 33). The pottery at Weasenham St Peter indicates that the settlement was founded during the Late Saxon period, presumably as a daughter settlement of Weasenham All Saints to the south, which surface finds suggest has earlier origins.[131]

The church at Weasenham All Saints and five other churches in the hundred — Beetley, Horningtoft, Tittleshall, and Great and Little Dunham — were surrounded by scatters of both Thetford-type wares and Ipswich ware, indicting that they were definitely Anglo-Saxon foundations but making it difficult to ascertain whether they were founded during the Middle Saxon or the Late Saxon period (Fig. 33).[132] In the case of Weasenham All Saints, for example, the church stands at the western end of a large scatter of Ipswich ware and the settlement was replanned and expanded greatly to the west of the church during the Late Saxon period. These scatters and the relationship with the Late Saxon foundation in Weasenham St Peter suggest that this church was a Middle Saxon foundation.[133] Similarly, in Horningtoft the church, which stands on the highest point in the valley, has an Ipswich ware scatter to its east, while the Late Saxon settlement expanded to the west. Again the church is located on the periphery of the Ipswich ware scatter, perhaps indicating a Middle Saxon foundation date.[134]

Two Launditch churches — Wellingham and Mileham — were associated solely with Ipswich ware scatters, indicating a Middle Saxon foundation date, to which can be added the Middle Saxon domestic and ecclesiastical features excavated at North Elmham (pp. 40–4).[135] Unlike some of the churches discussed here, which appear to have stood at the periphery of the Middle Saxon settlement, the site of Wellingham church was surrounded on all sides by Ipswich ware, indicating that it stood at the centre of a Middle Saxon settlement and confirming a Middle Saxon foundation date (Fig. 33).[136] The surface evidence from Mileham, however, provides the most clear-cut example of the Middle Saxon foundation date of a church being indicated by fieldwalking remains. A dense scatter of Ipswich ware was located to the east, south and west of the church, while the Late Saxon settlement lay to the north and was focused along the line of the main east–west road (Fig. 33). By Domesday Mileham was an important manorial centre, held by the king, having formerly been held by Archbishop Stigand, and had links with twenty other places in Norfolk. A substantial motte and bailey castle, the earthworks of which survive,

---

[129] Wade-Martins, *Village Sites*, pp. 29–32.
[130] *Ibid.*, pp. 76–7.
[131] *Ibid.*, pp. 65–70.
[132] Wade-Martins, 'Development of the Landscape', pp. 209–27, and *Village Sites*, pp. 19–23.
[133] Wade-Martins, *Village Sites*, pp. 59–64.
[134] *Ibid.*, pp. 24–8.
[135] Rigold, 'Anglian Cathedral'; Wade-Martins, *Excavations in North Elmham Park*.
[136] Wade-Martins, *Village Sites*, pp. 71–5.

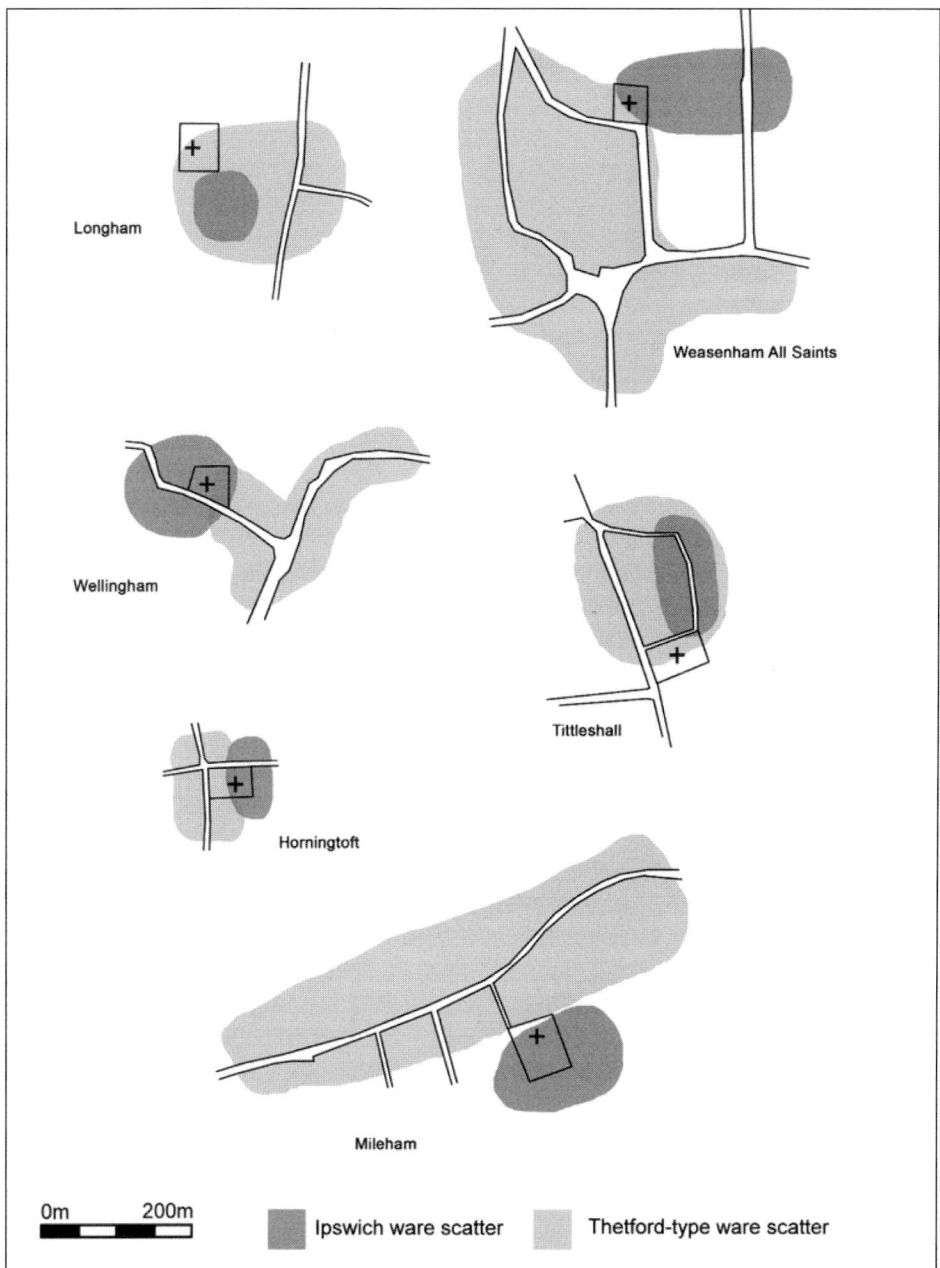

Longham

Weasenham All Saints

Wellingham

Tittleshall

Horningtoft

Mileham

0m   200m   ■ Ipswich ware scatter   ▨ Thetford-type ware scatter

Fig. 33: Middle and Late Saxon pottery scatters surrounding churches in Launditch Hundred (after Wade Martins, *Village Sites*).

Plate 13: An aerial view of Mileham from the east, 26 May 1995, showing the church (bottom left), the castle (top left) and the settlement in between. TF9119/AEV/HGZ14 (Derek Edwards). © *NMAS*

was constructed probably in about 1100 and straddles the main road.[137] Tellingly, the castle is located quite some distance to the west of the parish church, an indication of just how far the settlement focus had drifted by the Norman Conquest (Plate 13). The fact that the church was set back from the road and that its location bears little relation to the later settlement pattern led Wade-Martins to suggest that the church was demonstrably a Middle Saxon foundation.[138]

---

[137] Cushion and Davison, *Earthworks of Norfolk*, pp. 173–5.
[138] Wade-Martins, *Village Sites*, p. 41.

Many years later comprehensive fieldwalking in the parish of Fransham, also in Launditch, recovered a great deal more material than was revealed during the Launditch Hundred survey. The only Middle Saxon site located by this survey lay 800m east of Great Fransham parish church, while the church itself was associated with a scatter of Late Saxon pottery, as was that at Little Fransham, suggesting Late Saxon foundation dates for both of them.[139]

THE DEBEN VALLEY SURVEY

When renewed archaeological investigation began at Sutton Hoo in the 1980s it was decided that the work should be complemented by an extensive fieldwalking survey of the surrounding area. A 216km² study area, centred on Sutton Hoo and straddling the Deben valley, was thus defined (Fig. 31). Between 1983 and 1989 John Newman fieldwalked 42 per cent of this study area (65 per cent of the available arable land) in transects spaced 20m apart. Areas containing significant scatters were intensively resurveyed using a grid method.[140] Extensive prehistoric, Roman and Anglo-Saxon evidence was discovered, enabling much to be said about the changing settlement patterns of the area surrounding the Deben valley, not least the landscape setting of the area's churches.[141]

The Deben valley study area comprised twenty-nine whole or partial parishes; many of the peripheral parishes, such as Hollesley, were not walked to any great extent and consequently four of them have been classified here as having had no fieldwork conducted (Fig. 34). This is in contrast to the six parishes highlighted as containing 'no evidence', for these are the parishes which were extensively fieldwalked but in which the areas immediately around the parish church were inaccessible for reasons of ground cover or development. In the remaining nineteen parishes extensive fieldwalking was conducted in the vicinity of the parish church and any pottery scatters discovered have been used to ascribe a broad foundation date to the church in question. An additional element can be brought to the analysis, as Suffolk's churches were frequently recorded in Domesday Book, with more than 400 being mentioned. However, although the presence of a church in Domesday Book can be taken as an indication of its existence in 1086, it can be demonstrated by cross-referencing with other documentary sources that the absence of a record cannot be taken to indicate that a church had not yet been founded, for several churches known to exist in 1086 were not recorded.[142]

Following the same reasoning applied to the Launditch material, at three churches — Hasketon, Shottisham and Waldringfield — the absence of any Anglo-Saxon surface scatters suggests that they can be ascribed a post-Conquest foundation date. Waldringfield has already been mentioned: it was from this

---

[139] Rogerson, 'Fransham', pp. 101–62.

[140] Newman, 'Sutton Hoo before Rædwald', pp. 28–9; 'East Anglian Kingdom Pilot Study'; and 'Survey in the Deben Valley', pp. 478–9.

[141] Newman, 'Sutton Hoo before Rædwald', pp. 30–36, and 'Survey in the Deben Valley', pp. 480–83. Although these summaries of the Deben Valley project's finding have been published, the raw data have not. I am grateful to John Newman for providing me with a complete copy of his field notes and draft maps from the survey on which this analysis is based.

[142] Hoggett, 'Changing Beliefs', pp. 126–32.

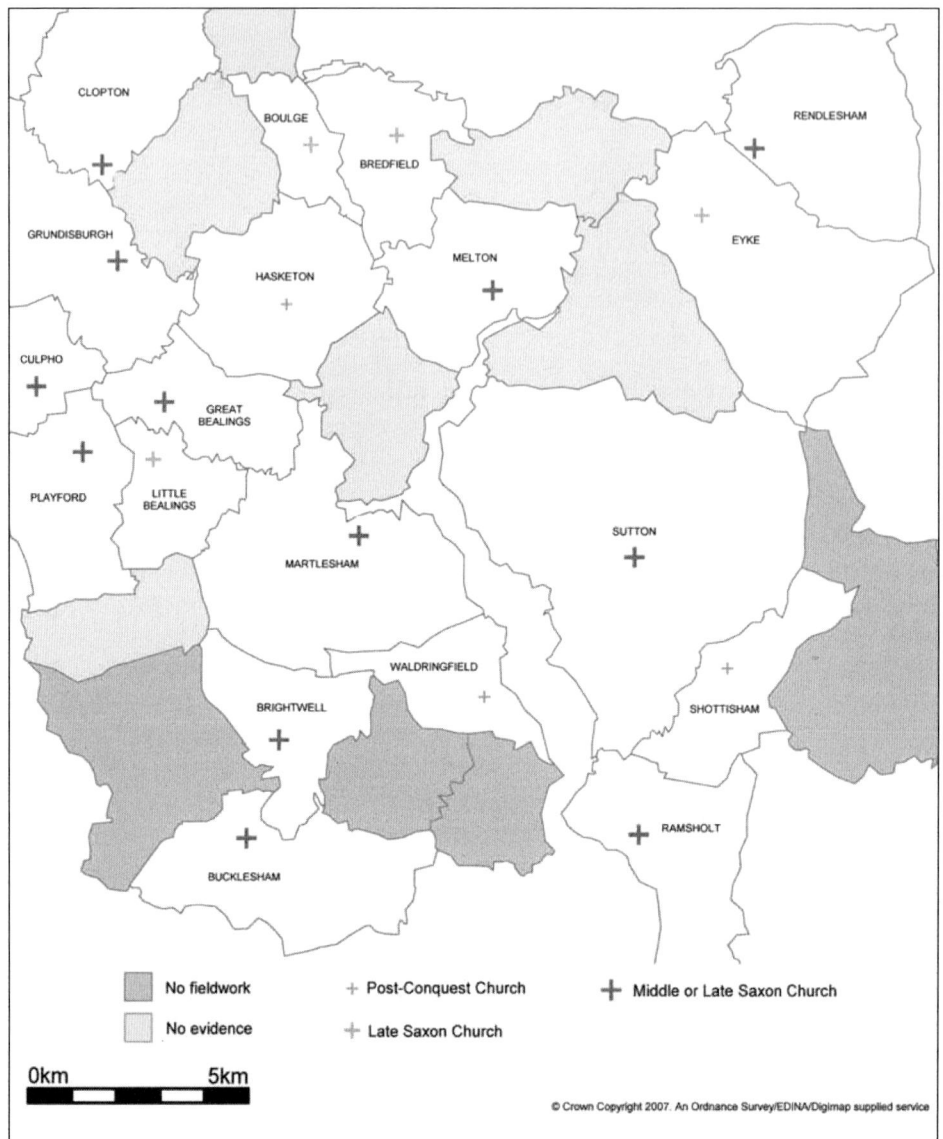

Fig. 34: The foundation dates of the parish churches in the Deben valley, as inferred from surrounding Middle and Late Saxon pottery scatters.

churchyard that an Early Saxon cremation urn was excavated in 1841 (pp. 143–5). The lack of any Middle or Late Saxon material serves to emphasise the coincidental nature of this discovery. Neither Hasketon or Waldringfield churches were mentioned in Domesday Book, but a church was recorded under the entry for Shottisham.[143] Given that much of the area surrounding Shottisham church is developed, it would seem that some Late Saxon evidence was potentially obscured in this instance.

[143] LDB f.324.

Surface scatters including Thetford-type wares allow the ascription of Late Saxon foundation dates to four churches: Little Bealings, Eyke, Boulge and Bredfield. A single Domesday entry for Bealings mentioned a church and probably referred, rather, to Great Bealings, while churches were also recorded for both Boulge and Bredfield.[144] Eyke was not recorded in Domesday Book at all, although the manor must have existed and the church has a substantial Norman core, but Williamson has convincingly argued that Eyke was actually referred to as Staverton in Domesday Book, the entry for which does include mention of a church.[145]

Mixed scatters of Thetford-type wares and Ipswich ware at the remaining twelve churches in the study area suggest Middle or Late Saxon dates for these foundations. Those churches are Brightwell, Bucklesham, Clopton, Culpho, Great Bealings, Grundisburgh, Martlesham, Melton, Playford, Ramsholt, Rendlesham and Sutton (Fig. 34). Eight of these churches are recorded in Domesday Book entries which each record a single church;[146] the four exceptions are Grundisburgh, Martlesham, Melton and Ramsholt, although absence from the record is no indication that a church was not in existence.

Unlike the churches of the Launditch Hundred, no Deben valley churches were associated solely with Ipswich ware, so no purely Middle Saxon dates can be ascribed on the basis of horizontal stratigraphy alone. However, the relative quantities of Middle and Late Saxon pottery might be employed to identify significant Middle Saxon sites. Sutton church, for example, was surrounded by a particularly dense spread of Ipswich ware, as was Clopton, while the relative quantities of pottery discovered at Melton and Martlesham suggest that they were of greater significance during the Late Saxon period. Rendlesham was the only church to have been surrounded by Roman, Early Saxon, Middle Saxon and Late Saxon scatters, suggesting a strong degree of continuity and a significant degree of importance within the local area.

Rendlesham was identified by Bede as having become a royal vill by the mid-seventh century; he recorded that the East Anglian king Æthelwold sponsored the baptism of Swithhelm of Essex, which took place in Rendlesham around 661 and was conducted by Bishop Cedd of the East Saxons (pp. 33–4).[147] If the present church and the venue of Swithhelm's baptism are one and the same, then Rendlesham church is one of the earliest documented foundations in the region, a conclusion that would seem to be supported by the archaeological evidence.[148] It is also significant that the royal church at Rendlesham is one of six East Anglian churches dedicated to St Gregory, the instigator of Augustine's mission to the Anglo-Saxons and ultimately the architect of the East Anglian conversion.

---

[144] LDB f.441v, f.319 and f.387v.
[145] LDB f.325; Williamson, *Sutton Hoo*, p. 40.
[146] Brightwell, LDB f.386; Bucklesham, LDB f.292; Clopton, LDB f.417v; Culpho, LDB f.346; Great Bealings, LDB f.441; Playford, LDB f.314v; Rendlesham, LDB f.307v, and Sutton, LDB f.318.
[147] *HE*, iii, 22.
[148] Newman, 'Sutton Hoo before Rædwald', pp. 34–6; Bruce-Mitford, *Aspects of Anglo-Saxon Archaeology*, pp. 73–113; Williamson, *Sutton Hoo*, pp. 96–101.

THE FENLAND PROJECT

The Fenland Project was founded in 1981 to systematically survey as much of the fen basin surrounding the Wash as possible in the six years allotted to the project.[149] The fenlands of west Norfolk cover a sizeable area, approximately 10 per cent of the area of the county, and comprise some 16 per cent of the total area of the fens, which also cover large parts of Cambridgeshire and Lincolnshire.[150] The survey concentrated on three main areas of the Norfolk fens: the marshland parishes lying immediately to the south of the Wash; the peat-filled valley of the River Nar, which flows westwards into the marshland; and the Wissey embayment, an area of peat fen to the south of the marshland (Fig. 31).[151] A number of significant scatters of Ipswich ware were discovered in the marshland parishes, spaced at regular intervals along the raised northern edge of the area, close to the coast. These sites were often on roddons — silted-up river channels which form areas of raised ground — and have been interpreted as being related to seasonal grazing or salt production. Many of these Middle Saxon sites were short-lived, although some were complemented by scatters of Thetford-type ware, suggesting their 'continued, if not continuous' occupation into the Late Saxon period.[152] One such Ipswich ware scatter, at Hay Green in the parish of Terrington St Clement, was exceptionally large, producing over 1,000 sherds.[153] Unfortunately, the other two areas of Norfolk examined by the Fenland Project were less illuminating. Of the Wissey embayment it was concluded that 'little useful comment can be made on the Saxon exploitation of the fen',[154] while the usefulness of the survey of the Nar valley to this study was hampered by the decision to concentrate on the bottom of the river valley and exclude the higher ground on either side where the settlements and churches are located.[155]

Only two sites examined by the Fenland survey are of direct relevance to this discussion. The first of these is West Walton, where Ipswich ware spreads were identified in the fields to the north and south of the parish church, suggesting that the church stood within a Middle Saxon settlement in a manner akin to some of the Launditch examples. The church is also associated with scatters of Late Saxon material, indicating either a Middle or Late Saxon foundation date for the church, although on balance the former seems more likely.[156] Subsequent metal-detecting at West Walton has revealed a 'productive site' to the north of the church, which has so far yielded numerous items of metalwork and a number of Middle Saxon coins.[157]

The second relevant site is Wormegay, which, owing to its location on an island in the Nar valley, was the only village centre to be surveyed.[158] A large Ipswich ware

---

[149] Silvester, '"The Addition of More-or-Less Undifferentiated Dots"'; Hall and Coles, *Fenland Survey*, pp. 7–12.

[150] Silvester, 'The Norfolk Fens'.

[151] Silvester, *Fenland Project 3* and *Fenland Project 4*.

[152] Silvester, 'The Norfolk Fens', p. 328, and 'The Addition of More-or-Less Undifferentiated Dots', pp. 27–8.

[153] Rogerson and Silvester, 'Middle Saxon Occupation' and *Fenland Project 3*, pp. 35–41.

[154] Silvester, *Fenland Project 4*, p. 91.

[155] Silvester, *Fenland Project 3*, pp. 169–73.

[156] Silvester, 'West Walton' and *Fenland Project 3*, pp. 88–96.

[157] Rogerson, 'Six Middle Anglo-Saxon Sites', pp. 118–21.

[158] Silvester, *Fenland Project 3*, pp. 172–3.

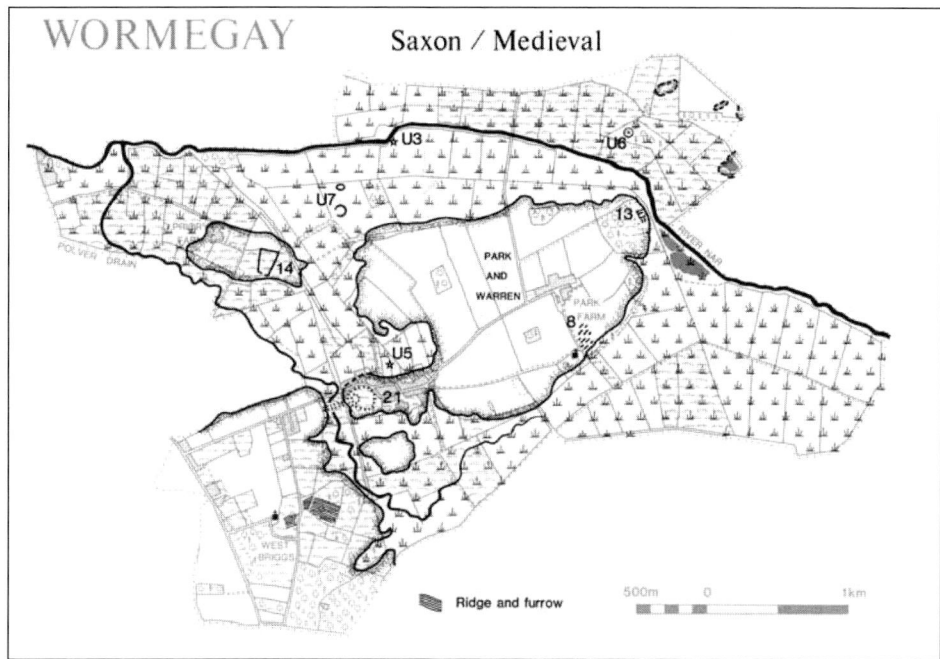

Fig. 35: The Saxon and medieval landscape of Wormegay, showing the topographic setting of the church with associated Middle Saxon pottery scatter (8) and the earthworks of the castle (21) (reproduced from Silvester, *Fenland Project 3*, fig. 109). © *NMAS*

scatter was found on the southern slopes of the island, adjacent to the parish church (Fig. 35). The scatter also contained a handful of Thetford-type ware, indicating that some occupation continued into the Late Saxon period, yet the settlement appears to have relocated to the western end of the island during the Late Saxon period and a castle was eventually founded there.[159] Metal-detecting at Wormegay has found that the Ipswich ware scatter is mirrored by a concentration of Middle Saxon metalwork, including styli, pins and coins. Intriguingly, a 'gap' has been identified in the Ipswich ware scatter which appears to correspond with a spread of human bone and it has been suggested that this might be remains of one or more ploughed-out burials.[160] These surface finds all indicate that the church at Wormegay was founded during the Middle Saxon period and that it was associated with a thriving settlement. The topographically isolated setting of the site is typical of some of the missionary stations discussed in Chapter 3 (pp. 71–7), and the church at Wormegay undoubtedly belongs to the first wave of Christian foundations in the region.

OTHER FIELDWALKING SURVEYS

In addition to the large-scale projects discussed above, a number of smaller fieldwalking surveys have concentrated on individual parishes or groups of parishes,

---

[159] *Ibid.*, pp. 143–50.
[160] Rogerson, 'Six Middle Anglo-Saxon Sites', pp. 118–21.

returning results akin to those already outlined.[161] In Norfolk many of these surveys were conducted by the late Alan Davison, whose single-handed contribution to our understanding of the Norfolk landscape cannot be overestimated. The conclusions of these surveys tell us many things, but their inclusion here is justified by the facts that numerous parish churches fell within the individual study areas and that several of them were associated with surface scatters of Anglo-Saxon material.

Fieldwalking in the three adjacent south-east Norfolk parishes of Hales, Loddon and Heckingham enabled these parishes to be studied as a single block of landscape (Fig. 31).[162] Although a Middle Saxon pin was discovered in the vicinity of Loddon church in 1948, today the church is entirely surrounded by later development and its environs could not, therefore, be fieldwalked. Hales church was hemmed in to the south by grassland, but ploughed fields lay to its north. Heckingham church is surrounded by farmland and could, therefore, be examined in detail. No conclusions could be drawn about the foundation date of Loddon church, while the total absence of any Late Saxon material from the vicinity of Hales church suggests a post-Conquest foundation date, a conclusion in keeping with its ornate Romanesque architecture.[163] However, a dense scatter of Ipswich ware was discovered surrounding Heckingham church, while the main concentration of Thetford-type ware lay 100m or so further to the north, with only residual traces of Late Saxon activity in the vicinity of the church.[164] Again, this evidence suggests a Middle Saxon foundation date for Heckingham church and indicates that the adjacent settlement had already begun to drift away from the church in the Late Saxon period.

An extensive fieldwalking survey of the south-west Norfolk parish of Barton Bendish revealed a number of Ipswich ware sherds in a field to the west of St Mary's church.[165] St Mary's was one of two Domesday churches recorded in the parish, although excavation demonstrated that a third Late Saxon church went unrecorded.[166] All three churches were surrounded by dense Late Saxon scatters, meaning that St Mary's should be considered a Middle or Late Saxon foundation, while both St Andrew's and All Saints' were clearly Late Saxon foundations. In the adjacent parish of Oxborough, fieldwalking on the site of the deserted medieval settlement of Caldecote revealed a concentration of Ipswich ware 200m north-east of the church and a dense scatter of Late Saxon pottery around the church itself, indicating a Late Saxon foundation date here too.[167] Fieldwalking in the parish of West Acre was less comprehensive because the areas to the west, south and east of

[161] Davison, 'Field Archaeology of Mannington and Wolterton', pp. 166–70; Lawson, *Archaeology of Witton*, pp. 70–72; Rogerson with Davison, 'Archaeological and Historical Survey of Barton Bendish', pp. 20–21; Silvester, 'Multi-Period Occupation', pp. 83–5; Davison, 'Archaeology of the Parish of West Acre', pp. 212–18; Davison *et al.*, *Illington*, pp. 3–4; Davison, 'Little Hockham'; Davison with Cushion, 'Archaeology of the Hargham Estate'; Davison, 'The Distribution of Medieval Settlement in West Harling', pp. 332–4.

[162] Davison, *The Evolution of Settlement*.

[163] *Ibid.*; Pevsner and Wilson, *Norfolk II*, pp. 375–6.

[164] Davison, *The Evolution of Settlement*, 16–22.

[165] Rogerson with Davison, 'Archaeological and Historical Survey of Barton Bendish', pp. 20–21.

[166] Rogerson and Ashley, 'Parish Churches of Barton Bendish', pp. 7–11, 52–3 and 63–4.

[167] Silvester, 'Multi-Period Occupation', pp. 83–5.

the church are either developed or under grass, but the open ground to the north produced both Middle and Late Saxon sherds, indicating a Middle or Late Saxon foundation date.[168]

Fieldwalking of the Mannington and Wolterton estates in north Norfolk incorporated the environs of five parish churches (Fig. 31). Of these, the churches of Wickmere and Mannington were found to be associated with both Middle and Late Saxon scatters, suggesting that they were either Middle or Late Saxon foundations, while limited fieldwork around Calthorpe church suggested that it was a Late Saxon foundation. Surrounding buildings prevented much work from being conducted at Little Barningham, although a church was recorded there at Domesday, while no Anglo-Saxon evidence was discovered in the vicinity of Wolterton church, suggesting that it was a post-Conquest foundation.[169] Also in north-east Norfolk, fieldwalking in Witton revealed a great number of Ipswich ware sherds in the vicinity of the church, suggesting a substantial Middle Saxon presence, although an even greater concentration of Thetford-type ware was found in the same area, making Witton a Middle or Late Saxon foundation.[170]

Fieldwalking in the Breckland parish of Illington revealed a dense concentration of Late Saxon material around the site of the church, while only a few Middle Saxon sherds were found some 400m to the west, indicating that Illington church was a Late Saxon foundation.[171] In the adjacent parish to the north, Little Hockham, fieldwalking revealed a concentration of Middle and Late Saxon pottery. Although there is no church on the site now, it would seem that one stood in the same area as this concentration, suggesting either a Middle or Late Saxon foundation date.[172] Fieldwalking nearby on the site of the deserted medieval village of Hargham, now in the south Norfolk parish of Quidenham, revealed a discrete scatter of Ipswich ware which was superseded by an elongated scatter of Thetford-type ware, demonstrating a gradual drift eastwards towards the site of Hargham church.[173] This must therefore have been a Late Saxon or even a post-Conquest foundation.

Four kilometres south of Illington and Hargham, the environs of the parish churches at West and Middle Harling were also examined. The absence of any Middle Saxon artefacts and the presence of Late Saxon artefacts clearly indicate a Late Saxon foundation for West Harling church, while a scatter of Ipswich ware, Thetford-type ware and ploughed-up human bone in Middle Harling was interpreted as the site of a former church which may have had a Middle or a Late Saxon foundation date.[174] Several years later part of the site was excavated after a hoard of Middle Saxon coins was discovered, suggesting that the Middle Saxon phase of occupation was the more significant and perhaps indicating a Middle Saxon foundation date for the church.[175]

[168] Davison, 'Archaeology of the Parish of West Acre', pp. 212–18.
[169] Davison, 'Field Archaeology of Mannington and Wolterton', pp. 166–70.
[170] Lawson, *Archaeology of Witton*, pp. 70–74.
[171] Davison *et al.*, *Illington*, pp. 3–4.
[172] Davison, 'Little Hockham'; Batcock, *Ruined and Disused Churches*, microfiche.
[173] Davison with Cushion, 'Archaeology of the Hargham Estate'.
[174] Davison, 'The Distribution of Medieval Settlement', pp. 332–4.
[175] Rogerson, *A Late Neolithic, Saxon and Medieval Site.*

*

This section has considered the two main categories of evidence from which, in the absence of excavation, we can hope to understand something of the foundation dates of the churches that populate the East Anglian landscape: artefacts recovered from churchyards and fieldwalking areas adjacent to churchyards. An examination of data from the former reveals that when it is actively sought Anglo-Saxon material can often be found in churchyards, disturbed from underlying contexts by the frequent digging and redigging of graves. We have seen that Early Saxon cremations have been revealed in this fashion, although reference to their wider landscape context and associated finds demonstrates that the juxtaposition of Early Saxon cremations and Christian churchyards is coincidental, their establishment often being separated by many centuries. Of greater significance to the argument developed here is the recovery of combinations of Middle and Late Saxon sherds and metalwork from churchyard soils, both of which, it has been argued, can be used to infer something of the underlying archaeology and, therefore, origins of the church in question. The major limitation of this category of evidence is the unsystematic nature of its survival and recovery, meaning that conclusions drawn from this material cannot be placed on a sound empirical footing. Fieldwalking evidence, by contrast, *is* systematically collected, enabling a comprehensive picture of settlement development to be built up, and, where the horizontal stratigraphy allows, even enabling the identification of distinct phases of occupation. The limitations imposed by the impossibility of fieldwalking churchyards themselves — and often their environs, if they are developed, obscuring areas in which survey would be desirable — are arguably far outweighed by the inferences that can be drawn from this material.

As we have seen, a number of East Anglian churches are associated with both Middle and Late Saxon artefact scatters. We cannot say whether these churches were founded during the Middle or Late Saxon period, but the presence of Middle Saxon material indicates that we are, at least, dealing with a settlement with seventh-century origins. It is extremely likely, therefore, that such Middle Saxon settlements had a Christian inhumation cemetery, and possible that this burial ground might have had an accompanying Middle Saxon church. We also know that not all the churches associated with Middle and Late Saxon material were founded during the Late Saxon period, because the association of churches solely with Middle Saxon material indicate with certainty that these churches at least — and potentially, therefore, others associated with a mix of material — are Middle Saxon foundations.

Conclusions

It is clear from the evidence examined in this chapter that the East Anglian landscape underwent a dramatic period of restructuring during the Middle Saxon period and that some of these upheavals, at least, can be a demonstrated to have occurred as a direct result of the conversion to Christianity. At the heart of these changes lay a fundamental shift in attitude towards the appropriate landscape setting for the dead, a shift which affected the structure and layout of settlements and cemeteries and, in turn, provides us with some of our strongest archaeological indicators of the range and progress of the East Anglian conversion.

The patterns which underlie the typical locations chosen for Early Saxon cemeteries and the spatial relationship between them and contemporary settlements have long been recognised and understood. Associations of cemeteries with ancient earthworks, especially Bronze Age barrows, are widespread and commonplace, as is the placing of cemeteries on valley sides; the distinguishing characteristic of greatest importance to this study is the distinct separation which existed between the settlements and cemeteries of the period. This separation could allow settlements and cemeteries to lie in close proximity, but they remained discrete entities. These patterns prevailed throughout the Early Saxon period, but were abandoned during the first half of the seventh century as part of the widespread religious change that is evident in the funerary landscape of Middle Saxon East Anglia.

Rather than following a linear course, as has often been suggested, it would appear that the changing Anglo-Saxon attitudes towards the treatment and placement of the dead resulted in the exploration in parallel of a number of different approaches to the creation and maintenance of cemeteries. As we have seen in this chapter, in a minority of cases new 'Final Phase' cemeteries were established, in which the frequency of furnished burials was lower than previously, although those burials which were furnished were furnished much more richly than had been the case. Most of the known examples of 'Final Phase' cemeteries remained separate from settlements, although intriguingly the integration of the 'Final Phase' cemetery into the settlement at Carlton Colville (Suffolk) suggests that this pattern is not absolute. Regardless of their locations, all these 'Final Phase' cemeteries were relatively short-lived and most appear to have fallen out of use by the early eighth century.

Contrary to popular belief, inferences drawn from the archaeological record suggest that once the traditional Early Saxon cemeteries and burial rites had been abandoned the vast majority of the population began to be buried in unfurnished, west–east-orientated inhumation cemeteries either situated within the newly established missionary stations or in churchyard-type cemeteries integrated into settlements. This, it is argued, is a physical reflection of the introduction of Christian ideology pertaining to the resurrection of the dead and the concept of intercessory prayer. Intriguingly, there are strong material indications that the notion of consecrated ground was also widespread in early Christian East Anglia: executed criminals were excluded from settlement-based cemeteries, instead being buried in separate cemeteries in peripheral locations which physically mirrored their social exclusion.

Tantalising excavated remains, surface scatters of artefacts and the overwhelming absence of Middle Saxon burials from the archaeological record all suggest that these churchyard-type cemeteries formed the precursors to many of the churches which later filled the medieval landscape. Unfortunately, the nature of church sites is such that these earlier layers are either firmly sealed beneath later buildings or have been destroyed by later burials. It would appear that in the majority of cases it was the churchyard-type cemetery which provided a Christian focus for a newly converted population and, in the absence of many excavated examples, we must assume that most examples of such cemeteries remain hidden.

What is more difficult to ascertain archaeologically is whether an attendant church was founded at the same time as the cemetery or whether it was a later addition, for here we begin to reach the limits of what can be inferred from the material evidence. In an attempt to understand the situation we must utilise the surface scatters of Ipswich ware, Thetford-type ware and other Middle and Late Saxon artefacts commonly discovered in association with churches, for they offer our only real hope of interpreting the developmental sequence of individual sites.

If each of the church sites associated with a Middle Saxon scatter possessed a Christian churchyard-type cemetery this would suggest that much of the population had become wholly and actively Christian during the seventh century. If this interpretation is taken to an extreme and all of these sites are assumed to have had Middle Saxon churches as well, then we are confronted with the possibility of a very densely populated seventh-century ecclesiastical landscape. Even adopting a more moderate view which assumes that only some of these sites had churches suggests that the number of seventh-century foundations would still be higher than might previously have been expected. On the strength of the archaeological evidence it would appear that Christianity was far from the preserve of Middle Saxon royalty; rather, it was widely practised at a grass-roots level and its popularity spread very rapidly.

Conclusion

The East Anglian Conversion

The coming of Christianity to seventh-century East Anglia was undeniably one of the most significant events in the kingdom's history. Not only did it reintroduce the written word, it also laid the foundations for an ecclesiastical system which was to shape lives and landscapes for the subsequent 1,400 years. Some would have us believe that the choice to convert to Christianity was a purely political decision on the part of the king, and was of little consequence to the vast majority of the population; yet, as this book has demonstrated, the archaeological evidence clearly indicates that this was far from the case. Although the initial stages of the East Anglian conversion were instigated and nurtured by the king, the consequent adoption of Christianity throughout the kingdom was both rapid and widespread and soon developed a momentum of its own. At a popular level the adoption of the new religion resulted in the introduction of missionary stations and attendant churches, major changes to funerary practices and a significant reorganisation of the Middle Saxon landscape, with regard, in particular, to the landscape settings chosen for cemeteries.

From the outset it has been acknowledged that religion is an abstract concept and that its more numinous aspects do not leave material traces. Therefore, we cannot study that part of the conversion process which is 'all in the mind' and cannot pass comment on the motivations of those who chose to convert. Such conclusions have traditionally led archaeologists to take a very pessimistic view of the archaeological study of religion and religious conversion, but, as we have seen, we are not dealing with a lost cause. Put simply, we can and do find material traces of ritualised behaviour encouraged by religious beliefs in the archaeological record and, with careful consideration and interpretation, these can and do tell us a great deal about the religious practices of the past. Similarly, the cessation and adaptation of existing practices and the introduction of new ones also leave traces in the archaeological record which provide us with strong indications of religious change.

As was explored in Chapter 1, the development of cognitive archaeology — a fusion of elements of processual and post-processual theory — gave rise to Renfrew's identification of five characteristic themes by which we might recognise religious practices in the archaeological record.[1] Multiple examples of all five of these themes are to be found in the East Anglian conversion-period archaeological record: these have been referred to explicitly in the preceding chapters and are implicit in much more of the material presented here. For example, attention-

---

[1] Renfrew, *Archaeology of Cult*, pp. 18–20, and 'Archaeology of Religion', pp. 51–2; Renfrew and Bahn, *Archaeology: Theories, Methods and Practice*, pp. 414–20.

focusing behaviour was exhibited in both the Early Saxon cremation and inhumations rites in the central importance placed on the burial tableau — the laying-out of the corpse in its grave or on a pyre — while the notion of demarcated ritual space underpins the Christian notion of sacred burial grounds and the exclusion of criminals therefrom. The themes identified by Renfrew are indeed very applicable to the East Anglian archaeological record and they have facilitated the identification and interpretation of a number of archaeological indicators of religious practices. Furthermore, the changes exhibited in these indicators during the course of the seventh century, especially in terms of funerary practices, have enabled a comprehensive picture of the East Anglian conversion to be drawn.

The research presented in Chapter 2 demonstrated that the historical evidence provided by Bede in the *HE*, the starting point for every study of the early Anglo-Saxon Church (including this one), was clearly derived from a number of different sources, very few of which were East Anglian in origin. It is important to remember that Bede was not an historian in the modern mould; he was first and foremost a theologian, and used his historical writing to present object lessons on good Christian living. As such, the *HE* is particularly focused upon the conversion of individual kings and kingdoms, the creation of the dioceses and the unification of the disparate strands of Christianity into a single entity. Despite these obvious biases, there is a strong tendency among those addressing the subject of the East Anglian conversion (and, indeed, the conversions of other regions) to rely unquestioningly on the historical framework presented by Bede in the *HE* and to take the information contained within its pages as a full and objective account of the conversion process. Consequently, most historical and archaeological discussions of the subject to date have comprised attempts to identify the people and places referred to by Bede with features in the archaeological record. Clearly the account of the East Anglian conversion derived from the documentary sources does not provide a comprehensive explanation of events; rather, it provides a framework against which the archaeological evidence can be measured, compared and contrasted.

The historical evidence suggests that the beginning of the East Anglian conversion was marked by the baptism *c.* AD 604 of King Rædwald at the behest of King Æthelberht of Kent, an event classified by Foote as the 'Conversion Moment' (Fig. 4).[2] Æthelberht was acting on the pope's instructions, and it would seem that Rædwald's acceptance was born out of political subordination, as his subsequent apostasy and probable burial at Sutton Hoo clearly attest. After this false start it was not until the AD 630s and the reign of Rædwald's son, Sigeberht, that the conversion of the East Anglian kingdom began in earnest. The intervening period might best be thought of as Foote's 'familiarisation' or Birkeli's 'infiltration' phase (see Fig. 4), during which the East Anglian kingdom was passively exposed to Christianity through economic and political ties, but not through direct missionary contact.[3] Sigeberht had grown up in exile in Christian Gaul, where he had accepted the faith, and on his return to East Anglia he brought with him a thorough understanding of Christianity. It was Sigeberht who initiated the

---

[2] Foote, 'Historical Studies', p. 137.
[3] Berkeli is cited in Lager, 'Runestones', p. 497; Foote, 'Historical Studies', p. 137.

'Institution/Consolidation' phase of the East Anglian conversion (Fig. 4), installing the Burgundian Bishop Felix in the new episcopal see at *Dommoc*, which can be confidently identified as the disused Roman fort of Walton Castle, from where his episcopal authority began to radiate out across the kingdom. The conversion was not concerned only with infrastructure; of greater importance was the widespread conversion of the general population, and so Sigeberht also supported the Irish missionary Fursa, giving him the site of *Cnobheresburg*. An examination of the sources clearly demonstrates that Fursa's story was included in the *HE* only because Bede had access to a copy of Fursa's *Life*, yet most traditional narratives would have us believe Fursa was the only missionary at work in East Anglia. Rather, Fursa is the only missionary recorded by Bede. Both the *Anglo-Saxon Chronicle* and the anonymous *Life of Ceolfrith* record at least one other missionary, Botolph, who founded a minster at Iken, and there must have been other missionaries like him. The archaeological evidence clearly demonstrates that many missionaries were active in East Anglia of whom the historical record tells us nothing.

Another recurring difficulty with the traditional narrative of East Anglian ecclesiastical development has also been rectified here. King Ælfwald's mid-eighth-century letter to Boniface was misread by Whitelock as referring to seven East Anglian monasteries,[4] a mistake which has percolated through a number of other works and caused authors to tie themselves in knots attempting to explain it away. Reference to the original sources quickly revealed that the letter referred to the seven canonical hours and not seven monasteries at all. Rather than referring to monasteries, Ælfwald was referring to the manner in which Boniface's name and those of others were to be praised during the monastic day.

It is clear from both the historical and archaeological records that many of East Anglia's Roman buildings remained abandoned until they were put to ecclesiastical use in the seventh century. Although not all instances of this reuse are documented, many of the reoccupations can be demonstrated to have been an active part of the evangelisation of East Anglia. As we have seen, the Roman fort at Walton Castle became the site of the episcopal see, while further north, the pair of forts flanking the Great Estuary, Burgh Castle and Caister-on-Sea, along with other sites with Roman connections, became the focus of Christian communities. In every case the walled enclosure, rather than the presence of any particular building within it, seems to have been of greatest importance to the occupiers. These enclosures were not used for defensive purposes — indeed, many would not have been defensible by the seventh century — but served to mark the boundary between the secular exterior world and the religious precinct within, while simultaneously providing a strong symbolic link with the Roman past.

Once the early ecclesiastics had occupied these Roman enclosures they became missionary stations from which the holy men could begin their work within the local population. A good indication of the degree of success enjoyed by early missionaries is provided by the presence and extent of the Christian cemeteries associated with these Roman sites. From the sheer quantity of burials discovered, particularly at Caister-on-Sea, it would seem that each of these missionary stations had a zone of

---

[4] Whitelock, 'The Pre-Viking Age Church', pp. 16–17.

influence which extended far beyond its walls, with individuals from the surrounding area being buried within or close to the fort.

While Roman sites were clearly attractive to the first wave of Christian missionaries, they were not occupied to the exclusion of other sites. Their finite number meant that many other sites were put to Christian use during the course of the conversion. Other types of ready-made enclosure, Iron Age earthworks in particular, were also reoccupied, and many important Anglo-Saxon churches were founded on the summits or shoulders of low hills, on promontories or on islands in marshy floodplains. Such sites, at once topographically separated from the surrounding world and yet fully integrated into the major riverine routes of communication, were ideally suited to the purposes of those who were seeking to combine a traditional life of monastic devotion with the proactive conversion of the surrounding population. A number of East Anglian religious foundations conform to these Roman and topographic models, suggesting that they were particularly early foundations which may have played an active role in the conversion.

By far our greatest insights into the nature and progress of the East Anglia conversion are provided by the enormous quantity of funerary evidence available to us; material which, according to the tenets of cognitive archaeology, has enormous potential to reflect religiously motivated behaviour.[5] The archaeological evidence for burials and cemeteries, unlike every other class of material evidence, dates from before, during and after the period of the conversion, providing us with a unique overview of the process. Cremation was predominant in Norfolk and north Suffolk during the Early Saxon period and has been demonstrated to have been an archetypal pagan rite, laden with religious imagery and requiring a large outlay of resources. The cessation of the cremation rite during the early seventh century is the most significant archaeological indicator of the conversion, as the Christian antithesis towards cremation and its use as a totemic pagan rite at Sutton Hoo testify. Here we see evidence for Insoll's 'displacement' phase of conversion, in which old rituals are ousted by new religious practices (Fig. 4).[6] The speed with which the cremation rite was abandoned and the size of the region within which this abandonment took place suggest that the conversion process was quick and widespread at a grass-roots level. It can be confidently stated that cemeteries which contain cremations represent communities that had yet to be converted and an absence of cremation is a necessary criterion for any identification of a Christian cemetery. However, the absence of cremation from a cemetery does not automatically signal Christian burial, for there were many demonstrably pre-Christian cemeteries which did not feature cremation either.

Several aspects of the inhumation rite can be used to chart the course of the East Anglian conversion. The increasingly regular adoption of a west–east alignment for burials is often cited as one such indicator, but within East Anglia this alignment was particularly common among the inhumations of the Early Saxon period and there was no radical change in this practice over time. While it is true that a west–east orientation is a necessary criterion for identifying a Christian burial and

---

[5] Renfrew, *Archaeology of Cult*, pp. 18–20, and 'Archaeology of Religion', pp. 51–2; Renfrew and Bahn, *Archaeology: Theories, Methods and Practice*, pp. 414–20.
[6] Insoll, 'Introduction'.

that burials which are not orientated west–east are not Christian, the uniformity of this practice both before and after the period of the conversion effectively rules it out as an indicator of Christianisation.

Unfurnished burial was practised to varying degrees throughout the Early and Middle Saxon periods and is therefore not a sound criterion for recognising conversion, but the cessation of the practice of burying grave-goods is often cited as an indicator of conversion. The deposition of grave-goods did not cease completely until the early eighth century, however, and therefore cannot have resulted from the adoption of Christianity, but grave-goods became rarer in the seventh century and there was a distinct change in their character — from a Germanic to a Romano-Byzantine influence — dubbed the 'Final Phase'. These changes clearly represent a radical change in wider spheres of influence and a growth of interest in *romanitas* which can be identified with the arrival of the Church. It seems that while the presence of Germanic grave-goods signals a non-Christian burial, the presence of Romano-Byzantine grave-goods, some of them bearing strong Christian iconography, is an indication of a converted population.

The composition of 'Final Phase' grave-good assemblages also suggests that there was a move away from grave-goods interpreted as equipment or provisions for the deceased, such as weaponry or food. Instead, grave-good assemblages came to comprise clothes fasteners and items of personal jewellery. This would seem to indicate that notions of equipping the deceased for an afterlife had changed. Similarly, the clearly defined biological and cultural stages of the Early Saxon lifestyle expressed via grave-goods also disappeared during the 'Final Phase', to be replaced by more uniform types of burial assemblages which were deemed suitable for all ages and which, it has been suggested, reflected the reaching of the Christian milestone of baptism in the life of the deceased. All these interpretations sit comfortably with the idea of a conversion process which took on and adapted existing local practices, changing their character but not banning them outright, and ultimately resulted in a uniquely East Anglian form of Christianity. The significance of such grave-goods is emphasised further when the landscape context of 'Final Phase' cemeteries is also considered.

The East Anglian landscape underwent a dramatic restructuring during the Middle Saxon period and some of these upheavals can be demonstrated to have occurred as a result of religious conversion. The adoption of Christian beliefs changed attitudes towards the appropriate landscape setting for the dead, a change which in turn affected the structure and layout of settlements and cemeteries and provides us with our strongest archaeological indicators of the progress of the East Anglian conversion. Early Saxon settlements and cemeteries were separate landscape entities, although some were situated in close proximity to one another, and a near-contemporaneous abandonment of all kinds of Early Saxon cemetery occurred during the first half of the seventh century. At the same time cremation ceased to be practised and 'Final Phase' grave-goods were adopted — both argued to be strong material indicators of conversion, as is the abandonment of Early Saxon cemeteries. These Early Saxon cemeteries were superseded by a number of different types of Christian cemetery which developed in parallel for some time.

In a few cases 'Final Phase' cemeteries were established; in these the frequency of furnished burials was lower than in Early Saxon cemeteries, although those burials which were furnished were furnished much more richly than previously. These cemeteries were founded on new sites, also away from settlements, although there is some evidence to suggest that some 'Final Phase' cemeteries might have been incorporated into settlements. Most 'Final Phase' cemeteries were relatively short-lived and most appear to have fallen out of use by the early eighth century. Crucially, the relatively small number of 'Final Phase' cemeteries cannot account for the entirety of the seventh-century population, the majority of whom were apparently buried elsewhere. We are particularly fortunate in the case of the Carlton Colville cemetery, for the overtly Christian nature of some of the grave-goods allows us to unequivocally identify the cemetery as being Christian. Indeed, given the timescale for the East Anglian conversion established in Chapter 2, which attributes the first major wave of conversion proper to the reign of Sigeberht in the AD 630s, it is likely that the cemetery at Carlton Colville was founded by one of the first generation of converts. The fact that Burgh Castle lies some 10km to the north of the site may be a telling factor in this respect.

The archaeological record suggests that once the Early Saxon cemeteries and burial rites had been abandoned the vast majority of the population were not buried in 'Final Phase' cemeteries, but actually began to be buried in unfurnished, west–east-orientated inhumation cemeteries either located within the newly established missionary stations or in new churchyard-type cemeteries which were integral parts of Middle Saxon settlements. This integration of domestic and funerary landscape elements has been argued here to be a physical reflection of Christian beliefs in the resurrection and the power of intercessory prayer. The exclusion of executed criminals from these new cemeteries and their burial at spiritually liminal sites on the edge of territories also provides a tantalising material suggestion that the notion of consecrated ground, or a variation thereof, may also have earlier origins than has thus far been supposed.

The archaeological record indicates that some of these early Christian cemeteries demonstrably did not have an attendant church, and thus these churchyard-type cemeteries appear to have been the religious precursors to many later churches. In the majority of cases it would seem to have been the cemetery itself which provided a Christian focus for a newly converted population, but what is more difficult to ascertain is whether an attendant church was founded at the same time as the cemetery or whether it was a later addition. A partial answer is provided by surface scatters of Middle and Late Saxon materials discovered in association with medieval parish churches, which enable us to say something about sites' developmental sequences.

As was argued in the previous chapter, if each of the medieval churches associated with a Middle Saxon scatter possessed at least a Middle Saxon Christian churchyard-type cemetery this would suggest that much of the Middle Saxon population had become wholly and actively Christian during the seventh century. If all of these sites could be demonstrated to have been equipped with attendant Middle Saxon churches as well, then the seventh-century ecclesiastical landscape would have been very densely populated indeed. Even the more moderate assumption that only some of these sites had attendant churches suggests that the number of seventh-century foundations would still be much higher than is traditionally suggested. It would appear, therefore, that Christianity was widely practised at a grass-roots level and its popularity spread very rapidly.

While the documentary evidence for the East Anglian conversion is poor, the material culture of Anglo-Saxon East Anglia is particularly rich and contains many strong indications of the nature and extent of the conversion process. By focusing on both categories of evidence and interpreting that material within its own regional frame of reference the attempt to understand the conversion of East Anglia presented in this book has succeeded where other attempts to find a unifying theory of Anglo-Saxon conversion have failed. This success has been achieved precisely because this study has focused on one region and has not become side-tracked by attempts to explain why Christianisation should have caused any particular practice to have been adopted or adapted in one region when the opposite was true in another. In its long history Christianity has demonstrated a remarkable ability to take on different cultural shadings as different peoples have adapted it to their world-views. As a consequence there is no universal set of Christian ideals or practices, for these varied in response to the nature of the converting population. During the course of conversion many compromises were made and existing practices integrated and adapted to suit the new religion. We should be thinking in terms of there being many Christianities and, although they are linked, the fundamental differences between them mean that the conversion of a people from one place and time cannot be expected to explain the conversion of a different people in another place and time. Each episode of conversion can be studied and appreciated only within its own, highly regionalised, terms. In fact, once the extent of the potential for local variation is accepted, many of the difficulties encountered in the traditional attempts to understand conversion can be explained. To take just one widely cited example, much discussion has centred upon explaining why the conversion to Christianity in the Frankish kingdoms coincided with the origin of the practice of richly furnishing burials, while in Anglo-Saxon England it was associated with the waning of the practice.[7] Yet, armed with an understanding of the infinitely adaptive and highly regionalised nature of conversion discussed here, we would not expect two different peoples to respond to conversion in the same way. Rather than being an awkward anomaly, this variation in approach to furnished burial becomes exactly the kind of diversity that we would expect to see.

Like all syntheses, this account of the East Anglian conversion is very much a product of the available evidence and has resulted in the development of a model of conversion which, while clearly applicable to East Anglia, may very well not be applicable to the conversion of other kingdoms or regions. Similarly, the methodological approaches employed are derived from a regionally specific archaeological record, and some of the classes of material utilised here are not available in other regions. That is not to say that the methodologies and interpretative frameworks promoted here could not be fruitfully employed in the study of other Anglo-Saxon kingdoms, or indeed further afield — merely that there

---

[7] e.g. James, 'Cemeteries' and 'Burial and Status'; Young, 'Myth of the Pagan Cemetery'; Geake, 'Persistent Problems'; Burnell and James, 'The Archaeology of Conversion'.

should not be an expectation that the conclusions drawn here should be able to be mapped directly onto the material record of other regions.

As regards the regional specificity of methods and materials, Ipswich ware, for example, ubiquitous in East Anglia, was not widely used outside the region and, where it is found, it tends to be associated with higher-status sites than is the case in the East Anglian heartlands.[8] Likewise, cremation was not practised across the entire country and its cessation cannot be used as an indicator of conversion in regions where it was not practised; but, in the cremating regions (primarily the Midlands and the eastern seaboard), links between the end of the rite and conversion might usefully be explored. Other evidence is of more widespread relevance: 'Final Phase' grave-good assemblages and cemeteries, for example, constitute a phenomenon which has been recognised across much of lowland England, and, on an even broader scale, the acquisition of abandoned Roman enclosures by early ecclesiastics is a pattern which has been recognised across western Europe. Of course, the opposite is also true, and many categories of evidence which have been readily employed elsewhere in studies of conversion are not applicable to East Anglia. Northumbria, for example, is rich in Anglo-Saxon architectural and sculptural survivals, classes of evidence almost entirely absent from East Anglia, while its surviving documentary sources, and those of many other kingdoms, far outstrip the meagre East Anglian historical record.[9]

The approaches to the East Anglian material presented here have resulted in an understanding of the conversion of the East Anglian kingdom, but they have also highlighted many areas in which further fieldwork and research would be desirable. One of the greatest difficulties encountered during this research was the lack of adequately published archaeological data, and a concerted effort should be made to address this shortcoming. Exemplary publications do exist — examples include the reports on the excavations at Sutton Hoo or McKinley's analysis of the cremated remains from Spong Hill — but such reports are few and far between and tend to concentrate on exceptional sites.[10] Many sites have never been adequately published: details of the 'Final Phase' cemetery excavated at Thornham, for example, were not included in the monograph which discussed the excavation of the earthwork enclosure, a note being included to the effect that full publication was to follow,[11] while the excavations of the Middle Saxon settlement and cemetery at Burrow Hill have only ever been published in summary form.[12] The excavations at Brandon conducted in the late 1980s are still best known from one short article,[13] although the publication of a full monograph is anticipated soon, and the short summaries published to date on the results of the Deben Valley survey do not do justice to the vast body of fieldwalking data collected by John Newman.[14] Other eagerly anticipated publications include a final interpretative volume on the

[8] Blinkhorn, 'Of Cabbages and Kings'.
[9] e.g. Taylor and Taylor, *Anglo-Saxon Architecture*; Hawkes and Mills, *Northumbria's Golden Age*.
[10] Bruce Mitford, *Sutton Hoo* (3 vols); McKinley, *Anglo-Saxon Cemetery at Spong Hill VIII*.
[11] Gregory and Gurney, *Excavations at Thornham*.
[12] Fenwick, 'Insula de Burgh'.
[13] Carr *et al.*, 'Middle-Saxon Settlement at Staunch Meadow'.
[14] Newman, 'Sutton Hoo before Rædwald'; 'East Anglian Kingdom Pilot Study'; and 'Survey in the Deben Valley'.

excavations at Spong Hill, the monograph on the 'Final Phase' cemetery at Coddenham and the final report on Paul Blinkhorn's Ipswich ware project. The results of the English Heritage-funded research project 'Anglo-Saxon England *c.* 580–720: The Chronological Basis' also have the potential to confirm or radically alter some of the conclusions presented here.

Having established a synthetic model for the East Anglian conversion, further fieldwork is needed to test the hypotheses developed here. It is clear that fieldwork examining the Middle Saxon reuse of the region's Roman forts would be extremely rewarding. The excavations conducted at Burgh Castle in the 1960s were poorly recorded and, despite Johnson's efforts in bringing them to publication, resulted in the loss of significant quantities of highly relevant data.[15] To date less than a quarter of the fort's interior has been excavated and the archaeological potential of this site remains very high. A renewed academic interest in the site could answer many questions about its Roman and post-Roman occupation, not least regarding the supposed association with Fursa's *Cnobheresburg*. Likewise, the archaeological potential of the fort at Brancaster is also high and here we know next to nothing about the fort's interior, except what can be plotted from aerial photographs. The patterns identified in this book strongly suggest that the fort would have been put to missionary use in the seventh century. Encouragingly, a renewed campaign of fieldwork is already underway at the Roman town of *Venta Icenorum*. Preliminary geophysical survey results have already increased our understanding of the town, while a detailed analysis of the aerial photographic evidence for the town is being undertaken by the Norfolk National Mapping Programme. One of this new project's main aims is to increase our understanding of the town's post-Roman development, and the excavations conducted in the churchyard within the walls have already proved illuminating; it will be interesting to see if further evidence to support the interpretations offered here is forthcoming.[16]

Despite the many fieldwalking surveys which have been conducted across the two counties, to date there has not yet been a comprehensive synthesis of those churches known to be associated with Ipswich ware and Thetford-type ware scatters. Many of the published examples have been mentioned here, but the Norfolk and Suffolk Historic Environment Records contain references to many other churches within or adjacent to substantial artefact scatters, which may allow something of their origins and early development to be ascertained. We should also be more pro-active in seeking opportunities to examine what lies beneath many of our parish churches through the examination of disturbed ground in churchyards, the observation of freshly dug graves and the archaeological monitoring of groundworks.

In a similar vein, much greater archaeological attention needs to be paid to the extensive evidence for Middle Saxon East Anglia that lies buried beneath modern-day settlements. We have seen here that such material has the potential to inform us about the origins of these settlements and provide information about the living and the dead. More specifically, this Middle Saxon material has the potential to answer

---

[15] Johnson, *Burgh Castle*.
[16] Bowden and Bescoby, 'The plan of *Venta Icenorum*'; Percival, 'Archaeological Evaluation at Caistor St Edmund'.

some of the questions raised here about the foundation and development of early Christian churchyard-type cemeteries, both with and without attendant churches. Today most archaeological fieldwork is conducted through the planning process and it is important that the potential of such work to address the research agenda outlined here is given due consideration in the development control process. It is only by collecting such data that we will be able to gain a greater understanding of the development of the Middle Saxon landscape, in which the conversion to Christianity has been demonstrated to have played such a large part.

Finally, on the subject of scale, a very broad-brush archaeological synthesis has been presented here, identifying a number of regional trends which signify the nature and progress of the conversion. Such an approach has proved very suitable for this study of the East Anglian conversion, but much could usefully be gained by adopting a sub-regional or even a highly localised approach to the subject, as exemplified by the discussion of the environs of *Venta Icenorum* presented in Chapter 5. For all of the similarities discussed here, there are also many differences between, for example, the archaeological records of north-west Norfolk and south-east Suffolk, while that of the eastern coast around the Great Estuary is different again. The variability of Christianity and its willingness to adapt and incorporate existing local practices in order to achieve conversion has been a recurring theme in this book, so it is appropriate that, as well as thinking in terms of one kingdom-wide East Anglian conversion, we should also consider the prospect of many smaller, more regionalised, East Anglian conversions.

In conclusion, it is safe to say that the surviving documentary sources merely provide an outline of the conversion of East Anglia which the archaeological evidence fleshes out, confirming the details of this sketch and indicating that the true picture of the East Anglian conversion is one of immense scale and variety. Far from supporting the notion of a nominal conversion on the part of the king which had little effect on the lower echelons of society, all of the different classes of evidence considered in this book point inexorably towards the same conclusion: once Christianity had been introduced to seventh-century East Anglia the conversion of the wider population was a significant and wide-reaching process which occurred very quickly and was exceedingly successful at a grass-roots level. The adoption of Christianity resulted in dramatic changes in the way that the living thought of and treated the dead, and precipitated a wide-scale restructuring of the East Anglian landscape, the effects of which still affect our daily lives some 1,400 years later.

Bibliography

Primary Sources

Alecto, *The Digital Domesday Book* [CD-ROM] (Hampshire, 2002)

Blake, E. (ed.), *Liber Eliensis* (London, 1962)

Bradley, S. (ed. and trans.), *Anglo-Saxon Poetry* (London, 2003)

Colgrave, B. (ed.), *The Earliest Life of Gregory the Great, by an Anonymous Monk of Whitby* (Cambridge, 1968)

—, (ed.), *Felix's Life of Saint Guthlac* (Cambridge, 1956)

—, and Mynors, R. (eds), *Bede's Ecclesiastical History of the English People* (Oxford, 1969)

Emerton, E. (ed. and trans.), *The Letters of Saint Boniface* (New York, 1940)

Erbe, T., *Mirk's Festival* (London, 1905)

Fairweather, J. (ed. and trans.), *Liber Eliensis* (Woodbridge, 2005)

Foley, W. and Holder, A. (eds and trans), *Bede: A Biblical Miscellany* (Liverpool, 1999)

Haddan, A. and Stubbs, W. (eds), *Councils and Ecclesiastical Documents Relating to Great Britain and Ireland*, vol. 3 (Oxford, 1871)

Hamilton, N. (ed.), *Willelmi Malmesbiriensis monachi De gestis pontificum Anglorum libri quinque* (London, 1870)

Hardwick, C. (ed.), *Thomas of Elmham: Historia Monasterii S. Augustini Cantuariensis*, Rolls Series 8 (London, 1858)

Heaney, S. (trans.), *Beowulf* (London, 1999)

Jack, G. (ed.), *Beowulf: A Student Edition* (Oxford, 1994)

Krusch, B. (ed.), *Monumenta Germaniæ Historica, Scriptores Rerum Merovingicarum, 4: Passiones vitaeque sanctorum aevi merovingici* (Hannover, 1902)

Luard, H. (ed.), *Bartholomew Cotton: Historia anglicana (A.D.449–1298)*, Rolls Series 16 (London, 1859)

Lumby, J. (ed.), *Polychronicon Ranulphi Higden monachi Cestrensis*, vol. 6, Rolls Series 41, 6 (London, 1876)

McClure, J. and Collins, R. (eds), *Bede: The Ecclesiastical History of the English People* (Oxford, 1999)

Martyn, J. (ed. and trans.), *The Letters of Gregory the Great*, 3 vols (Toronto, 2004)

Mynors, R., Thomson, R. and Winterbottom, M. (eds and trans), *Gesta regum Anglorum by William of Malmesbury* (Oxford, 1998)

Plummer, C. (ed.), *Venerabilis Baedae Opera Historica*, vol. 1 (Oxford, 1896)

—, and Earle, J. (eds), *Two of the Saxon Chronicles Parallel* (Oxford, 1898)

Preest, D. (trans.), *The Deeds of the Bishops of England by William of Malmesbury* (Woodbridge, 2002)

Rackham, O. (ed. and trans.), *Transitus Beati Fursei* (Norwich, 2007)

Saunders, H. (ed.), *The First Register of Norwich Cathedral Priory* (Norwich, 1939)

Tangl, M. (ed.), *Die Briefe des Heiligen Bonifatius und Lullus* (Berlin, 1916)

Wallis, F. (trans.) *Bede: The Reckoning of Time* (Liverpool, 2004)

Webb, J. and Farmer, D. (eds and trans), *The Age of Bede* (London, 1998)

Whitelock, D. (ed. and trans.), *Anglo-Saxon Wills* (Cambridge, 1930)

—, (ed. and trans.), *English Historical Documents c.500–1042*, 2nd edn (London, 1979)

—, Douglas, D. and Tucker, S. (eds and trans), *The Anglo-Saxon Chronicle* (London, 1961)

Secondary Sources

Abrams, L., 'The Anglo-Saxons and the Christianization of Scandinavia', *Anglo-Saxon England* 24 (1995), pp. 213–49

—, 'Conversion and Assimilation', in D. Hadley and J. Richards (eds), *Cultures in Contact* (Brepols, 2000), pp. 135–53

Abramson, T., *Sceattas: An Illustrated Guide* (Great Dunham, 2006)

Albone, J., Massey, S. and Tremlett, S., 'The Archaeology of Norfolk's Coastal Zone', unpublished report for English Heritage (2007)

Allan, T., *The Archaeology of the Afterlife* (London, 2004)

Allen, J. and Fulford, M., 'Fort Building and Military Supply along Britain's Eastern Channel and North Sea Coasts: The Later Second and Third Centuries', *Britannia* 30 (1999), pp. 163–84

Allen, J., Fulford, M. and Pearson, A., '"*Branodunum*" on the Saxon Shore (North Norfolk): A Local Origin for the Building Material', *Britannia* 32 (2001), pp. 271–5

Anderson, S., 'The Human Skeletal Remains from Caister-on-Sea', in M. Darling with D. Gurney, *Caister-on-Sea: Excavations by Charles Green 1951–55*, East Anglian Archaeology 60 (Gressenhall, 1993), pp. 261–8

—, *The Human Skeletal Remains from Staunch Meadow, Brandon, Suffolk*, unpublished Ancient Monuments Laboratory Report 99/90 (1990)

—, and Birkett, D., 'The Human Skeletal Remains from Burgh Castle', in M. Darling with D. Gurney, *Caister-on-Sea: Excavations by Charles Green 1951–55*, East Anglian Archaeology 60 (Gressenhall, 1993), pp. 256–60

Andrews, P., 'Middle Saxon Norfolk: Evidence for Settlement 650–850', *Norfolk Archaeological and Historical Research Group Annual* 1 (1992), pp. 13–28

Ariès, P., *The Hour of Our Death* (London, 1981)

Armstrong, G. and Wood, I. (eds), *Christianizing Peoples and Converting Individuals* (Turnhout, 2000)

Arnold, C., *An Archaeology of the Early Anglo-Saxon Kingdoms* (London, 1997)

—, 'Wealth and Social Structure: A Matter of Life and Death', in P. Rahtz, T. Dickinson and L. Watts (eds), *Anglo-Saxon Cemeteries 1979*, BAR British Series 82 (Oxford, 1980), pp. 81–142

—, and Wardle, D., 'Early Medieval Settlement Patterns in England', *Medieval Archaeology* 25 (1981), pp. 145–9

Ashbee, P., 'Changing Prehistoric Configurations', in C. Barringer (ed.), *Aspects of East Anglian Pre-History* (Norwich, 1984), pp. 1–11

Aston, M., *Monasteries in the Landscape* (Stroud, 2000)

Avent, R., *Anglo-Saxon Garnet Inlaid Disc and Composite Brooches. Part i: Discussion* (Oxford, 1975)

Bachelard, G., *The Psychoanalysis of Fire* (Boston, 1964)

Bagge, S. and Nordeide, S., 'The Kingdom of Norway', in N. Berend (ed.), *Christianization and the Rise of Christian Monarchy* (Cambridge, 2007), pp. 121–66

Bahn, P. (ed.), *Tombs, Graves and Mummies* (London, 1996)

Bales, E., Horlock, S. and Tremlett, S., 'Norwich, Thetford and A11 Corridor NMP Project
—, Recent Results and Highlights', *The Annual: The Bulletin of the Norfolk Archaeological and Historical Research Group* 18 (2009), pp. 23–32

Barker, P., *Techniques of Archaeological Excavation*, 3rd edn (London, 1993)

Barnard, L., 'Bede and Eusebius as Church Historians', in G. Bonner (ed.), *Famulus Christi* (London, 1976), pp. 106–24

Barrett, J., 'Agency, the Duality of Structure, and the Problem of the Archaeological Record', in I. Hodder (ed.), *Archaeological Theory Today* (Cambridge, 2001), pp. 141–64
—, 'Towards an Archaeology of Ritual', in P. Garwood, D. Jennings, R. Skeates and J. Thomas (eds), *Sacred and Profane* (Oxford, 1991), pp. 1–9

Barrowclough, D. and Malone, C. (eds), *Cult in Context: Reconsidering Ritual in Archaeology* (Oxford, 2007)

Bartlett, R., 'From Paganism to Christianity in Medieval Europe', in N. Berend (ed.), *Christianization and the Rise of Christian Monarchy* (Cambridge, 2007), pp. 47–72

Bassett, S., 'In Search of the Origins of Anglo-Saxon Kingdoms', in S. Bassett (ed.), *The Origins of Anglo-Saxon Kingdoms* (Leicester, 1989), pp. 1–27

Batcock, N., *The Ruined and Disused Churches of Norfolk*, East Anglian Archaeology 51 (Gressenhall, 1991)

Bell, T., 'Churches on Roman Buildings: Christian Associations and Roman Masonry in Anglo-Saxon England', *Medieval Archaeology* 42 (1998), pp. 1–18
—, *The Religious Reuse of Roman Structures in Early Medieval England*, BAR British Series 390 (Oxford, 2005)

Bellinger, R. and Sims, J., 'Caistor St Edmund Fieldwalking Project 1992–1994', *Norfolk Archaeological and Historical Research Group Annual* 5 (1996), pp. 11–20

Berend, N. (ed.), *Christianization and the Rise of Christian Monarchy* (Cambridge, 2007)

Bertemes, F. and Biehl, P., 'The Archaeology of Cult and Religion: An Introduction', in P. Biehl and F. Bertemes with H. Meller (eds), *The Archaeology of Cult and Religion* (Budapest, 2001), pp. 11–24

Bieler, L., 'Ireland's Contribution to the Culture of Northumbria', in G. Bonner (ed.), *Famulus Christi* (London, 1976), pp. 210–28

Binford, L., 'Archaeology as Anthropology', *American Antiquity* 28 (1962), pp. 217–25

Binski, P., *Medieval Death* (London, 1996)

Blair, J., 'Anglo-Saxon Minsters: A Topographical Review', in J. Blair and R. Sharpe (eds), *Pastoral Care Before the Parish* (Leicester, 1992), pp. 226–66
—, *The Church in Anglo-Saxon Society* (Oxford, 2005)
—, 'Ecclesiastical Organization and Pastoral Care in Anglo-Saxon England', *Early Medieval Europe* 4 (2) (1995), pp. 193–212
—, 'A Handlist of Anglo-Saxon Saints', in A. Thacker and R. Sharpe (eds), *Local Saints and Local Churches in the Early Medieval West* (Oxford, 2002), pp. 495–565
—, 'Minster Churches in the Landscape', in D. Hooke (ed.), *Anglo-Saxon Settlements* (Oxford, 1988), pp. 35–58
—, (ed.), *Minsters and Parish Churches* (Oxford, 1988)
—, and Sharpe, R. (eds), *Pastoral Care Before the Parish* (Leicester, 1992)

Blair, P., *The World of Bede* (Cambridge, 1990)

Blinkhorn, P., 'Early and Middle Saxon Pottery', in G. Hey (ed.), *Yarnton: Saxon and Medieval Settlement and Landscape* (Oxford, 2004), pp. 267–73

—, 'Of Cabbages and Kings: Production, Trade, and Consumption in Middle-Saxon England', in M. Anderton (ed.), *Anglo-Saxon Trading Centres* (Glasgow, 1999), pp. 4–23

Blomkvist, N., Brink, S. and Lindkvist, T., 'The Kingdom of Sweden', in N. Berend (ed.), *Christianization and the Rise of Christian Monarchy* (Cambridge, 2007), pp. 167–213

Boddington, A., 'Models of Burial, Settlement and Worship: The 'Final Phase' Reviewed', in E. Southworth (ed.), *Anglo-Saxon Cemeteries: A Reappraisal* (Stroud, 1990), pp. 177–99

Bond, J., 'Burnt Offerings: Animal Bone in Anglo-Saxon Cremations', *World Archaeology* 28 (1996), pp. 76–88

—, 'The Cremated Animal Bone', in J. McKinley, *The Anglo-Saxon Cemetery at Spong Hill, North Elmham. Part VIII: The Cremations*, East Anglian Archaeology 69 (Gressenhall, 1994), pp. 121–35

Bonner, G. (ed.), *Famulus Christi* (London, 1976)

Bonney, D., 'Early Boundaries and Estates in Southern England', in P. Sawyer (ed.), *English Medieval Settlement* (London, 1979), pp. 41–55

—, 'Early Boundaries in Wessex', in P. Fowler (ed.), *Archaeology and the Landscape* (London, 1972), pp. 168–86

—, 'Pagan Saxon Burials and Boundaries in Wiltshire', *Wiltshire Archaeological and Natural History Journal* 61 (1966), pp. 25–30

Bowden, W. and Bescoby, D., 'The Plan of *Venta Icenorum* (Caistor-by-Norwich): Interpreting a New Geophysical Survey', *Journal of Roman Archaeology* 21 (2008), pp. 324–34

Bowie, F., *The Anthropology of Religion*, 2nd edn (Oxford, 2006)

Bradley, R., *Ritual and Domestic Life in Prehistoric Europe* (London, 2005)

Branston, B., *The Lost Gods of England* (London, 1957)

Brink, S., 'New Perspectives on the Christianization of Scandinavia and the Organization of the Early Church', in J. Adams and K. Holman (eds), *Scandinavia and Europe 800–1350* (Turnhout, 2004), pp. 163–75

Brookes, S., 'Walking with Anglo-Saxons: Landscapes of the Dead in Early Anglo-Saxon Kent', *Anglo-Saxon Studies in Archaeology and History* 14 (2007), pp. 143–53

Brothwell, D., *Digging Up Bones*, 3rd edn (London, 1981)

Brown, D., 'Swastika patterns', in V. Evison (ed.), *Angles, Saxons and Jutes* (Oxford, 1981), pp. 227–40

Brown, G. H., *Bede the Educator*, Jarrow Lecture 1996 (Jarrow, 1996)

Brown, M. A., 'Grave Orientation: A Further View', *Archaeological Journal* 140 (1983), pp. 322–8

Brown, M. P., *How Christianity Came to Britain and Ireland* (Oxford, 2006)

—, *The Life of St. Fursey* (Norwich, 2001)

Brown, P., *The Rise of Western Christendom*, 2nd edn (London, 2003)

Brown, T. and Foard, G., 'The Saxon Landscape: A Regional Perspective', in P. Everson and T. Williamson (eds), *The Archaeology of Landscape* (Manchester, 1998), pp. 67–94

Browne, T., *Hydriotaphia, Urne-Buriall, or, A Discourse of the Sepulchrall Urnes lately found in Norfolk* (London, 1658)

Bruce-Mitford, R., *Aspects of Anglo-Saxon Archaeology* (London, 1974)

—, *The Sutton Hoo Ship-Burial*, vol. 1 (London, 1975)

—, *The Sutton Hoo Ship-Burial*, vol. 2 (London, 1978)

—, *The Sutton Hoo Ship-Burial*, vol. 3 (London, 1983)

Brück, J., 'Ritual and Rationality: Some Problems of Interpretation in European Archaeology', *European Journal of Archaeology* 2 (3) (1999), pp. 313–44

Brugmann, B., 'The Role of Continental Artefact-Types in Sixth-Century Kentish Chronology', in J. Hines, K. Høilund Nielsen and F. Siegmund (eds), *The Pace of Change* (Oxford, 1999), pp. 37–64

Brush, K., 'Adorning the Dead: The Social Significance of Early Anglo-Saxon Funerary Dress in England', unpublished PhD thesis, University of Cambridge (1993)

Buckberry, J., 'Missing, Presumed Buried? Bone Diagenesis and the Under-Representation of Anglo-Saxon Children', *Assemblage* 5 (2000)
http://www.shef.ac.uk/assem/5/buckberr.html, last accessed 1 June 2009

Bullough, D., 'Burial, Community and Belief in the Early Medieval West', in P. Wormald (ed.), *Ideal and Reality in Frankish and Anglo-Saxon Society* (Oxford, 1983), pp. 177–201

Burnell, S. and James, E., 'The Archaeology of Conversion on the Continent in the Sixth and Seventh Centuries: Some Observations and Comparisons with Anglo-Saxon England', in R. Gameson (ed.), *St Augustine and the Conversion of England* (Stroud, 1999), pp. 83–106

Butler, L., 'The Churchyard in Eastern England, AD 900–1100: Some Lines of Development', in P. Rahtz, T. Dickinson and L. Watts (eds), *Anglo-Saxon Cemeteries 1979*, BAR British Series 82 (Oxford, 1980), pp. 383–9

—, and Morris, R. (eds), *The Anglo-Saxon Church*, CBA Research Report 60 (London, 1986)

Bynum, C., *The Resurrection of the Body* (New York, 1995)

Cabot, S., Davies, G. and Hoggett, R., 'Sedgeford: Excavations of a Rural Settlement in Norfolk', in J. Hines, A. Lane and M. Redknap (eds), *Land, Sea and Home* (Leeds, 2004), pp. 313–24

Cambridge, E. and Rollason, D., 'The Pastoral Organisation of the Anglo-Saxon Church: A Review of the "Minster Hypothesis"', *Early Medieval Europe* 4 (1) (1995), pp. 87–104

Camden, W., *Britannia* (Oxford, 1695)

Campbell, J., (ed.), *The Anglo-Saxons* (London, 1982)

—, 'Bede I', in J. Campbell (ed.), *Essays in Anglo-Saxon History* (London, 1986), pp. 1–28

—, 'Bede II', in J. Campbell (ed.), *Essays in Anglo-Saxon History* (London, 1986), pp. 29–48

—, 'Bede's Words for Places', in P. Sawyer (ed.), *Names, Words and Graves* (Leeds, 1979), pp. 34–54

—, 'The East Anglian Sees before the Conquest', in I. Atherton, E. Fernie, C. Harper-Bill and H. Smith (eds), *Norwich Cathedral: Church City and Diocese 1096–1996* (London, 1996), pp. 3–21

—, 'Rædwald (d. 616×27)', *Oxford Dictionary of National Biography* (Oxford, 2004) http://www.oxforddnb.com/view/article/23265, last accessed 20 Oct 2009

—, 'Sigeberht (fl. 630/31–654)', *Oxford Dictionary of National Biography* (Oxford, 2004) http://www.oxforddnb.com/view/article/25531, last accessed 20 Oct 2009

Carnegie, S. and Filmer-Sankey, W., 'A Saxon "Cremation Pyre" from the Snape Anglo-Saxon Cemetery, Suffolk', *Anglo-Saxon Studies in Archaeology and History* 6 (1993), pp. 107–12

Carr, R., 'The Archaeological Potential of Bury St Edmunds', *East Anglian Archaeology* 1 (1975), pp. 46–56

—, Tester, A. and Murphy, P., 'The Middle-Saxon Settlement at Staunch Meadow, Brandon', *Antiquity* 62 (1988), pp. 371–7

Caruth, J., 'Ipswich, Hewlett Packard plc, Whitehouse Industrial Estate (IPS247)', *Proceedings of the Suffolk Institute of Archaeology and History* 38 (4) (1996), pp. 476–9

Carver, M., 'Boat-Burial in Britain: Ancient Custom or Political Signal?', in O. Crumlin-Pedersen and B. Munch Thye (eds), *The Ship as Symbol in Prehistoric and Medieval Scandinavia* (Copenhagen, 1995), pp. 111–24

—, 'Burial as Poetry: The Context of Treasure in Anglo-Saxon Graves', in E. Tyler (ed.), *Treasure in the Medieval West* (York, 2000), pp. 25–48

—, 'Conversion and Politics on the Eastern Seaboard of Britain', in B. Crawford (ed.), *Conversion and Christianity in the North Sea World* (St Andrews, 1998), pp. 11–40

—, (ed.), *The Cross Goes North* (York, 2003)

—, (ed.), *In Search of Cult* (Woodbridge, 1993)

—, 'Kingship and Material Culture in Early Anglo-Saxon East Anglia', in S. Bassett (ed.), *The Origins of Anglo-Saxon Kingdoms* (Leicester, 1989), pp. 141–58

—, 'Pre-Viking Traffic in the North Sea', in S. McGrail (ed.), *Maritime Celts, Frisians and Saxons* (York, 1990), pp. 117–25

—, *Sutton Hoo: A Seventh-Century Princely Burial Ground and its Context* (London, 2005)

—, *Sutton Hoo: Burial Ground of Kings?* (London, 1998)

—, and Fern, C., 'The Seventh-Century Burial Rites and Their Sequence', in M. Carver, *Sutton Hoo: A Seventh-Century Princely Burial Ground and its Context* (London, 2005), pp. 283–313

Chadwick, H., 'The Sutton Hoo Ship Burial VIII: Who Was He?', *Antiquity* 14 (1940), pp. 76–87

Chaney, W., *The Cult of Kingship in Anglo-Saxon England* (Manchester, 1970)

Chatwin, C., *British Regional Geology: East Anglia and Adjoining Areas*, 4th edn (London, 1961)

Chester, G., 'Notice of a Gold Cross found at Wilton, Norfolk', *Norfolk Archaeology* 3 (1852), pp. 374–6

Chester-Kadwell, M., *Early Anglo-Saxon Communities in the Landscape of Norfolk*, BAR British Series 481 (Oxford, 2009)

—, 'Metal-Detector Finds in Context: New Light on 'Dark Age' Cemeteries in the Landscape of Norfolk', *Archaeological Review from Cambridge* 20 (1) (2005), pp. 70–96

—, 'Metallic Taste: Archaeologists and the Treasure Hunters', in D. Barrowclough (ed.), *Our Precious Past* (Cambridge, 2004), pp. 49–68

Church, S., 'Paganism in Conversion-Age Anglo-Saxon England: The Evidence of Bede's Ecclesiastical History Reconsidered', *History* 93 (2008), pp. 162–80

Clark, G., *Archaeology and Society*, 3rd edn (London, 1960)

Clarke, D., *Analytical Archaeology* (London, 1968)

—, 'Archaeology: The Loss of Innocence', *Antiquity* 47 (1973), 6–18

Clarke, R., 'Norfolk in the Dark Ages 400–800: Part II', *Norfolk Archaeology* 27 (1940), pp. 215–49

Collingwood, W. G., 'The Whissonsett Cross', *Norfolk Archaeology* 15 (1904), pp. 316–23

Costambeys, M., 'Willibrord [St Willibrord] (657/8–739)', *Oxford Dictionary of National Biography* (Oxford, 2004) http://www.oxforddnb.com/view/article/29576, last accessed 1 June 2009

Cowdrey, H., 'Stigand (d. 1072)', *Oxford Dictionary of National Biography* (Oxford, 2004) http://www.oxforddnb.com/view/article/26523, last accessed 1 June 2009

Cox, J., 'Ecclesiastical History', in W. Page (ed.), *The Victoria History of the County of Suffolk*, vol. 2 (London, 1907), pp. 1–52

Cozens-Hardy, B., 'The Early Days of the Society', *Norfolk Archaeology* 29 (1946), pp. 1–7

Crabtree, P., 'The Symbolic Role of Animals in Anglo-Saxon England: Evidence from Burials and Cremations', in K. Ryan and P. Crabtree (eds), *The Symbolic Role of Animals in Archaeology* (Philadelphia, 1995), pp. 20–26

Cramp, R., *Wearmouth and Jarrow Monastic Sites*, vol. 1 (London, 2005)

Crawford, B. (ed.), *Conversion and Christianity in the North Sea World* (St Andrews, 1998)

Crawford, S., 'Anglo-Saxon Women, Furnished Burial, and the Church', in D. Wood (ed.), *Women and Religion in Medieval England* (Oxford, 2003), pp. 1–12

—, *Childhood in Anglo-Saxon England* (Stroud, 1999)

—, 'Children, Death and the Afterlife in Anglo-Saxon England', *Anglo-Saxon Studies in Archaeology and History* 6 (1993), pp. 83–91

—, 'Children, Grave Goods and Social Status in Early Anglo-Saxon England', in J. Derevenski (ed.), *Children and Material Culture* (London, 2000), pp. 169–79

—, 'Votive Deposition, Religion and the Anglo-Saxon Furnished Burial Rite', *World Archaeology* 36 (2004), pp. 87–102

—, 'When do Anglo-Saxon Children Count?', *Journal of Theoretical Archaeology* 2 (1991), pp. 17–24

Crawley, P., 'An Archaeological Excavation and Watching Brief at Uplands, Caister-on-Sea, Norfolk: Assessment Report and Updated Project Design', unpublished NAU Archaeology client report 1878a (2009)

Cremation Society of Great Britain, *The History of Modern Cremation in Great Britain from 1874* (London, 1974)

Cronyn, J., *The Elements of Archaeological Conservation* (London, 1990)

Crowfoot, E., 'The Textiles', in R. Bruce-Mitford, *The Sutton Hoo Ship-Burial*, vol. 3 (London, 1983), pp. 409–79

Cubitt, C., *Anglo-Saxon Church Councils c.650–c.850* (London, 1995)

Cuming, G. (ed.), *The Mission of the Church and the Propagation of the Faith* (Cambridge, 1970)

Cunliffe, B., 'The Saxon Shore – Some Problems and Misconceptions', in D. Johnson (ed.), *The Saxon Shore* (York, 1977), pp. 1–6

Cusack, C., *Conversion Among the Germanic Peoples* (London, 1998)

Cushion, B. and Davison, A., *Earthworks of Norfolk*, East Anglian Archaeology 104 (Gressenhall, 2003)

Dahl, L., *The Roman Camp and the Irish Saint at Burgh Castle* (London, 1913)

Dales, D., *A Light to the Isles* (Cambridge, 1997)

Dallas, C., 'Middle and Late Saxon Pottery', in M. Darling with D. Gurney, *Caister-on-Sea Excavations by Charles Green, 1951–55*, East Anglian Archaeology 60 (Gressenhall, 1993), pp. 218–22

—, 'The Post-Roman Pottery', in S. Johnson, *Burgh Castle, Excavations by Charles Green 1958–61*, East Anglian Archaeology 20 (Gressenhall, 1983), pp. 104–8

Daniell, C., *Death and Burial in Medieval England, 1066–1550* (London, 1997)

Dark, K., *Civitas to Kingdom* (Leicester, 1994)

—, and Dark, P., *The Landscape of Roman Britain* (Stroud, 1997)

Darling, M. with Gurney, D., *Caister-on-Sea Excavations by Charles Green, 1951–55*, East Anglian Archaeology 60 (Gressenhall, 1993)

Darvill, T. and Russell, M., *Archaeology after PPG16* (London, 2002)

Davies, J., *Venta Icenorum* (Norwich, 2001)

Davies, W., 1992. 'The Myth of the Celtic Church', in N. Edwards and A. Lane (eds), *The Early Church in Wales and the West* (Oxford, 1992), pp. 12–21

Davison, A., 'The Archaeology of the Parish of West Acre. Part 1: Field Survey Evidence', *Norfolk Archaeology* 44 (2003), pp. 202–21

—, 'The Distribution of Medieval Settlement in West Harling', *Norfolk Archaeology* 38 (1983), pp. 329–36

—, *The Evolution of Settlement in Three Parishes in South-East Norfolk*, East Anglian Archaeology 49 (Gressenhall, 1990)

—, 'The Field Archaeology of the Mannington and Wolterton Estates', *Norfolk Archaeology* 42 (1995), pp. 160–84

—, 'Little Hockham', *Norfolk Archaeology* 40 (1987), pp. 84–93

—, with Cushion, B., 'The Archaeology of the Hargham Estate', *Norfolk Archaeology* 43 (1999), pp. 257–74

—, Green, B. and Milligan, B., *Illington: A Study of a Breckland Parish and its Anglo-Saxon Cemetery*, East Anglian Archaeology 63 (Gressenhall, 1993)

Davison, K., 'History of Walton Priory', in S. West, 'The Excavation of Walton Priory', *Proceedings of the Suffolk Institute of Archaeology* 33 (2) (1974), pp. 141–9

Dearmer, P., *The Parson's Handbook*, 12th edn (Oxford, 1949)

Department of the Environment, *Planning Policy Guidance Note 16: Archaeology and Planning* (London, 1990)

Dickens, A., Mortimer, R. and Tipper, J., 'The Early Anglo-Saxon Settlement and Cemetery at Bloodmoor Hill, Carlton Colville, Suffolk: A Preliminary Report', *Anglo-Saxon Studies in Archaeology and History* 13 (2006), pp. 63–79

Dickinson, T. and Speake, G., 'The Seventh-Century Cremation Burial in Asthall Barrow, Oxfordshire: A Reassessment', in M. Carver (ed.), *The Age of Sutton Hoo* (Woodbridge, 1992), pp. 95–130

Dowden, K., *European Paganism* (London, 2000)

Downes, J., 'Cremation: A Spectacle and a Journey', in J. Downes and T. Pollard (eds), *The Loved Body's Corruption* (Glasgow, 1999), pp. 3–29

Draper, S., 'Roman Estates to English Parishes? The Legacy of Desmond Bonney Reconsidered', in R. Collins and J. Gerrard (eds), *Debating Late Antiquity in Britain AD 300–700*, BAR British Series 365 (Oxford, 2004), pp. 55–64

Dumville, D., 'The Anglian Collection of Royal Genealogies and Regnal Lists', *Anglo-Saxon England* 5 (1976), pp. 23–50

Dunn, M., *The Christianization of the Anglo-Saxons, c.597–c.700* (London, 2009)

Dunning, G., Hurst, J., Myres, J. and Tischler, F., 'Anglo-Saxon Pottery: A Symposium', *Medieval Archaeology* 3 (1959), pp. 1–78

Eaton, T., *Plundering the Past: Roman Stonework in Medieval Britain* (Stroud, 2000)

Edwards, D., 'The Archaeology of Religion', in M. Díaz-Andreu, S. Lucy, S. Babić and D. Edwards, *The Archaeology of Identity* (London, 2005), pp. 110–28

Edwards, D.A. and Green, J., 'The Saxon Shore Fort and Settlement at Brancaster, Norfolk', in D. Johnson (ed.), *The Saxon Shore*, CBA Research Report 18 (York, 1977), pp. 21–9

Effros, B., *Caring for Body and Soul* (Philadelphia, PA, 2002)

—, *Merovingian Mortuary Archaeology and the Making of the Early Middle Ages* (London, 2003)

Ekwall, E., *The Concise Oxford Dictionary of English Place-Names*, 4th edn (Oxford, 1960)

Emery, A., *Greater Medieval Houses of England and Wales, 1300–1500. Volume II: East Anglia, Central England and Wales* (Cambridge, 2000)

Evans, A., *The Sutton Hoo Ship Burial* (London, 1994)

Everitt, A., *Continuity and Colonization* (Leicester, 1986)

Evison, V., 'An Anglo-Saxon Cemetery at Holborough, Kent', *Archaeologia Cantiana* 70 (1956), pp. 84–141

Ewing, T., *Gods and Worshippers in the Viking and Germanic World* (Stroud, 2008)

Fairclough, J. and Hardy, M., *Thornham and the Waveney Valley* (Great Dunham, 2004)

Fairclough, J. and Plunkett, S., 'Drawings of Walton Castle and Other Monuments in Walton and Felixstowe', *Proceedings of the Suffolk Institute of Archaeology and History* 39 (4) (2000), pp. 419–59

Faulkner, N., *Hidden Treasure* (London, 2003)

Faull, M., 'The Location and Relationship of the Sancton Anglo-Saxon Cemeteries', *Antiquaries Journal* 56 (1976), pp. 227–33

Fenwick, V., 'Insula de Burgh: Excavations at Burrow Hill, Butley, Suffolk 1978–1981', *Anglo-Saxon Studies in Archaeology and History* 3 (1984), pp. 35–54

Filmer-Sankey, W. and Pestell, T., *Snape Anglo-Saxon Cemetery: Excavations and Surveys 1824–1992*, East Anglian Archaeology 95 (Ipswich, 2001)

Finneran, N., *The Archaeology of Christianity in Africa* (Stroud, 2002)

Flannery, K. and Marcus, J., 'Cognitive Archaeology', in D. Whitley (ed.), *Reader in Archaeological Theory* (London, 1998), pp. 35–48

Fletcher, R., *The Conversion of Europe* (London, 1997)

Foot, S., 'Anglo-Saxon Minsters: A Review of Terminology', in J. Blair and R. Sharpe (eds), *Pastoral Care Before the Parish* (Leicester, 1992), pp. 212–25

—, *Monastic Life in Anglo-Saxon England, c.600–900* (Cambridge, 2006)

—, 'What was an Early Anglo-Saxon Monastery?', in J. Loades (ed.), *Monastic Studies* (Bangor, 1990), pp. 48–57

Foote, P., 'Historical Studies: Conversion Moment and Conversion Period', in A. Faulkes and R. Perkins (eds), *Viking Revaluations* (London, 1993), pp. 137–44

Fox, G., 'Romano-British Suffolk', in W. Page (ed.), *The Victoria History of the County of Suffolk*, vol. 1 (London, 1911), pp. 279–320

Frend, W., *The Rise of Christianity* (London, 1984)

Frere, S., 'The Forum and Baths at Caistor by Norwich', *Britannia* 2 (1971), pp. 1–26

Fry, D., 'The Art of Bede: Edwin's Council', in M. King and W. Stevens (eds), *Saints, Scholars and Heroes*, vol. 1 (Collegeville, 1979), pp. 191–207

Gallyon, M., *The Early Church in Eastern England* (Lavenham, 1973)

Gameson, R. 'Augustine of Canterbury: Context and Achievement', in R. Gameson (ed.), *St Augustine and the Conversion of England* (Stroud, 1999), pp. 1–41

Gannon, A., *The Iconography of Early Anglo-Saxon Coinage* (Oxford, 2003)

Garrow, D., Lucy, S. and Gibson, D., *Excavations at Kilverstone, Norfolk: An Episodic Landscape History* (Cambridge, 2006)

Geake, H., 'Burial Practice in Seventh- and Eighth-Century England', in M. Carver (ed.), *The Age of Sutton Hoo* (Woodbridge, 1992), pp. 83–94

—, 'The Control of Burial Practice in Anglo-Saxon England', in M. Carver (ed.), *The Cross Goes North* (York, 2003), pp. 259–69

—, 'Invisible Kingdoms: The Use of Grave-Goods in Seventh-Century England', *Anglo-Saxon Studies in Archaeology and History* 10 (1999), pp. 203–15

—, 'Persistent Problems in the Study of Conversion-Period Burials in England', in S.

Lucy and A. Reynolds (eds), *Burial in Early Medieval England and Wales*, Society for Medieval Archaeology Monograph 17 (London, 2002), pp. 144–55

—, *The Use of Grave-Goods in Conversion-Period England c.600–c.850*, BAR British Series 261 (Oxford, 1997)

—, 'When were Hanging Bowls Deposited in Anglo-Saxon Graves?', *Medieval Archaeology* 43 (1999), pp. 1–18

Geary, P., *Living with the Dead in the Middle Ages* (London, 1994)

Gejvall, N.-G., 'Cremations', in D. Brothwell and E. Higgs (eds), *Science in Archaeology* (London, 1963), pp. 379–90

Gelting, M., 'The Kingdom of Denmark', in N. Berend (ed.), *Christianization and the Rise of Christian Monarchy* (Cambridge, 2007), pp. 73–120

Genrich, A., 'A Remarkable Inhumation Grave from Liebenau, Nienburg, Germany', in V. Evison (ed.), *Angles, Saxons and Jutes* (Oxford, 1981), pp. 59–71

Gilchrist, R., 'Magic for the Dead? The Archaeology of Magic in Later Medieval Burials', *Medieval Archaeology* 52 (2008), pp. 119–59

—, and Sloane, B., *Requiem: The Medieval Monastic Cemetery in Britain* (London, 2005)

Gittos, H., 'Creating the Sacred: Anglo-Saxon Rites for Consecrating Cemeteries', in S. Lucy and A. Reynolds (eds), *Burial in Early Medieval England and Wales*, Society for Medieval Archaeology Monograph 17 (London, 2002), pp. 195–208

Goodier, A., 'The Formation of Boundaries in Anglo-Saxon England: A Statistical Study', *Medieval Archaeology* 28 (1984), pp. 1–21

Gransden, A., *Historical Writing in England c.550 to c.1307* (London, 1974)

Gräslund, A.-S., 'The Conversion of Scandinavia – A Sudden Event or a Gradual Process?', *Archaeological Review from Cambridge* 17 (2) (2000), pp. 83–98

Green, B. and Rogerson, A., *The Anglo-Saxon Cemetery at Bergh Apton, Norfolk*, East Anglian Archaeology 7 (Gressenhall, 1978)

Green, B., Milligan, W. and West, S., 'The Illington/Lackford Workshop', in V. Evison (ed.), *Angles, Saxons and Jutes* (Oxford, 1981), pp. 187–226

Green, B., Rogerson, A. and White, S., *The Anglo-Saxon Cemetery at Morning Thorpe, Norfolk*, East Anglian Archaeology 36 (Gressenhall, 1987)

Green, C., 'East Anglian Coast-line Levels Since Roman Times', *Antiquity* 35 (1961), pp. 21–8

Green, C. S. and Gregory, T., 'Surface Finds', in J. Hinchcliffe with C. Green, *Excavations at Brancaster 1974 and 1977*, East Anglian Archaeology 23 (Gressenhall, 1985), pp. 190–221

Greene, J., 'Strategies for Future Research and Site Investigation', in G. Keevill, M. Aston and T. Hall (eds), *Monastic Archaeology* (Oxford, 2001), pp. 4–8

Gregory, T. and Gurney, D., *Excavations at Thornham, Warham, Wighton and Caistor St Edmund, Norfolk*, East Anglian Archaeology 30 (Gressenhall, 1986)

Gurney, D., 'A Note on the Distribution of Metal-Detecting in Norfolk', *Norfolk Archaeology* 42 (1997), pp. 528–32

—, *Outposts of the Roman Empire* (Gressenhall, 2002)

Hadley, D., *Death in Medieval England* (Stroud, 2001)

—, 'Equality, Humanity and Non-Materialism?', *Archaeological Review from Cambridge* 17 (2) (2000), pp. 149–78

Hall, T., *Minster Churches in the Dorset Landscape*, BAR British Series 304 (Oxford, 2000)

Halsall, G., *Early Medieval Cemeteries* (Glasgow, 1995)

Hamant, Y. (ed.), *The Christianization of Ancient Russia* (Paris, 1992)

Hamerow, H., *Early Medieval Settlements* (Oxford, 2002)

—, 'Settlement Mobility and the 'Middle Saxon Shift': Rural Settlements and Settlement Patterns in Anglo-Saxon England', *Anglo-Saxon England* 20 (1991), pp. 1–17

—, '"Special Deposits" in Anglo-Saxon Settlements', *Medieval Archaeology* 50 (2006), pp. 1–30

Härke, H., 'Anglo-Saxon Laminated Shields at Petersfinger – A Myth', *Medieval Archaeology* 25 (1981), pp. 141–4

—, 'Changing Symbols in a Changing Society: The Anglo-Saxon Weapon Burial Rite in the Seventh Century', in M. Carver (ed.), *The Age of Sutton Hoo* (Woodbridge, 1992), pp. 149–66

—, 'The Circulation of Weapons in Anglo-Saxon Society', in F. Theuws and J. Nelson (eds), *Rituals of Power* (Leiden, 2000), pp. 377–99

—, 'Early Saxon Weapon Burials: Frequencies, Distributions and Weapon Combinations', in S. Hawkes (ed.), *Weapons and Warfare in Anglo-Saxon England* (Oxford, 1989), pp. 49–59

—, 'Knives in Early Saxon Burials: Blade Length and Age At Death', *Medieval Archaeology* 33 (1989), pp. 144–8

—, 'Material Culture as Myth: Weapons in Anglo-Saxon Graves', in C. Jensen and K. Høilund Nielsen (eds), *Burial and Society* (Aarhus, 1997), pp. 119–27

—, '"Warrior Graves"? The Background of the Anglo-Saxon Weapon Burial', *Past and Present* 126 (1990), pp. 22–43

Harrod, H., 'Excavations made at Burgh Castle, Suffolk, in the Years 1850 and 1855', *Norfolk Archaeology* 5 (1859), pp. 146–60

—, 'On the Site of the Bishopric of Elmham', *Proceedings of the Suffolk Institute of Archaeology* 4 (1) (1864), pp. 7–13

Harrold, B., *An Enigma of Ancient Suffolk* (Colchester, 2003)

Haslam, J., '*Dommoc* and Dunwich: A Reappraisal', *Anglo-Saxon Studies in Archaeology and History* 5 (1992), pp. 41–5

Hassall, M., 'The Historical Background and Military Units of the Saxon Shore', in D. Johnson (ed.), *The Saxon Shore* (York, 1977), pp. 7–10

Hawkes, C., 'Archeological Theory and Method: Some Suggestions from the Old World', *American Anthropologist* 56 (1954), pp. 155–68

Hawkes, J. and Mills, S., *Northumbria's Golden Age* (Stroud, 1999)

Hawkes, S., 'The Archaeology of Conversion: Cemeteries', in J. Campbell (ed.), *The Anglo-Saxons* (London, 1982), pp. 48–9

—, 'Orientation at Finglesham: Sunrise Dating of Death and Burial in an Anglo-Saxon Cemetery in East Kent', *Archaeologia Cantiana* 92 (1976), pp. 33–51

—, and Wells, C., 'Crime and Punishment in an Anglo-Saxon Cemetery?', *Antiquity* 49 (1975), pp. 118–22

Healy, F., *The Anglo-Saxon Cemetery at Spong Hill, North Elmham. Part VI: Occupation during the Seventh to Second Millennia BC*, East Anglian Archaeology 39 (Gressenhall, 1988)

Hefner, R., 'Introduction: World Building and the Rationality of Conversion', in R. Hefner (ed.), *Conversion to Christianity* (Oxford, 1993), pp. 3–44

Hey, G., *Yarnton: Saxon and Medieval Settlement and Landscape* (Oxford, 2004)

Heywood, S., 'The Ruined Church at North Elmham', *Journal of the British Archaeological Association* 135 (1982), pp. 1–10

Higham, N., *The Convert Kings* (Manchester, 1997)

—, *An English Empire* (Manchester, 1995)

Hill, D., *An Atlas of Anglo-Saxon England* (Oxford, 1981)

Hill, P., *Whithorn and St Ninian* (Stroud, 1997)

Hill, R., *The Labourers in the Field*, Jarrow Lecture 1974 (Jarrow, 1974)

Hills, C., *The Anglo-Saxon Cemetery at Spong Hill, North Elmham. Part I: Catalogue of Cremations 20–64 and 1000–1690*, East Anglian Archaeology 6 (Gressenhall, 1977)

—, 'Anglo-Saxon Cremation Cemeteries, with Particular Reference to Spong Hill, Norfolk', in P. Rahtz, T. Dickinson and L. Watts (eds), *Anglo-Saxon Cemeteries 1979*, BAR British Series 82 (Oxford, 1980), pp. 197–207

—, 'The Archaeology of Anglo-Saxon England in the Pagan Period: A Review', *Anglo-Saxon England* 8 (1979), pp. 297–329

—, and Penn, K., *The Anglo-Saxon Cemetery at Spong Hill, North Elmham. Part II: Catalogue of Cremations 22, 41 and 1691–2285*, East Anglian Archaeology 11 (Gressenhall, 1981)

—, and Wade-Martins, P., 'The Anglo-Saxon Cemetery at The Paddocks, Swaffham', *East Anglian Archaeology* 2 (1976), pp. 1–44

—, Penn, K. and Rickett, R., *The Anglo-Saxon Cemetery at Spong Hill, North Elmham. Part III: Catalogue of Inhumations*, East Anglian Archaeology 21 (Gressenhall, 1984)

—, Penn, K. and Rickett, R., *The Anglo-Saxon Cemetery at Spong Hill, North Elmham. Part IV: Catalogue of Cremations 30–2, 42, 44a, 46, 65–6, 2286–799, 2224 and 3325*, East Anglian Archaeology 34 (Gressenhall, 1987)

—, Penn, K. and Rickett, R., *The Anglo-Saxon Cemetery at Spong Hill, North Elmham. Part V: Catalogue of Cremations 2800–3334*, East Anglian Archaeology 67 (Gressenhall, 1994)

Hinchcliffe, J. with Green, C., *Excavations at Brancaster 1974 and 1977*, East Anglian Archaeology 23 (Gressenhall, 1985)

Hines, J., *The Anglo-Saxon Cemetery at Edix Hill (Barrington A), Cambridgeshire*, CBA Research Report 112 (York, 1998)

—, 'Religion: The Limits of Knowledge', in J. Hines (ed.), *The Anglo-Saxons from the Migration Period to the Eighth Century: An Ethnographic Perspective* (Woodbridge, 1997), pp. 375–410

—, *The Scandinavian Character of Anglian England in the Pre-Viking Period*, BAR British Series 124 (Oxford, 1984)

—, 'The Sixth-Century Transition in Anglian England: An Analysis of Female Graves from Cambridgeshire', in J. Hines, K. Høilund Nielsen and F. Siegmund (eds), *The Pace of Change* (Oxford, 1999), pp. 65–79

Hirst, S., 'Death and the Archaeologist', in M. Carver (ed.), *In Search of Cult* (Woodbridge, 1993), pp. 41–3

Hoare, P. and Sweet, C., 'A Grave Error Concerning the Demise of "Hunstanton Woman"', *Antiquity* 68 (1994), pp. 590–96

Hodder, I., *The Archaeological Process* (Oxford, 1999)

—, 'Post-Processual and Interpretive Archaeology', in C. Renfrew and P. Bahn (eds), *Archaeology: The Key Concepts* (London, 2005), pp. 207–11

—, *The Present Past* (London, 1982)

—, and Hutson, S., *Reading the Past*, 3rd edn (Cambridge, 2003)

Hodges, H., *Artifacts: An Introduction to Early Materials and Technology*, 2nd edn (London, 1976)

Hodges, R., *The Anglo-Saxon Achievement* (New York, 1989)

—, 'An Unusual (?) Tating Ware Vessel', in J. Hinchcliffe with C. Green, *Excavations at Brancaster 1974 and 1977*, East Anglian Archaeology 23 (Gressenhall, 1985), pp. 125–6

Hofstra, T., Houwen, L. and MacDonald, A. (eds), *Pagans and Christians* (Groningen, 1995)

Hoggett, R., 'Changing Beliefs: The Archaeology of the East Anglian Conversion', unpublished PhD thesis, University of East Anglia (2007)

—, 'Charting Conversion: Burial as a Barometer of Belief?', in S. Semple and H. Williams (eds), *Early Medieval Mortuary Practices*, Anglo-Saxon Studies in Archaeology and History 14 (Oxford, 2007), pp. 28–37

—, 'The Origin and Early Development of Sedgeford, Norfolk', unpublished MA dissertation, University of Bristol (2001)

Høilund Nielsen, K., 'From Society to Burial and from Burial to Society?', in C. Jensen and K. Høilund Nielsen (eds), *Burial and Society* (Aarhus, 1997), pp. 103–10

—, 'The Schism of Anglo-Saxon Chronology', in C. Jensen and K. Høilund Nielsen (eds), *Burial and Society* (Aarhus, 1997), pp. 71–99

Holdsworth, C., 'Bishoprics, Monasteries and the Landscape *c*.AD 600–1066', in D. Hooke and S. Burnell (eds), *Landscape and Settlement in Britain AD 400–1066* (Exeter, 1995), pp. 27–49

Holtrop, P. and McLeod, H. (eds), *Missions and Missionaries* (Woodbridge, 2000)

Hooke, D., *The Landscape of Anglo-Saxon England* (Leicester, 1998)

Howlett, R., 'The Ancient See of Elmham', *Norfolk Archaeology* 18 (1914), pp. 105–28

Huggett, J., 'Imported Grave Goods and the Early Anglo-Saxon Economy', *Medieval Archaeology* 32 (1988), pp. 63–96

Hughes, K., 'The Celtic Church: Is This a Valid Concept?', *Cambridge Medieval Celtic Studies* 1 (1981), pp. 1–20

Hurst, J., 'The Pottery', in D. Wilson (ed.), *The Archaeology of Anglo-Saxon England* (Cambridge, 1976), pp. 283–347

—, and West, S., 'An Account of Middle Saxon Ipswich Ware', *Proceedings of the Cambridgeshire Antiquarian Society* 50 (1957), pp. 29–42

Hutcheson, A., 'The Origins of King's Lynn? Control of Wealth on the Wash Prior to the Norman Conquest', *Medieval Archaeology* 50 (2006), pp. 71–104

Hutton, R., *The Pagan Religions of the Ancient British Isles* (Oxford, 1993)

Hyslop, M., 'Two Anglo-Saxon Cemeteries at Chamberlains Barn, Leighton Buzzard, Bedfordshire', *Archaeological Journal* 120 (1963), pp. 161–200

Insoll, T., 'Archaeology of Cult and Religion', in C. Renfrew and P. Bahn (eds), *Archaeology: The Key Concepts* (London, 2005), pp. 45–9

—, *The Archaeology of Islam* (Oxford, 1999)

—, *Archaeology, Ritual, Religion* (London, 2004)

—, 'Are Archaeologists Afraid of Gods? Some Thoughts on Archaeology and Religion', in T. Insoll (ed.), *Belief in the Past*, BAR International Series 1212 (Oxford, 2004), pp. 1–6

—, (ed.), *Case Studies in Archaeology and World Religion*, BAR International Series 755 (Oxford, 1999)

—, 'Introduction: The Archaeology of World Religion', in T. Insoll (ed.), *Archaeology and World Religion* (London, 2001), pp. 1–32

James, E., 'Archaeology and the Merovingian Monastery', in H. Clarke and M. Brennan (eds), *Columbanus and Merovingian Monasticism*, BAR International Series 113 (Oxford, 1981), pp. 33–55

—, 'Burial and Status in the Early Medieval West', *Transactions of the Royal Historical Society* 5th series 39 (1989), pp. 23–40

—, 'Cemeteries and the Problem of Frankish Settlement in Gaul', in P. Sawyer (ed.), *Names, Words and Graves* (Leeds, 1979), pp. 55–89

—, *The Franks* (Oxford, 1988)

James, S., Marshall, A. and Millett, M., 'An Early Medieval Building Tradition', *Archaeological Journal* 141 (1984), pp. 182–215

Jensen, C. and Høilund Nielsen, K., 'Burial Data and Correspondence Analysis', in C. Jensen and K. Høilund Nielsen (eds), *Burial and Society* (Aarhus, 1997), pp. 29–61

Jesch, J., 'Scandinavians and "Cultural Paganism" in Late Anglo-Saxon England', in P. Cavill (ed.), *The Christian Tradition in Anglo-Saxon England* (Woodbridge, 2004), pp. 55–68

Johnson, M., *Archaeological Theory: An Introduction* (Oxford, 1999)

Johnson, S., *Burgh Castle, Excavations by Charles Green 1958–61*, East Anglian Archaeology 20 (Gressenhall, 1983)

Jones, P., *A Concordance to the Historia Ecclesiastica of Bede* (Cambridge, 1929)

Jones, P. and Pennick, N., *A History of European Paganism* (London, 1995)

Jones, T., *The English Saints: East Anglia* (Norwich, 1999)

Jordan, D., Haddon-Reece, D. and Bayliss, A., *Radiocarbon Dates* (London, 1994)

Kelly, S. E., 'Anna (d. 654?)', *Oxford Dictionary of National Biography* (Oxford, 2004) http://www.oxforddnb.com/view/article/39123, last accessed 20 Oct 2009

Kendall, G., 'A Study of Grave Orientation in Several Roman and Post-Roman Cemeteries from Southern Britain', *Archaeological Journal* 139 (1982), pp. 101–23

Kennett, D., *Anglo-Saxon Pottery* (Aylesbury, 1989)

Keynes, S., 'Rulers of the English, c.450–1066', in M. Lapidge, J. Blair, S. Keynes and D. Scragg (eds), *The Blackwell Encyclopaedia of Anglo-Saxon England* (Oxford, 2001), pp. 500–520

Kilbride, W., 'Why I Feel Cheated by the Term "Christianisation"', *Archaeological Review from Cambridge* 17 (2) (2000), pp. 1–17

Kirby, D., *Bede's Historia Ecclesiastica Gentis Anglorum: Its Contemporary Setting*, Jarrow Lecture 1992 (Jarrow, 1992)

—, 'Bede's Native Sources for the Historia Ecclesiastica', *Bulletin of the John Rylands Library* 48 (1966), pp. 341–71

—, *The Earliest English Kings* (London, 1991)

Knight, J., *The End of Antiquity* (Stroud, 1999)

Lager, L., 'Runestones and the Conversion of Sweden', in M. Carver (ed.), *The Cross Goes North* (York, 2003), pp. 497–507

Laistner, M., 'The Library of the Venerable Bede', in A. Thompson (ed.), *Bede: His Life, Times and Writings* (Oxford, 1935), pp. 237–66

Lane, P., 'The Archaeology of Christianity in Global Perspective', in T. Insoll (ed.), *Archaeology and World Religion* (London, 2001), pp. 148–81

Lane-Fox, R., *Pagans and Christians* (Harmondsworth, 1986)

Lapidge, M., *The Anglo-Saxon Library* (Oxford, 2006)

Larwood, G. and Funnell, B. (eds), *The Geology of Norfolk* (Norwich, 1961)

Lawson, A., *The Archaeology of Witton*, East Anglian Archaeology 18 (Gressenhall, 1983)

—, Martin, E. and Priddy, D., *The Barrows of East Anglia*, East Anglian Archaeology 12 (Gressenhall, 1981)

Leahy, K., *Anglo-Saxon Crafts* (Stroud, 2003)

Lee, C., *Feasting the Dead: Food and Drink in Anglo-Saxon Burial Rituals* (Woodbridge, 2007)

Leeds, E., *Early Anglo-Saxon Art and Archaeology* (Oxford, 1936)

Lethbridge, T., *A Cemetery at Lackford, Suffolk* (Cambridge, 1951)

—, *A Cemetery at Shudy Camps, Cambridgeshire* (Cambridge, 1936)

—, *Recent Excavations in Anglo-Saxon Cemeteries in Cambridgeshire and Suffolk* (Cambridge, 1931)

Levison, W., 'Bede as Historian', in A. Thompson (ed.), *Bede: His Life, Times and Writings* (Oxford, 1935), pp. 111–51

Loveluck, C. and Atkinson, D., *The Early Medieval Settlement Remains from Flixborough, Lincolnshire: The Occupation Sequence, c. AD 600–1000* (Oxford, 2007)

Lubbock, J., *Pre-Historic Times* (London, 1865)

Lucy, S., *The Anglo-Saxon Way of Death* (Stroud, 2000)

—, 'Changing Burial Rites in Northumbria AD 500–750', in J. Hawkes and S. Mills (eds), *Northumbria's Golden Age* (Stroud, 1999), pp. 12–43

—, *The Early Anglo-Saxon Cemeteries of East Yorkshire*, BAR British Series 272 (Oxford, 1998)

—, 'Housewives, Warriors and Slaves? Sex and Gender in Anglo-Saxon Burials', in J. Moore and E. Scott (eds), *Invisible People and Processes* (Leicester, 1997), pp. 150–68

—, 'The Significance of Mortuary Ritual in the Political Manipulation of the Landscape', *Archaeological Review from Cambridge* 11 (1) (1992), pp. 93–103

—, Tipper, J. and Dickens, A., *The Anglo-Saxon Settlement and Cemetery at Bloodmoor Hill, Carlton Colville, Suffolk*, East Anglian Archaeology 131 (Cambridge, 2009)

—, Newman, R., Dodwell, N., Hills, C., Dekker, M., O'Connell, T., Riddler, I. and Walton Rogers, P., 'The Burial of a Princess? The Later Seventh-century Cemetery at Westfield Farm, Ely', *Antiquaries Journal* 89 (2009), pp. 81–141

McClure, J., 'Bede and the Life of Ceolfrid', *Perita* 3 (1984), pp. 71–84

MacGregor, A., 'A Seventh-Century Pectoral Cross from Holderness, East Yorkshire', *Medieval Archaeology* 44 (2000), pp. 217–22

McKinley, J., *The Anglo-Saxon Cemetery at Spong Hill, North Elmham. Part VIII: The Cremations*, East Anglian Archaeology 69 (Gressenhall, 1994)

—, 'Cremations: Expectations, Methodologies and Realities', in C. Roberts, F. Lee and J. Bintliff (eds), *Burial Archaeology: Current Research, Methods and Developments*, BAR British Series 211 (Oxford, 1989), pp. 65–76

Malim, T. with Penn, K., Robinson, B., Wait, G. and Welsh, K., 'New Evidence on the Cambridgeshire Dykes and Worsted Street Roman Road', *Proceedings of the Cambridgeshire Antiquarian Society* 85 (1997), pp. 27–122

Markus, R., *Bede and the Tradition Of Ecclesiastical History*, Jarrow Lecture 1975 (Jarrow, 1975)

Marsden, B., *The Early Barrow-Diggers* (Aylesbury, 1974)

Marshall, A. and Marshall, G., 'Differentiation, Change and Continuity in Anglo-Saxon Buildings', *Archaeological Journal* 150 (1993), pp. 366–402

—, 'A Survey and Analysis of the Buildings of Early and Middle Anglo-Saxon England', *Medieval Archaeology* 35 (1991), pp. 29–43

Martin, E., *Burgh: Iron Age and Roman Enclosure*, East Anglian Archaeology 40 (Ipswich, 1988)

—, 'St Botolph and Hadstock: A Reply', *Antiquaries Journal* 58 (1978), pp. 153–9

—, 'Soil Regions', in D. Dymond and E. Martin (eds), *An Historical Atlas of Suffolk*, 3rd edn (Ipswich, 1999), pp. 20–21

—, 'Suffolk and the East Anglian Kingdom', in D. Dymond and E. Martin (eds), *An Historical Atlas of Suffolk*, 3rd edn (Ipswich, 1999), pp. 22–3

—, and Satchell, M., *Where Most Inclosures Be. East Anglian Fields: History, Morphology and Management*, East Anglian Archaeology 124 (Ipswich, 2008)

Marzinzik, S., *Early Anglo-Saxon Belt Buckles*, BAR British Series 357 (Oxford, 2003)

Mayr-Harting, H., *The Coming of Christianity to Anglo-Saxon England*, 3rd edn (Philadelphia, PA, 1991)

—, *Two Conversions to Christianity: The Bulgarians and the Anglo-Saxons* (Reading, 1994)

Mays, S., *The Archaeology of Human Bones* (London, 1998)

Meaney, A., 'Anglo-Saxon Pagan and Early Christian Attitudes to the Dead', in M. Carver (ed.), *The Cross Goes North* (York, 2003), pp. 229–41

—, 'Bede and Anglo-Saxon Paganism', *Parergon* new series 3 (1985), pp. 1–29

—, 'Felix's Life of St Guthlac: Hagiography and/or Truth', *Proceedings of the Cambridgeshire Antiquarian Society* 90 (2001), pp. 29–48

—, *A Gazetteer of Early Anglo-Saxon Burial Sites* (London, 1964)

—, and Hawkes, S. *Two Anglo-Saxon Cemeteries at Winnall, Winchester, Hampshire* (London, 1970)

Mellor, V., 'Archaeological Evaluation on Land at Church Close, Whissonsett, Norfolk', unpublished Archaeological Project Services client report 128/04 (2004)

Meyvaert, P., 'Bede the Scholar', in G. Bonner (ed.), *Famulus Christi* (London, 1976), pp. 40–69

Mills, K. and Grafton, A. (eds), *Conversion in Late Antiquity and the Early Middle Ages* (New York, 2003)

—, (eds), *Conversion: Old Worlds and New* (New York, 2003)

Moreland, J., 'The Significance of Production in Eighth-Century England', in L. Hansen and C. Wickham (eds), *The Long Eighth Century: Production, Distribution and Demand* (Leiden, 2000), pp. 69–104

Morris, R., *Churches in the Landscape* (London, 1989)

—, *The Church In British Archaeology*, CBA Research Report 47 (York, 1983)

—, and Roxan, J., 'Churches on Roman Sites', in W. Rodwell (ed.), *Temples, Churches and Religion*, BAR British Series 77 (Oxford, 1980), pp. 175–209

Murphy, P., 'Appendix II: The Carbonised Plant Remains from the Cremations', in J. McKinley, *The Anglo-Saxon Cemetery at Spong Hill, North Elmham. Part VIII: The Cremations*, East Anglian Archaeology 69 (Gressenhall, 1994), microfiche

—, 'Coastal Change and Human Response', in T. Ashwin and A. Davison (eds), *An Historical Atlas of Norfolk*, 3rd edn (Chichester, 2005), pp. 6–7

Myres, J., *Anglo-Saxon Pottery and the Settlement of England* (Oxford, 1969)

—, *A Corpus of Pagan Anglo-Saxon Pottery* (Oxford, 1977)

—, 'Some Anglo-Saxon Potters', *Antiquity* 11 (1937), 389–99

—, and Green, B., *The Anglo-Saxon Cemeteries of Caistor-by-Norwich and Markshall, Norfolk* (London, 1973)

Naylor, J., *An Archaeology of Trade in Middle Saxon England*, BAR British Series 376 (Oxford, 2004)

Neill, S., *A History of Christian Missions*, 2nd edn (Harmondsworth, 1986)

Newman, J., 'The Anglo-Saxon Cemetery at Boss Hall, Ipswich', *Sutton Hoo Research Committee Bulletin* 8 (1993), pp. 33–5

—, 'East Anglian Kingdom Pilot Study', in M. Parker Pearson and R. Schadla-Hall (eds), *Looking at the Land* (Leicester, 1994), pp. 10–15

—, 'Exceptional Finds, Exceptional Sites? Barham and Coddenham, Suffolk', in T.

Pestell and K. Ulmschneider (eds), *Markets in Early Medieval Europe* (Macclesfield, 2003), pp. 97–109

—, 'The Late Roman and Anglo-Saxon Settlement Pattern in the Sandlings of Suffolk', in M. Carver (ed.), *The Age of Sutton Hoo* (Woodbridge, 1992), pp. 25–38

—, 'Metal Detector Finds and Fieldwork on Anglo-Saxon Sites in Suffolk', *Anglo-Saxon Studies in Archaeology and History* 8 (1995), pp. 87–93

—, 'New Light on Old Finds – Bloodmoor Hill, Gisleham, Suffolk', *Anglo-Saxon Studies in Archaeology and History* 9 (1996), pp. 75–9

—, 'Survey in the Deben Valley', in M. Carver, *Sutton Hoo: A Seventh-Century Princely Burial Ground and its Context* (London, 2005), pp. 477–88

—, 'Sutton Hoo before Rædwald', *Current Archaeology* 180 (2002), pp. 498–505

Newton, S., *The Origins of Beowulf and the Pre-Viking Kingdom of East Anglia* (Cambridge, 1993)

—, *The Reckoning of King Rædwald* (Colchester, 2003)

Norwich Survey, *The Norwich Survey 1971–1980* (Norwich, 1980)

O'Brien, E., *Post-Roman Britain to Anglo-Saxon England: Burial Practices Reviewed*, BAR British Series 289 (Oxford, 1999)

Otto, R., *The Idea of the Holy* (Oxford, 1928)

Owen, G., *Rites and Religions of the Anglo-Saxons* (London, 1981)

Owen-Crocker, G., *Dress in Anglo-Saxon England* (Manchester, 1986)

Pader, E.-J., 'Material Symbolism and Social Relations in Mortuary Studies', in P. Rahtz, T. Dickinson and L. Watts (eds), *Anglo-Saxon Cemeteries 1979*, BAR British Series 82 (Oxford, 1980), pp. 143–59

—, *Symbolism, Social Relations and the Interpretation of Mortuary Remains*, BAR British Series 130 (Oxford, 1982)

Page, R., 'Anglo-Saxon Paganism: The Evidence of Bede', in T. Hofstra, L. Houwen and A. MacDonald (eds), *Pagans and Christians* (Groningen, 1995), pp. 99–129

Paor, L. de, *Saint Patrick's World* (Dublin, 1996)

Parker Pearson, M., *The Archaeology of Death and Burial* (Stroud, 1999)

—, 'The Powerful Dead: Archaeological Relationships between the Living and the Dead', *Cambridge Archaeological Journal* 3 (1993), pp. 203–29

—, and Richards, C., 'Architecture and Order: Spatial Representation and Archaeology', in M. Parker Pearson and C. Richards (eds), *Architecture and Order* (London, 1994), pp. 38–72

—, van de Noort, R. and Woolf, A., 'Three Men and a Boat: Sutton Hoo and the East Saxon Kingdom', *Anglo-Saxon England* 22 (1993), pp. 27–50

Parsons, B., *Committed to the Cleansing Flame* (Reading, 2005)

Parsons, D., *Books and Buildings: Architectural Description Before and After Bede*, Jarrow Lecture 1987 (Jarrow, 1987)

—, 'Sites and Monuments of the Anglo-Saxon Mission in Central Germany', *Archaeological Journal* 140 (1983), pp. 280–321

Pearson, A., *The Construction of the Saxon Shore Forts*, BAR British Series 349 (Oxford, 2003)

Penn, K., *An Anglo-Saxon Cemetery at Oxborough, West Norfolk: Excavations in 1990*, East Anglian Archaeology Occasional Paper 5 (Gressenhall, 1998)

—, *An Anglo-Saxon Cemetery at Shrubland Hall Quarry, Coddenham, Suffolk*, East Anglian Archaeology (forthcoming)

—, 'The Early Church in Norfolk: Some Aspects', in S. Margeson, B. Ayers and S. Heywood (eds), *A Festival of Norfolk Archaeology* (Norwich, 1996), pp. 40–46

—, 'Early Saxon Settlement (*c*.AD 410–650)', in T. Ashwin and A. Davison (eds), *An Historical Atlas of Norfolk*, 3rd edn (Chichester, 2005), pp. 30–31

—, *Excavations on the Norwich Southern Bypass, 1989–91. Part II: The Anglo-Saxon Cemetery at Harford Farm, Caistor St Edmund, Norfolk*, East Anglian Archaeology 92 (Gressenhall, 2000)

—, and Brugmann, B., *Aspects of Anglo-Saxon Inhumation Burial: Morning Thorpe, Spong Hill, Bergh Apton and Westgarth Gardens*, East Anglian Archaeology 119 (Gressenhall, 2007)

Percival, J., 'Villas and Monasteries in Late Roman Gaul', *Journal of Ecclesiastical History* 48 (1997), pp. 1–21

Percival, J.W., 'An Archaeological Evaluation at Caistor St Edmund Churchyard, Norfolk', unpublished draft report for the Caistor Roman Roman Town Project (2009)

Percival, S., 'Caistor St Edmund Metal-Detector Survey 1993', *Norfolk Archaeological and Historical Research Group Annual* 5 (1996), pp. 21–3

Pestell, T., 'The Afterlife of "Productive" Sites in East Anglia', in T. Pestell and K. Ulmschneider (eds), *Markets in Early Medieval Europe* (Macclesfield, 2003), pp. 122–37

—, 'An Analysis of Monastic Foundation in East Anglia *c*.650–1200', unpublished PhD thesis, University of East Anglia (1999)

—, *Landscapes of Monastic Foundation* (Woodbridge, 2004)

—, and Ulmschneider, K. (eds), *Markets in Early Medieval Europe* (Macclesfield, 2003)
Pevsner, N., *Suffolk* (London, 1975)

—, and Wilson, B., *Norfolk I: Norwich and North-East* (London, 1997)

—, and Wilson, B., *Norfolk II: North-West and South* (London, 1999)

Plunkett, S., *Suffolk in Anglo-Saxon Times* (Stroud, 2005)

Pluskowski, A. and Patrick, P., '"How do you Pray to God?" Fragmentation and Variety in Early Medieval Christianity', in M. Carver (ed.), *The Cross Goes North* (York, 2003), pp. 29–57

Price, N. (ed.), *The Archaeology of Shamanism* (London, 2001)

Prothero, S., *Purified by Fire* (London, 2001)

Radford, C., 'Pre-Conquest Minster Churches', *Archaeological Journal* 130 (1973), pp. 120–40

Rahtz, P., 'Buildings and Rural Settlement', in D. Wilson (ed.), *The Archaeology of Anglo-Saxon England* (Cambridge, 1976), pp. 49–98

—, 'Grave Orientation', *Archaeological Journal* 135 (1978), pp. 1–14

—, 'Late Roman Cemeteries and Beyond', in R. Reece (ed.), *Burial in the Roman World*, CBA Research Report 22 (London, 1977), pp. 53–64

Ravn, M., *Death Ritual and Germanic Social Structure (c.AD 200–600)*, BAR International Series 1164 (Oxford, 2003)

—, 'Theoretical and Methodological Approaches to Migration Period Burials', in M. Rundkvist (ed.), *Grave Matters*, BAR International Series 78 (Oxford, 1999), pp. 41–56

Rees, E., *Celtic Saints in their Landscape* (Stroud, 2001)

Reid-Moir, J., 'The Excavation of Two Tumuli on Brightwell Heath, Suffolk', *Journal of the Ipswich and District Field Club* 6 (1921), pp. 1–14

Renfrew, C., *The Archaeology of Cult* (London, 1985)

—, 'The Archaeology of Religion', in C. Renfrew and E. Zubrow (eds), *The Ancient Mind* (Cambridge, 1994), pp. 47–54

—, 'Cognitive Archaeology', in C. Renfrew and P. Bahn (eds), *Archaeology: The Key Concepts* (London, 2005), pp. 41–5

—, 'Ritual and Cult in Malta and Beyond: Traditions of Interpretation', in D.
    Barrowclough and C. Malone (eds), *Cult in Context* (Oxford, 2007), pp. 8–13
—, 'Towards a Cognitive Archaeology', in C. Renfrew and E. Zubrow (eds), *The
    Ancient Mind* (Cambridge, 1994), pp. 3–12
—, *Towards an Archaeology of the Mind* (Cambridge, 1982)
— and Bahn, P. (eds), *Archaeology: The Key Concepts* (London, 2005)
— and Bahn, P., *Archaeology: Theories, Methods and Practice*, 4th edn (London, 2004)
— and Zubrow, E. (eds), *The Ancient Mind* (Cambridge, 1994)
Reynolds, A., *Anglo-Saxon Deviant Burial Customs* (Oxford, 2009)
—, 'Burials, Boundaries and Charters in Anglo-Saxon England: A Reassessment', in S.
    Lucy and A. Reynolds (eds), *Burial in Early Medieval England and Wales*, Society for
    Medieval Archaeology Monograph 17 (London, 2002), pp. 171–94
—, 'The Definition and Ideology of Anglo-Saxon Execution Sites and Cemeteries', in G.
    De Boe and F. Verhaeghe (eds), *Death and Burial in Medieval Europe*, vol. 2 (Zellik,
    1997), pp. 33–41
—, *Later Anglo-Saxon England: Life and Landscape* (Stroud, 1999)
Reynolds, N., 'The Rape of the Anglo-Saxon Women', *Antiquity* 62 (1988), pp. 715–18
Richards, J., 'Anglo-Saxon Symbolism', in M. Carver (ed.), *The Age of Sutton Hoo*
    (Woodbridge, 1992), pp. 131–47
—, 'Funerary Symbolism in Anglo-Saxon England: Further Social Dimensions of
    Mortuary Practices', *Scottish Archaeological Review* 3 (1984), pp. 42–55
—, *The Significance of Form and Decoration of Anglo-Saxon Cremation Urns*, BAR
    British Series 166 (Oxford, 1987)
—, 'Style and Symbol: Explaining Variability in Anglo-Saxon Cremation Burials', in S.
    Driscoll and M. Nieke (eds), *Power and Politics in Early Medieval Britain and
    Ireland* (Edinburgh, 1988), pp. 145–61
—, 'What's so Special about "Productive Sites"? Middle Saxon Settlements in
    Northumbria', *Anglo-Saxon Studies in Archaeology and History* 10 (1999), pp. 71–80
Richardson, A., *The Anglo-Saxon Cemeteries of Kent*, BAR British Series 391 (Oxford, 2005)
Rickett, R., *The Anglo-Saxon Cemetery at Spong Hill, North Elmham. Part VII: The Iron
    Age, Roman and Early Saxon Settlement*, East Anglian Archaeology 73 (Gressenhall, 1995)
Rigold, S., 'The Anglian Cathedral of North Elmham, Norfolk', *Medieval Archaeology* 6
    (1962), pp. 67–108
—, 'Further evidence about the site of "*Dommoc*"', *Journal of the British
    Archaeological Association* 37 (1974), pp. 97–102
—, '*Litus Romanum* – The Shore Forts as Mission Stations', in D. Johnson (ed.), *The
    Saxon Shore*, CBA Research Report 18 (York, 1977), pp. 70–75
—, 'The Supposed See of Dunwich', *Journal of the British Archaeological Association* 24
    (1961), pp. 55–9
Rippon, S., *Beyond the Medieval Village* (Oxford, 2008)
Roberts, J., *Guthlac of Crowland, a Saint for Middle England* (Norwich, 2009)
Rodwell, W., 'The Archaeological Investigation of Hadstock Church, Essex: An Interim
    Report', *Antiquaries Journal* 56 (1976), pp. 55–71
—, *The Archaeology of Churches* (Stroud, 2005)
—, 'Churches in the Landscape: Aspects of Topography and Planning', in M. Faull (ed.),
    Studies in Late Anglo-Saxon Settlement (Oxford, 1984), pp. 1–23
—, and Rodwell, K., *Historic Churches: A Wasting Asset*, CBA Research Report 19
    (London, 1977)

Roesdahl, E., 'The Archaeological Evidence for Conversion', in B. Sawyer, P. Sawyer and I. Wood (eds), *The Christianization of Scandinavia* (Sweden, 1987), pp. 2–5

Rogerson, A., 'Fransham: An Archaeological and Historical Study of a Parish on the Norfolk Boulder Clay', unpublished PhD thesis, University of East Anglia (1995)

—, *A Late Neolithic, Saxon and Medieval Site at Middle Harling, Norfolk*, East Anglian Archaeology 74 (London, 1995)

—, 'Middle Saxon Norfolk (*c*.AD 650–850)', in T. Ashwin and A. Davison (eds), *An Historical Atlas of Norfolk*, 3rd edn (Chichester, 2005), pp. 32–3

—, 'Rural Settlement *c*.400–1200', in S. Margeson, B. Ayers and S. Heywood (eds), *A Festival of Norfolk Archaeology* (Norwich, 1996), pp. 58–64

—, 'Six Middle Anglo-Saxon Sites in West Norfolk', in T. Pestell and K. Ulmschneider (eds), *Markets in Early Medieval Europe* (Macclesfield, 2003), pp. 110–21

—, and Ashley, S., 'The Parish Churches of Barton Bendish', in A. Rogerson, S. Ashley, P. Williams and A. Harris, *Three Norman Churches in Norfolk*, East Anglian Archaeology 32 (Gressenhall, 1987), pp. 1–66

—, with Davison, A., 'An Archaeological and Historical Survey of the Parish of Barton Bendish, Norfolk', in A. Rogerson, A. Davison, D. Pritchard and R. Sylvester, *Barton Bendish and Caldecote*, East Anglian Archaeology 80 (Gressenhall, 1997), pp. 1–42

—, and Lawson, A., 'The Earthwork Enclosure at Tasburgh', in J. Davies, T. Gregory, A. Lawson, R. Rickett and A. Rogerson, *The Iron Age Forts of Norfolk*, East Anglian Archaeology 54 (Gressenhall, 1991), pp. 31–58

—, and Silvester, R., 'Middle Saxon Occupation at Hay Green, Terrington St Clement', *Norfolk Archaeology* 39 (1986), pp. 320–22

Rose, E., 'A Note on the Demolition of the Walls of the Roman Fort', in J. Hinchcliffe with C. Green, *Excavations at Brancaster 1974 and 1977*, East Anglian Archaeology 23 (Gressenhall, 1985), pp. 188–9

Rousseau, P., *The Early Christian Centuries* (London, 2002)

Rumbelow, P., 'Finds on a Roman Site at Caister-on-Sea, Norfolk', *Norfolk Archaeology* 26 (1938), pp. 178–82

Rundkvist, M., 'Early Medieval Burial Studies in Scandinavia 1994–2003', in S. Semple and H. Williams (eds), *Early Medieval Mortuary Practices*, Anglo-Saxon Studies in Archaeology and History 14 (Oxford, 2007), pp. 47–55

Russell, J., *The Germanization of Early Medieval Christianity* (Oxford, 1994)

St Joseph, J., 'The Roman Fort at Brancaster', *Antiquaries Journal* 16 (1936), pp. 444–60

Sawyer, B., Sawyer, P. and Wood, I. (eds), *The Christianization of Scandinavia* (Alingsas, 1987)

Sawyer, P., 'The Process of Scandinavian Christianization in the Tenth and Eleventh Centuries', in B. Sawyer, P. Sawyer and I. Wood (eds), *The Christianization of Scandinavia* (Alingsas, 1987), pp. 68–87

Scarfe, N., *Suffolk in the Middle Ages* (Woodbridge, 1986)

—, *The Suffolk Landscape* (Bury St Edmunds, 1987)

Schülke, A., 'On Christianization and Grave-Finds', *European Journal of Archaeology* 2 (1) (1999), pp. 77–106

Scole Committee, *Ipswich: The Archaeological Implications of Development* (Ipswich, 1973)

Scull, C., 'Before Sutton Hoo: Structures of Power in Early East Anglia', in M. Carver (ed.), *The Age of Sutton Hoo* (Woodbridge, 1992), pp. 3–23

—, 'A Cemetery of the 7th and 8th Centuries at St Stephen's Lane/Butter Market, Ipswich', in G. De Boe and F. Verhaeghe (eds), *Death and Burial in Medieval Europe*, vol. 2 (Zellik, 1997), pp. 97–100

—, *Early Medieval (Late 5th–Early 8th Centuries AD) Cemeteries at Boss Hall and Buttermarket, Ipswich, Suffolk* (Leeds, 2009)

Semple, S., 'Burials and Political Boundaries in the Avebury Region, North Wiltshire', *Anglo-Saxon Studies in Archaeology and History* 12 (2003), pp. 72–91

—, 'A Fear of the Past: The Place of the Prehistoric Burial Mound in the Ideology of Middle and Later Anglo-Saxon England', *World Archaeology* 30 (1998), pp. 109–26

Shearman, F., 'Excavation, Examination and Conservation of Anglo-Saxon Jewellery from Boss Hall, Ipswich', *The Conservator* 17 (1993), pp. 26–33

Sherlock, D., 'The Post-Roman Coins and Jettons', in M. Darling with D. Gurney, *Caister-on-Sea Excavations by Charles Green, 1951–55*, East Anglian Archaeology 60 (Gressenhall, 1993), pp. 68–71

Silvester, R., '"The Addition of More-or-Less Undifferentiated Dots to a Distribution Map"? The Fenland Project in Retrospect', in J. Gardiner (ed.), *Flatlands and Wetlands*, East Anglian Archaeology 50 (Gressenhall, 1993), pp. 24–39

—, *The Fenland Project Number 3: Marshland and the Nar Valley, Norfolk*, East Anglian Archaeology 45 (Gressenhall, 1988)

—, *The Fenland Project Number 4: The Wissey Embayment and the Fen Causeway, Norfolk*, East Anglian Archaeology 52 (Gressenhall, 1991)

—, 'Multi-Period Occupation at Caldecote, West Norfolk', in A. Rogerson, A. Davison, D. Pritchard and R. Sylvester, *Barton Bendish and Caldecote*, East Anglian Archaeology 80 (Gressenhall, 1997), pp. 77–90

—, 'The Norfolk Fens', *Antiquity* 62 (1988), pp. 326–30

—, 'West Walton: The Development of a Siltland Parish', *Norfolk Archaeology* 39 (1985), pp. 100–117

Smedley, N. and Owles, E., 'Excavations at the Old Minster, South Elmham', *Proceedings of the Suffolk Institute of Archaeology* 32 (1) (1970), pp. 1–16

—, 'Some Suffolk Kilns: IV. Saxon Kilns in Cox Lane, Ipswich, 1961', *Proceedings of the Suffolk Institute of Archaeology* 29 (3) (1963), pp. 304–35

Smith, A., *English Place-Name Elements* (Cambridge, 1956)

Smith, R., 'Anglo-Saxon Remains', in H. Doubleday (ed.), *The Victoria History of the County of Norfolk*, vol. 1 (London, 1901), pp. 325–51

—, 'Anglo-Saxon Remains', in W. Page (ed.), *The Victoria History of the County of Suffolk*, vol. 1 (London, 1911), pp. 325–55

Speake, G., *A Saxon Bed Burial on Swallowcliffe Down* (London, 1989)

Staecker, J., 'The Mission to the Triangle: The Christianisation of the Saxons, West Slavs and Danes in a Comparative Analysis', *Archaeological Review from Cambridge* 17 (2) (2000), pp. 99–116

Stenton, F., 'The East Anglian Kings of the Seventh Century', in P. Clemoes (ed.), *The Anglo-Saxons* (London, 1959), pp. 43–52

Stevenson, F., 'St Botolph and Iken', *Proceedings of the Suffolk Institute of Archaeology* 18 (1924), pp. 30–52

Stoodley, N., 'From the Cradle to the Grave: Age Organization and the Early Anglo-Saxon Burial Rite', *World Archaeology* 31 (2000), pp. 456–72

—, 'Multiple Burials, Multiple Meanings? Interpreting the Early Anglo-Saxon Multiple Interment', in S. Lucy and A. Reynolds (eds), *Burial in Early Medieval England and Wales*, Society for Medieval Archaeology Monograph 17 (London, 2002), pp. 103–21

—, *The Spindle and the Spear*, BAR British Series 288 (Oxford, 1999)

Taylor, A., *Burial Practice in Early England* (Stroud, 2001)

Taylor, H. and Taylor, J., *Anglo-Saxon Architecture*, 2 vols (Cambridge, 1965)

Taylor, M., *Wood in Archaeology* (Aylesbury, 1981)

Taylor, T., *Time Team 1999: The Site Reports* (London, 1999)

Thacker, A., 'Monks, Preaching and Pastoral Care in Early Anglo-Saxon England', in J. Blair and R. Sharpe (eds), *Pastoral Care Before the Parish* (Leicester, 1992), pp. 137–70

—, 'Wilfrid [St Wilfrid] (c.634–709/10)', *Oxford Dictionary of National Biography* (Oxford, 2004) http://www.oxforddnb.com/view/article/29409, last accessed 1 June 2009

Thomas, C., *The Early Christian Archaeology of North Britain* (Oxford, 1971)

Thompson, A. (ed.), *Bede: His Life, Times and Writings* (Oxford, 1935)

Thompson, V., *Dying and Death in Later Anglo-Saxon England* (Woodbridge, 2004)

Thurston, H., 'Christian Burial', *The Catholic Encyclopaedia*, vol. 3 (1908) http://www.newadvent.org/cathen/03071a.htm, last accessed 1 June 2009

Toy, J., 'St Botolph: An English Saint in Scandinavia', in M. Carver (ed.), *The Cross Goes North* (York, 2003), pp. 565–70

Traboulay, D., *Columbus and Las Casa* (Lanham, 1994)

Trigger, B., *A History of Archaeological Thought* (Cambridge, 1989)

Trimble, G. and Hoggett, R., 'An Archaeological Evaluation on Land at North View Drive, Whissonsett, Norfolk (Amended)', unpublished NAU Archaeology Client Report 1185 (2010)

—, 'An Archaeological Excavation at Church Close, Whissonsett: Assessment Report and Updated Project Design', unpublished NAU Archaeology Client Report 1159a (2010)

Turner, S., *Making A Christian Landscape* (Exeter, 2006)

—, 'Making a Christian Landscape: Early Medieval Cornwall', in M. Carver (ed.), *The Cross Goes North* (York, 2003), pp. 171–94

Ucko, P., 'Ethnography and Archaeological Interpretation of Funerary Remains', *World Archaeology* 1 (1969), pp. 262–80

Ulmschneider, K., 'Archaeology, History and the Isle of Wight in the Middle Saxon Period', *Medieval Archaeology* 43 (1999), pp. 19–44

—, 'Central Places and Metal-Detector Finds: What are the English "Productive Sites"?', in B. Hårdh and L. Larsson (eds), *Central Places in the Migration and Merovingian Periods* (Lund, 2002), pp. 333–9

—, *Markets, Minsters and Metal-Detectors*, BAR British Series 307 (Oxford, 2000)

—, 'Settlement, Economy and the "Productive" Site: Middle Anglo-Saxon Lincolnshire AD 650–780', *Medieval Archaeology* 44 (2000), pp. 53–80

Urbańczyk, P., 'Christianisation of Early Medieval Societies: An Anthropological Perspective', in B. Crawford (ed.), *Conversion and Christianity in the North Sea World* (St Andrews, 1998), pp. 129–33

—, 'The Politics of Conversion in North Central Europe', in M. Carver (ed.), *The Cross Goes North* (York, 2003), pp. 15–27

Vésteinsson, O., *The Christianization of Iceland* (Oxford, 2000)

Wacher, J., *Roman Britain* (Stroud, 1998)

—, *The Towns of Roman Britain* (London, 1976)

Wade, K., 'Anglo-Saxon and Medieval (Rural)', in J. Glazebrook (ed.), *Research and Archaeology: A Framework for the Eastern Counties. 1. Resource Assessment*, East Anglian Archaeology Occasional Paper 3 (Norwich, 1997), pp. 47–58

—, 'The Later Anglo-Saxon Period', in D. Dymond and E. Martin (eds), *An Historical Atlas of Suffolk*, 3rd edn (Ipswich, 1999), pp. 46–7

Wade-Martins, P., 'The Development of the Landscape and Human Settlement in West

Norfolk from 350–1650 AD, with particular reference to the Launditch Hundred',
unpublished PhD thesis, University of Leicester (1971)

—, *Excavations in North Elmham Park 1967–1972*, East Anglian Archaeology 9
(Gressenhall, 1980)

—, *Village Sites in Launditch Hundred*, East Anglian Archaeology 10 (Gressenhall, 1980)

Wallace-Hadrill, J., *Bede's Ecclesiastical History of the English People: A Historical
Commentary* (Oxford, 1988)

—, *The Frankish Church* (Oxford, 1983)

Wallis, H., 'Excavations at Church Loke, Burgh Castle, 1993–4', *Norfolk Archaeology* 43
(1998), pp. 62–78

Warner, J., 'Notices of the Original Structure of the Roman Fortifications at Brancaster (the
Ancient *Branodunum*) Norfolk', in *Memoirs Illustrative of Norfolk and the City of
Norwich* (London, 1851), pp. 9–16

Warner, P., *The Origins of Suffolk* (Manchester, 1996)

Watkins, J., 'Anglo-Saxon Grave Mystery', *Heritage Today* (September 2006), pp. 40–42

Watkins, P., 'An Archaeological Strip, Map and Sample Excavation at Wimbotsham,
Norfolk: Assessment Report and Updated Project Design', unpublished NAU
Archaeology Client Report 1320 (2007)

Watts, V. (ed.), *The Cambridge Dictionary of English Place-Names* (Cambridge, 2004)

Webster, L. and Backhouse, J. (eds), *The Making of England* (London, 1991)

Welch, M., *Anglo-Saxon England* (London, 1992)

—, 'Cross-Channel Contacts between Anglo-Saxon England and Merovingian Francia',
in S. Lucy and A. Reynolds (eds), *Burial in Early Medieval England and Wales*,
Society for Medieval Archaeology Monograph 17 (London, 2002), pp. 122–31

—, 'Rural Settlement Patterns in the Early and Middle Anglo-Saxon Periods', *Landscape
History* 7 (1985), pp. 13–25

Wells, C., 'A Study of Cremation', *Antiquity* 34 (1960), pp. 29–37

— and Green, C., 'Sunrise Dating of Death and Burial', *Norfolk Archaeology* 35
(1973), pp. 435–42

Werner, J., 'A Review of *The Sutton Hoo Ship Burial: Volume 3*', *Anglo-Saxon Studies in
Archaeology and History* 5 (1992), pp. 1–24

West, S., *The Anglo-Saxon Cemetery at Westgarth Gardens, Bury St Edmunds, Suffolk*,
East Anglian Archaeology 38 (Bury St Edmunds, 1988)

—, *A Corpus of Anglo-Saxon Material From Suffolk*, East Anglian Archaeology 84
(Ipswich, 1998)

—, 'The Early Anglo-Saxon Period', in D. Dymond and E. Martin (eds), *An Historical
Atlas of Suffolk*, 3rd edn (Ipswich, 1999), pp. 44–5

—, 'The Excavation of Dunwich Town Defences, 1970', *Proceedings of the Suffolk
Institute of Archaeology* 33 (1) (1973), pp. 25–37

—, 'The Excavation of Walton Priory', *Proceedings of the Suffolk Institute of
Archaeology* 33 (2) (1974), pp. 131–52

—, 'Excavations at Cox Lane (1958) and at the Town Defences, Shire Hall Yard,
Ipswich (1959)', *Proceedings of the Suffolk Institute of Archaeology* 29 (3) (1963),
pp. 233–303

—, *West Stow: The Anglo-Saxon Village*, East Anglian Archaeology 24 (Bury St
Edmunds, 1985)

—, *West Stow Revisited* (Bury St Edmunds, 2001)

—, Scarfe, N. and Cramp, R., 'Iken, St Botolph, and the Coming of East Anglian

Christianity', *Proceedings of the Suffolk Institute of Archaeology and History* 35 (4) (1984), pp. 279–301

White, R., *Roman and Celtic Objects From Anglo-Saxon Graves*, BAR British Series 191 (Oxford, 1988)

Whitehouse, R., 'Ritual Objects: Archaeological Joke or Neglected Evidence?', in J. Wilkins (ed.), *Approaches to the Study of Ritual* (London, 1996), pp. 9–30

Whitelock, D., 'Bede and His Teachers and Friends', in G. Bonner (ed.), *Famulus Christi* (London, 1976), pp. 19–39

—, 'The Pre-Viking Age Church in East Anglia', *Anglo-Saxon England* 1 (1972), pp. 1–22

Whitley, D., 'New Approaches to Old Problems', in D. Whitley (ed.), *Reader in Archaeological Theory* (London, 1998), pp. 1–28

—, and Keyser, J., 'Faith in the Past: Debating an Archaeology of Religion', *Antiquity* 77 (2003), pp. 385–93

Whitley, W., 'Botulph's Ycean-Ho', *Journal of the British Archaeological Association* 36 (2) (1931), pp. 233–8

Whyman, M., 'Emporia and Early Medieval Settlement', in D. Perring (ed.), *Town and Country in England*, CBA Research Report 134 (York, 2002), pp. 92–106

Wilkins, J. (ed.), *Approaches to the Study of Ritual* (London, 1996)

Williams, H., 'Ancient Landscapes and the Dead: The Reuse of Prehistoric and Roman Monuments as Early Anglo-Saxon Burial Sites', *Medieval Archaeology* 41 (1997), pp. 1–32

—, 'Animals, Ashes and Ancestors', in A. Pluskowski (ed.), *Beyond Skin and Bones? New Perspectives on Human-Animal Relations in the Historical Past*, BAR International Series 1410 (Oxford, 2005), pp. 19–40

—, 'Artefacts in Early Medieval Graves: A New Perspective', in R. Collins and J. Gerrard (eds), *Debating Late Antiquity in Britain AD 300–700*, BAR British Series 365 (Oxford, 2004), pp. 89–101

—, 'Assembling the Dead', in A. Pantos and S. Semple (eds), *Assembly Places and Practices in Medieval Europe* (Dublin, 2004), pp. 109–34

—, 'Cemeteries as Central Places – Place and Identity in Migration Period Eastern England', in B. Hårdh and L. Larsson (eds), *Central Places in the Migration and Merovingian Periods* (Lund, 2002), pp. 341–62

—, *Death and Memory in Early Medieval Britain* (Cambridge, 2006)

—, 'Death Warmed Up', *Journal of Material Culture* 9 (3) (2004), pp. 263–91

—, 'An Ideology of Transformation: Cremation Rites and Animal Sacrifice in Early Anglo-Saxon England', in N. Price (ed.), *The Archaeology of Shamanism* (London, 2001), pp. 193–212

—, 'Keeping the Dead at Arm's Length: Memory, Weaponry and Early Medieval Mortuary Technologies', *Journal of Social Archaeology* 5 (2) (2005), pp. 253–75

—, 'Material Culture as Memory: Combs and Cremations in Early Medieval Britain', *Early Medieval Europe* 12 (2) (2003), pp. 89–128

—, 'Monuments and the Past in Early Anglo-Saxon England', *World Archaeology* 30 (1998), pp. 90–108

—, 'Placing the Dead: Investigating the Location of Wealthy Barrow Burials in Seventh-Century England', in M. Rundkvist (ed.), *Grave Matters*, BAR International Series 781 (Oxford, 1999), pp. 57–86

—, 'Remains of Pagan Saxondom? – The Study of Anglo-Saxon Cremation Rites', in S. Lucy and A. Reynolds (eds), *Burial in Early Medieval England and Wales*, Society for Medieval Archaeology Monograph 17 (London, 2002), pp. 47–71

Williamson, T., *England's Landscape: East Anglia* (London, 2006)

—, *The Origins of Norfolk* (Manchester, 1993)

—, *Sandlands* (Macclesfield, 2005)

—, *Shaping Medieval Landscapes* (Macclesfield, 2003)

—, 'Soil Landscapes', in T. Ashwin and A. Davison (eds), *An Historical Atlas of Norfolk*, 3rd edn (Chichester, 2005), pp. 8–9

—, *Sutton Hoo and its Landscape* (Oxford, 2008)

Wilson, D., *Anglo-Saxon Paganism* (London, 1992)

— (ed.), *The Archaeology of Anglo-Saxon England* (Cambridge, 1976)

Wilson, D. R., 'Air-Photography and *Venta Icenorum*', in P. Wilson (ed.), *The Archaeology of Roman Towns* (Oxford, 2003), pp. 251–7

Wood, I., 'Boniface [St Boniface] (672 × 5?–754)', *Oxford Dictionary of National Biography* (Oxford, 2004) http://www.oxforddnb.com/view/article/2843, last accessed 1 June 2009

—, 'The Conversion of the Barbarian Peoples', in G. Barraclough (ed.), *The Christian World* (London, 1981), pp. 85–98

—, 'The Mission of Augustine of Canterbury to the English', *Speculum* 69 (1) (1994), pp. 1–17

—, *The Missionary Life* (Harlow, 2001)

—, *The Most Holy Abbot Ceolfrid*, Jarrow Lecture 1995 (Jarrow, 1995)

—, 'Pagan Religions and Superstitions East of the Rhine from the Fifth to the Ninth Century', in G. Ausenda (ed.), *After Empire* (Woodbridge, 1995), pp. 253–79

—, 'Some Historical Re-identifications and the Christianization of Kent', in G. Armstrong and I. Wood (eds), *Christianizing Peoples and Converting Individuals* (Turnhout, 2000), pp. 27–35

Wood, P., 'Afterword: Boundaries and Horizons', in R. Hefner (ed.), *Conversion to Christianity* (Oxford, 1993), pp. 305–21

Woodward, B., 'The Old Minster at South Elmham', *Proceedings of the Suffolk Institute of Archaeology* 4 (1) (1864), pp. 1–7

Wymer, J., 'The Excavation of a Ring-Ditch at South Acre', in J. Wymer (ed.), *Barrow Excavations in Norfolk, 1984–88*, East Anglian Archaeology 77 (Gressenhall, 1996), pp. 58–89

—, 'Surface Geology', in D. Dymond and E. Martin (eds), *An Historical Atlas of Suffolk*, 3rd edn (Ipswich, 1999), pp. 18–19

Yorke, B., 'The Adaptation of the Anglo-Saxon Royal Courts to Christianity', in M. Carver (ed.), *The Cross Goes North* (York, 2003), pp. 243–57

—, *The Conversion of Britain* (Harlow, 2006)

—, *Kings and Kingdoms of Early Anglo-Saxon England* (London, 1990)

—, 'The Reception of Christianity at the Anglo-Saxon Royal Courts', in R. Gameson (ed.), *St Augustine and the Conversion of England* (Stroud, 1999), pp. 152–73

Young, B., 'The Myth of the Pagan Cemetery', in C. Karkov, K. Wickham-Crowley and B. Young (eds), *Spaces of the Living and the Dead* (Oxford, 1999), pp. 61–85

Zadora-Rio, E., 'The Making of Churchyards and Parish Territories in the Early-Medieval Landscape of France and England in the 7th–12th Centuries: A Reconsideration', *Medieval Archaeology* 47 (2003), pp. 1–19

Zubrow, E., 'Cognitive Archaeology Reconsidered', in C. Renfrew and E. Zubrow (eds), *The Ancient Mind* (Cambridge, 1994), pp. 187–90

Index

Numbers in italics signify figures and plates

ANGLO-SAXON STUDIES